Doli Incapax

Doli Incapax

Cleopatra Jones

Published by Tablo

Table of Contents

Doli Incapax – Incapable of guilt

Doli Incapax is an archaic legal maxim that refers to a child being incapable of committing a crime, under legislation or common law, because there is a presumption that they are too young to know the wrongness of their actions.

Doli Incapax is, however, a rebuttable presumption which means that if the Crown wishes to prosecute against children between the ages of 10 and 14, then they need to prove that the child had the necessary mens rea(guilty mind) meaning that they had knowledge of the seriousness or criminality of their actions, not just that they knew they were being naughty or mischievous. The Crown has the burden to prove this beyond all reasonable doubt.

I say Doli Incapax must die; it originated in England but, after the James Bulger case, even England saw fit to abolish it and have held the age of criminal responsibility at 10 ever since.

I say there is no such thing as 'child's play.' Children know the difference between right and wrong and the seriousness of their actions and, in modern day Australia in 2018, they know it well before 10 years old.

Doli Incapax is a book about what sexual assault really looks like when brave victims come forward. Until our sexual assault laws change, the only legally and morally responsible advice for a lawyer to give to survivors of sexual assault in 2019 is 'keep quiet.'

***

Doli Capax– capable of guilt

Means that a child is considered capable of forming the intent to commit a crime or tort, especially by reason of age (10 years old or older).

***

Nolle Prosequi– be unwilling to pursue (unwilling to prosecute)

Look out for my next book in my legal trilogy Nolle Prosequi – true stories from my angry clients about their own (and/or their children's) sexual assault cases that didn't get prosecuted and tells why in shocking detail. It also includes important legal updates on the various legal chapters contained in this book.

You will be outraged about the extent to which our Australian child protection, criminal law and family law jurisdictions do not dovetail and do not bring justice when it comes to sexual assault! It will leave you convinced not to step foot near a court room or a police station.

Acknowledgement

To my new family of fellow victims of sexual abuse; clients and friends who have replaced my extended paternal family, love and thanks to you, my new lifeline, 'my brothers and sisters from another mother.' Your bravery inspires me to keep on fighting until victims have the right to a lawyer in the criminal justice system.

I'll never be quiet until I can be a victim's lawyer where it matters most – in the criminal courts – until I can be your lawyer from start to end, not just for VOCAT, Royal Commissions and civil justice, the latter of which one can seldom afford, but especially when you're a victim of childhood sexual abuse and your life follows one inevitably tragic trajectory. Let the voice of my experience smash the lies like a hammer to an eggshell.

To my beautiful parents who are the best parents in the world, beyond a shadow of a doubt, and to my husband, my rock.

To my wonderful children Christopher, Declan, Kate and Alexander. This book is for you, for your children and for your grandchildren. Always stand up for yourself, and for others when they can't themselves, and remember that I love you, always.

Photo from left:
Cleopatra, Kate, Christopher, Declan and Alexander (in foreground)
Mother's Day 2011, Lake Provincial, Conservative Town

Prologue

In the pages of this book, you will find unreserved and unashamed criticism of my immediate family, my extended family, the Catholic Church and our current Australian Legal System. My knowledge and opinions are well founded in my professional experience as a current practising lawyer in family law, intervention orders, child protection, VOCAT (Victims of Crime Assistance Tribunal), civil law and Royal Commissions. As a board member of a Family Violence Support Agency in Conservative Town for many years and a duty lawyer in the Family Violence Court, I can attest to the fact that the cycle of violence is still cycling and if you pick up a newspaper, you will see the statistics are worsening. How many more women can 'accidentally' slip off a balcony and fall to their death or be 'accidentally' shot by a loved one? I have also learned a great deal about our criminal injustice system from my own experience as a bewildered police complainant and from my criminal lawyer husband.

I participated in the Royal Commission into Family Violence as a stakeholder and as a victim. I also represented clients in the Royal Commission into Institutional Responses to Child Sexual Abuse, some of whom have trampled a similar path as I with the police and courts. I also represented complainants in the police case against Cardinal Campeius and many other clergy members. As a former Catholic who has since denounced my religion, I see that many people are also leaving the church over the shameful and sinful Catholic cover-

up. However, in the Catholic stronghold that is Conservative
Town, I also see a disturbingly strong growth in Catholic
education, with a new Catholic primary school built by a
Diocese that says it has no money to compensate victims of
clergy abuse. I see a community fund drive established for
Campeius' legal defence. I see an infamous cathedral
prematurely taking down the Loud Fence ribbons in a
clandestine manner. I see churchmen who were complicit in
covering up abuse remaining on our local Catholic school
boards. Certainly, the persistent denial and desperate cover-up
of child sexual abuse is very concerning, particularly in light of
what we know now about what they knew then and their
responses now.

Overwhelmingly though, what has informed and motivated
the writing of this book is my hugely uncomfortable personal
experience of our legal system as a denied and angry client
who has been given multiple servings of law but absolutely no
justice.

Lady Justice pictured on the outside wall near the entrance
of the County Court in Big Smoke, the only person in the
Court precinct speaking the truth, reminding me, 'You're
going in blind, lady. Enter at your own risk.' Forget about
impartiality; there's a gender war going on daily inside
courtrooms across this country and women are losing almost
without fail. This happens even if your eyes are wide open
without a blindfold on but especially if you're a confident,
intelligent woman who knows what's going on inside all that
sandstone, glass and architectural veneer. This gender war is
also taking place outside the courtroom and the sexual assaults
and homicides on the daily news reveal the winner day after
day. Violence is undoubtedly gendered, but so are the
responses to it, including the recent #MeToo movement. I can

say without a shadow of a doubt that women are their own best advocate.

Whilst my cousin's sexual abuse of me and his reprehensible behaviour since my disclosure, showing no remorse whatsoever, together with my family's subsequent deplorable treatment of me, has caused the greatest emotional pain, the legal system has run a close, photo-finish third. Its systems abuse for breakfast, lunch and dinner at my table. The anger I still very much feel has been generated first by the actions of my cousin and abuser – hereafter referred to as King Claudius – and his ridiculous, untenable stance and second by our legal system, happily and deliberately reinforcing his untouchable status, the new preying patriarch of our family (and that is not a typo despite his Catholicism). This has happened in each jurisdiction that I have turned to; Criminal, Civil, VOCAT and in my application to revoke a Suppression Order that both King Claudius and the law turned into a Machiavellian plot.

Why does the law continue playing this game and anoint him winner every time, even when I won with final Orders in my favour, including full costs, twice? Furthermore, what, if anything, does the Catholic Church have to do with it? Why am I so misunderstood by my legal brethren as if what I'm asking for, basic respect and acknowledgement of what happened to me, is legally unattainable? No one can rightly explain to me what's happened in my case. My story is met with utter disbelief from every lawyer I've engaged or spoken with, every barrister I've briefed and seemingly, no one is able put things right, including a Queen's Counsel. I've learned that it's up to me, the victim of crime with a lawyer hat on, as sadly, I discovered that only I am passionate enough to fight for me properly, with the attention to detail that is required to win or get anywhere near a taste of justice. I wanted to be a client and stay a client, but the bumbling legal fools around me had to go and so I had to put my lawyer hat on again at a time when I was most vulnerable.

My aim in writing this book is to do more than simply spill the beans on the Australian Legal System's incompetence, impotence and blatant denial of sexual abuse as a crime that deserves to be properly punished. It is to inform, advise and bolster other victims of childhood sexual abuse and to support them in making the best decision for them about what to do with that all-consuming, sad and negative energy they often carry. Ultimately, I say going to the police is currently a total waste of time. Going to court is also a total waste of time and money.

I'm afraid to say that today, in 2018, the pursuit of justice, acknowledgement, redress and apology are all concepts foreign to the law and mostly out of reach in a courtroom when it comes to sexual abuse. Why though, when those things are relevant and comparatively easy to achieve in other areas of the law? If I slipped over on a banana in Coles tomorrow, more would happen and in far less time, family would visit me with flowers, fritole (Croatian doughnuts) and Cadbury Roses and I'd be compensated. There is no industry built around shame and 'she's lying' there.

In my case, like all other cases of sexual assault, there's a presumption that 'he's not lying' for our legal system says that he's innocent until proved guilty. So, it also follows that if you can't prove someone's guilty, they're deemed not guilty. It's the trappings of the law that create a courtroom drama where guilt is seldom proved. Currently, only a very small number of cases go to committal and trial and in most of those cases, the accused are found 'not guilty'. All the other police reports not prosecuted are as good as proved 'not guilty' too, for they net the same result; the perpetrator goes unpunished 97 per cent of the time despite being brave and doing everything right as legally prescribed.

But there is nothing inevitable about the way we process serious crime and we need to change it, or we can absolutely forget about sexual abuse, especially historic sexual abuse, being a crime that's prosecuted and ends with a conviction. Just look at the current statistics around criminal convictions for sexual assault; the rates are shamefully low! There is a conviction rate of six per cent which reduces to three per cent after one takes into consideration successful appeals.[1] If the OPP were a private organisation, it would surely be out of business, for its core aim, to prosecute crime and bring justice to victims, is far from met. Moreover, it's harder still to gain any semblance of justice in a civil jurisdiction when the accused is an individual with no institution able to be held legally responsible. Just look at John Ellis and what he went through. Similarly, victims are usually unemployed or low-paid workers at best who can't afford to go to court for years to sue their perpetrator. And even thought the Statute of Limitations and the Ellis Defense have been abolished, a complainant still needs to overcome the 'passage of time unfairly prejudices the defendant' argument.

This is my story without embellishment, but I admit, at times, this book may seem to belong in the fiction section because what has happened to me in the last five years and to many of my clients is so outrageous. How I wish it was all just one of my PTSD nightmares and my extended paternal family would surround me in support and the legal system would finally hold my cousin responsible for his actions, but my reality is to the contrary and my nightmare plays out every day since I disclosed it.

In this book, I will attempt to provide the answer to how sexual abuse can be properly and adequately recognised by the law, that I have come to learn the hard way, and I make numerous recommendations to change the law in this area completely. A total revamp is needed as we need to start from scratch, with a victim-informed process. Adults having sex with children is a crime. Children having sex with other children is also a crime. There is no such thing as 'child's play'. If you have sex with a child, whoever you are, you should be guilty of a crime. The victim of childhood sexual abuse does not care how old the perpetrator is, whether they used an object or a body part to assault you, or whether there was penetration or not. Only the judge, the OPP and the defense lawyer care about these facts and the defences to them, such as doli incapax. So why are these facts the framework that underpins our laws about sexual abuse? Because it's not victim focussed. This book brings the focus back to where it should be – with the victim.

Why is it that sexual assault, the worst crime against a surviving victim, rarely gets any legal traction? Why did all the specialist lawyers practising in sexual assault and institutional abuse desperately try to dissuade me from suing my cousin? Because the legal path is insane. I was told by a wonderful lawyer friend, 'It would amount to me stealing money from you and you'll have a pyrrhic victory at best.' She was speaking the truth and I respected her for that, but how can that possibly still be the truth in 2019?

Sadly, I see the police as being about as useful in a criminal case of sexual assault as they are when they come speeding in at the end of a blockbuster film, with flashing lights and sirens and a box of iced doughnuts thrown in for good measure, generally after the victim has already saved herself out of necessity. The findings from the IBAC Inquiry[2] in 2016 reveal Conservative Town Police Station as one of the worst in Australia. Similarly, The Lindt Café siege is another fine example of the deplorable state of current Australian policing. Who in their right mind would wait for the police to save you? The same can certainly be said for waiting for justice from the courts. Forget it.

The Royal Commission into Institutional Responses to Child Sexual Abuse has now made their recommendations and the vital thing is that the government adopts their recommendations, but do we really need a Royal Commission to tell us that having sex with a child is a crime? Sadly, it seems we do. On 12 November 2017, the Western Australian reported that a 14-year-old boy was found guilty of raping a 9-year-old boy, but the judge gave him a twelve-month sentence fully suspended plus sixty hours of community service[3]. To a victim, this means he got away with it. Cases with outcomes like this are the norm, not the exception, as the courts are seldom tough on sex offenders, but they are the lucky ones for most reported cases don't even proceed.

My brilliant career – yeah, right. I'm as tough as nails and I fight the good fight every day, but my like-minded and I should be winning the battle by now, case by case. My criminal lawyer husband should use his fine legal mind, present the plea . . . and then rightly lose. Why does he net excellent results time and time again, day after day, when his client is almost certainly guilty despite their instructions, which often predictably change to a plea of guilty at the last minute anyway? Why aren't our finest legal minds working for the betterment of victims and society? Why isn't that legally desirable? What is our preoccupation with the bad guy and his trajectory? Yes, he's entitled to representation, but why, in cases of sexual assault, does he win 97 per cent of the time? Because victims have no lawyer and no legal standing.

As a nation, we have been brought up to revere the bad guy. Ned Kelly, a horse thief and violent murderer, is possibly our greatest hero! It seems that lawyers who can get the bad guy off have some sort of hero status, some sort of sexy or naughty image in synchrony with their client, so clever to outsmart the police and get away with the crime. In contrast, why are we victims stuck with the departmental hacks at the OPP or DHHS, where the truth is deemed redundant and sits in someone's in tray under mountains of red tape? Lawyers flock to practise in crime in droves, but they can't represent the victim as the victim is merely a witness for the police; they currently have no legal standing and no right to a lawyer. Even in civil matters, there's seemingly very few who know how to competently fight for the plaintiff or even want to because it's just too hard. I suspect that it would knock their ego anyway if the bench wasn't regularly onside with them, for the judiciary also aims to keep the criminals at liberty despite societal outrage about it. Sadly, I see it every day. It's a lawyer's game and everyone gets to be onside, with the victim conveniently absent from the courtroom most of the time as police tell them they don't need to be there! They are a non-party, which makes it easier for those feeding off their pain to dehumanise them.

I say don't wait in vain for the legal system to save you; save yourself instead. Engage with a good counsellor, nurture yourself and work on your lost childhood sooner rather than later. Find where you were broken and rebuild. Don't wait for strangers in the legal system to understand you or believe you as they rarely do and it's insulting, frustrating and financially crippling. I could have gone around the world three times first class with my family of six for the time I've devoted and the money I've spent on legal fees and a fourth time for the money saved by the tasks I did when representing myself over the past four and a half years. Don't be a principled fool like me. No one cares if you're right or telling the truth; truth gains no traction. It just gives you a whopping great legal bill while the defence lawyers gloat at their success, not because of great lawyering but because of the armchair ride given to them and their client by the legal system.

What role, if any, does the Catholic Church play in all this unsightly legal mess? As I discovered, it's playing the lead role so, as I see it, there is absolutely no separation between the State, the Church and the Law: the unholy trinity. Through my work in the Royal Commission into Institutional Responses to Child Sexual Abuse, I discovered that the outcomes in my own legal matters, by chance running contemporaneously, were brought to me care of the Catholic Church. It sounds like a crazy conspiracy theory, I know, but it's certainly not. It's a shameful cover-up, but I'll let you be the judge.

This book is about how a creative little girl from Conservative Town, with a love of expression and social justice, found herself at the butt end of the legal system, as an adult and as a lawyer, and explains what I intend on doing about it so that my clients, both current and future, do not follow in my footsteps. As I have painfully discovered, it's best for victims to look where police, courts and lawyers are and run as fast as possible in the opposite direction – at least for now until the system works for victims. Don't be led to believe you should report to SOCIT; why would you bother with a 3 per cent conviction rate? Being brave doesn't work and the truth doesn't work. The select cases aired in the media are politically acceptable to keep the "justice illusion" alive, to keep the criminal justice industry alive, to keep government looking 'tough on crime'. The rape stories are about those who go to trial, cases like Saxon Mullins, but what about cases that reflect the masses of complainants who are knocked out well before then. Why don't we focus on the 97% of brave complainants, who are mainly women, who get absolutely nowhere, and investigate that intelligently. Just look at the news stories about the ABC and Melbourne University Press and one really questions the existence of independent media.

Before you begin reading my story, I need to explain my use of the words victim and survivor. I see myself as a victim and so, as author, I have opted to use this term about myself. However, I am mindful and sensitive to the fact that many people who have been sexually abused find the term offensive. I absolutely understand the issues people have with the word victim, including that it has a sense of disempowerment to it. It suggests one stays forever victim to their perpetrator. It implies that one cannot survive their experience. Arguably, it shares one's status with those who have died prematurely through foul play; victims are often also dead. I wholeheartedly celebrate those who have survived their traumatic experience and re-brand as 'survivors'.

Notwithstanding this, I still say I am a victim. Then and now. I was a victim to King Claudius as a child. I survived. I am a victim to King Claudius' lies now as an adult. I am a victim to the law's re-victimisation. I have died, not in body but in spirit. I have died a social death. I am alive but invisible, a walking dead of sorts, to my own flesh and blood, dead to my clan. But I have survived and society is listening – just not members of my Croatian family. Ironically, members of other families support me, but they likely don't support their own who have been sexually abused. How sad is misplaced love and compassion? Like a deer that deserts its dying fawn or a do-gooder parishioner visiting sick members of the parish with a hearty casserole but who heartlessly turn their back on their own children who allege clergy abuse.

In my view, 'survivor' sanitises the loss, the pain, the hurt, the trauma and the isolation through its positive flavour. 'Survivor' implies, 'I've survived, albeit with scars.' It suggests one has transcended one's experience and needs to draw on their resilience to 'bounce back'. I don't believe that is truly possible – or at least not for me. Life is forever altered. You are alive, but you need to learn to rethink, reinterpret and renew, which is all positive, but the childhood lens often remains. Having said that, life is a little like the Nancy Drew children's adventure books I read as a child – choose your own ending. I choose to speak out and make a path for children that leads them to destinations far better than Hansel and Gretel had – lost in the forest, abandoned by family or eaten by a wicked stranger. The ugly truth is that there is currently no clear legal path for sexual-assault victims and the signposts keep getting switched by police, lawyers, judges and politicians. And so, I use the words victim and survivor interchangeably as appropriate.

My Use of Pseudonyms

I have had many a moment of mental anguish as to whether I should use pseudonyms for my family members, but I believe for authenticity that I should use real names. There is little point in hiding from this story in any way. But alas, for good old legal reasons, I have had to use a pen name, Cleopatra

Jones, and give all my family members fake names.

In the circumstances, I thought it appropriate to turn my story into a Shakespearean tragedy as that's what it is, so it wasn't too difficult although frustrating. I have more happily used pseudonyms for the legal eagles because it doesn't matter to me who they are as individuals but rather the position of power they have and the duplicitous role they play through legal process. At risk of being sued, I have had to de-identify my photographs and documents wherever possible, which is beyond galling, including the necessity to remove specific dates. How ridiculous is it that I can't speak the truth in case I embarrass someone?

I apologise for the confusion I will undoubtedly cause to some readers as I have used Shakespearean names from different plays within the one family unit at times. Some Shakespearean character traits are a perfect match for my family members and in other cases, I just randomly picked another Shakespearean name to fill the large Croatian family tree.

I also sincerely apologise for offending anyone in this process, referring to lawyers as bird brains and my family members as Shakespearean narcissists, sinners and schemers.

As Dida always used to say, 'In my way, in my way, I no offend, I no offend,' when what he really meant to say was 'I don't mean to offend you, but now I'm about to offend you, so look out because here comes the insult.'

Part 1

My Conservative Town Childhood, 1980 B.D. (Before Death/Disclosure)

Axiom's hit song 'A Little Ray of Sunshine'[4] came out in 1970 and three years later my parents' little ray of sunshine did too – little me, their "brown-eyed girl."[5] The hippie artist he was, my dad picked some wild flowers growing through a neighbour's fence on the way to St Vincent's Private Hospital in Melbourne to welcome me into the world, ten little pink fingers and ten little pink toes, in the shape of a girl.

Chapter 1

You Be Good Girl

'You be good girl. Be good to Mudda, Fudda, dis one, dat one,' spluttered Dida, my devout Catholic Croatian grandfather, Bruno Pavlovic, the unrefined patriarch of our large new-Australian family, dictating the way I should behave. He repeated this caution almost every time I saw him with monotonous regularity, accidentally spitting his home-made, watered-down wine on me as he spoke. He usually recited this speech to me from his stage at Villa Pavlovic, the front porch, sitting on the white Italianate cast-iron chair with one leg tucked up under his bottom, invariably chain-smoking.

I never knew the full importance of his words 'You be good girl' until I dared to do something that would change the family forever and disrupt its very core: I told my secret.

My secret seems almost boring now as I say it, as if the facts have gone stale like yesterday's news; I was sexually abused by my first cousin King Claudius for four years, from when I was seven years old and in grade two at school until the end of grade five, a few months after my eleventh birthday. It took me thirty-three years to tell my secret to my parents, but I had already told two other people before them: my ex-husband Gallus and my husband Antony. I knew my secret was safe with them; there'd be no consequence in telling them. I knew that telling my parents would mean action and ramifications, so I held onto my pain for such a long time until I burst, and it literally blurted from by lips like vomit. But my news has since been ignored by the police, the Courts and the extended Pavlovic family. Life goes on; King Claudius remains the king of the castle, without so much as a scratch.

Like my Dida, the Law also orders, 'You be good girl'– be good to your abuser, be good to the police, be good to the magistrate, be good to the judge, don't say this, just say that (and in the way we tell you to say it, Ms Jones!) and kindly agree to our lukewarm plan for diversion for your rapist cousin. Water things down so that your experience is nicely sanitised for us please victims, including in your statement of claim and in your victim impact statement, and don't say anything too dramatic. Follow the legal processes for years and years like a good little girl, but we'll understand and be all too glad if you give up along the way. Girls get tired after all, the weaker sex, 'the second sex', so aptly put by my mentor, the late French feminist philosopher Simone de Beauvoir.[6]

'She was vengeful' or 'She was lying,' the law concludes time after time as another criminal is routinely acquitted, branded 'not guilty'. It must have been a case of mistaken identity, a witch hunt of this poor innocent man, like many 'innocent' men I see daily on the news, guilty yet walking away deemed free men by the courts.

The Church also commands, 'You be good girl' too by the fourth commandment: 'Honour thy father and thy mother'. I suspect that is what Dida meant – you be a good girl and don't bring shame to the family. In other words, the good reputation of our family relies on you and all the Pavlovic girls behaving themselves, staying virgins and not getting pregnant; keep your mouths and legs shut unless prised open by a member of our family. For the sake of our family – namely, the bad men in our family – kindly shut up, including at your own expense. Be kind and forgive him; it's better for you to live in secret shame. Don't seek to punish him as that's God's job alone. Be a good girl and confess your sins, for you are to carry his sins like Jesus did for us. Good Girl School will teach you how to do this, to martyr your life away as if a nun; nod nicely, smile slightly, blush lightly and speak politely!

Thinking back now, I never did hear 'You be good boy' directed at the young males in our family, not from Dida or from my grandmother, Baba, nor from anyone else. And I'm still waiting to hear it . . .

And while I'm waiting, I ask you this; if it is true that there are so many good men out there during this pandemic of men's violence against women, why did not one man – one grandfather, uncle, brother, son, nephew, cousin, friend, lawyer, barrister, policeman, prosecutor, magistrate, or judge – tell King Claudius to do the right thing?

Why did they all still tell me, 'You be good girl' instead, in this highly educated First World country of ours?

Chapter 2

Me, the 1980s Girl

I was born in the year 1973, but I really belong to the 1980s. I loved the '80s. Well, not really.

Fashion? Yes.

Music? Yes.

School? Yes.

Ballet? Yes.

King Claudius? No.

The '80s were legendary and fun in a gaudy way. Mullets were cool, puff sleeves and shoulder pads were ace, fluoro was hot and trendy men wore pastel clothes and white sandals. Princesses were real; kindergarten teacher Diana turned into a princess like magic, appearing bejewelled and complete with tiara on the cover of Women's Day. The Smurfs, Holly Hobbie and Strawberry Shortcake came to town and the smells of her and her friends wafted strongly through my bedroom. Every girl's delight was my bedroom, full of dolls and trinkets displayed in true OCD style on my antique dressing table, all pieces lovingly kept in mint condition, never misplaced. My wallpaper had sweet little birds twittering on crab-apple blossoms, the perfect backdrop for my antique bed and a happy little girl... on the outside.

I remember sizzling summer afternoons going to the pool, playing on my neighbour's slip-and-slide, or going to the milk bar to get a Skona or a Funny Feet ice cream. I had a yellow hula hoop that smelled of dreamy banana. I remember making 'shrinkies' out of chip packets and writing to my pen pal in China, Carolyn Tan, exchanging novelty stickers with her. I had a pink cartridge pen I used to sign my letters with, using my most unfortunate, self-appointed nickname, Ring, with a heart replacing the dot over the letter i– cringe; what was I thinking and where was my dictionary? I drew pictures endlessly with my massive tin of seventy-two Derwent pencils and loved reading the names of the colours aloud: 'magenta, deep vermilion, chartreuse, Naples yellow'. Wham and Spandau Ballet – the nouveau romantics were my favourite bands and I still remember buying my first cassette tape, Bop Girls, a compilation of hits from all the rock chicks I loved like Pat Benatar and Bananarama. My pink-and-yellow ice-cream brooch, with a bite out of it, was my favourite thing inside my twirling-ballerina jewellery box.

I also remember freezing cold Conservative Town mornings going running down Crow Hill or mushrooming with my dad in the paddocks and mullock heaps around our home, in the last street of Birdville, on the fringe of Conservative Town. It was such a thrill to find the next mushroom or fairy ring and we'd bring back my treasures to show Mum, including blackberries, rabbit skulls and sheep bones. Mum took them to work as subject matter for her life drawing classes. I also remember collecting garden snails for Baba, fresh from her suburban garden, ready for her cooking pot, some garlic broth, a toothpick and then slurp and down the hatch. 'Mangia mangia, puž' (pronounced 'Munja, munja, pooja', meaning 'Eat, eat, snail!'), she would say. Simple things, happy moments.

However, most of my primary school years, from

Christmas Day 1980 to the end of 1984, were also characterised by the sexual abuse of me by my cousin King Claudius, my sad parallel world running alongside my happy world. I worked hard at playing along, skipping between the two worlds as required. Children are so good at keeping secrets and instinctively hold adult interests above their own. They also listen to and obey children older than them as if they were adults and are often manipulated, groomed, bossed and bullied into submission. They work out very quickly the currency of their existence and survival. If I do A, B will happen. If I do C, D will happen.

Initially, I chose the path of least resistance: no resistance. It was a subconscious choice though. In the later years of the abuse, I said 'No' and asked, 'Do we have to?' to no avail, but that was the most I ever said to him to verbalise my dissent. The rest of the time, I just let sexual acts happen to me, giving him answers I hoped would please him to get it over with as quickly as possible.

'Does this feel like a snake?' he'd ask as he touched me.

'Yes,' I'd reply.

'Does this feel good or bad?' he'd enquire.

'Yes,' I'd say again robotically, not making any sense and not answering his question.

My answers were given as if I were in a trance of sorts, automated responses like saying sorry to someone when in fact, it is them who have crashed into you with their shopping trolley, a non sequitur.

My developing child brain overanalysed so many things to try to make sense of my frightening experience. I associated my suffering with Jesus' and played word games in my head, trying to give meaning to the letters 'INRI' on the crucifix, which I imagined stood for 'I now rest injured', 'I never ran inside', 'I never resisted immediately', or 'I never really imagined'. That's what I'd think about when I'd go to chapel at school and stare at the big cross behind the altar. I later learned in Latin classes that the phrase 'Jesus of Nazareth, the King of the Jews' would have been translated as 'Iesus Nazarenus, Rex Iudaeorum' and the first letter of each word creates the abbreviation INRI.

Sadly, I also associated my name with my perpetrator's name for far too many years; Cleopatra and Claudius both start with the letters C and L, but moreover, we also share the letter A, which is even worse. I thought it was my predetermined fate, as if I was somehow chosen by King Claudius through the shared letters in our names. I was reminded of this flawed thought process recently at a wedding down on the peninsula of Victoria, when the lovable mother of the groom commented on how well the bride and groom complemented each other, proved by the fact that their first initials, S and Z, were mirror images.

These are the things spinning in a little girl's mind, word associations no crazier than fun methods of determining love compatibility based on numbers and letters, still used by children and adults alike today. As an adult, I consider that turning to astrology and numerology is a little bit of childish fun and I admit that I still check the star guide from time to time, usually when I'm feeling desperate along with buying a Tatts ticket. However, I have left behind any association with King Claudius, be it literal or otherwise; we have nothing in common now and I have made sure of that. I had to, to survive. Surviving during the abuse and surviving after the abuse are two different things entirely.

Needless to say, I missed the remainder of her wedding speech as my mind had now trailed off, staring down at my perfectly applied nail polish, thinking back to 1990. I had to write King Claudius' name out beautifully when I was asked to design the cover of the church booklet (Order of Service) for his wedding and to write out the place cards in calligraphy; such was my friendship with the bride, Tamora, and her family too, who were already old family friends of ours from when our fathers were at primary school together. A task that should have been a simple pleasure to a girl with a love of art, design and calligraphy became my introduction to the land of passive-aggressive people pleasing.

The first time King Claudius touched my private parts was on Christmas Day 1980. Baba had invited everyone to her house for Christmas and the relatives were down from Bundaberg, Queensland. We all feasted on spit roast, salad and Vienna bread under the watchful eye of Jesus and his disciples at The Last Supper, framed purposefully in the kitchen. I used to love Baba's cooking and her red wine vinegar was so delicious on a simple lettuce salad. But Dida's home-made wine tasted disgusting to little me. Baba would always give me a little bit in a glass, saying, 'Pisti, isti' (meaning 'Drink, eat'). I would take a pretend sip and promptly escape to the lounge room, tipping the remainder into one of her pot plants.

Baba's niece Angelica, her husband and her children, Perdita and Othello, were staying at Baba's house during the Christmas holidays. Those children were older than King Claudius. They came with scary ghost stories I hadn't heard before, which I listened to intently until something distracted me; King Claudius' fingers were touching my vagina. Just like that. We children were all squashed into Baba's sewing room and it happened in the dark. No words were spoken. It was sudden. This happened again when we were playing chasey and hide-and-seek outside. This was the start of my body not being my own.

Chapter 3

Appi Burzday!

The song "Mad World" by Gary Jules[7] plays in my head as I recall events to write this chapter.

Looking through the cake album at Violet's Cake Shop, I decided that I wanted the pretty pink ballerina cake, so Mum ordered it for my 9thBirthday party, complete with sprinkles, silver chaos and fancy swathes of icing. My invitations had gone out weeks earlier and the whole school class was coming, but my invites weren't from Hallmark. Oh no, there was no chance of that with artistic parents! Instead, Mum carved out a linocut of my face and the words "Cleopatra invites…" Each invite was an original black lino print on thick expensive art paper, but to tell you the truth, back then I would have been much happier with Kermit or Miss Piggy on the invite, like all the other kids had. All I ever wanted to do was blend in, but blending was never possible for me.

'How many more sleeps?', I asked Mum excitedly.

'Only two more, then straight after ballet it's party time. Do you want to have pass the parcel?', Mum enquired.

My brain flashed to what normally happens straight after ballet, like stills from a photo booth.

'Pass the parcel?' she repeated. 'What can we wrap up as the present?', asked Mum.

'Um, um…stickers…and Smurf mini figures. And a flashing yo-yo would be ace!', I said, quickly returning back to the present.

And with that, Mum bought a spirograph set. Of course she did, another uncommon choice that kids didn't really want compared to a Disney trinket.

When my special day finally came around I was so nervous. I couldn't wait to have my party and had been waiting all year, counting down the days, but I started worrying about my friends teasing me about the nude paintings hanging on our walls. But then Baba and Dida arrived during the party and the birthday song took the cake of embarrassment:

'Appi Burz-day to yooo

Appi Burz-day to yooo

Appi Burz-day Cle-a-pat-traaaaaaa

Appi Burz-day to yooo

Ip Ip Ooo-ray, Ip Ip, Ooo-ray.",

they sang in their best Croatian peasant tone.

Baba and Dida had dropped past on their way back from mowing the lawn at our beach house, unaware that it was my birthday. They amused and outsung everyone, mispronouncing the words spectacularly, but why after decades of living in Australia do Croatians seem to have so much trouble with the letter 'H' I wonder?

And at my party, Baba's singing continued as she played the baby clapping game with my baby brother Romeo in his highchair:

'Batti le manine

Ore viene papa

Portera boborne

Romeo mangera'

And then my German grandparents Oma and Opa arrived

and Oma sang another song, but this time with a strong German accent and in German, with baby Romeo bobbing up and down on her knee:

'Hopa hopa reita,
Ven der velt den shreiter,
Velt der in den graben,
And hacken in de raben,
Velt der in den sumpf,

Der – macht - der - Romeo...**plumps!**", at which Romeo was bounced off her lap, squealing with delight.

And twelve years later, my 21stBirthday party was still a day of clashing sounds, a battle of the bands really. The Croatian family band in the studio made up of my Uncles on piano accordions and guitars that echoed traditional folk songs off Dad's bluestone walls, walls like Montsalvat, whilst outside in the garden we tried to drown out the 'wog' music with the cousins 'Aussie' band, playing Jimmy Barnes and U2 songs. Sampson brought his guitar and his big personality and there was a tribe of young adults who joined in, but we didn't stand a chance against the bellows from the Croatian squeezebox.

My best friend Teresa Jam from Crescent College brought her boyfriend who ripped his pants and so he had to wear a pair of Terese's pants for the rest of the night and was so embarrassed as they were far too small for him and the zipper kept undoing. My other friends from Crescent College including Mary O'Leary, Sam O'Reily and Maria Stefani were there too, getting a massive dose of Croatian culture, one liqueur glass at a time, for our Rakia-home-brew could knock you out in one shot!

My parents gave me a big 21st Key that they had a craftsman in Conservative Town make, using Opa's original key mould from his electroplating days. It was the same as Opa had made for his own children and I will have the same keys made for my children in the years to come. I love carrying on our family traditions, including paying homage at the cemetery.

I am absolutely convinced that Croatians love cemeteries and funerals. I suspect that its part of the important ritual that heralds their loved one's entry to Heaven and all must attend to witness it and mourn loudly. I am slightly different in that I like the cemetery post funeral but not the funeral itself. Germans love cemeteries too and my Mum told me that visiting them on a Sunday is common in Germany. Like my Oma and Opa, many have an open grave where a garden grows. Mum keeps her little garden fork between the graves, to tend and weed between the annuals. My family planted camelias and boy did they flourish to the quality found in a botanical garden. Oma and Opa's grave is so beautiful that it's included in the cemetery tour run by the National Trust.

Every year, I go to Baba's grave on her birthday to wish her a Appi Burzday and I give my greeting with a passion out aloud! Anyone walking past would think I'm crazy. I always take bright orange or deep red roses for her, for she liked strong coloured flowers the best. I look at her grave photo and I see the angels keeping her safe from the devil but not from the vandals unfortunately, as one year the angels were beheaded on all the Pavlovic graves, the same fate as Marie Antoinette.

Croatians don't celebrate birthdays much, in fact, they don't place much importance on it at all. The big deal to be celebrated is Gospa Velika and our own Saints Day, decided when you choose your Saints name for your confirmation. I chose Saint Katherine but when you are young, your birthday means everything to you. My dad was really lucky and had two birthdays; the real one and the day his birth was registered by Dida, although his parents never really celebrated either of them. Dida explained to Dad that he had to walk many kilometres into Zadar to do it; roughly two weeks later. We have always celebrated Dad on the registered day, but it has become somewhat of a family joke that his real birthday is in May, not June. And as for Saint Katherine's Day, I never knew the date and my family certainly never celebrated it. But I liked that name Katherine because it was my first taste at having a normal English name. Years later I learned that she had counselled Joan of Arc which endears me to her but with the burning of Joan of Arc at the stake, I figure that my Saint Katherine must have gone into early retirement! Still, I named my daughter after her.

The night of my 17thbirthday, which was also the night before Baba died, Baba called our house, inviting us to come over. Some family friends had arrived from interstate in anticipation of her big party the next day and she wanted us all to come over, but we were in the middle of having my own birthday dinner and so we declined. What was the urgency anyway at eight o'clock at night? We were due to see her and celebrate her birthday the next day in any event and we figured she was simply letting birthday party excitement get to her.

In the morning we received another call, again from Baba's house, but this time from Uncle King Lear, telling us to come quickly as Baba was dying. We raced to Villa Pavlovic and Dad went straight into her bedroom where she lay in the final minutes of her life. My Dad held her hand together with his siblings and talked to her and they said their goodbyes as her great heart stopped beating and her body went from warm to cool… and then to stone cold. She had known.

Chapter 4

My Ballet Days

Madame Gulbis, svelte and reliably dressed in black, commanded respect naturally. She was disciplined, confident, measured and sharp. 'Holly-Jane, don't hold your arm like a coat hanger!' she would often exclaim to a fellow ballerina. Madame was always in control and had very high standards of her dancers. I admired her, but I was absolutely scared of her. I worked hard at pointing my toes, keeping my hands elegant and my arms elongated. I really tried to please her. When learning ballet theory, I was so nervous about getting an answer wrong that those French words like grand battement, chassé and pas de bourrée occupied my thoughts at night like counting sheep. I learned them in her strong Latvian accent.

My favourite cousin, Goneril, King Claudius' sister, did ballet with me and being the same age, we were in the same classes. I started ballet when I was just three years old as I had flat feet and the doctor recommended I do ballet to improve my arches and foot strength. In the early days, I remember being asked by Madame to pretend I was a butterfly and to freely dance as I wished while Madame watched us all fluttering around with a keen ballet eye. I loved the freedom of movement, the classical music and I enjoyed being with Goneril as she was like a sister to me, a sister I didn't have. I developed a love of Tchaikovsky's The Nutcracker[8], ballet costumes, make-up, ribbons and ballet shoes. I kept my first pair of pointe shoes and all the old Anna Gulbis Ballet annual recital programs in case I had a daughter one day to pass them on to. Ironically, my daughter quit classical ballet before she could appreciate them, for modern dance is more her thing. That's my Kate!

Madame's studio was on the top floor of the old Hollywood Cinema in Conservative Town. I remember there were many flights of stairs to climb to get to Madame's studio, seemingly more when I was running late for class. My father would collect Goneril and me after ballet classes on Saturdays and there was a health food shop a few doors up where Dad would get apricot soft-serve frozen yoghurts for us as an after-ballet treat. Then Dad would take us to the house of Uncle King Lear and Aunty, King Lear's wife, in Cambridge Street South and I would be left to play there for the afternoon with Goneril and Regan, her younger sister. 'Cool bananas!' Sadly, it was this innocent after-ballet plan that provided King Claudius with endless opportunities to continue to regularly sexually abuse me and he did for four years.

King Claudius was their brother, almost five years older than Goneril and me and eight years older than Regan. He was a tall boy and seemed like an adult to me as he was so much bigger than me and looked like an adult in his St Michael's College uniform. He was the most influential of the cousins and everyone did as he told them to, including me. He was certainly the boss, with many siblings and many, many first and second cousins in our massive Croatian extended family. He always appointed himself "'it'" when we cousins played chasey and hide- and- seek and no one ever dared to challenge him.

I loved having girls to play with on Saturdays as I was an

only child until my brother was born just before Christmas in 1981, when I was eight. My cousins' house adjoined Baba and Dida's house as their backyards were connected by a gate. How very 'new Australian' to build houses on adjoining blocks as if establishing a Croatian settlement. At every family celebration, the children would run through one property to the other, playing chasey or hide-and-seek or playing at the house of Uncle King Lear and Aunty King Lear's wife instead, while the adults gathered at Baba and Dida's. I know that it was a well-trodden path between the two, with Baba constantly going over to criticise Aunty for the mess in her house first thing in the morning daily. Lucky Aunty!

But with so much going on all the time at those two houses, no one noticed when King Claudius started sexually abusing me. There was too much laughter and shouting and too many children darting around. There were piano accordions, guitars and loud guttural singing. The men were often playing a card game, Scopa, or talking – make that shouting – politics. There was the female dishes brigade in the kitchen and fritole overflowing. There were multiple languages being spoken at the same time: Croatian, some Italian, English and a weird combination of the lot. There was no known reason for anyone to doubt my safety, surrounded by my loved ones in this big, caring, demonstrative family that gave double kisses with every greeting.

King Claudius was an opportunistic child with the cunning of the Artful Dodger. He was not an innocent child; he was a sex abuser and a child. For some, this may be difficult conceptually, but it's not to me. When I was in Year 2 at Conservative Town Grammar, he was in Year 7 at St Michael's College, Conservative Town and when I was in Year 5, he was in Year 10. He sexually abused me on numerous occasions over four years, more than one hundred times, any chance he could get after ballet and at the many family celebrations we'd have, no matter how fleeting. We had at least twenty family occasions each year; such was our large family, with many birthdays and religious events to celebrate at St Michael's Cathedral, Conservative Town. We were also related to many other Croatians in Conservative Town, including the Zipic and Daric families, who had come from the same Croatian village and we often attended their celebrations too and other events at the Croatian Club.

Looking back now, I suspect that King Claudius may also have been sexually abused by someone, someone from the clergy perhaps. He and his siblings went to primary school at St Vincent's, the same primary school that Cardinal Carlisle went to as a child, years earlier, when he was sexually abused as a child. King Claudius lived just a few streets away from the Carlisle family home, where Cardinal Carlisle would have stayed at and visited many times over the period of fifty years that his family lived there, in that house over the road from the primary school. Perhaps Cardinal Carlisle or his nephew Cameron Carlisle abused King Claudius. King Claudius was only two years younger than Cameron Carlisle. When Cameron Carlisle was eighteen, he sexually abused a survivor named Jacques DeBoys, who was fourteen years old at the time. This happened in 1984, the same year that my sexual abuse stopped. Cardinal Carlisle stopped sexually abusing Cameron in 1982, according to Cameron. So, our sexual abuse was going on contemporaneously. Was it merely a coincidence?

Or perhaps King Claudius was abused by someone else? According to Harry Percy, another survivor of Conservative Town clergy abuse, King Claudius was also the favourite altar boy of Cardinal Campeius and would be required to serve at all important ceremonies at St Michael's Cathedral, Conservative Town, including at the Bishop of Ely's funeral. King Claudius also attended secondary school at St Michael's College, Conservative Town, from 1981 to 1985. This is the very school where serial paedophiles in priestly garb lurked, including Cardinal Carlisle, Cardinal Wolsey, the Bishop of Winchester, the Bishop of Lincoln, Brother Friar and Brother Parsons Nose. These clergymen taught there and sexually abused children there, including some of my clients, such as Jack Cade and John Bates, the latter in the same year at school as King Claudius and a few years ahead of King Claudius' brother Hamlet. Perhaps King Claudius was abused by one of the clergy at his school.

The 1981 school magazine of St Michael's College, Conservative Town, The Holy Grail', confirms that King Claudius began Year 7 there. The 1982 and 1983 school magazines reveal that Father Lennox was the school chaplain and Cardinal Campeius was a rowing coach. In 1983, King Claudius was in Form 3 and Hamlet was in Form 1. King Claudius was involved in the college concert band and the athletics team. Hamlet was in junior hockey. In that same year, 1983, there were the following nine boys named O'Bourke at the school: Form 1, Aaron O'Bourke; Form 4, Abraham O'Bourke of Conservative Town and Agrippa O'Bourke of Conservative Town; Form 5, Boyet O'Bourke of Cleartown and Alonso O'Bourke of Mount Horizon; and Form 6, Angelo O'Bourke of Polotown. In 1984, there were extra boys named O'Bourke at the school in addition to those named above: Amiens O'Bourke of Birdville, Angus O'Bourke of Conservative Town and Agamemnon O'Bourke of Coaltown.

I initially suspected that one of those O'Bourke boys must

be the boy Obe in the bedroom during the group sexual assault, the same boy King Claudius' mum identified as O'Bourke when I disclosed my abuse, whom she told King Claudius to stop hanging around with at the time, for she told me she considered O'Bourke to be a bad influence. The police only ever made enquiries of one man named O'Bourke during the police investigation, Grumio O'Bourke. The trouble was he went to Birdville Technical School in Conservative Town and although he remembered King Claudius and admitted he had been to his house many times, he told police that he did not remember me. The police investigation of any O'Bourke ended there and then. However, it is likely that Grumio was the boy I knew as Obe in the bedroom as I later learned that King Claudius intended calling him as a witness at trial.

In the 1984 school magazine, The Holy Grail', there is a picture of young boys admiring Brother Parsons Nose's budgies. He would have been popular with the children, no doubt, using those birds as a draw card like many paedophiles use a game, a puppy, or lollies to attract and lure children. The same magazine reveals that King Claudius was involved in cadets, athletics and rowing and played the flute in 1984. Those activities would have brought him into even further contact with these known paedophiles than just his regular school classes. In that same year, Cardinal Campeius opened a new administration wing of the school and attended a school dinner.

The sad fact is that King Claudius orchestrated years of sexual abuse for his sisters and me and possibly other cousins who may not have disclosed their abuse. On one occasion, I was a victim of a group sexual assault with two other victims and two other perpetrators who used various equipment on us in turn. What child orchestrates sexual assaults like this without being taught or having seen this behaviour before? Goneril told me this group sexual assault happened to us twenty to thirty times in her memory and was surprised when I only recalled it happening to us once. Obviously, she remembers my abuse and my being there during the sexual assaults more than once, despite her subsequent statement to police to the contrary.

Sadly, ballet classes were my main, regular connection to King Claudius and being sexually abused, so I quit ballet at the end of grade five so there would be far less opportunity for contact between us. To convince my parents that I wanted to quit, I begged to get my hair cut in the summer school holidays, just to be sure, as I determined that cutting off my long ballet hair would mean the end of hair buns and ballet days and the end of King Claudius abusing me. I started grade six with a bob haircut and did not re-enrol at ballet.

To my surprise, my plan worked as he stopped sexually abusing me after this. Notwithstanding the resulting avoidance of after-Saturday-ballet abuse, I thought he'd continue abusing me at family events but, to my enormous relief, he didn't. My ballet medal collection stopped there with the end of my ballet classes, a forever reminder of my successful survival technique, like a war medal. Lest we forget – if only I could.

During the years of sexual abuse, the song 'Romeo and Juliet'[9] by Dire Straits started playing on the radio. Goneril and I talked about how cool it was to have a song with her parents' names in it. This song reminds me of the Cambridge and Oxford Street days and how anxious, sick and scared King Claudius made me feel while sexually abusing me. I think of him, not Uncle and Aunty, whenever I hear that song. Unfortunately, Conservative Town radio station Time Warp still plays it often.

Chapter 5

My Black

During my primary school years, there were more black-dressed figures like Madame Gulbis in my world, but I feared them much more than Madame: Dracula; Stari, the Croatian 'bad man'; and my Uncle Petruchio's shiny black multiple-headed sculpture stationed on my cousin's fence, a troll of sorts, daring us to cross.

Black was everywhere I looked as a child and that shade dominated my childhood world; my ballet leotard was black, my leg warmers were black, my violin case was black, King Claudius' cat, Mutchka, was black, my tetkas (aunties) back in Croatia all wore black, Baba wore black, Baba's squid-ink pasta was black, the mussels we collected at Portarlington Beach were black, marble gravestones for my family members were black, the hearses were black, the coffins were black, the priests wore black, the charcoal my parents used for life drawing was black, the nib ink at Goldrush School was black and Baba's hair was religiously dyed black. Always. I could even make black on demand when I closed my eyes to hide from King Claudius, but that worked like broken block-out blinds.

Stari could always be seen from the kitchen window of our beach house in Portarlington. 'Stari' was really just the branches of a cypress tree masquerading as the silhouette of a long-nosed man, belonging to a line of trees in the distance. It was unmistakably Stari though, no matter how much you stared critically and thoughtfully at that tree as a child from the safety of the kitchen. Baba always told me, 'You be good girl, or Stari will get you.' I believed her. Goneril believed her. We Pavlovic girls all believed her, and he was still watching us every time we peered out the window to check.

Ironically, the Devil wasn't one of the black figures I feared. From an early age, I decided the Devil wasn't real and that there was no Hell. Aunty Lady Macbeth, my cousin Banquo's mum, was a believer though. Aunty considered my cousin Desdemona the Devil personified after the seance. Poor Desdemona seriously considered the possibility and I remember parting her hair when she desperately asked me to check her head for the '666' as, by sad chance, her birth date also contained the Devil's number. In fact, all the cousins were scared into checking one another's heads for the Devil's number. Aunty Macbeth told Desdemona she was a black snake, the Devil and pure evil; such was her anger at Desdemona for conducting a seance in her parents' cellar.

Desdemona organised it with the elder cousins shortly after Banquo's death. We cousins were secretly huddled in the dank, dark cellar, with Uncle's smoked pršut hanging around our heads for added scare, while they willed the glass to move. Desdemona claimed Banquo spoke to her via the Ouija board that night, but I never saw the glass move. I quickly learned that superstition and Catholicism don't mix. Nor did little Cleopatra and Catholicism.

Under the black of night, I used to have recurring dreams that I could fly, not way up high like the Flying Nun but rather hovering over things – but only if I flapped my wings madly. I could fly low over the coffee table and then change direction across to the incredible couch and then swoop under the ugly

'70s arched wall through to the kitchen and down the passage with its sliding door of hideous amber glass and back around again. I never went far, seemingly just around the safe and familiar environment of my home.

On my journey, I would stop and stare at objects like the louvred pantry door and be anxious not to stop for too long or else I'd fall, but one time, I woke up to a crash landing, right on the dining table. In this dream, my tummy had brushed the surface, not getting the angle of the descent right and then I hovered for too long, watching a one-legged magpie out the window, a regular visitor we named Mack the Maggie. I was never sure when I woke up, whether my dream had been real, but I was always suspicious, and on this occasion, I raced to the lounge room window to see if my magpie friend was still there. Through the aluminium window, I saw the trunk of an enormous white gumtree and a frosted lawn leading to Dad's bluestone studio, but there was no bird in sight.

In hindsight, it's surprising that I didn't dream about ways of getting revenge on King Claudius. I was addicted to Prisoner, including the theme song, and knew that there were horrendous, violent ways of getting back at people, like bashing them or burning their hand in an ironing press – my favourite episode. I learned about the law and what happens when you break it but also about hierarchy, pecking order and corruption in the ranks from Queen Bea, Lizzie and 'the Screws', especially 'Vinegar Tits' and 'The Freak'.[10]

I assume that my lack of wanting revenge on King Claudius was because when I was a child, I didn't see what he did to me as a crime. I knew what he was doing to me all the time was wrong and forbidden, and very secret, but my child brain categorised it away from the stuff that meant handcuffs and police like a shooting or a bank robbery attracts. It wasn't until

I was older that I started to see the connections between sex and law: crusty old judges determining that prostitutes and wives can't be raped, that 'no often means yes' and other pearls of wisdom from the bench.

I always wanted to be a lawyer and I remember doing work experience in Year 10 at a reputable law firm that stood for social justice, for the underdog. I remember assisting with filing and observing cases in the old Magistrates' Court and being so ridiculously impressed with what I saw there that I stared at the barristers in awe, dreaming of the suits I'd wear and the shrewd retorts I'd give. However, in my university years, I also thought about how close that law firm was to the brothel every time my tram went past. Was it purely coincidental, or was there a secret internal door on their shared wall? Is it just another coincidence that the strip clubs are within metres of the Court precinct?

I still remember my school headmistress, Mrs Strict, justifying to a group of us wannabe debutantes why our school did not and will not hold debutante balls. 'I can think of nothing worse – young ladies dressed up, ready for a meat market!', she admonished. Despite my wanting to be a princess for a day back then, I now determined that Mrs Strict had been right - meat markets were everywhere I looked: the catwalks, the child-modelling pageants, the Victoria Secret catalogues, the Miss Worlds, the parade queens and the black-market versions. Suddenly, the meat market at Victoria Market didn't look or smell so bad anymore. The ghastly hocks, the garish pigs' heads and the grotesque rib cages lined in rows were just the same, hooked and hanging for the hungry consumer like the coquettish bony models for the designers and fashion magazines.

At school, I studied the artist Ivan Durrant and remember

writing about his meat paintings and his shocking performance art in the 1970s: the dumping of a slaughtered cow carcass[11] outside the National Gallery of Victoria, a reflection of the way we have become immune to and conveniently overlook, the horror of killing in modern-day society.[12] I think it's time for another installation as we appear to care more about the conditions of sheep for live export than the way we treat women. Those sad lamb's eyes return in the black of my mind. My black is indelible.

Chapter 6

Portarlington

Our basic fibro beach house in Summer Street, Portarlington was the scene of many happy family times; travelling down in our panel van for lazy summer days, splashing in the water, the smell of coconut oil in the air, the smell of moth balls in the cupboards and bait in the pantry, stale Lattice biscuits from the time before, the odd mouse trap. The Brady Bunch was often on TV, framed by a large monsteria.

Dida could always be found in the backyard digging up the vegetables or picking figs and lemons. Some things seen were quite unsavoury though, like me spying Baba cleaning intestines to cook tripe and polenta in the outside laundry. She certainly knew how to use every part of an animal to feed her large family, such was her resourcefulness, learned from her stone farm days in Croatia, but the stench was utterly putrid.

We children would cluster around the kitchen table, kneeling up on the old orange vinyl chairs so our arms could reach, hovering around the cauldron-sized aluminium pot of mussels like starving seagulls. It was an uncomplicated affair to share in a meal of mussels: no manners; no cutlery; no crockery required; a simple dipping sauce of garlic, olive oil and lemon; no bowl for the discarded shells, much too civilised, unnecessary. But we had to earn it; all the effort happened down on the beach. The children were directed by

Baba to collect the mussels, no time for sandcastles on our summer holidays. Our buckets and spades were used to hunt and gather for utilitarian purpose. There were mussels to collect and crabs to hunt. There were fish to catch too and many days spent on Uncle King Lear's boat, nibbling on Salada crackers to stave off seasickness while the fish bit and the men gutted.

Tragically, Portarlington Beach would claim my cousin Banquo, the beautiful little olive-skinned boy with jet black eyes, and take him away in front of us all. It was Australia Day weekend. We were playing in the waves which, at Portarlington Beach, a bay beach, seldom consist of more than a ripple. Safety in numbers – at least twenty members of our family there on the beach. 'Where's Banquo? Have you seen Banquo?' Aunty called out in panic. Banquo had been snorkeling near Goneril and me. He was our age, 7, and we hung out together at our many family get-togethers. Dad was his godfather, a serious title in our devout Roman Catholic family.

From the beach, Banquo looked like a white buoy, floating. His white T-shirt could have been mistaken for a seagull or a plastic bag. A stranger brought him in and back onto the beach and it was the most traumatic thing to see – endless 'Omo' suds being expelled from his limp body like an overflowing washing machine. 'What's all that Omo?' I asked Dad, who had affectionately called the crashing waves Omo in our excitement during my childhood. The consensus is that Banquo had an asthma attack whilst in the water. There was no saving him despite everyone's desperate efforts. We, his flesh and blood, all huddled around him in shock and loss. Deep chills in the heat of a hot summer's day. Aunty screaming. Adults wailing. Children crying. The inviting water now empty. The seam of our family lost like unravelling knitting before our very eyes. My beautiful mate was gone; the boy I had naughtily jumped on my parents' bed with was lifeless.

I saw Banquo for the last time at the viewing. Such is our religion, we kiss our loved ones' goodbye in open coffin. As a result, I saw death as a natural thing. I saw each step in the process. It was somehow tangible. There was no mystery in my mind other than the mystery of the faith. His skin made sense to me; he still had sea salt on his cheeks and stuck in his eyelashes. He was buried with his little fishing rod and looked just the same to me. My father lifted me up over the side of his coffin and I kissed my cousin's cold little cheek.

Black mussels were replaced with black rosary beads. My extended family turned to the Church and became more pious – if that were even possible; such was their steely devotion to Catholic dogma already. Banquo's bedroom became a shrine, beaches were black banned and out came the black clothes again. The family beach house died with my cousin and was eventually sold. Our Pavlovic family never recovered; however, could it?

Banquo was buried in the same plot with my Uncle King Claudius, who had died in a cycling accident in 1966, well before I was born. Uncle was only 20 years old when he died.

Born three years after Uncle died, in 1969, my cousin King Claudius, my abuser, was named after Uncle King Claudius. A lot carried with that name.

Chapter 7

Bucket Down the Well

There was another burial later that same year for my dog
Spotty, a little Jack Russell. He died while I was overseas;
'choked on a chicken bone' was what Baba told me. I was
getting used to this 'cycle of life' thing. Two accidental deaths.
God couldn't save Banquo or Spotty or bring them back to life
no matter how many Hail Marys.

In June 1981, my parents, both art teachers, went on long
service leave and off we went to Europe; Germany, Austria,
France, Italy and Croatia were now on my childhood map. I
wrote a daily diary and I still have it, it's so precious to me.
King Claudius' family gave it to me and King Claudius signed
his name in the front of it. Reading it reminds me of the little
things we notice as children that adults don't see. After all,
adults are too tall and too busy. Idle moments, spent bored and
waiting, sitting in the back of cars, wondering why our parents
are having to drive so far as if to the end of the earth, where
rainbows hide. From each hotel we stayed in, I took mini sugar
packets, mini jams and butters just in case I was peckish. I
collected bottle tops, pressed wild flowers, kept receipts,
napkins, ticket stubs, matchboxes, stones from the beach and
used postage stamps along the way. An inexpensive ring from
the marketplace in Split was my prized souvenir.

Dračevac, Zadar, the small village on the Adriatic Coast in

Croatia, where my dad and all his eight siblings were born. Two babies had died in utero, Adriana and Cassandra, so Baba had been pregnant at least ten times. In 1981, when we visited, the old family home was still without electricity and without running water. The kitchen was simple; a clay bell over a wood fire and sacks of flour and sugar was about it. Eggs from the chickens pecking around us, vegetables from the garden, milk from the cow and meat from the farmyard animals as required – subsistence living at its best.

I remember sitting on the stone front doorstep with a lady I called Baba Pava out of respect, who was Dad's aunty. Together, we spent time plucking feathers from a chicken in preparation for the evening's repast. This was organic farming without the organic price tag. The bread was made each morning by Baba Pava and Tetka Sorka and tasted like heaven; nothing here in Australia comes even close to that crust and smell. I met my loving and generous extended family, rode their donkey and we were made to feel so welcome throughout the little village. We ate with them, walked with them, swam with them and went to church with them, of course. They were humble, unsophisticated people with an abundance of generosity and would give you their last crumb if they were starving. Women in black mourning the death of their husbands long gone is Dračevac, very Catholic, like Conservative Town.

'Tomi!' shouted Tetka in anger and the rest, she uttered in Croatian. Tomi was a relative of mine, the son of Tetka Sorka. He was a boy only a little older than me. There was trouble in the town; the bucket had been dropped down the well, causing all manner of calamity. The story goes that I dropped the bucket down the well, but the truth is Tomi did it and blamed me. I had been shown how they get water with the bucket and rope and I had a turn. It was so exciting to me and Dad helped me carry that water to the house in a container; who needed a trip to Tourist Hill now?

My dad translated into English for me that Tomi said I did it when faced with his mother's accusations and in turn, the village believed Tomi. Little did I know then, as a 7-year-old girl, that this simple event would foreshadow what was in store for me back in Australia:

Boys are believed over girls.
Men are believed over girls and boys.
Men in the law change the narrative of women and children.
Men are believed over women.
Women take the blame.
Smart women take the blame with pride.
Troublesome women don't.
Brave women don't, but they are deemed insane.
They tread a lonely path . . . and I've found it.

Saturday 18.7.81
Baba Pavo and
tetka Sorka
cook for us
every day.
Tetka Sorka
bakes bread
every morning.
First she makes
a fire on bricks.
Then when it's
hot she brushes
the coals aside.
She puts the
dough on the
hot bricks and
puts a clay bell
on top of it.

Sunday 19·7·81.
I helped mum do
the washing
today. We have to
get all water from
the well. We do the
washing by hand

Chapter 8

My First Communion

Spring lamb on the spit for the celebration feast of my first
Eucharist didn't happen easily. My parents had a massive fight
over the lamb. They had agreed that lamb would be on the
menu, but Mum couldn't cope with Dad buying a live lamb to
be slaughtered and I remember Mum and I walking home
from that farm distraught and in tears. The lack of mental
connection then to what we eat on our plate and where it
comes from is hugely embarrassing now. I just don't think
Mum thought it through and I was easily caught up in her
distress. We left poor Dad to deal with it, but it made it to the
rotisserie somehow.

I remember feeling really nervous about going to the
Church and felt anxious about what seem like trivial things
now, like remembering which hand to take the holy host in as
I was rather unfamiliar with mass generally, only attending
Chapel at my Anglican school, which held a different mass to
the Catholic mass. I was concerned about my not knowing the
same replies to prayers and I knew different hymns too. I do
remember the holy host getting stuck on the roof of my mouth
and discreetly trying to dislodge the tasteless, Clag-like wafer
with my tongue whilst kneeling in silent prayer or in silence
anyway.

After the Communion Mass at St Michael's Cathedral in

Conservative Town, it was a casual backyard affair and we had all the tables set up outside in the warm Spring weather, but I still had butterflies in my tummy. There were vases of flowers, cakes and plenty of bread, the essential ingredient of every good Croatian party. I received Bibles, rosary beads and statues of Mary and baby Jesus, but I don't think I understood that I was sharing in eating the body of Christ that day though. It was too foreign a concept to me, just like a lifeless piece of roast lamb that tasted great was unrelated to that bleating lamb with big eyes that was looking at me at that farm.

However, I had other things on my mind that trumped the lamb that day and caused the butterflies: if and when King Claudius would strike. It happened again behind my bedroom door. Under my beautiful white communion dress. Nowhere was safe anymore. I had no 'barley' anymore.

Chapter 9

Sunday Mornings

Unlike the extended family, we rarely went to Church, only for special occasions, so Sundays were essentially free. Sunday mornings meant sleeping in, jogging with Dad, reading the papers, cooking pancakes and listening to records like Lou Reed and Bob Dylan up loud. We'd usually have family over for lunch and I'd help Mum with the cooking, using the voice of Bruce Springsteen to keep us chopping, mixing and baking.

One Sunday morning, I awoke to a loud banging at the front door, right behind my bedroom wall.

'Julio!' I could hear Baba's voice calling Dad's nickname.

Mum came racing into my bedroom and said, 'Quick, get up. Baba's here.'

I turned my sleepy head and my clock told me it was 7:10 a.m. – the Croatian visiting hour, apparently. I pulled back the curtains and saw Baba's brown Holden Statesman in our driveway and Dida approaching with an old lady I didn't recognise. I heard Mum say to Dad, 'Keep them at that end of the house while I make the beds!' and on went the happy hour. I was lost in translation, but I could easily decipher that this was a kind Croatian woman who was genuinely delighted to meet our family, especially my brother and me. Although I knew it was rude to stare, I fixated on her gold tooth as she smiled at me. We toured the house, showing our extended

relative Dad's paintings: portraits and landscapes acceptable to
Le Salon, intermixed with totally unacceptable oils of antique
dolls heads, twisted male and female bodies entwined in all the
wrong places, horse heads, Croatian flags and other flotsam
jetsam – very Dali.

Some years later, I recall going to a Vali Myers[13] exhibition
in Daylesford and meeting the eccentric artist herself, another
weirdo friend of my dad, who had a tattoo of a Dali-esque
moustache above her top lip. The persistence of memory . . .
shared by artists and sexual assault victims.

After the art tour around our house, we chatted over coffee
and cake, the Sunday-morning German breakfast served to
Croatians today. Then Baba turned to me and said, 'Dami
lollol' and I played lucky dip in her handbag, reaching for a
wrapped caramel, a ritual I was used to. I decided that she
must have bought all the Columbines in the world, for she
never ran out, and the same can be said for Teddy Bear biscuits
from the red-and-yellow melamine cookie container she had.
The grandchildren would always make a beeline for that
barrel, but she kept it well stocked.

When I was a child, I didn't want these surreal walls of my
home, for at my birthday parties, my school friends would say
things like 'That's rude!' pointing to a breast or a vagina. I
would retort, 'That's art!' but my rose blush gave me away.
Pictures of baskets of fruit, beautiful lakes, or benign sailing
boats didn't exist at our house. And whilst on topic, I didn't
want a surreal father either, who tied his hair back in a
ponytail, had a moustache and wore masseur sandals and a sari
to a Grammar School picnic. That was a day-mare, not a
nightmare, and I had many of those involving my wog
surname, late-arriving parents at school pickup – and by panel
van, might I add – and a lunchbox with a Band-Aid for a name

label! Or I had the choice of a yellow V8 Monaro collecting me that my friends could hear miles off and would yell out, 'Cleopatra, your grandfather's coming!' Joyous, character-building times for me at Conservative Town Grammar.

And I recall in the playground too. I always wanted to be Princess Leia as I had a crush on Luke Skywalker; we all did. However, despite my Leia buns and monkey loops, the boys decided that I should be Chewy, for I had the longest hair, so I had to spend playtime in the 'pinies', making weird monosyllabic noises. Damn, I was so jealous of you, Lyndal, and with your blonde hair and blue eyes; you were the Olivia in Grease too, the lead heroine again!

I still remember your birthday slumber party where, after watching Grease for the first time, we went running though the water drains of Conservative Town without your parents knowing. As a reward for getting away with it, we got to order whatever we liked from your parent's pub The Endless Pint and sat in the Ladies Lounge eating our dinner amongst the public on our own, like big grown-ups. That night began my love affair with chicken Kiev.

One day in 2009, I decided to reminisce and so I took my children to have some 1980s fun – down to the drains in Westbourne Street. We'd get off the screens and play real life Ninja Turtles! I safely lowered each child down the side of the high stone wall, and then, figuring it was doable, I jumped all the way down, but on landing I lost my balance and knocked all my children over like skittles, causing a cut, a graze and a few bruises. I must admit that I have always been challenged by physical pursuits!

Anyway, most Sunday mornings as a child, I would often be playing outside in the garden or in the lounge room when I'd see a large group of approximately thirty to forty children, boys and girls of various ages, walking past our house. I'd stop what I was doing to watch them walking en masse, in the middle of the road and I'd often wave at them and some would wave back. Sometimes I said hello coyly from our driveway. They were always singing sweetly, all in time, an angelic vision dressed in white smocks like a moving choir. Mum and Dad had explained to me that they were from St Crispin's Boys Home, the orphanage just up the road.

St Crispin's was an ominous-looking place, bordered by large Cypress trees. It looked formal and old, the type of building you'd expect to see a ghost in when you looked up at a window. Dad and I would go past often on our runs and I'd catch glimpses of the children from time to time. I thought they were so happy as they certainly presented that way. I hated being an only child and I used to think to myself how lucky they all were, always having someone to play with. I thought they had more fun than me. Little did I know what life was really like for them, not until I met Sir Hugh Evans, 'Hughsy', in 2015.

During the Royal Commission into Institutional Responses to Child Sexual Abuse, I discovered that Hughsy had lived there in the 1950s and 1960s and it was nothing short of hell for him with the depraved physical and sexual abuse that he was forced to endure. All these years, I thought it had been a happy place and I remember when it closed in 1980 as the children stopped coming past. I asked Mum and Dad what happened to them and they told me they'd found homes to live in and the orphanage was closing down. I had been satisfied with that outcome and did not question this any further. My cousin Hecate had her wedding reception there in the old chapel in the 1990s, when it was the function centre Foxglove Forest, but I did not give the orphaned children living there, all those years earlier, another thought.

In 1980, when St. Crispin's closed, I was an only child. Sarah, my best friend at school at the time, had two sisters and a brother and her family had just bought a pop-top caravan. This was my ultimate dream, to have siblings and a pop-top caravan. I begged my parents to get one too, to no avail as Mum was no camper. Uncle King Lear and Aunty, King Lear's wife, also had a caravan that I used to play Mums and Dads in and it was the coolest thing ever. Game shows like The Price is Rightand Sale of the Century gave out pop-top caravans as prizes at that time. I still associate caravans with big happy families and lots of children. I remember it was a time of mission brown and orange Tupperware, jelly and junket, housewives and women's magazines, perms and colour televisions, sibling rivalry and messy rooms – all the things I didn't have. But in 1981, my baby brother was growing in my mummy's tummy. Unreal banana peel![14]

I thought big families meant automatic happiness, country picnics on checked blankets and ribbon sandwiches like I thought babies meant bunny rugs, burps and maternal bliss. I never knew cousins and siblings could mean sexual abuse. I never knew family could mean sexual abuse. I was naive, but that is all I could be then as a 7-year-old who loved making daisy chains and paper fortune tellers. Yet notwithstanding my own sexual abuse, I was determined to have a big happy family too and to have my children in close succession. I was pregnant with Declan on Christopher's first birthday. I was on track. Christopher was not going to be an only child. And after Declan came Kate, followed by Alexander. Four children - far out brussel sprout![15] I was designing my happiness, which had children, brothers and sisters, at its core.

My four beautiful children give me eternal happiness, but

I'm not sure that they give one another this, at least not some of the time. They often complain that they have no one-on-one time with me and it's a fair complaint to make as they rarely do. In my case, a big family means a happy but mostly exhausted mum. I have realised I can't have it all and especially not at the same time. That is something only men can do and seemingly rather easily. I need a housewife, a chef, a cleaner, a gardener and a personal secretary, but I can't afford all that! Nor would most men if they paid for what women in their personal lives do for them and their children. And I also need a stylist, a personal trainer . . .

Chapter 10

My Confirmation

My Confirmation was an event that passed almost beyond my recall. It took place under the same Gothic arches as my First Communion four years earlier. Another new white dress from Calico, Lace and Flowers and a new opal necklace as a gift from my maternal grandparents Oma and Opa; no gold cross for me! More religious classes back at St Vincent's Primary School to prepare me to drink the blood of Christ from the fancy gold chalice.

Yet one factor that changed everything was absent: King Claudius. Maybe he was there, or maybe he wasn't there. Maybe he was sick or on school camp. Whatever the reason, whether he was there or not, I don't remember anything bad happening to me that day.

I was worried about the germs from other people's mouths on that church cup though, from drinking someone else's saliva. I remember talking about the chance of 'backflush', as we called it, giggling with Lizzie and my other girlfriends. A normal childhood day for me at long last.

My mum recalls noticing a change in me during grade six. She distinctly remembers suggesting to me that we stop for coffee at the house of Aunty, King Lear's wife, on the way home numerous times and me not wanting to go. She now recalls she thought it odd at the time as I was usually super keen to see Goneril and Regan and missed seeing them since quitting ballet. Apparently, I continued to find lame excuses to not want to visit there, such as saying I was too tired from school or had too much homework. Mum never knew the real reason why but probably didn't worry further as I still had playdates with Goneril and Regan but only at my house from then on, never again at their house.

Obviously, I tried to reduce the number of occasions I'd see King Claudius any way I could. I still saw him at our many regular family celebrations, including at Baba and Dida's house, but for some unknown reason, King Claudius stopped sexually abusing me. Maybe he saw an increased resistance in me; I am not sure. Maybe he was scared I'd tell now that I was older. Maybe he'd moved on to his younger sister Regan as Aunty, King Lear's wife, suggested to Regan when I disclosed my abuse and she disclosed hers in turn. Certainly, by the time Aunty and Uncle moved into the new house they built at Rosencrantz Lane, the sexual abuse had stopped. I remember King Claudius' new bedroom in the turret of their new house, decorated with posters of Arnold Schwarzenegger, his hero. I remember feeling relieved that their new house was not on the way home like their old house was.

I also remember a hymn I regularly sang at my school chapel at that time:

'What a friend we have in Jesus,
    All our sins and griefs to bear!
    What a privilege to carry
    Everything to God in prayer!
    Oh, what peace we often forfeit!
    Oh, what needless pain we bear!
    All because we do not carry

Everything to God in prayer!

Have we trials and temptations?
　Is there trouble anywhere?
　We should never be discouraged.
　Take it to the Lord in prayer.
　Can we find a friend so faithful
　Who will all our sorrows share?
　Jesus knows our every weakness.
　Take it to the Lord in prayer.

Are we weak and heavy laden,
　Cumbered with a load of care?
　Precious Saviour, still our refuge –
　Take it to the Lord in prayer.
　Do thy friends despise, forsake thee?
　Take it to the Lord in prayer!
　In His arms, He'll take and shield thee.
　Thou wilt find a solace there.'[16]

It was as if my connection to King Claudius and my sexual abuse rekindled during school chapel with the flickering candle near the altar. This song was a trigger for my sexual abuse and I remember trying to disguise my tears in chapel during this hymn. But the tears were involuntary and the more anxious I became about not crying, the more the tears welled and streamed. I thought Jesus knew what had happened to me, even if no one else around me did. The irony is that I didn't really believe in Jesus and God by then as the more I learned about evolution in science at school and discussed it with my parents, the more I rejected Catholicism. But that song served as a weekly reminder that someone knew, no matter how illogical. Someone knew and cared.

I could not regulate my emotions at chapel, but I certainly tried to. I remember trying to think of serious things to distract my mind, like one teacher Mrs Wilcox yelling at me loudly and sternly, 'Cleopatra Pavlovic, return to the Blue House area now!' when I was talking to my friends in the Red House camp on Athletics Day. It was the first and only time I was told off in primary school to my recollection, so I remember it well because I was mortified, the goody two shoes that I was. I also tried to focus on the colours in the stained-glass windows of the chapel and follow the leadlight pattern with my eye in an attempt to ignore the words of the hymns that seemed to go right to the heart of my secret and my soul. I tried to avoid chapel any time I could because it undid my perfectly happy world at school, where I felt safe and free of King Claudius. It was like the truth was tapping me on the shoulder and I couldn't cope with the reminder.

Chapter 11

The Changing Face of My Black

Years later, my childhood black returned to my world at Traditional University in the form of my academic gown at Crescent College, worn for dinner, and then again at my university graduations and Supreme Court admissions. This was what I considered legitimate black though, the silver lining on the black mussel shells of my childhood. Black now attached to positive things in my world: the ubiquitous little black dress, the colour of my newborn's gollywog hair after their first bath, delicacies like liquorice and caviar and my car and work suits. All legitimate and all good. I reclaimed it; I needed to, living in Big Smoke where black is the 'new black' eternally. But fully reconciling the black of my childhood years would be a long way off yet.

My baba and dida had taught me that black meant respect, dignity, honour, tradition, death. It was a colour to be revered. It meant something important was happening. Baba would tell me and her other granddaughters to remember to wear a black dress (and forbade us wearing pants) to her funeral when she died. She told us this in the prime of her life, when there was no hint of ill health. She was a product of her times, a good Croatian lady, a subservient Croatian daughter at the heart of her adult being. This woman had a significant impact on me, but I imagine I am an utter failure and village prostitute in her eyes for shaming the family. It was King Claudius though, not me, who shamed our family, without a shadow of a doubt.

I never really knew what Baba thought of me – she never told me in words – but I could read between the lines, for she adored her boys, her Pavlovic men. Having had a massive heart attack on her birthday, which is one day after my birthday; there would be no "Appi Burzday!" that year and she was buried wearing her finest black lace dress.

As a child, I thought we must be so alike to have our birthdays a day apart, both Librans, with the scales of justice as our star sign. Even my twenty-first birthday cake was decorated with those damn scales of justice, a foreshadowing of my bright legal future; a painful legal quest, in chocolate ganache.

I will, however, claim the good traits of Baba. I share her outgoing nature, her love of her family, her positive can-do attitude, her determination, her resilience, her industriousness and her love of cooking. I also have her loud voice that's missing the same volume control button. However, she did not push boundaries where she could have done. She worked with what she had, accepted her lot in life and seemingly didn't dream of more. Maybe she didn't dare to. Certainly, she did not raise her men to respect women but rather to rule them. She accepted her role and played it well.

Thankfully, my father had his own beautiful mind and a heart set to a different beat, so he failed to adopt her mantra, either domestically or religiously. When Dad graduated from university as a mature-aged student, the first in the family to do so and the only sibling to do so, Baba appeared again in black dress with her bright brick-red lipstick to match. She was beamingly proud of him, but would she have felt the same way at my own graduations had she still been alive then? For I'm a mere girl after all and according to Baba, that's a shame in of itself.

Baba was progressive in some ways though – getting her driver's license in Australia, learning and speaking English and leaving her family in Croatia. She was brave leaving her home country, but for all her confidence, she betrayed me and all the other girls in my family. She considered it bad luck that I wasn't a boy when I was born. She told my Mum, 'Better luck next time – have boy.' So, it's bad luck to be a girl, according to Baba.

I may have grown up to believe this were true had my mum also been a good Croatian lady, but my wonderful German mum, with a work ethic second to none, illustrated the falsity of this in her life as a teacher and as a mother. Autonomy, she always said, was the key. Her mother, my oma, had told her the worst thing you can do is sit at home, wondering how to pay the bills with no money. If you want something, you must work for it; don't hold your hand out to anyone but especially not to your husband.

So, albeit married, my mum worked and determined the path of her life and was the best role model a girl could ever have. My dad was a teacher too and unconsciously a feminist and supported my mum to have her career just as he had his. I knew I could be whatever I dreamed; my parents believed it, my maternal grandparents believed it, my friends believed it, my teachers believed it and most importantly, I believed it, absolutely. However, my dad's family seemed to be at cross purposes, modelling and preaching something else entirely.

My brother Romeo and I were the only Pavlovic cousins to go to Conservative Town Grammar School. All my other cousins went to Catholic primary and Catholic senior schools Good Girl School and St Michael's College in Conservative

Town. One cousin, Desdemona, did attend Grammar off and on but only at her deranged father's whim, but that same cousin started a rumour amongst the cousins that I thought I was better than everyone else. She had nothing to be jealous of but remains that sort of person and has supported King Claudius to the end of the court case, just as Cardinal Campeius supported Cardinal Carlisle! What a proud moment for her last year, to be the crutch of a paedophile.

I started at Conservative Town Grammar in three-year-old kinder in 1977 and went all the way through to Year 12 in 1991. I absolutely loved my school. My teachers gave me structure, order and sanity. The opportunity for hope and a path forward was intoxicating and I was hungry for self-determination and knowledge. I was fiercely independent from a very young age and have been 'on a mission' for as long as I can remember. My friends said I would walk to the library at a noticeably fast pace and even going to the canteen to get a sausage roll involved a brisk, purposeful walk. I aimed high and achieved high with social justice in my core. My world at Grammar made sense to me and I believed what they told me about the outside world. What the teachers said even came true – for a while.

I was only dished up the alternative form of 'girl' at Pavlovic family gatherings, where I quickly learned that I didn't fit in with the other girls from that finishing school by the lake. My mum didn't fit in with the in-laws either. For starters, none of them worked outside the home. They complained they never had any money, for they believed it was their husband's money after all. Cake recipes were really their only common ground. Once ballet died, so too did my frame of reference to my girl cousins.

I couldn't sew at all and had only done one semester of

textiles in Year 7. Good Girl School seemed to prescribe cooking and sewing classes as compulsory subjects while I was busy learning subjects at Grammar like Latin and Legal Studies instead. Clearly, Good Girl School was where good Croatian girls were made, the kind Dida had exhorted me to be. On one occasion, my Aunty Lady Macbeth invited me to a sewing day at her house as a way of rectifying my obviously gaping absence of good wife and homemaker qualities. Aunty taught me other things too, quite by accident, unknowingly putting me on the spot when inviting me to say grace at the dinner table. I honestly didn't know what to say, so she kindly prompted me through it.

I remember embarrassing poor Aunty Lady Macbeth one time I will never forget. One of our extended relatives, another woman in black, was over from Croatia. We had gathered at Baba and Dida's to meet her when Aunty turned to me and said,

'Can you say something in Croatian for her, please, draga?'

I smiled and confidently said, 'Eh crago!'

Aunty said, 'Oh darling, no, no, something else, please.'

I tried again – 'Courbina cher?' with concerning intonation.

Aunty's reaction was one of utter horror, for I had just told the visitor to go to hell and that she should fornicate with God. I was banished to the lounge room. I was like a client who, in a nanosecond, undoes their own case proudly from the witness box, swearing and admitting that they were there at the scene of the crime and saw someone else do it despite giving firm instructions to the contrary for six months. I had just committed a crime without knowing it, for the words I had used were the ones I heard Baba and Dida say to each other all the time. I knew others too like *courutz*, *issusati borgaty* and *prasits*, but they would have dug me a deeper grave. *Dobro* was the safe word I was looking for but couldn't find.

'Toy rata,' said Aunty with a look of disgust. I knew what those words meant and gently closed the door behind me in a cloud of disgrace. Then the grandfather clock told me off, as if for Dida –'Ding, ding, ding, ding, ding, ding, ding, ding, ding, ding, ding!' I passed the time until lunch by playing with Dida's cigarette keeper box, triggered into recalling the times I'd heard the clock chimes from the bedroom while I was being sexually assaulted. No wonder I never wanted that grandfather clock as an inheritance.

Baba and Dida were a complicated couple. They swore at each other relentlessly as they went about their daily rituals of housewife and worker. Those words popped out with passion at breakfast, when Baba would prepare his European breakfast bowl of milky coffee bread – slops for pigs, basically – or outside in the hothouse where the tomatoes reddened, and tempers flared. Most things involved a heated argument or at least nasty words, words I didn't hear at home. This unnecessary din betrayed the otherwise calm serenity and order of Baba's kitchen: meat roasting, bones broiling, soup bubbling – all timed perfectly for the family's return for lunch after Church, and the stunning white Hoya absolutely thriving and flowering amongst it all.

'When I young, I eat two pig!' Dida would often boast. This was a Croatian saying that meant that he was as strong as an ox and could eat enough food to feed a village for a year in one day. Dida was a tireless worker and his enormous, strong and calloused hands showed it; his wiry body also showed it. He and his sons built houses all over Conservative Town. But Baba worked equally hard and had the same strong hands that did mend, darn, sew, cook, clean, garden and fix. White doilies, family photographs, indoor plants, '60s kitsch and crochet toilet paper dolls reflected my Baba. She loved jewellery too and always wore gold, boldly exclaiming, 'Gold is best, is specialie!' but it weighed down her pierced ears so much so that the original holes appeared as deep linear cuts. A funny thing she always did was say, 'Baka baka,' and contemporaneously flick my head firmly with her giant fingers. I don't know if she thought I had nits, but there seemed to be no reason for her to do so other than as a show of her affection. And when it was time to go, a hug that could crush your insides and a pat on the back that would wind me. I knew that I was loved!

Returning to the topic of my inability to sew, Mum didn't know how to sew either, for she bought clothes with her money earned through teaching instead. My cousins would talk about their sewing projects and I would have nothing to add or relate to. I made some attempts, but my interest was fleeting, just to temporarily fit in. I have never had a cooking class, but I could cook very well without home economics as I learned the recipes of my parents at home every day. My father shared the cooking with my mother, healthy German and Mediterranean meals mainly and always a salad but no grace. Dad also changed my nappies as a baby, much to Baba's disgust. Admittedly, Mum did do the bulk of housework, but there was no assumption that it was her work to do; rather, a level of German pride was at play more than anything else.

This was in stark contrast to life for my cousins; their mothers concerned themselves with pleasing their husbands with dinner on the table at six o'clock sharp, cleaning the house and all chores and child-related jobs done by them alone. Their fathers were born to relax at home after work and be pleased by twenty-four-hour wifely servitude. Meanwhile, my cousins complained that their dads got their names mixed up with their other siblings and that they didn't really know their fathers and vice versa. They even feared their fathers. They told me my parents were 'so cool' and they wished theirs were more like mine. These were the two models of family life presented and juxtaposed, but it was an easy choice for me to make.

My parents are irreligious, artistic, intelligent, loving, educated, kind and extremely generous. They modelled consideration, compassion and the importance of family. They taught me by example how to belong yet maintain one's individual thought and action. I learned that at times, it's important to go with the flow and not to rock the boat for the sake of family harmony. In this way, Dad's elder brothers got their way, first choice in things like the best rooms in the family beach house, best plots of land in Croatia and the ability to trump upcoming weddings and occasions with that of their own. Put simply, privilege based on patriarchy and primogeniture, something I considered completely offensive and irrelevant in my life as an educated woman in Australia. I would not subscribe to their hierarchy, but I had to reconcile the difference which has continued to be a costly exercise to my heart and soul. I had to fight for respect because Dad himself hadn't challenged the status quo.

Rather than seeking to be critical of my dad, I say that this dynamic is true in most families, for I have noticed that it seems that no matter how accomplished one becomes in their life, in their careers, in their accumulation of fancy material possessions, one cannot easily transcend the family pecking order, which makes family gatherings at Christmas and Easter such a painful experience for so many. It seems that one is almost stuck in one's birth order, forever seeking transcendence or approval in vain, attempting to not be the oft-forgotten 'middle child' or whatever the case may be. For even when one transcends this childhood hierarchy in one's adult life, it seems to remain fixed when it comes to one's extended family life. The youngest child whom no one listened to transforms into the confident speaker, whose expertise makes them a millionaire, who then morphs back into the unheard child as the original pecking order is reimposed at Christmas time. If they try to assert their new persona, it often leads to a family fight and someone leaving Christmas lunch early.

I continued to butt heads with tradition and patriarchy in my later years. My aunties claimed my boyfriend Gallus, who would later become my husband, could not be in a significant family photo taken at Baba's funeral in 1990 because we were not yet married. Baba's death also caused King Claudius' first wedding to be postponed out of respect but at the expense of the bride's parents, whereby they lost their wedding deposits. Yet when Dida died in March 1998, Witch One's wedding went ahead only a month later, for some traditions seem to be abandoned when it suits the Pavlovic brothers, especially when it's their money that is at stake. Moreover, my Uncle Macbeth claimed his daughter's wedding should go two weeks before mine simply because she was older than me. Stone farm philosophy!

At the time that I booked my wedding at Crescent College Chapel and Quat Quatta in Melbourne, more than a year in advance notice was required and my cousin wasn't even engaged yet. Still, she had to have her Conservative Town Tack-o-rama Room Wedding on Anzac Day, the only available Saturday; such was their rush and short notice. Our family connection to the Cathedral enabled her to have her wedding on Anzac Day itself, which was far from kosher. Still, she got her way simply because her father was older and richer than mine, which was so frustrating as Gallus and I had saved and paid for our wedding mostly ourselves. Moreover, it was a similar guest list with only one weekend in between, which took the momentum for ours away.

This became a patriarchal pattern that I desperately tried to unpick at every opportunity. I did wear black to Baba's funeral though, as was her living and dying wish, for some traditions cost nothing to follow and are a pleasure, especially when the choice to follow them is made freely.

In Year 12 at school, I painted a large mural in acrylic entitled 'What Style of Woman Are You?'[17] and I won the Jessie Merritt Art Award. I used various artistic styles to express the different personalities and traits of women: post-modernists, traditionalists, expressionists and those who'd succumbed to The Beauty Myth[18]. Clearly, I had a lot to say back then too, but I wasn't shut down then. I loved debating and public speaking too, but no one turned off my microphone then.

In Year 12, I also wrote an English essay not dissimilar from the early chapters of this book. I wrote about my maternal and paternal grandparents, my childhood, my family traditions, but I stopped short of the sexual abuse. In hindsight, I wonder if this was the beginning of me trying to tell, an innocent foreshadowing of the disclosure that was to come more than twenty years later after I wrote that essay.

At university, I blossomed. I did a double major in Fine Art History and Women's Studies in my Arts Degree and Frida Kahlo, Simone de Beauvoir and Jocelyn Scutt became my new heroes. My new bibles included The Second Sex[19], The Bell Jar[20], Who's Afraid of Virginia Wolf?[21] and one fabulous text book: Women and the Law[22]. At university, my favourite subject was family law, which is no surprise, and I remember Dr Scutt coming to Macquarie University to speak to us law students. She earned my instant respect and admiration. During a trip to Paris in 2013, for my fortieth birthday, I visited de Beauvoir's and Sartre's grave, but unlike the Pavlovic graves in the Roman Catholic section in Conservative Town, I found no angels guarding them in black granite. I left my mentor some beautiful lilies, as pale as the granite of her headstone, and softly whispered, 'No one knows me or loves me completely. I have only myself'[23]. I thought to myself, No one knows me in Paris!

Like the great philosophers, I was ahead of my time at university, on an exciting new path to fight for women's rights on a new wave of feminism, but when I told people I had a major in Women's Studies, they asked, 'What's that?' My subjects included 'The Changing Place of Women in Society' and 'Women in Organisations', and from thereon, I proudly branded myself a feminist and kept fighting for change at a time when many of my privileged female contemporaries thought feminism was a dirty word, an unnecessary fight and necessitated having hairy armpits.

Whilst at Traditional University, I lived on campus at Crescent College, designed by Sir Walter Burleigh Griffin, with the great dining-hall dome the main architectural marvel. My cousins Hamlet and Goneril resided there too, with Goneril attending the Victorian College of the Arts for dance. I worked part time in the College kitchen under the management of Mrs Parsimony, who was certainly a shrewd business lady. My shifts included Saturday lunch: ham steaks and ice-cream blocks and, of course, everyone wanted chocolate topping. But the problem was that Mrs Parsimony ordered equal quantities of chocolate, strawberry, caramel and butterscotch topping, so when I asked for more chocolate to be ordered, as I was at the coalface fielding the complaints about no chocolate topping, she said firmly in her shrill German accent, 'No, zere's plenty of topping. I'm not buying any more until it's all run out.' There's one way to keep the topping budget down!

I returned to Crescent College to get married in its architecturally magnificent Chapel in 1998 for the sentimental significance and for the beautiful sandstone backdrop for the photographs. I also returned to religious ceremony at St Michael's Cathedral in Conservative Town with the Christenings of my children, but I can't explain why I even bothered other than for tradition's sake. Although I do remember my mum telling me about how boring Catholic conversion classes were for her when she, a Protestant, was preparing to marry Dad; essentially listening to a drunk old priest for hours while Dad and the priest took turns at nodding off. She suggested her grandchildren be Christened for convenience, just in case. I was certainly happy to be caught up in the celebration of all these religious events, ordering wonderful Castle cakes made by Carmel, wrapping themed bonbonnière and dressing my children into the beautiful heirloom christening gown my parents bought for my first child, Christopher.

It may be shallow of me, but it's true; I loved an excuse for a party, but there was no religious aim. King Claudius' mum, King Lear's wife, would come and discuss the importance of the sacrament to us each time, being the parish sponsor, but it was a nice cuppa and a catch-up as I went through the motions of paperwork, choosing godparents and booking BH's (Beautiful Hotel) over the road for the celebrations. When I have coffee at BH's now and see all those Loud Fence ribbons flying brightly, I feel so heartened by so many. Talk about a themed frame for my life!

After I disclosed my abuse, my Croatian uncles considered that my father had failed in his duty to silence me and Uncle Cassius considered that I should be muzzled. This was Neanderthal nonsense simply dovetailing with my belief in evolution and providing proof of same. Similarly, my Uncle Macbeth disgraced himself when he told my parents in an undignified crouching position, 'She shitting on family like this,' after he learned that I'd told the police. At that point, I considered him to be representative of one of the earliest monkeys depicted on the chart of evolutionary development of mankind.

My closest aunty at the time, Emilia, even applied for an Intervention Order against me in a vain attempt to silence me. Imagine that, in 2013, just one week before Christmas, my antiquated 70-year-old aunty finally got with the times and found her way to the Conservative Town Magistrates' Court, an idea spawned by her daughter Desdemona, no doubt. I'm surprised that her Croatian donkey and cart could get her there. It's ironic after all the years of family violence bestowed on her by her husband, including at least one massive black eye, that she never found her way to the Courthouse sooner when there was actual cause to seek safety and from the man who supposedly loved her. Rather, she was seeking safety from the truth I was telling.

My colour black returned in the form of Aunty's eye. At the time of her black eye, I talked to my father about it but never received a satisfactory answer as he didn't wish to pry; such was his gentle, non-confrontational nature. I always suspected my brutish uncle was responsible. Aunty was always more martyr than sense. She waited until after my uncle's death in 2013 to sing in a choir as she'd always wanted to do.

She thought she was smarter than my other aunty Lady
Macbeth, who had sung in the church choir for forty years,
albeit at the annoyance of her husband. She explained that she
considered herself smarter for not bringing that kind of marital
disharmony to her life and so denied herself whilst convincing
herself that this was the correct thing to do. How sad to wait
fifty years to sing? Such is the nature of family violence.

I remember Aunty Emilia yelling at me in response to my
disclosure, 'You think you are the only one [that was abused].
You want to change it, you are on your own!'

My relationship with her abruptly ended that day, never to
return. I was dead to the family now, ironically not King
Claudius, so on White Ribbon Day in 2013, I wrote an open
letter to the family titled 'Eulogy to the Pavlovic Family — On
the Sad Loss of Cleopatra, Julius Caesar and Calpurnia'[24]. At
that stage, I didn't include my brother Romeo in the eulogy as
he was still in contact with some of our cousins who were his
age, so it wasn't appropriate. I also never gave the Eulogy to
King Lear and his wife or Goneril and Regan, or to Brutus and
Portia, because at that time they all believed me. They all
believed me until they learned that the police were involved.

Chapter 12

Saturday Mornings

Saturday mornings in Clarence Street for violin lessons and then Hollywood Cinema for ballet lessons were a beautiful thing, but Saturday afternoons were a black ink blot on the landscape of my childhood. I had a lot to think about on Saturdays; remembering my music book, my ballet shoes and wondering what King Claudius would do to me today.

My violin teacher, Mrs. Moritz, lived in a big old house in Diggers Rise, a suburb tucked in behind the Conservative Town railway station. She was Japanese and was married to Mr. Henry Moritz, one of Mum and Dad's teachers at art school. She taught me violin by Suzuki method until she died in 1985, when I was in Grade six at school. She was a lovely lady who was softly spoken, encouraging and had a warm and gentle nature. I can still remember the old tunes and sometimes show off to my children that I can still play from memory, without knowing the notes or how to read music. Listening to violins in an orchestra is still music to my soul, as if I have an ear for it for life.

There was another Moritz in my life because of my constant childhood word associations: a naughty German boy called Moritz. The mischievous adventures of Max and Moritz[25] and Struwwelpeter (or Shock-headed Peter)[26] were my bedtime stories; old, didactic German tales, most often

ending in death and I have read these same stories to my
children at bedtime. What's wrong with that? Bugger Spot and
Dr. Seuss!

I especially loved the story of 'Sucker Thumb', who sucks
his thumb when his mother is out despite his mother warning
him not to and sure enough, the great Scissor Man comes and
cuts his thumb right off! Or poor Paulinchen, the girl who's
warned not to play with matches yet strikes another match and
she catches alight and burns to death, of course, leaving a pile
of ashes and her little red shoes, which don't burn with her for
some strange reason I could never understand and always
commented on to Mum, who'd translate the stories she read
from her books written in German.

It was those stories or Dracula tales told by Dad from his
imagination, not from a book, that put me to sleep, but the
mental images he painted through descriptive language were
spectacularly scary. Sadly, for me, there was a space behind the
'incredible couch' that we owned, the same couch John
Farnham had, according to the salesman and his pitch, that left
just enough room for Dracula's coffin. Dad would tell me how
Dracula would come out of his coffin at night-time, hungrily
looking for blood. I would go to bed covering my neck each
night, the doona pulled right up to my chin, including on the
hottest summer nights. I loved Dad's stories though and I'd
beg him to tell me another and another. He'd sometimes
pause, I suspect to think of Dracula's next move in the ad-lib
plot, and I'd impatiently yell out, 'Keep going!' Dad's tales of
Transylvanian terrors were wonderfully chilling, but I don't
know how he came up with so many new storylines now that
I'm a tired parent myself.

I was quite critical of my storybooks as a child though,
particularly when the pictures on the page didn't match the

words on that page. I'd complain that what I was hearing and the pictures together didn't make sense. The pictures would show earlier events or scenes yet to be described. I liked things to make sense. It really annoyed me, and I told my parents that when I was a grown-up, I'd make proper picture books. What a precocious pain!

I suspect that my mind must have formed its OCD pattern in my primary school years. A pattern that benefitted me in my school studies, my university studies, my working years, my family organisation – a challenge with work and four children. I run everything to plan in disciplined order and leave nothing to chance. I write to-do lists and create charts at home and at work. I'm sure that I drive everyone crazy.

This need for predictability and control of my environment, to never be late, to never miss a beat, is it the real me or the me I had to become to cope with the sexual abuse? A way to know that each time, immediately after the abuse, there was still a reason to live, to keep going about my day as if nothing bad had happened? But the dancing died. And with the death of Mrs. Moritz, so too did violin. And in case you were wondering, the book characters Max and Moritz died too - turned into chicken pellets as a result of their cruel mischief to chickens amongst other things. My earliest lesson in karma. No wonder I was a goody two shoes!

Yes, sexual abuse forever changes you, but you never know who you were before it started. Maybe it's different if you've been abused when you are older, but how do you know who you were before the abuse when you were a young child when it started? My husband, Antony, is adopted and I sometimes wonder if he asks similar rhetorical questions: who would I be if I had been raised by my biological parents? I seem to be on a quest to find my original, true self. I can see who I am as a mother, as a wife, as a daughter, as a sister, as a friend and as a lawyer. But when I see myself out of context, if I were to just sit on a park bench around the lake, I honestly don't know who I am. Who was I before the abuse? Like the confused bunyip in the children's picture book The Bunyip of Berkeley's Creek[27] by Jenny Wagner and brilliantly illustrated by my parent's friend Ron Brooks, who repeatedly asks, 'What am I?'as he gazes at his own reflection.

My passions, my hopes and my dreams for a better world for my children are all focused on stopping the sexual abuse of children. I'm like a one-policy party. Yes, I do care about the environment and the sad state that it is in. I care about the shameful unequal distribution of wealth and the declining quality of life that so many people in my local community of Conservative Town are experiencing, lives plagued with poverty, crime, drug abuse, loss of motivation, marital breakdown, children in State care, homelessness and unemployment. But through my lens of child sexual abuse, I believe that stopping sexual abuse would go a long way to resolving relationship breakdown, drug abuse, suicide, family violence in all its guises, homicide, overcrowded jails and a bulging health budget.

Sexual abuse is at the core of one's wounded soul. Without it, lives would be lighter, hearts would be freer, families would be happier and premature deaths would be fewer. I could truly dance again when I hear the Nutcracker Suite[28] at Christmas time or read the story to my children without tears welling. I wouldn't have to change the station when I hear Romeo and Juliet[29] on the radio.

And the cycle of life continued. I said goodbye to Madame Gulbis on Thursday, 31 August 2017, at the interment of her ashes in Conservative Town. Born in 1920, she was 97 years old when she died. A remarkable lady, strong through wartime, brave in a new country, artistic and disciplined. I thank her for bringing the magic and love of dance to my childhood, the dance of the sunflowers. I will never forget her.

Chapter 13

My Christmas and Easter

'Wake up, Cleopatra, wake up. It's time to go,' said Dad as I jumped into action. I can't believe that I had gone to sleep whilst waiting despite all my excitement. I sat up, already dressed and ready, grabbed my coat and hurried to the car with Mum and Dad. It was pitch black and the streets were empty as we drove to Midnight Mass. As we parked in Friar Street, there was a sea of people, marching like lines of ants, all heading silently in the one direction: to St Michael's Cathedral in Conservative Town.

There's something really intoxicating about Midnight Mass to a child. It's so dramatic to go to Church in the middle of the night. It's freezing and seemingly even colder inside the austere, dimly lit church. For many years, we had standing room only because it was so packed or perhaps because we were so late; I'm not sure. Yet my extended family members were never late, always taking pride of place in the front five pews. I remember not being able to see the altar and tall adults blocked my view of the important priests. I remember the distinctive smell of that church incense, singing hymns and snuggling up to Mum and Dad, huddled between them to keep warm in the cold, draughty pews. I remember staring closely at people's coat buttons and handbags as that's what I saw at eye level. Afterwards, Dad would take the long way home, driving around, looking for Christmas tree lights that were still on that late at night.

This crazy night-time exodus from home happened on one other notable occasion in my childhood: when my brother Romeo was born. I was woken in the middle of the night and driven to Oma and Opa's house when Mum went into labour. That was more than exciting. It was like being in a time warp, tired yet euphoric with excited anticipation at finally having a brother or sister! My eight long years as an only child would soon be over.

There were other exciting late-night escapades too, like leaving for the airport to collect Aunty Beatrice arriving from Florida or going to the old Southern Drive-In just up the road from our house. Mum and Dad would load me into the car in my pyjamas, dressing gown and slippers, together with blankets and pillows. When we got there, I would be propped up between them in the middle of the front seat, sitting on the driver's console on a stack of pillows and doonas and wrapped in my white satin-edged blanket. I remember Dad resting the little speaker in the window and going to the diner-type café to get movie snacks for us like hot chips and hot chocolate. I barely remember watching the movie and when I did, it was often through Conservative Town rain and windscreen wipers on, with the car all fogged up, distracted by the environment around me. I would fall asleep at some point though, waking up to go home, seated back in my seatbelt. I loved the ritual; never mind the movie.

We always made it to Midnight Mass and to Church again only hours later for Christmas Day because Mum's family Christmas never clashed with my dad's. Mum's family celebrated the European way, on Christmas Eve, which finished just in time for midnight mass and Dad's family always gathered there and again on Christmas Day.

Mum told me that when she was young, her dad, my opa, would ring the bell for her and her four younger siblings to tell them all that the Christmas celebration was starting. They'd rush into the lounge room to see the room magically transformed into a German Christmas scene: the tree, the Christmas plates and a brass angel candleholder that spun from the heat as the candle burned. Opa rang the bell for his grandchildren too on the occasions that we still went to his house for Christmas Eve when I was young.

Their Guildenstern Christmas was all about the Christmas Tree, certainly not religion. 'O Tannenbaum, o Tannenbaum, Wie treu sind deine Blätter!'[30] Everything was silver on a real, live fir tree: silver baubles, silver lametta (tinsel) laid strand by strand and a silver star or angel on top. Every ornament was made of glass and there were real candles arranged on the branches by metal clip holders. In 1977, our tree set alight, but after people were stupidly blowing on it, fueling the fire, it was put out with wet towels before houses were inbuilt with the fuss of smoke detectors, alarms and fire engines to follow.

When I was a young child, I preferred the bright plastic Christmas tree decorations that my friends and Dad's family had. They had colourful lights that flashed, brightly coloured satin-covered bells on plastic Christmas trees, complete with a colourful tinsel garland. I just think children love colour and seemingly, the brighter the better. Plastic and colour was certainly 'in', just not at our house.

As an adult, I carry on the silver-only tree tradition, not to be monotone in a fashionable way but just for tradition's sake, for Opa, for Mum, for me, not a drop of colour and every year, I search for another ornament to hang on the tree. It's now crammed full of Venetian glass baubles, silver bells and silver frosted pinecones, but electric candle-style lights have replaced real candle and flame (and wax drips on the carpet). I have another tree for the children's hand-made decorations and the more colourful items.

Under our tree are the presents and on the coffee table in front are the chocolate plates. These plates are a German tradition and the ones we had originally were from Germany and made of hardy, fluted cardboard, decorated in vintage Christmas design. These have been replaced over the years with metal ones. These plates are laden with liqueur chocolates, mixed nuts still in their shells, gingerbread iced biscuits called pfeffernüsse, speculaas and three pieces of fruit: one orange, one apple and one banana. Mum told me that fruit was scarce in wartime Germany, so that's why we had to have what I saw as boring pieces of everyday fruit taking up too much room on the plate that should be reserved for sweeter, more decadent things. I remember biting into my first liqueur bean, breaking through the crisp sugar shell and releasing the cherry or orange liqueur inside and spitting the lot out onto the carpet. They don't make those same liqueur beans anymore, but I found them in France recently, so I brought boxes of them back to Australia. I loved looking at the colourful decorative chocolates carefully arranged on the top: foil umbrellas, ladybugs, angels, stars, stacked presents tied with string, coins and the obligatory Santa Claus. When I was young, these plates held the colour of Christmas I wanted, not the tree.

Willy Schneider[31] and Elvis Presley[32] Christmas records were played ritualistically. We had to listen to the bells of the Cologne Cathedral in Germany on that record before we could open our presents. The presents were opened in an orderly fashion, with one person handing out all the presents one by one as we'd listen to the German Boys' Choir that played on your heartstrings and gave you goose bumps.

Christmas in 1979 was memorable for all the wrong reasons though. There was a near drowning just two years before my cousin Banquo drowned. We had gone to Sydney to spend Christmas with my maternal Aunt Rosalind and Uncle Orlando and their two young boys. We were having a wonderful time when Aunty received a phone call from Oma, who was back in Conservative Town, some 950 kilometres away. She told Aunty that she'd had a premonition that Leonardo was drowning in the pool. Mum and I were inside with Aunty and baby Horatio when Aunty dropped the phone and raced outside to find Leonardo, whom we thought was safe outside with his dad, who was cooking the BBQ. Aunty looked at the pool and Leonardo was in it, all right, at the bottom. He was saved in seconds, but we couldn't work out how he'd got through the locked pool fence and escaped the view of Uncle, moreover how Oma knew about it. Oma always had a sixth sense about her and no one can tell me that it was a coincidence. No one in the family can explain it to this day. I'm happy to say that my cousin Leonardo, four years my junior, is alive and well, fit as a fiddle and just as cheeky as he was when he was little. He's a 'top bloke', as Opa would say in his strong German accent.

Christmas today carries strong traditions for my family, but they're certainly not religious. It's still all about the tree, but there's no Midnight Mass. Or daytime Mass. There's no Church, no prayer, private or otherwise, and there's certainly no confession of 'sins'. After all, we are not 'sinners' and certainly not from birth. We bake, we decorate, we sing, we plan, we shop, we wrap, we dream and we count down the days. We still go Christmas tree hunting at night, with everyone yelling out, 'There's one!' It's all about togetherness and not taking one another for granted.

Assembling the tree used to be a tradition the whole family participated in until the teenagers lost interest and left it to the eldest and youngest members of the family. It's a high-energy affair to get all the Christmas boxes down and decorate the tree and the house. There're boxes of baubles to sort and arrange, unhinged bells to fix and restring that got tired last year. Miraculously, the lights are always tangled, no matter how well they were packed away last year. I don't know if it's Christmas elves at play or my children or bloody Stari, but someone certainly tangles them up!

Christmas is still absolutely magical for us. We religiously play Elvis and Willy Schneider, for it wouldn't be Christmas without them and Opa's German potato salad, his recipe perfected by all of us out of sheer desperation to replicate that exact taste that Opa made using the right quantities of potato, pickled herring, pickled cucumbers, potatoes, mayonnaise and eggs, adorned with Viennese frankfurts with German mustard! Some years, I've made an advent calendar out of gingerbread men, decorating them with the children and numbering each one in icing and wrapping them in individual cellophane bags. Each one of my children takes it in turns to gobble up the next one. They get six each and the lucky child gets a seventh on Christmas Day!

We also keep to the tradition of making a gingerbread house each year, with lollies glued into place with royal icing. We have marshmallow rooves, lattice windows, mint-leaf borders, pineapple edges, milk-bottle fences, freckle paths and a Jaffa door handle. We even have figurines of a little witch and Hansel and Gretel for completeness.

Easter was another time of competing family traditions, the

religious ones upheld by my extended family versus the creative ones upheld by my immediate family, like Mum and Dad visiting churches overseas for their history and architectural splendour but certainly not to pray. The German tradition of Easter focusses on us making hand-dyed Easter eggs and hanging them on branches of twisted willow arranged in a vase, the rainbow centrepiece of our Easter table. We blow all the yolk and egg white through pin holes, far from fun as it gives you a headache and then we seal the holes with wax. Then layer by layer and colour by colour, we use beeswax to draw on each colour layer before we dye it again with the next colour. We have special wood and copper hand tools that we use to draw and drip the wax onto the egg over each layer of colour. At the end, we gently and carefully burn off all the wax, revealing all the previously kept colours. The final product is amazing. My children really look forward to this Good Friday holiday tradition at Peaceful Creek each year and the decadent brunch and egg hunt that follows on Easter Sunday.

In contrast, on Good Friday, Dad's family wakes up early to walk the Stations of the Cross and sometimes we went too. My Uncle Cassius and late Aunty Cassius' wife would host a brunch of hot cross buns afterwards at their home at the top of the hill, the end of the pilgrimage in Scenic Street, Religious Hill. We die-hard Conservative Town Catholics would brave the predictably cold mornings and meet at St George's Church in Church Street North, Conservative Town, and follow the Jesus cross and the Church van, the type a pervert would drive, with an old-fashioned loudspeaker blaring out the awful sound of an old screeching crone sitting atop the van, intoning the liturgy. It was bloody painful listening to her as the van rattled along, so I'd keep an ear-safe distance behind at the back of the pack, talking to my cousins as we dawdled along in the three-to four-hundred-odd crowd. Dad would often take Mum and me along begrudgingly, just to catch up with all the relatives in his family. Sometimes, if I was lucky, we'd be running so late that we'd miss the holy pilgrimage and meet at Uncle's house just to see everyone, which I always loved.

Despite being an atheist myself, my own family still celebrates Easter and Christmas for our own meaning and tradition. We lavish in it, family times imbued with childhood excitement over finding eggs in the garden and seeing all the presents under the tree. These festive events mean seeing Aunties, Uncles, cousins and grandparents, now only on my Mum's side since I disclosed by abuse. Extra chairs, extended tables, extra food, extra cutlery. White tablecloths to be starched and ironed, a once-per-year session I happily spend with an iron and an ironing board so that everything looks just right. Candelabra in position. My heirloom Whitehill silver cutlery in place. Delicatessen shopping to buy cake glazes, egg dyes, pickled herrings and other hard-to-find ingredients.

And specifically, at Christmas time, making a gingerbread house, truffle trees, advent calendars, Christmas biscuits, poppy-seed cake, streusel cake, baked cheesecake decorated with freshly glazed strawberries and adults-only tiramisu using a whole bottle of Tia Maria. A hazelnut torte that uses Nutella called Silvia's Cake, named after my Aunty Silvia Daric, which has become a family favourite. Butter cake baked in a Kugelhopf tin, filled with my parents' freshly picked cherries and raspberries, loganberries, gooseberries and red currants, all from my parents' garden. Raspberry macarons also make it to the table, fresh from the Melbourne institution that is Brunetti, not from my oven. I am yet to master that temperamental almond delight!

And at Easter time, Croatian Easter bread and fritolethat

Dad makes, Croatian liqueurs like Slivovitz, Kruskovac and Maraschino. They are very sentimental to me as my baba used to work in that Croatian liqueur factory! A German fruit and marzipan yeast ring that Mum makes, the hand-dyed egg tree, the dyed boiled eggs, shined with bacon fat and ready for our Easter egg smashing fight. Special jams like gooseberry, fig and Rübenkraut for our croissants. Platters of deli meats like pastrami, salami, hams, wheels of soft cheeses like double brie and the obligatory liverwurst. 'Wunderbar!'

As my children have grown older, they have commented how things seemed so much more exciting to them as a young child. They remembered Oma and Dida's house to be a bushland adventure so much bigger than it appears now. They loved the excitement of the big presents like train sets, Tonka trucks and dolls prams and mountains of wrapping paper. With exchanges of money in cards being the desired present as children get older, there's a loss of surprise, a loss of the careful thought previously required to find the little things that ascribe meaning, that show that the giver truly knows who the receiver is at heart.

So I will continue to go in the festive season search for the little things that matter: the gnome for Christopher, to remind him of his 3-year-old cheeky self who smashed the garden gnome as I told him the gnome reports to me whenever he pulls baby Declan's hair; the savoury treats for Declan, who was born missing a sweet tooth and the tiniest gifts for him to match his love of micro Lego or micro anything; dance gear or science-y things for Kate, including chemicals or anything in a bottle that loves to permanently stain carpet; and for Alexander, anything from the Poppy Shop, perhaps another mouse in a box like Tim to keep him company. The little things that fit into a stocking seem to hold the most meaning now. Little surprises from big hearts are the things my older children now yearn for.

When I was young, my brother Romeo and I always got what we wanted for Christmas, but we weren't spoilt. Baby Alive, Barbie, or roller skates for me. Lego, an electric train set, or rollerblades for Romeo. Our wish was always granted. But here's the thing: we received one gift. We never had a stocking as well or money or multiple gifts. Just one expensive gift, the thing we wanted most, and we thought we had the world. I do believe that we give our children far too much, and we need to cut back and learn to be happy with less. People, our family, our traditions, our funny moments and memories make Christmas. Money in a card is rather sad, in my opinion, but it's not the physically big presents either. Seemingly, it's the little things wrapped in string that are my favourite things. I'm with Julie Andrews on this. I wonder what my children will cling to in their own family traditions in the years to come. It certainly won't be the Church, a dying structure of abuse and corruption now perfectly wrapped in Loud Fence ribbons for all occasions.

Part 2

My Brave New World, 2013 A.D. (After Death/Disclosure)

Police are good. Police believed me. My cousin admits. Admits to me. My cousin denies. Denies to family. Denies to police. 'No comment' interview. Law protects him. Law hides truth. Innocent till guilty. Innocent don't confess. King Claudius did confess. No one cared. What the hell?

Chapter 14

An Extraordinary Mother/Daughter Day

I was shopping with Mum in Big Smoke when we decided to have lunch at Café Mia, a little Italian restaurant in the laneway off Fancy Arcade, and I knew I was finally ready to tell her my secret. The words came out surprisingly easily with a little wine and pasta and her advice was as I expected all along –'Go to the police, for heaven's sake. What are you waiting for?' The same advice my husband, Antony, had given me. Full support and understanding – the best mum in the world. She believed me and later that night, back in Conservative Town, so did Dad. And in an instant, I was a little girl again, nestled there between my parents like I used to be, snuggled up to them in front of the heater as a child, drinking hot chocolate in my two-handled Bunnykins mug, where I felt loved, safe and protected.

Chapter 15

Finding the Courage to Go to the Police

Like many of my clients and people before me, I stepped into the SOCIT unit at Conservative Town, my dad by my side, laden with fear and hope, hope that someone would believe me, fear that they wouldn't. It was June 2013, some thirty-three years after the abuse had started. Apparently, that's the average time it takes to disclose childhood sexual abuse: thirty-three years. I made the average, spot on.

But Dad was an outlier. Days after I disclosed, so did my Dad. Aversa, Italy, was the scene of the crimes against him: little 7-year-old Dad, working at the cinema, bleeding, coming home hurting. He didn't tell a soul. He wounded his own instead. Immigrating to Australia when he was 10 years old prevented any further sexual abuse. Unlike me, he didn't have to invent a way to make it stop.

During our trip overseas in 1981, we went to Aversa – of course we did – just like I drive by Cambridge and Oxford Streets, Conservative Town, past Villa Pavlovic. The wrought-iron sign remains a sad reminder of what went on in there. Just like the girl Jenny throwing stones at the house in the movie Forrest Gump[33], one often returns to the scene of the crime to reconcile their past trauma. The beautifully melodic yet triggering song 'Streets of your Town'[34] by the Go-Betweens plays in my head and the tears roll.

I was so shocked that both Dad and I were sexually abused at the same age, 7 years old. Magic number seven. When my daughter Kate turned 7 in May 2013, my childhood was zoomed in on and I went right back there to Cambridge Street, my little brown almond eyes focusing on my micro world: the texture of the carpet, the scuffs on the skirting board, the dust in the gap between the carpet and the skirting board. I turned my head away and focussed on the minutiae when he was touching me. I studied mini beasts lying down in the grass during hide-and-seek, the ants and the ladybirds, the bark on the tree trunk, the texture of the cement between the bricks as I ran my finger along, the pattern on my stockings. I tried to hold my breath, so he couldn't hear my heart beating and find my hiding place.

It was stark and obvious to me now. There was no grey area. I saw my 7-year-old self in Kate and I saw my older boys, Christopher and Declan, with similar age gaps to Kate as between King Claudius and me. Having my own children illustrate the dynamic gelled everything into place and solidified my resolve to tell. I tried to fathom my abuse from this new perspective, to somehow understand why, but I was lost. My older boys had nothing to do with Kate now, as if boys and girls don't mix. They were at different developmental stages entirely. She was young, playing with dolls and Play-Doh and they were four and six years older than her, playing soccer and riding scooters at the skate park with their friends. Their birthday parties had turned into 'boys only'. In primary school, that's a lot, five years. It makes an enormous difference. If you don't believe me, think of a girl in Year 5 you know in primary school and a Year 10 boy you know in secondary school and picture them in sexual acts together. Solved?

Kate is now 11 and in grade five; my abuse would stop at

the end of this grade-five year. I look at her and her little freckles, just like mine, and wonder how I behaved and appeared from grade two to grade five, four long, sad and anxious years of primary school bearing stomach aches and constant butterflies. Shy, nervous, self-conscious, studious, quiet and embarrassed was little Cleopatra. Two words, painfully shy, the only evidence of my abuse contained in my school reports and the high marks, hid the problem. I hid the problem. I knew I had to. I knew King Claudius was bad to do this to me. I knew it was wrong, but somehow, I made it my job to keep it a secret, to not get him into trouble. If this meant me losing confidence and being called 'self-conscious', so be it. Telling was not an option. I knew they would believe King Claudius and they all did, thirty-three years later.

While giving evidence at the Royal Commission into Institutional Responses to Child Sexual Abuse[35], Associate Professor Carolyn Quadrio explained,

About 20 to 40 per cent of children who have been abused won't show any symptoms at all and that's because some of them are what we describe as resilient, children who somehow survive trauma and make a reasonably good development. But some of those apparently non-symptomatic children become symptomatic later on. That's called the sleeper effect: that they look fine at the time and then some years later, something else triggers it.[36]

I must have been just that, a 'sleeper', and I suspect that my own children were the trigger. But there was another trigger too: King Claudius himself. At Uncle Iago's funeral in April 2013, King Claudius did not even say hello to me. This was the first time ever that he had completely ignored me. A seemingly small thing perhaps, possibly a faux pas, but not to me. We were no more than a few centimetres away from each other,

and we were there for hours at the church and at the wake at
the Conservative Town Bowling Club, but he ignored me. It
was as if he didn't even need to make an effort to acknowledge
me anymore. For years, I had listened to him give speeches at
family occasions, watched him carry coffins and represent our
family whilst biting my tongue. Now this. He had gotten away
with it and had become smug. He obviously had no need to
keep me onside or afford any respect to me or even pretend to.
He must have considered himself utterly invincible, like his
hero Arnold Schwarzenegger all those years ago. It was the last
straw.

What made me more resilient than most other survivors
though? Why had I survived when others hadn't? I was going
through the same stuff as someone who had overdosed on
drugs, yet being the overachieving extrovert and putting
myself centre-stage in the family, as if overcompensating,
seemed to work for me for a very long time. But it all caught
up with me, for I could not outsmart my own memories.

I went to Paris for my fortieth birthday with my husband,
Antony, a belated honeymoon to get away from the fallout
after my disclosure, hoping the Parisian air would rejuvenate
me and provide some big-picture perspective, away from the
needs of my four children, just for a few weeks. Countryside
France was amazing and Paris was every girl's dream:
macarons in Ladurée, beautiful fashion, fancy dogs, perfectly
trimmed topiaries, simple meals of baguette and the finest
gourmet gooey cheeses from Île Saint-Louis and magnificently
sparkling Moulin Rouge dancers; that took me back to my
ballet days, right back to Conservative Town. Sylvia Plath was
so right, because wherever I was, from Café de Flore in Paris to
Brunetti back home, I felt trapped and silenced under
soundproof walls, in my own 'Bell Jar'[37] feeling the misery of

injustice.

In Paris, I learned that the brain remembers and the nightmares play no matter how far you fly away, no matter how crammed full your life is with current-day happiness. I've switched to fight mode ever since and have dredged up the past; I had to, to survive.

Chapter 16

Going to CASA

Anger and sadness. Grief and pain. Family is lost. Anger and frustration. Memories and pain. Nightmares and insomnia. Anger and anger. Appointments with psychologists. Brave with clients. Fighting for clients. Fighting for me. Preoccupied with truth. Present-day suffering. My children proud. Coping in Conservative Town. Just.

I was fooling myself thinking I could vicariously heal, saving everyone but myself through legal practise. I was destined to fail and inevitably, I started to unspin.

It was time to become a client. In fact, it was long overdue. 'Time to open a file for me this time. This is not a client referral.' I laughed on the phone to CASA, but the remainder of the time, I cried at CASA. A lot. Piecing together truth, hurt, anger, history, events, people, actions, words and lies was an exhausting and sad process. Poring over photo albums with my parents, retracing our lives through a new lens of innocence lost. These were the hardest days of my life, trying to balance the present with the past. Functioning as a lawyer in a client matter one day and in my own the next, with a break for children, washing, meals and anxiety in the middle at night-time. I dragged my family through all this. My heartbroken parents, my concerned children and my exhausted husband.

When I arrived at Gospa Velika, Feast of Our Lady, on 15 August 2013, I felt like a suicide bomber, laden with explosives, ready to detonate. The table was set with wonderful Croatian dishes, white tablecloth, flowers and liqueurs from Zadar, the capital near our Pavlovic hometown. I told everyone I had something to say and then said it, just like that. 'King Claudius and Hamlet sexually abused Goneril, Regan and me years ago, when we were young.' My Neanderthal Uncle Macbeth tried to make light of it and said, laughing, 'Well, at least no one died.' Aunty Emilia got up and left, taking her precious fritolewith her in her urgency to get out of there, but my Uncle King Lear said,

'Whether it's Rolf Harris or my son, he has to face the consequences. If I'd known at the time, I would have killed them.'

When I disclosed my abuse to the family, the news had just broken worldwide about Rolf Harris and his escapades with his 'extra leg'. Uncle King Lear believed me then, but there weren't any consequences for his son King Claudius that followed, and the Catholic lie campaign set to work in full swing, more willing women covering up the mess of men. My university-educated cousins, many with children of their own, quite unbelievably believing the lies – or pretending to – and protecting the holy one, King Claudius, with Desdemona rolling out the red carpet for him at every turn.

At first, my extended family tried the old divide and conquer. They declared my mum was evil and I was her daughter, so I was inevitably evil too. Unoriginal virgin/whore stuff was all . . . boring. Notably, there was no mention of my dad's genetic contribution at that point. They lied to my dad, tried to blackmail him and my brother into submission, with the sole purpose of protecting King Claudius, protecting the family name Pavlovic and having access to my latest thoughts and intentions. They pressured him for me to drop it. They bribed them with paid work. They have always considered Dad the weakest link, a real softie.

On one occasion, my Uncle Cassius came to my house and berated me at my front door. I told him that I had heard the lies he'd been spreading about me and said he should say it to my face instead. He then had a conversation with my father out the front on the nature strip. I watched them through the blinds of my bedroom window and I could hear them talking. Uncle was trying to browbeat my dad, telling him that he needed to shut me up. They talked for about an hour whilst I listened in secret, angry and appalled. He told Dad that if I kept fighting this, it would go on forever. At that time, I didn't know why, but now I do; seemingly, the relationship between King Claudius, our family and Catholic clergymen would keep it going for years and years, with no end in sight.

At the time, I fought back and stressed to my dad that I would fight alone if I had to. The fence sitters later sided with me, but it took some time for them to detach themselves from the family and show loyalty and it was initially very hurtful to me. King Claudius had the entire family on side; surely, he didn't need my dad and my brother too. And why did they need the family so badly anyway and at the expense of supporting me? King Claudius and the family tried to take what little support I had so I'd fall apart and drop it. They failed. They messed with the wrong girl.

Chapter 17

The Legal Labyrinth

Days off work. Days at court. Documents to draft. Affidavits to swear. Memories to trawl. Reports to tender. Letters to write. Finding my voice. They don't listen. Police are wrong. Police are corrupt. The clock ticks. My hope fades. I am silenced. I walk alone. The tears roll. The phone rings. A caring friend. Bright fresh flowers. My mum's hugs. My dad's wisdom. I fight on. The years pass. My children grow. The clock ticks. The court slows. My husband angers. I grow angrier. Clients grow angrier. Stronger yet wearier. Feeding the law. With our money. With our time. With our energy. With the truth. Following all Orders. Finding no justice. Ready and resolute. Battling for change. Four long years. Years before too. When I pretended. I am tired. Truth tires you. In our system. The injustice system. Perpetrators know this. The legal system knows this. They lie in wait for you to die.

'There is little encouragement for survivors to participate in the criminal justice system if it does not have truth as its fundamental objective. Why risk potential re-traumatisation, a risk which materialises in many cases, to merely be a player in a sophisticated lawyers' game?'[38]

— The Honourable Justice Peter McClellan,
   Modern Prosecutors Conference, April 2017

Introduction

For more than four years, over four jurisdictions, for four years
of abuse, I tried to find justice. Justice can be a subjective and
elusive concept admittedly, but it shouldn't be this hard. I only
wanted the acknowledgement of what happened to me. I had a
taste of it twice, once from King Claudius during the pretext
call and a second time from Goneril and Regan, when they
validated my experience with their own because we shared the
same perpetrator. But the law didn't cause this. The law has
never assisted me, not even once. The law has worked its
working day, boxes have been ticked, documents have been
drafted, everyone's done their job, but it hasn't led to justice
but rather to yet another mention of my matter in Court. The
law works well but for its own ends, not for justice. Everyone
gets respected by the law except for the victim.

Like my dida, the law orders me, 'You be good girl' too,
albeit without the Croatian accent. Although I don't remember
having to say I would be a good girl at my Supreme Court
Admission in 1999, it must have been implied or declared
when I wasn't listening . . . or when I wasn't watching. It
certainly crept in from somewhere though, unbeknown to me,
or did it creep up and out of the very foundation stones of the
Court building? I swore I'd be of good character, but so did the
men being admitted as lawyers too that day. My mentor,
Simone de Beauvoir, prepared me for this double standard, not
the female lawyer and Pavlovic family friend Constance who
moved my admission.

The law calls it the 'Burden of Proof', but the burden is too great. It ensures guilt-free offending; whether it intended to or not is beside the point. The fact is it does. The police briefs are often completely inept. They are mostly put together by departmental hacks of low intelligence and mediocrity, essentially school dropouts. Charges laid are often incorrect, charges are dropped unceremoniously, or the brief is approved with errors and then successfully defended by the best in the legal profession. Fait accompli. It's inevitable; it's no surprise when one looks at the formula. If we really do want the pathetically low conviction rates to change, surely, we need to change this formula. Essentially, when you have government enterprise versus private enterprise, it's a no-brainer. Moreover, when you have an adversarial system where one party, the complainant, is unrepresented and not even considered a party with their own legal interest, it can hardly be a 'fair trial'.

So it goes something like this if you want to play the game of law: statements to police, pretext calls, letters to write, emails to read, cost and disclosure statements to sign, affidavits to swear, documents to draft, documents to serve, documents to file, documents to peruse, advice/instructions to give or receive, correspondence to peruse, transcripts to request, fees to request, court forms to complete, barristers' fee slips, court-filing fees, briefs to barristers, file notes to keep, back sheets to prepare, chronologies to order, indexes to create, jury fees payable, Orders to follow, Notice of Hearing, media to contact, articles to write, genograms to draw, dramatis personaes to draft, mind maps to draw, phone calls to make, cases to research, reasons for decision to read, psychologists' offices to attend and their reports to tender, subpoenas to serve, freedom of information to seek, conferences with barristers, briefs to advise and further, for lucky me, changing lawyers three times, parking fines in Big Smoke, many children's events missed, nearly five years of my life gone on legal servitude and procedure without a gold star or even a tick in the right box.

And thirty-three years before this sordid and sorry legal chapter began, by walking into the police station and telling my secret, my childhood gone. That's cumulative too, just like the sentencing, but the difference is I don't get a discount. Mine is cumulative in the other direction, for my years are added on, not subtracted. Cumulative harm, all right . . .

So, there I stood in [DATE] 2014 in the Big Smoke Magistrates' Court at the Committal Hearing, the victim of crime unrepresented in the courtroom. There's no one at the bar table for the victim in criminal law. There's no lawyer for the victim at all at any point. This is the only area of law where this happens. All sex abuse victims are equal in the eyes of the law, all right – equally unrepresented, that is, rich or poor. Pity that can't be said for defendants where legal aid funds the impecunious criminals and the rich ones brief the likes of Queen's Counsels Lord Biggot and Philip Fulconbridge.

And then more injustice inside the courtroom; adjournments given to King Claudius, Orders contravened by him, second chances given to him (now up to one hundred plus), OPP and Defence in collusion for him, judges working for him, judges arguing case law supporting him in his absence, corruption in the ranks, all allowable because of the presumption of innocence or because of the connection to senior Catholic clergy. Who knows? But the pretext call absolutely defies his innocence! Why didn't the law allow the presumption to be rebuffed when he admitted what he did?

I admit, the great King Claudius must have had his trials too though. I admit he must have been under pressure swanning around at family events, giving holier-than-thou speeches to family, being wrapped in cotton wool and honoured by everyone, including the judiciary. Surely, being the unquestioned, popular king of the castle is a tough gig though, for how does he keep up with his lies? How does he look at his victims like me and not break down? Sociopathy? What has he said to keep everyone on side? That I'm the dirty rascal? Or did they even bother to ask him, the king of the castle?

More importantly still, how has he kept the law on side? I deny he has had to utter more than seven words in more than four years in a courtroom and has only shown up twice and that's part of the answer. In 2013 and 2014, during the criminal matter, 'No comment', 'Not guilty' and through his counsel, Strut-Bittern, Esq, 'He's lost for words'. How illuminating after he admitted to the allegations in the pretext call.

In 2015, he fought my application to revoke a Suppression Order to keep me silenced and to keep his offending secret. He lost that battle, but strangely, I was still denied costs by Magistrate Quail, as if to punish me for being right. Costs always follow a win, but not when I win. There's seemingly nothing worse to the law than a woman who is right. The law doesn't like it, so it admonishes every female who dares to enter the ring through unjust and untenable outcomes or disparaging comments.

In 2016, King Claudius became unnecessarily involved in my VOCAT application, such was his great desire to deny me any compensation. I mean, the money does not come from him in a VOCAT application, for when an Award is made, it's paid to the victim by the government, so what's it to him anyway? I say that I should at least be granted my legal costs by VOCAT because I should not have to pay for my right to freedom of speech to be restored when it was taken from me as a result of being a victim of crime who simply spoke up.

In 2016, he also finally filed his defence in the civil matter I brought against him after his lawyer initially refused to accept service of the writ as part of his great campaign adopted from the Catholic Church: deny, delay and deprive. What angers me most is that the legal profession is unashamedly complicit in this game. It makes money from the vulnerability of victims, caught up in a shitty process brilliantly designed to fail where victims of sexual abuse are concerned. And each year the legal year begins with 'Red Mass' held in the Catholic Church - hardly impartial!

In 2017, King Claudius continued to fetter the civil litigation process at every juncture to cause me delay, to bleed me dry. Moreover, when he got tired of playing the game, the law took over for him without him even asking. Even when he and his lawyer, Barnaby Bustard-Braggart, failed to appear in the County Court twice, consecutively, without excuse reasonable or otherwise and he was in breach of three sets of court orders, totalling fourteen separate breached orders, including those made by consent, the judge was still there working hard for King Claudius in the courtroom. Instead of striking his defence out, which he rightly should have, he was intrigued by his absence. He argued case law for him and adjourned it again and again despite no appearance from the defence for two consecutive mentions. His lawyer wasn't there, his barrister wasn't there, and he certainly wasn't there; no one stood at the bar table for him. No medical excuses were there on file; no affidavits were filed by him. I was there though, paying for everyone in that courtroom, keeping the legal cogs nicely turning. 'His Honour', all right – King Claudius' honour! What about mine? Answer: a good girl's job is to protect men's honour, so suck it up and remember, 'You be good girl!' As I listened to the judge prattle on, I quietly asked myself, Was Dida reincarnated, or are all men in positions of power really like this?

Worse still, when final orders were finally made in my favour, including costs for the entire proceeding, King Claudius sought a judicial review, summonsing me back to court and successfully had the default judgement set aside; a new interlocutory timetable was set and a new trial set for April 2018. I was wronged and livid. Seemingly, Jesus had turned water into wine again, but someone was certainly plotting out of session!

Seemingly, my cousin has the resolve and the bank funds of the Catholic Church – or funds directly from the Catholic Church, as I suspect. He's singing from the same hymn sheet as them, the one I tore up years ago. Halleluiah! However, I have the will of John Ellis and the determination of Chrissie and the late Anthony Foster and every wave of feminism inside me. I'm also telling the truth. King Claudius' denial is a blatant lie. King Claudius' recorded admission is the truth. Surely that should count for something to the legal eagles; alas, no, but it should. So, it's game 'to be continued' until I gladly declare the legal game over. I will never give up on eliciting the truth and this book is my appeal to the law. Someone must fight for the truth. I can't understand why so many of my colleagues have forgotten this is the purpose of legal practise, to illicit the truth. Otherwise, it seems we're simply going to law school to learn how to pervert the course of justice for perverts, creating more unjust trials for our children and future children. As I keep saying, 'I'm your daughter. I'm everyone's daughter.'

What sane person would want to build a career out of aiding, abetting and perverting the course of justice and, in turn, ironically often use the money made in legal fees to send their children to the best private schools, where their girls are taught that they too can achieve their hearts' desire, just like the boys? This isn't the truth from where I'm sitting though. Maybe girls' school fees and university fees should be discounted at the rate they are paid wages or promoted.

Sadly, these same clever, confident schoolgirls, the duxes and the captains of the finest learning establishments, are also told to be good girls too when the real world hits them. They are kept quiet by the system even if they are outspoken and smart and have the courage to report when and if raped and abused by men they know – in their family, at school, on their university campus, at work, or by a stranger's random attack from behind a bush. Sadly, the latter is the only crime that gets any real traction with police, the media, or the courts.

The Animal That Is Man

Man is a sophisticated animal, or so we like to think. Neanderthals, Cro-Magnon Man, Homo sapiens: men are still animals, no matter the carbon dating.

Just look at how sophisticated we haven't become. The recent rape case of Lazarus v New South Wales Director of Public Prosecution [2015] NSWSC 1116 (21 August 2015)[39] raises the perpetual issue of a woman's consent. I ask, is this not every virgin girl's dream, to have anal sex first before vaginal sex and outside the back of a nightclub for all to see? It makes perfect sense, doesn't it, considering that the clitoris, labia and vagina have rarely been important to men? Hence, anal sex is good for a virgin girl too, from a male perspective, because it's not about her, her pleasure, or what she consents to. Throughout history, sex has rarely been about more than anything but men's pleasure and seemingly, any vessel will do, consent or no consent. Seemingly, the lack of consent is even more thrilling to the hunt and chase. Animal kingdom stuff is playing out here as I see it and alarmingly, the law still relies on the question of consent of the woman determined by whether the animal of man thought she was consenting. Preposterous legal nonsense!

Similarly, the barbaric act of female circumcision is still used on some women today, to steal and deny female sexual pleasure so that their body is only used for male sexual pleasure and reproduction. The same can be said for drugging rape victims and buying child sex slaves over the Internet; having sex with a drugged out, under-aged girl can hardly be about her pleasure or her consent. So, what is it about?

Just look at the statistics around family violence and the pathetically soft approach around criminal behaviour towards women there, so soft that on average one woman is murdered each week by their current or ex-partner. In addition there are the daily physical and sexual assaults and attempted murder of women too. As Rosie Batty says, this is the real terrorism and this is what should weigh on the defence budget. With every new terrorist attack, most recently in the UK and France, people forget about their local terrorists living next door in suburbia. In this way, our Prime Ministers can continue to remain silent about family violence and the big boys can play battleship and army men again.

This truth is that the situation of pandemic family violence could be changed in a very short period. In 2014, laws were passed on 'coward's punch' in just five weeks in Victoria. We obviously like to protect our young men from being knocked unconscious by drunken louts. We made it clear that you are guilty of a crime if you king-hit someone and they die because of your blow. We changed the laws on operating hours on pubs and clubs. We changed the laws around admitting intoxicated patrons into multiple venues. Why can't we adopt the same approach where abused women are concerned? Imagine if we simply sent these violent men responsible for coward's punch to a men's behaviour change program so it wouldn't happen again in the future. If we gave them a free hit for the first punch, there would be mass outrage. Yet we do this with our abused women day after day. Simone de Beauvoir was right; we women are certainly the second sex, or at least we're still treated as such now, today.

The advertising campaigns against family violence are powerful, but I fear they are largely preaching to the converted. The recent television ad where the football hits the mum's head is excellent. 'She can take it,' says the father to their son. That's exactly the mentality we're dealing with and the same attitude was condoned by the judge in the Lazarus case; she can take it (up the arse) and the judge was female. Members of the legal fraternity assist the law to uphold excuses for men's criminal behaviour against women. Why was the female victim of Luke Lazarus left crying in court that day? I know exactly how she feels and I left the County Court the same sad way, crying my heart out just last week, and I've been crying at court for more than four years now.

On 23 June 2013, The Age published an article by Annabel Crabb, 'The Expectations We Have of Women Who Are Assaulted', where she states as follows:

'Physical and sexual assault against women is – globally – a common event. In a report released on Friday, based on interviews with 24,000 women, the World Health Organisation concluded that more than a third of all women will be physically or sexually abused at some

point, usually by someone they know.

What is truly unusual about these crimes, though, is the extent to which, once committed, they tend to produce a rather unique secondary problem for the victim.

A woman assaulted by someone known to her is, in many cases, assaulted again by conflicting expectations. There is the expectation from the offender that she will forgive him/lighten up/stop provoking him. And there is the expectation from others that she will speak out/press charges/stand up for herself and victims everywhere.

How cosmically unfair it is that this double jeopardy – whatever she does will earn her contempt or disappointment or retribution from someone – occurs precisely when the victim is least able to cope with it and might feel entitled, understandably, to a bout of trauma-induced irrationality or deep self-pity.[40]

How is it that my extended family expects me to fight – fight King Claudius, fight their lies, fight their ignorance, fight the law, fight their beloved church and fight their beloved clergy friends? The answer is, they don't. They're praying for me to die.

How do they think it's possible for me to maintain my marriage, my children, my relationships with my parents, with my brother, Romeo and his partner, Juliet, my work, my fight and my health – and contemporaneously? The answer is, they don't. They're praying for me to die.

How is it that they can live with their own lies, ignorance and shame of being complicit in King Claudius' attempts at my destruction? The answer is, they don't. I suspect that they confess their sins at confession and then consider themselves absolved. How convenient. Then before bed, on their rosary, on their knees, they pray for me to die.

But I have no intention of dying. They'll have to pray a bit harder or ask their clergy friends to say a quick prayer for them. I'll keep fighting. They'll keep lying.

So, what do prominent Australian men have to say about the animal that is man? Former Prime Minister Tony Abbott once said when discussing women being underrepresented in institutions of power in Australia,

'If it's true, Stavros [interviewer], that men have more power, generally speaking, than women, is that a bad thing?'[41]

Another person added to the conversation that she wanted her daughter to have as much opportunity as her son, to which Mr Abbott replied,

'Yeah, I completely agree, but what if men are, by physiology or temperament, more adapted to exercise authority or to issue command?'[42]

Following this, would Mr Abbott then concede that men, by physiology or temperament, are more inclined to kill their partner and children, judging from the statistics?

Genetics doesn't explain everything, but it certainly explains something. It's telling that men have become accustomed to a sense of entitlement through social conditioning. If there is no rightful genetic basis to their superiority complex, then let's see equality in practise by men respecting women in their families, in their workplace and in their world.

Making a Statement to the Police

On 10 June 2013, shortly before I was about to turn 40 in October, I reported my childhood sexual abuse to the Conservative Town police and made a statement. Senior Detective Jacob Rosser was the Informant. I talked, the police typed and then I signed. It was a totally exhausting and relieving day, a day of truth, a 'This is your life' moment. I thought the hard part was now over, but how wrong I was; it was merely the very start of the beginning.

King Claudius' Confession — Pretext Call

Following the report, Rosser suggested to me that I make a pretext call to King Claudius and I did. Rosser discussed with me how pretext calls work. He suggested that it may be useful to try as cases of historic sexual abuse are the hardest to prove because it often comes down to 'he said, she said.' He explained that the rules of evidence have been relaxed to allow for pretext calls when it comes to cases of historic sexual abuse. DSC Rosser asked me whether I had ever discussed the abuse with the defendant before. I said I hadn't. He said that's good because pretext calls work best when it's a call made from out of the blue, providing a greater chance for an unguarded, spur-of-the-moment admission.

After I had made my statement to the police, I returned approximately a week later to make the pretext call. My father came with me to SOCIT in Conservative Town as a support again. The police gave me a micro-cassette recorder and a piece of paper that had a blurb on it that I was asked to read out immediately before and then immediately after the call. It said words to the effect of

'My name is Cleopatra Jones. I am about to make a call to a number I believe to be that of King Claudius. I will now make the call.'[43]

I was ushered into a room in the SOCIT unit and I was left alone to make the call. I had no one with me when I made the call because I was told by Rosser that I wasn't allowed to, so my dad had to wait in the waiting room.I called King Claudius' mobile number that I had been provided with by my father. When I called that number, it was answered by King Claudius as I immediately recognised his voice. I spoke to King Claudius for approximately seven minutes until he said that he couldn't talk to me any longer as there were people with him in the car and that he would call back and speak to me later. I never spoke to anyone other than King Claudius, and no one other than King Claudius spoke to me during that call. Furthermore, I never heard anyone in the background at any time during the call.

The pretext call annexed at the end of this book is the entire call; there is no part missing from it. At the end of the call, I read out the blurb and then pressed the Stop button on the micro-cassette recorder. I then left the room and gave the micro-cassette recorder to DSC Rosser, who was waiting with my father in another room in SOCIT where I had originally been together with them.

I was in total shock. I told my father and DSC Rosser that King Claudius had admitted to sexually abusing me. I couldn't believe it as I thought he would try to deny it or hang up on me. DSC Rosser then left my father and me for a while and then returned a short while later, telling me they have all they need to charge him now. DSC Rosser told me I was very lucky because it is extremely rare for a perpetrator to make full admissions and apologise. I then left SOCIT with my father and went home emotionally exhausted.

The stress involved in making that call was humongous. I had run through different scenarios in my head days before as to how the call would go. I wondered whether he'd just hang up on me, deny it, abuse me or even yell at me. I don't think I ever believed that he'd simply admit to it and say he was sorry. King Claudius told me he had someone with him in the car at the time, but I doubt it. Rather, I think that he wanted to invent an excuse to end the call. These are some of the things he said to me during the pretext call that clearly show that he remembers, that he knows what I'm talking about, despite the considerable passage of time that had passed since the offences:

'I think there are certain things that happen when people are young . . . It was silly kids.'

'Absolutely, that's one of the things I've always regretted in my life. Always.'

'So – and I want you to know that – so it's not something that you can sort of say you can put things behind you. No. It's not.'

'I don't want you to think that's reflective of who I am or what I am, and, ummm, I'm more than happy for me to look back at those times.'

'I'm sorry.'[44]

King Claudius said he was sorry at the end, of his own volition, without prompting. Obviously, it's much more devoid of emotion in typed words, and it's far better hearing it as one can tell a lot from tone, intonation and expression. When I listen to it, it makes me cry; it's so heartfelt. It really has me in a very vulnerable position, which is the last thing you want to be in with your perpetrator again. I can also hear the cool calm in King Claudius' voice, the ease with which he speaks, his concern for the preservation of his own image above all else – words of a sociopath minimising the sexual assaults.

Now that I know how it all works with pretext calls, why on earth didn't the police tell me to meet with him and wear a wire? I would have been in a far better position to go into intimate details of the sexual abuse then if I knew this level of detail was necessary. I never even knew that I needed to link specific details of my abuse with my allegations and somehow get him to confess to each one.

King Claudius tried calling me later that day, as he suggested in the pretext call, but I did not answer that call. I had asked Rosser about how I should handle any contact from him and they said now that he had confessed, there was no need to talk any further with him. Rosser told me there's no need for me to have any further discussions with King Claudius at all. But this was patently wrong as here was a further opportunity to get the specifics of what the police later said they needed for a successful prosecution. What fatal, erroneous advice to have given me.

I could have asked King Claudius further questions about the individual sexual assaults and the group sexual assault. I could have asked him about the equipment he used on us, where he got it from, what the name of the other offending boy was, especially if I'd known that was all required. I could have continued where I left off about Hamlet, Goneril and Regan and discussed how they've coped after the group sexual assault. Moreover, I could have asked him why he did it and whether he was sexually abused himself and if so, by whom.

Why suggest making a pretext call at all if it's only going to re-traumatise you? It's currently like playing legal 'pin the tail on the donkey', blindfolded and blindsided without knowing the objective of the game. Survivors and victims should be told exactly how to do it, so they know it'll be worth it or at least know what they must try to obtain to make it worth it. They have a right to make a fully informed decision about it, surely. The only reason victims aren't told how to make a pretext call is due to the conflict of interest created by police bringing the action and victims, as police witnesses, having no independent legal standing.

I say urgently change the law to give sexual abuse survivors a lawyer, so we can start getting some decent convictions and sentences. I'd simply love to practise in this area; it would give me great satisfaction and would leave police free to catch the criminals they want to catch, the easy stuff, the Mars Bar thieves. Leave the victims of child abuse to me, please. They need a lawyer to give them independent legal advice and avoid these costly stuff-ups. I know and care about family violence. Remember, that's where the bulk of sex abuse happens – within the family unit. The community already has stranger danger and victims of random crime covered and while often just as heinous, it's not denied by family and the OPP.

Police, by their own admissions, are legally prevented from assisting victims with pretext calls; otherwise, it's deemed inadmissible. Police are independent investigators and in fulfilling that role, they cannot possibly represent the victim and herein lies the problem. Police need to do their job and a lawyer for victims can then do theirs. Imagine if a defendant's alibi evidence was deemed inadmissible if the law simply said that the defendant having a defence lawyer deemed any alibi inadmissible as it's arguable that the defence lawyer suggested you create an alibi as part of the carefully crafted false narrative. We need to stop treating victims with suspicion because of the presumption of innocence afforded to the defendant. It is not for the police to believe a victim's story, but rather, victims need a lawyer who can act on their instructions.

It takes a sensitive and informed approach to catch these sex abusers; we're not looking for Adrian Bayley types here; the lazy-eyed albino psycho that jumps out from behind a

bush. We're looking for mayors, priests, policemen, coaches –
prominent men in the community. Fathers in the leafy suburbs
who easily fly under the radar in those positions that come
with a 'good guy' carapace. The police need to act with
unbiased integrity here, regardless of who the alleged
perpetrator is. Then we need a new specialised sexual assault
judiciary that wants to make just decisions in this area. This
means more convictions, scrapping suspended sentences,
immediately jailing criminals – and with maximum sentences,
for a change – awarding punitive damages most of the time
and, awarding compensation to victims without putting them
through hell on earth first in the form of a costly, lengthy legal
game that takes years to play . . . and with the victim losing 97
per cent of the time. Anyone for a game of chess where you
have no queen, but I do?

Survivors of historic sex abuse don't keep their DNA-
soaked underpants from their school days, 'sorry'. We have no
evidence on us anymore, we often have no witnesses and we
often have no proof. The law needs to adjust and be led by
social sciences here. The law is not the expert; it is a relic.
Listen to the victims to design the best path forward because
the criminal justice model is entirely unjust. If the model
doesn't lead to prosecutions, change the model. Don't expect
victims to morph into what they can't be, an unemotional and
unaffected being; use the system, get a manifestly unjust
outcome and then turn around and tell them, 'At least that was
cathartic for you and you gave it your best shot. There's power
in that. Well done. Now off to CASA with you!' What a load of
rubbish. It's the destination, not the journey. The journey is re-
traumatising and leaves you far worse off, so it can't be about
'the journey' in these sexual assault matters. The legal
outcome matters. Why do we want any less for victims of such

a heinous crime that changes you and scars you for life? If I took people's cars from them with a 3 per cent success rate of compensation or replacement, there would be mass outrage. Men would go nuts. But we've nicely sorted car insurance, for men love their cars, so there's a successful and straightforward path to use to get your stolen car back or a replacement. Ask yourself, what matter is more important and what matter costs society more in the long run?

Until the law changes, I offer my own cheat sheet[45] for victims in the Criminal Justice System as they desperately need legal advice.

'One Thousand Sorrys a Day'

On 26 September 2013, I heard the doorbell ring. It was my Aunty, King Lear's wife. She said she had just been dropped off by Uncle King Lear, who had to run an errand, and said she thought she'd come to visit us as she and Uncle occasionally did. We went into our home office to talk away from the hearing of my children. Aunty discussed with Antony and me how sorry she was about what King Claudius had done to me. She said, 'One thousand sorrys a day wouldn't make up for what he's done.' She wondered how I found the courage to disclose my abuse at Gospa Velika and thanked me repeatedly, grasping my hands in hers when doing so. She told me, 'You're lucky you have a good, strong husband to support you through this,' and I agreed.

Sitting beside me, Aunty looked me right in the eye and said, 'It's taken me to 70 years old to find out what's wrong with my own children as none of them had ever said anything,' yet she always felt like there was an elephant in the room. She just couldn't thank me enough, and I told her I don't blame her at all, explaining that it could happen in my house too with my own children and I wouldn't know. She left after about half an hour on good terms once Uncle King Lear returned to collect her. Uncle had bought a Jackaroo Ute and had got it for a competitive price and was happy to show Antony, who, being a car person too, was most interested.

Later that day, I received a call from my parents telling me that Aunty and Uncle had been to visit them too, at their house in Peaceful Creek. Like me, this was the first time they had seen Aunty and Uncle since Gospa Velika. Aunty told my parents that King Claudius was wrong to do this to me and said that King Claudius saying he's sorry once is not enough. However, they also told my parents that King Claudius was always a very delicate, sensitive child and then attempted to excuse his behaviour on his heart condition, pulmonary arrhythmia, as if his dodgy heartbeat somehow led to his sexually abusive behaviour. According to my parents, Uncle and Aunty seemed to be looking for sympathy towards King Claudius rather than expressing sympathy for me. At no time did they offer any kind of intention for King Claudius to take ownership of his actions.

While Dad and Uncle were desperately trying to build bridges, discussing the quality of Dad's latest batch of home-made wine, Mum and Aunty were dealing with the reality of the situation. Mum remained unconvinced and did not concur with the Catholic-style narrative that Aunty, King Lear's wife, was providing. Aunty then urged Uncle King Lear that they best leave as she could see that they could not find any common ground as Mum was very critical of their son King Claudius and as a mother myself now, I say rightly so. Aunty edged towards the door and Uncle and Aunty soon left, never to return.

Interestingly, the alpha male in the room, my Uncle King Lear, talked about everything but the sexual abuse. He was no leader; he was a cleaner, a cover-up man, one who smooths things over by his mere presence and Dad towed the line, being his younger brother.

Mum was the fly in the wine, the pea in the princesses' mattresses, the ripple that starts a tidal wave. She was also the grain of sand in an oyster that makes a pearl. Thank you, my wonderful mum. Thank you for standing up for me in those very lonely, early days too, always.

Charging King Claudius

For a while, I told the police I didn't want them to charge King Claudius because he had confessed and that's what I wanted, the acknowledgement and apology for what he had done to me for all those years. That's all I needed. However, despite his admissions during the pretext call, he subsequently denied the abuse to our extended family, which shocked me after hearing his initial apology. I then changed my mind and asked the police to charge him, which they did. They charged him with four counts of rape in October 2013. I thought the police knew what they were doing, but I was sadly mistaken.

The police investigation was stunted and strange. They took three long months to find and speak to King Claudius despite having his work and residential address in central Big Smoke, which I supplied them, along with his telephone number and telephone numbers of my cousins Goneril and Regan. The police never even interviewed his brother Hamlet as they could not get their manager to sign off on the flights to Remote Island, where he lives. Then they told me they could only interview him if Regan and Goneril came forward too;

otherwise, he'd possibly incriminate himself. It's fair to say that the police became less interested in my matter and more interested in seeing if I could get Goneril and Regan on board too as I understand that King Claudius was over 18 for some of the time he abused Regan. I said I didn't understand; I have five witnesses to the sexual abuse of me alone (King Claudius, Hamlet, Goneril, Regan, boy O'Bourke) and a taped confession. That should be enough. I shouldn't have to take Goneril and Regan hostage to disclose their own abuse. The police had previously assured me they could prosecute my matter alone, without them also coming forward, as we had his confession, which was declared by police and the court as fully admissible. I remember Regan talking to my husband, Antony, about the criminal consequences of King Claudius' abuse of her, were she to come forward too, but she was scared about the possibility of him going to jail as he was over 18 where some of her offences were concerned.

Before this, the police had asked me to speak to his sister Regan to see if she would also make a pretext call to King Claudius, her brother, about his sexual abuse of her. I talked to her at length about what's involved, and Regan said she would process it all and consider doing it as her partner at that time, Duke of Cornwall, was encouraging her to tell the police too. I gave her Senior Detective Jacob Rosser's contact details, but she never called him. Rosser tried many times and left messages for her to no avail.

Some text messages between Regan and I are as follows:

9.9.'13 Cleopatra to Regan
Hi Regan, I really appreciated our talk the other day and I am so sorry for what happened to you, I hope you are relieved as I am that

we have support in each other, as horrible as it is. I have just left you a voice message as I really need to speak to you. Let me know when it's a good time to call you. Thanks, Cleopatra

9.9.'13 Regan to Cleopatra

Hi Cleopatra, Sorry I missed your call. I finished work late tonight, but will be up for the next half hour if you're still awake? I'll be finishing late for the next 2 nights but will have Thursday off if you'd prefer to chat during the day. Speak soon, Regan x

11.9.'13 Cleopatra to Regan

Hi Regan, hope you're hanging in there. Let me know when a good time is to call you. I can come to Big Smoke instead if that suits as it might be nice to talk in person. Up to you, happy with whatever you are comfortable with. Love, Cleopatra

11.9.'13 Regan to Cleopatra

Hi Cleopatra, I just left a msg on your home phone. I'm home sick today so am free to chat anytime between 11am-5pm or after 7pm x I am also coming to Conservative Town for an appointment on Monday if you'd like to catch up for a cuppa in the morning around 10.30am? Hope you're ok? Regan x

11.9.'13 Cleopatra to Regan

Hi again, Sorry about all this. Jacob Rosser is the name of the policeman, he's from Conservative Town specialist sex offences unit and he's very lovely, non-pushy, no male ego or anything at all. He asked if tomorrow morning would be ok time to call you?? No pressure Regan, I understand if I'm alone on this. You can say nothing or whatever u r comfortable with. It's totally up to you. Thinking of you, call anytime if u need me for anything. Cleo xx

11.9.'13 Regan to Cleopatra

thanks Cleopatra, I'm really under the weather today so will process the information and be in touch x

20.9.'13 Cleopatra to Regan

Hi Regan, Thanks for calling me yesterday with the update. While I respect Goneril and your position, mediation is not the answer for me. Good luck with it and I hope it brings you peace. Wish Goneril the best from me too. Xx

27.9.'13 Regan to Cleopatra

Hi Cleopatra, I've just sent you Goneril's contact numbers. She tried to get in touch with you last week end but you didn't return her call. Ive sent you her home number just now also. So if you need to speak with her I suggest you call her as communication works both ways. We are just as upset with the situation as you are and she is about 3 stages behind you so I think it would be important for you to call her as you have not done so. I am working really long hours at the moment but if you need to speak with me I will get back to you ASAP if I don't pick up right away. Hope you are doing ok, love Regan x

27.9.'13 Cleopatra to Regan

Hi Regan, omg. I have just checked my 101 and there was Goneril's message last Sunday. This is the first I heard it, honestly. I feel bad to think you thought I wouldn't call her, total opposite, but I understand. I will call her right away and explain. Also, your Mum came past yesterday which was sad but good. I'm ok, in school holiday mode with kids, all good. Talk soon. What time is it in Faraway? Too early to call? Cleo

27.9.'13 Regan to Cleopatra

Coolio. That would be great if you could call her. They are 2 hours behind so maybe wait a little *xxx*

27.9.'13 Cleopatra to Regan

I just sent her a text re best time to call her and explaining that I would have called her straight away. Your mum must have thought it strange when I said Goneril must not want to go back into the past etc. if she knew Goneril had been trying to talk to me. Anyway, I thank you for following up on it. I don't live by this phone, normally call me on the home number coz often not charged etc xx

27.9.'13 Regan to Cleopatra

Thanks for the update xx

2.10.'13 Regan to Cleopatra

Hi Cleo, sorry for the late reply, thanks for the update and have a safe journey. Regan x

6.11.'13 Cleopatra to Regan

Hi Regan, I left you a voicemail message earlier re Tamora called me a liar to my face. She says she doesn't believe a word of it, she says she's close to King Claudius and believes him, has told her kids I'm a liar. I'm furious and totally amazed. Easy to lose faith in people. Call me when you get a chance. Cleo x

On several occasions, Regan and I talked about a way forward and we were waiting to see what Goneril wanted to do upon her return from work in Canada. Goneril told me she wanted mediation, but I did not agree to that. Regan followed her sister's lead; she stopped returning my calls, had a baby shower and invited everyone but my family and me and proceeded to completely ignore me. She continues to deny me, my abuse and my existence, as does Goneril. I honestly don't know how they live with themselves or how they sleep at night. I no longer know who they are.

I heard nothing more from them after a while. After that, I knew that I would have to do this alone and that they weren't strong enough to do anything. They ended up siding with King Claudius and, to the best of my knowledge, they have carried on attending family events as if nothing has ever happened and completely turned their back on me with the rest of the pitiful Pavlovic family. They are now as bad as King Claudius and Hamlet in my eyes. I hope they are very happy or appi, as the Croatians say.

The last time I communicated with both Goneril and Regan was on [DATE] 2014. I left them separate telephone voice messages. I called them from the café near the Big Smoke Magistrates' Court immediately after the special mention to tell them that their brother King Claudius had just got away with it as the OPP had withdrawn all charges against him, no thanks to them. I discuss the special mention more fully further along in this book. I was really hurt by them and their lack of any care whatsoever towards me in the face of them knowing what he'd done to all of us. They never returned my calls. What good little Pavlovic girls. Baba and Dida would be so proud of you. You saved your brother, a paedophile. Well done. I hope the #MeToo movement regularly pricks your conscience.

So, in summary, although I made my statement to the police in June 2013, the police did not question King Claudius until October 2013. It took them four months to interview him about my allegations. This delay felt like an eternity and I spent many days calling the police to see if he'd been charged. It's not like any other delay I've experienced in life as you have zero control over it. Nothing else compares, not even waiting for the birth of my children, heavily pregnant and totally over it. At least then, you have some control and can ask for an epidural, drugs, caesarean, etc. I also wondered whether he'd just show up at my door one day to apologise and I kept my eye on passing traffic on weekends, on the sad chance I'd see his big black car pull up in my driveway. Fool Cleopatra!

He was finally questioned about my statement and the pretext call I made, to which he gave a 'no comment' interview, simply answering each question with 'No comment'. The police charged him with four counts of rape and he was bailed to reappear at the Conservative Town Magistrates' Court on January 2014. Everything was in order, or so I thought, but as you can see from the previous paragraphs, things were not right and certainly did not go well.

Going to Court

When the matter returned to court, King Claudius' lawyers applied for a suppression order and for a transfer of the matter to Big Smoke Magistrates' Court as I usually appeared in the Conservative Town Magistrates' Court. I did not take issue with either the transfer of the matter or the Suppression Order as it's standard protocol to ensure a fair trial. However, although I was told about it, I was never served with a copy of the Suppression Order at any time. That's because I'm not considered to be a party to the proceeding as a complainant. Complainants never are. Yet this is a glaring omission in the legislation as all people, whether strictly parties or not, to whom the order applies, should surely be served with the order as they are in all other jurisdictions. This, most importantly, includes complainants.

The very fact that complainants aren't served is testament

to the traditional focus of Suppression Orders being on the protection of the defendant despite the supposed intention of the legislation, the wording and the spin. If I am wrong, it is certainly one great whopping oversight of our Parliament and it brings huge risk of legal and cost consequences to complainants and other non-parties who are nevertheless subject to its conditions. Most importantly, I say that one can't be guilty of a breach of a Suppression Order if one is not served with the order, for unless a person knows about the order, as proved by an Affidavit of Service, they cannot be said to have known about it. A court order is only active once it's served. I say until the law is changed, victims of crime should not be afraid to use their freedom of speech. Test the law and force the change, for the status quo is legally ridiculous. Speak up and demand the law justifies itself, particularly as the reason for the Open Courts Act (2013)[46] is allegedly to protect freedom of speech! I have my doubts.

Section 15 of the Open Courts Act 2013 (No. 58 of 2013) covers the Review of Orders as follows:

The Court or tribunal that made a suppression order may review the order –

>*on the Court's or tribunal's own motion; or*
>*on the application of –*

>>*the applicant for the order;*
>>*a party to the proceeding in connection with which the order was made;*
>>*the Attorney-General;*
>>*the Attorney-General of another State or Territory or of the*

>>>*commonwealth;*
>>>*a news media organisation; and*

> *any other person who, in the opinion of the Court or*
> *tribunal, has a sufficient interest in the question of*
> *whether the order should be confirmed, varied or revoked.*
> *Each of the persons specified in subsection (1)(b) is entitled to appear*
> *and be heard by the Court or tribunal on the review of a*
> *suppression*
> *order.*
> *On a review under subsection (1), the Court or tribunal –*
> *may confirm, vary, or revoke the suppression order; and*
> *in addition, may make any other order that the Court or*
> *tribunal may make under this Act.* [47]

As above, there should be a similar list of people specified in relation to the service of the Order on all relevant parties as the Service and Execution of Process Act(1992)[48] also omits to make provision for Service of Suppression Orders, as above, but both lists should include service on the complainant in a criminal matter.

Unbeknown to me at the time, this Suppression Order in my matter would become a live issue a year on, but more about that later.

The Filing Hearing was uneventful, as was the Committal Mention, and things were on track – or so I was led to believe – with a Committal Hearing scheduled for [DATE] 2014.

Lead Up to the Committal Hearing

On Monday, [DATE] 2014, Kylie from OPP witness assistance service sent me a text about arranging a time to meet with the OPP lawyers in preparation for the Committal Hearing scheduled for [DATE] 2014. On [DATE] 2014, I was told by Kylie that the solicitor assigned to my matter was Mr Tom

Murphy. On [DATE] 2014, I was told by Kylie that the meeting
was booked in for [DATE].

On [DATE] 2014, I met with the OPP lawyers in Big Smoke
for the first time. We met at eleven thirty the morning after
my family and I returned from a week's holiday in Fiji. In
attendance were the following people: Senior Detective Jacob
Rosser; myself; Antony, my husband; Mary O'Sullivan from
witness support as Kylie was sick; and solicitor Virginia Raven
as Murphy had hurt his ankle. I was told Raven now had
carriage of my matter. I was told by Raven that Sir Donald
Dodo of counsel was briefed in the matter and that he was
very experienced and that the OPP brief him regularly because
he's one of the best.

I brought a list of questions that we went through together.
I confirmed that I did not want to use the remote witness
facility as I was more than happy to go in the witness box
because I'd been waiting a long time for the truth to be heard.
Also, I was a lawyer and certainly familiar with a courtroom,
but most importantly, I was no longer scared of King Claudius
and I wanted to show him that. I asked if they'd heard from the
defence; they said no, they hadn't. I told them of my
willingness to consider a reasonable offer, being a plea of guilty
to a lesser charge than rape, e.g. sexual penetration or indecent
assault. I explained that for me, it's more about the plea of
guilt, his confession and his acknowledgement that he did this
to me. This would show his remorse. I cared less about what
the offences are legally classified as per the charges. King
Claudius had already said sorry to me on the phone, but it's
meaningless unless he admits to the family that he did it. All a
private sorry does is make him feel better and it keeps it secret.
How could that possibly assist me?

I asked DS Rosser if my cousins Goneril and Regan had

made statements to the police yet and he said they had. I said great, but he said no, it's not great. 'They don't support what you say, but I can't tell you any more than that.' I understood why he couldn't and although very disappointed, I explained that I wasn't surprised they opted to do that. I said they probably say they don't remember anything, adopting a sit-on-the-fence position. I said if pressure from family has silenced them, so be it. They obviously don't want to be responsible for what happens to King Claudius. I told myself that I still have the truth and I'm doing this for myself; I can't be responsible for their journeys as well.

Raven told me that after I give my evidence, I can leave court, go shopping, etc. I was shocked by her lack of insight into the functioning of victims. I explained that I want to stay till the very end, of course; how could I feel like leaving and do anything else but to be there? It's not like I can switch off and say, 'Ah, now for a spot of shopping!' Do the OPP not understand how much mental energy it takes to walk the victim or survivor-seeking-justice path? One day at court can drain you for weeks as it takes so much energy to show a brave face to others and to go through the motions of legal process. The fact is I doubt they wanted me there because the less I know, the more control they have.

They told me that the Directions Hearing would be the next day and that's when the trial date would be set down. They said I didn't need to be there for that and that they'd let me know the date for the trial by phone. I told them no, I'd be there for that too. They seemed surprised that I'd want to be there. I was surprised that they were surprised. This is my case, not theirs, and I think they forget that as criminal matters are prosecuted by the Crown and victims are not a party to the proceeding. Notwithstanding this, I'm almost certain that any survivor who reports the crime thinks that the criminal case is about them. Sadly, it's not, and herein lies this inbuilt irony and inbuilt problem.

I immediately booked the Radisson Hotel, opposite Royal Gardens, for my husband and myself for the night of [DATE] 2014. The OPP said everything is set and ready to go and to call them if I had any questions. They told me to take breaks when giving my evidence, give short answers, don't take things personally, answer wildcard questions and just move on. I told them I was very prepared for cross-examination through my own work as a lawyer. I'd also been reading the book Crazy Court Days by Dr Mary Smith[49], whom I later learned is married to former priest-psychologist Dr Butts, the spiritual counsellor, employed by the Catholic Church and appointed to its Special Issues Committee, the committee formed for the purpose of advising the bishop about child sexual abuse complaints against clergy.

They asked if I wanted to meet the prosecutor after explaining that his role is very small, just to get my statement sworn in. He'd be asking three or four questions; that's about it. After their advice, I said not really, clearly no need. They said, 'If you meet him at 9:00 a.m., then there's half an hour to meet and ask any last-minute questions.' I said that's fine. Then I said, 'I have a few things I'd like to edit in my statement that don't go to anything substantive, just for the sake of clarity.' I discussed the proposed revisions and Raven said to email them to her, which I did. On [DATE] 2014, I sent Raven an email with the revisions to my police statement and seeking confirmation where we'd be meeting on [DATE] 2014 at 9:00 a.m., at court or at the OPP office. She never replied to my email.

On [DATE] 2014, I received a text message from DS Rosser,

police informant, that the OPP wanted a meeting with me on [DATE] 2014. He said he had no idea what it's about. I told him Monday was fine as I had matters for clients of mine in the Federal Circuit Court in Big Smoke on [DATE] and [DATE], so either day at lunchtime or after 4:00 p.m., when court rises for the day. DS Rosser later called me back and said Monday should be fine with the OPP. I was hoping it was about an offer to settle as I had told the OPP at the previous conference that I was willing to accept an offer to a plea of guilty to a lesser charge as I don't care what they call it in the 1980s versus today. I only want the acknowledgement that he did it! Rape, sexual assault, indecent act – I don't care which.

On [DATE] 2014, DS Rosser sent me a text at 9:24 a.m., confirming a 4:15 p.m. conference at OPP office, which I said was fine. 'See you there.' At 1:04 p.m., my husband, Antony Jones, who was working in our Conservative Town law office, sent me a text stating that DS Rosser had contacted him, stating the OPP wanted him to be there today at the conference too and he offered to take him to Big Smoke with him in the police car, which he did. DS Rosser said he had no idea why the OPP asked this of Antony. Antony then called my mum to organise school pick-ups for our four children and cancelled his afternoon appointments at short notice to be there.

The meeting started just after 4:30 p.m. at the OPP office in Big Smoke on [DATE]. Those present were myself, Antony, DS Rosser, Kylie from OPP's witness protection and Raven, the OPP solicitor. We sat down, and Raven said, 'I'm afraid we have some bad news for you.' I said, 'What bad news?' She said, 'We are no longer running your case after much review by two senior crown solicitors.' I said, 'You're joking. This can't be right. What message does this send to the community about historic child sexual abuse matters, men's violence towards women, my right to have my matter heard, the seriousness of the matter, the fact that I have never been told until now about any doubts or weaknesses in my case?'

Raven said it's nothing I'd done but that it was to do with uncharged acts in my statement to police. I said, well, just make the extra charges then as I know these negotiations happen all the time; dropping and adding charges is something my husband negotiates with police every day. She said no, the decision is final; it's been made and there's nothing I can do about it. She said she was very sorry and said I'd make a great witness in the top three people in two hundred witnesses in her estimation. Kylie said I was rare; only a handful opt to go in the witness box and I'm strong and brave etc. I said, 'Then get the director Edmond Friarbird to meet with me to see for himself.' She said, 'I'm afraid that's not possible.'

I was shattered and told them what I thought of them, that I'd be embarrassed and mortified to be a lawyer working here. 'You do not meet your vision and mission statement of the OPP. Stick it where the sun don't shine!' I passionately exclaimed. I asked them for a feedback sheet and she said they didn't have one. I said, 'You should make such a complaint pro forma as a matter of priority and put that on your OPP website rather than telling me how the OPP are a leader for victims' rights and that you adhere to the Victim's Charter' that they have on their website. What a joke. I made such a song and dance, told them they had wasted my time, let down all child sexual abuse victims, made a mockery of all the hard work the police had put into my case. I asked if there was at least 1 per cent chance that it would run, but she couldn't even give me that. It was hopeless. I told them I'd be going to the media about this; how they treat sexual assault victims is no better than the rapist!

I then asked the security guard in the foyer at the front desk to call and see if someone, anyone, in the OPP office would see me. He tried, was very polite and, as expected, said no one was available. So, there I stood in the foyer of the OPP with my bags of truth, just like seemingly 'crazy' clients who enter my office with their bags of truth, folders full of the law gone wrong. This happens time and time again. I was now that 'crazy' client, intelligent and right but with nowhere to go. There was nothing else for me to be. Rosser then drove Antony and I back to Conservative Town in the police car. I was very thankful but warned him I was feeling like shit and wouldn't be good company. He was apologetic, professional and accommodating like always during the time I've known him. I called my lawyer friend Clarice and bitched about the OPP the whole way home and why wouldn't I?

The next day, I sent some texts to Kylie at the OPP reiterating my sentiments, including saying that I had never encountered such injustice and incompetence and I would never recommend that my clients go to the police for serious crimes against the person. They had just raped me again! I said I surely had a right of review and that it's a magistrate's role to decide if there's enough evidence for it to proceed to trial after the committal has run and they've heard the evidence, not for the OPP to cut me off at the courtroom door.

Once I had finished my Federal Circuit Court matter for my family law client, a denied grandparent seeking time with her grandchildren, I went straight to the OPP office and camped there in the foyer with my trolley and bags of folders for the second time in two days, asking to see Raven. I was feeling like a homeless person with everything that I was, everything that mattered to me, on my person, like a snail with its home on its back; my bags of truth could at best serve as an overnight pillow in the OPP foyer. Kylie kindly met with me and explained that Raven was in a meeting about my case. I waited and talked with her off and on in a meeting room and she assured me that Raven was doing her best to convince the Director of the OPP that my matter should run. I checked the court list on my laptop and my matter was still listed on the Magistrates' Court website. I had hope. I begged them to keep it listed on the court list.

No word until about 4:45 p.m., when Raven said she'd just come out of her meeting and the case was going to go ahead but that the director plans to review it immediately after the Committal, so it's likely that it will not proceed past the committal. She said they had the power to pull the pin at any time and she wanted me to not get my hopes up. Despite this, I was still relieved and heartened and thanked them with Croatian enthusiasm, arranging to meet the next day at court at 9:00 a.m. The eternal flame at my old school chapel was still flickering for me, after all.

The Aborted Committal Hearing

The next day, [DATE] 2014, we got to the court at 9:00 a.m., saw my ex-husband, Gallus, there, who was there as he was to be called as a witness of first complaint. No one else was there yet. DS Rosser arrived at 9:45 a.m. At 10:00 a.m., Raven and Kylie arrived with Sir Donald Dodo, the barrister that the OPP had briefed. He briefly introduced himself and said he was sorry for being late, that he'd had a Directions Hearing in the County Court over the road. I wondered why someone more junior or a solicitor wasn't attending to that. I had never met him before and a Committal Hearing is certainly far more important and complicated than a Directions Hearing. Clearly, he knew prior to this that my matter was not going to run that day. Then he left with Raven, explaining that they were off to have discussions with the defence counsel Strut-Bittern, Esq. All good – so I thought.

No word until 11:45 a.m., when I was asked to come and have a chat with them all. I was in a conference room with Sir Dodo, DS Rosser and Raven. I was told by Sir Dodo that the defence had made an offer. I said that's great and told him that I wasn't sure if he knew but that I had already told the OPP that I was certainly open to an offer to settle. Great, I thought. Then he said they're offering diversion and he asked me if I knew what it was. I said yes, what someone gets in Children's Court if they steal a Mars Bar. He then said curtly, 'So my role is to bring you the offer,' and I said, 'Yes, I know, and I reject it. It's an insult.'

Sir Dodo said there will be one new charge of unlawful assault and the rape charges were being dropped. Then he said there will be no conviction recorded and he said that DS Rosser would now draft up the agreed new statement from King Claudius, which is 'I pulled down your pants and touched you on the pubic bone with my finger once'. I said, 'What the hell is that?' It's someone else's file and story; it's not what happened. I said, 'Tell them, the defence and the OPP, that I vehemently reject it.'

Sir Dodo then blurted out, 'You have a weak case.' I disagreed and reminded him about the good evidence I have, like the taped confession. What more did they possibly need? Sir Dodo turned and said to me, 'So what? What's sexual abuse to King Claudius and you are two different things.' I was so shocked. I said no one says sorry and they have regretted it for all their life unless they did it. He did it; that's why he confessed. Sir Dodo was unmoved and said, 'I will now take that offer to the OPP and if they think it's a reasonable offer, that's what's going to happen.' He was cocky and arrogant and had the people skills of a dead cat, to be frank. I got up and said, 'I'm out of here so you can make your little zipped-up deal. What a joke,' and I stormed out. DS Rosser, Raven and Sir Dodo remained in the room, I imagine patting one another on the back for a job well done.

I then told a barrister friend of mine who had come to court to support me. He said he'd go and talk to them because he thought I'd got the offer wrong as they wouldn't get diversion for this as, in his opinion, it's completely unsuitable. When he went to speak to them about it, Sir Dodo was feeling challenged by my friend and asked how many trials he had done, especially when my friend said the presumption of doli incapax wouldn't get up as he was 14 and 15, nearly 16 years old, when some of the sexual abuse took place. Sir Dodo asked how long my friend had been at the bar and was quite defensive, to hide his own incompetence, I imagine. It was so pathetic and he completely embarrassed himself.

The OPP left and then returned, asking to speak to me. I asked if this time, I could bring my barrister friend with me and they still said no, just me, on my own. Of course, remain unrepresented, Cleopatra. You're a no one and you're on your own, just as my Neanderthal Auntie Emilia had forewarned in a familial context. I sat down with Raven, Sir Dodo and DS Rosser. Sir Dodo then said in the most patronising, arrogant way; 'Like I said, this matter is going for diversion and so you will get a call from the diversion coordinator in about two weeks.' I sat there with tears in my eyes and said, 'I don't agree.' He said, 'It's not your decision.' Raven agreed and said it's been reviewed and checked over. I asked, 'Is there anything

I can do?' and Sir Dodo said no, taking great delight in saying it. I said my husband has never heard of a matter like this being recommended for diversion, nor had my friend and they are criminal lawyers. Sir Dodo then said, 'So you can go now. There's nothing more happening. It's out of your hands. There's no need to be here.' I said I was disgusted with all of them, that I hoped he didn't have a daughter. I told him he'd wasted police time and was the most pitiful barrister I'd encountered. He was unmoved, arrogant and unapologetic. I thought to myself, Of course, this is the barrister the OPP regularly brief, a misogynist taking great delight in causing social injustice.I suspect that he's briefed because he's willing to compromise his long-buried principles, clearly the prerequisite and resulting carapace of an OPP lawyer.

I raced out of that court anteroom crying and my friend came over and consoled me as I told him what was said away from the other group, in a quiet row of chairs on the other side. He told me Sir Dodo definitely isn't working for me – he's a shocker – and suggested we go and have a coffee and debrief as there's nothing we can do about this today. However, he said I should make a formal complaint against the OPP and let the diversion coordinator know my thoughts, which they consider when making their decision. He offered to help me with this, which I gratefully accepted. Then we promptly left without talking to anyone further. Raven and DS Rosser were telling my dad, ex-husband and husband what was happening and they saw we were leaving, so they also left. Raven and Rosser remained behind. Antony told me that he said to them it was such an utter disgrace and said the next time the Police bring charges of rape, he'll expect the OPP will accept diversion for his clients too! All I could think is, What an easy job it is to be a criminal barrister like Strut-Bittern, Esq.

As I was leaving court, I saw my Uncle King Lear with a great big smile on his face as if he had won Tattslotto, with all his teeth on display. Apparently, his bad boy was still a good boy. Praise the Lord! Good men had seen to that. Good men and bad boys, all cooperating, gathered at court as if on a golf course. Perhaps I should have been in the club kitchen instead, making scones for their afternoon tea. I would have been respected there with my apron on. Or back in the bedroom perhaps, where this all started. Uncle King Lear had convinced himself that his boy was a good boy. There was no room for the truth in his mind. The law had provided him with a new narrative and he was clinging to it for dear life.

My dad, Antony and I returned to court at 2:00 p.m., unbeknown to the OPP gang, slipping into the back of the court unnoticed. I wanted to see for myself what was going to happen because, as a lawyer myself, I know how important it is for all parties to be at court to get the best possible resolution and it's in your best interests in case something different happens. Court is always unpredictable and there's seldom any consistency. Also, I had absolutely no trust in the OPP and wasn't sure if I was being lied to. I smelt a rat.

The clerk was in there, but H. Honour Woodpigeon had not come on the bench yet. I was listening to defense counsel and Sir Dodo talking about the dodgy deal, including the 'allegedly agreed' new charge of unlawful assault and the date of this supposed new assault being 1 Jan 1981 (the first day in the date range of 1981 to 1984 inclusive). That's four years of offending reduced to one act on the first day. Minimising at its best – well done, 'learned' gentlemen! I could hear them as they were talking near one of the microphones on the bar table, but I couldn't see their L plates, for they do have so much to learn about strong women and psychology. Once they noticed me, they relocated outside the courtroom to continue their low-brow discussions. No one spoke to me or acknowledged me, not Sir Dodo, Raven, or DS Rosser. I saw them as a pack of redundant idiots sitting there. I had no respect for them; they looked like incompetent departmental hacks because that's exactly what they were. A whole bar table full! Of course, I wasn't acknowledged; how stupid of me to have forgotten that I'm not a party to the proceeding. This is not my matter. I have no legal standing in it at all. I'm merely the victim, an unrepresented nobody, a mere observer like anyone else in the public gallery, crying in the back row.

H. Honour Woodpigeon came onto the bench and the OPP explained that the matter had settled and that it was being recommended for diversion. OPP and Defence lawyers each gave a brief submission and then there was the usual pause in proceedings whilst the clerk was looking for a date for the diversion coordinator. During this pause, I spontaneously stood up from one of the back rows and said, 'Excuse me, Your Honour, could I please say something?' I am certain that my body moved before my brain told me to as I had no idea what I was about to say or do, but I suspect that my survival instinct had kicked in. H. Honour said, 'I take it that you are Ms Jones,' and I said, 'I am, Your Honour.' In a few sentences, I explained that although Sir Dodo just explained that the matter had settled and all parties agreed, I was not in agreement nor happy about it and that I had been bullied by the OPP over the last two days trying to stop my case from being heard.

H. Honour Woodpigeon then said that they would like to hear from me. Sir Dodo quickly jumped up at the bar table and said, 'I can ask the complainant if she'd like to give a written submission,' but H. Honour asked if I would prefer to give oral evidence from the witness box or from the body of the court if

I was more comfortable. I thanked H. Honour and opted to give my evidence from the witness box.

H. Honour Woodpigeon read out the legislation on diversion to the court to help me understand what he must consider making such a recommendation or not. One thing he said was that the new statement must reflect the current police statement, which it didn't; it wasn't even close. I was sworn in and then H. Honour asked me to tell the court about my experience with the OPP and what my view was on the appropriateness of diversion. He assured me that he had heard the pretext call I made to King Claudius. I was so relieved. A glimmer of hope flickered in my heart.

I first thanked H. Honour Woodpigeon for the opportunity to be heard. I said that it was an insult to me and to every woman for this matter to be recommended for diversion. How can four counts of rape possibly be reduced to one count of unlawful assault?

I explained that my husband is an experienced criminal lawyer, as is my barrister friend, who both say diversion is not appropriate and have never heard of this for charges of rape in their experience.

I complained that if the OPP will not run my case, I don't have the opportunity to have a top barrister like Strut-Bittern, Esq, or any lawyer for that matter. I deliberately said in vain, 'I want a Mr Strut-Bittern!'

I explained that Sir Dodo has been consistently rude and arrogant towards me.

I complained how Sir Dodo minimised what happened to me, telling me that it is a 'historic matter' and I was 'playing with the boys' elsewhere first, implying that I consented to what happened to me. What a pig!

I explained that I shouldn't be criticised for taking time to come forward, mentioning the men of Boys Town in Queensland and how common it is for victims to take until they are in their 40s to disclose childhood sexual abuse.

I complained that this new agreed statement of 'I pulled down her pants and touched her on the pubic bone once leaving her half naked'is not true, isn't my story and couldn't happen like that in any event as I was wearing a ballet leotard with stockings and no underpants before the group sexual assault. It is normal in ballet not to wear underpants – ask any ballerina – so I was fully naked in his false new statement because you must take off a leotard first before you can pull down stockings. Why on earth can the law allow this group of men to rewrite my history, the truth, into their untrue words? Where was the victim's experience in this new sanitised crap written by men, agreed to by the perpetrator?

I explained that I am a family lawyer and my experience includes being duty lawyer for years in the Family Violence Court and the Department of Human Services Child Protection Lawyer. I thought if I helped everyone else, it would heal me, but I had to help myself, so here I am, after CASA counselling etc. Now my work and values dovetail with my inner self. No point helping clients if I'm part of the silence protecting perpetrators.

I explained that I understand that I am not the OPP' s client, that the police informant is, but I was in a similar position when working for the Department of Human Services, where my client is the social worker known as the 'protective worker', not the 'at risk' child. I explained to H. Honour that it would be incongruous to work for DHS unless I respected and was working for the common good of the 'at risk' child.

This brings me to a crucial point. In no area of law – other than criminal law – is a party unrepresented. Importantly, it's the most important person in the matter who is unrepresented: the victim. In Children's Court matters, the DHHS brings the application like the OPP does in a criminal matter, yet in the DHHS matter, everyone is individually represented – the child, each sibling, the biological parents, the foster parents, the DHHS social worker, the grandparents and any other interested party. It is not unusual to have ten lawyers at the bar table in child protection matters. Well, the victim in a criminal matter remains unrepresented to this day. There is no one in the courtroom for them. Why? No answer is satisfactory to me in any event. I say there is nothing inevitable about having the complainant unrepresented in criminal law. It needs changing urgently, without delay, and I dare anyone more or less learned to correct me on this.

Shockingly, the Royal Commission into Institutional Responses into Child Sexual Abuse does not recommend this despite all the evidence they've heard across Australia and despite complainants being legally represented in the Royal Commission itself. If victims truly don't need legal representation, why were they afforded it in the Royal Commission, I ask, at a notably huge expense to the commonwealth? More about this paradox is discussed in later chapters.

I **explained** to H. Honour the guilt I feel that my disclosure has fractured the family. I referred to my aunty and uncle in court today and how I don't blame them as it's likely that I too wouldn't know if it happened with my own children in a back room in my house. I explained how my parents and I have been ostracised from the entire family as it's easier to blame the victim and just pretend it didn't happen. I referred to my poor dad sitting in court in the back row and how he's lost his entire extended family.

I **explained** how children don't tell because they won't be believed and look at this courtroom now, no better than the Catholic Church, silencing victims with lies and cover-up.

I **explained** how my aunt had thanked me for disclosing as it was the beginning of healing her family, yet now she denies it to everyone and plays happy families. I spoke about how Regan had called me, saying she's sorry and she should have told me when she confronted King Claudius two years ago about what he'd done to her and she'd told him to apologise to his victims. She knew there were many other victims including me. I said how she's pregnant and fleeing to Faraway to be with the other victim, her sister Goneril, to which her parents laughed. What sort of relationship they all have with each other in the face of this is rather puzzling and far from funny to me. Perhaps they can explain why their girls have been virtually absent from family events since they left home. And why do they live so far away in Faraway?

I **complained** about the OPP, saying I was prepared for Mr Strut-Bittern here today to cross-examine me but not for the OPP to be doing his job for him! I'd lose my practising certificate if I represented clients like this. But I was wrong there. The OPP did represent their client, the police, very well that day. Someone in the police wanted my matter dropped, but why start an investigation in the first place if my matter had no reasonable prospect of success as Friarbird's letter claims? DS Rosser or DPP Edmond Friarbird or someone in between needed it hidden. Or someone godlike, high above them all?

H. Honour Woodpigeon thanked me for my courage and eloquence and I sat back down in the body of the court, well away from the OPP as I had before. H. Honour then asked if

King Claudius wanted to say anything and after taking some quick instructions, Strut-Bittern Esquire said, 'He's lost for words!' H. Honour then asked Mr Strut-Bittern if he wanted to say anything further in response and Mr Strut-Bittern said, 'No, I'll leave it, Your Honour.' What legal mindfulness, well worth the briefing fee, clearly.

H. Honour Woodpigeon then said he would not be recommending Diversion as the law didn't allow him to and it wasn't appropriate considering all things. I was shocked and delighted. I had turned it all around myself, the victim, with no legal representation. The bar table full of about four lawyers with a combined legal experience of one hundred years minimum had lost. They were as thick as thieves and all wrong. I won. That's well and good for me, but the problem is, how many victims who aren't lawyers would have done this or even known that they could? Most victims would have gone home, as told by the OPP, and any who would stay would not have the confidence to speak for themselves in a courtroom for justified reasons. I am rare, but that's my point; a proposition for Diversion for sexual assault should lose every time. Moreover, it should not be put as an argument in the first place as it's inappropriate and insulting and second, it certainly should not be accepted by the OPP when a defence lawyer tries their luck and scrapes the bottom of the barrel in negotiations.

Strut-Bittern, Esq, asked for a sentencing indication and H. Honour said a good behaviour bond but that in a matter like this, it must be 'with conviction'. Finally, a good man who respected me. Woodpigeon was my hero. His words 'with conviction' rang in my ears for the rest of the day and for the next two weeks. For the first time ever, I felt vindicated. H. Honour clearly understood the matter, understood what I needed from my cousin and his decision was appropriate and in proportion. An acknowledgement, not necessarily a prison sentence. I remember H. Honour saying he hoped today would be a 'book end' for both my cousin and me. Fair and appropriate. An acknowledgement – nothing more, nothing less – is all that I personally needed. Others may need more, but that's what I wanted, hence my original direction to the police to not charge him when I thought he'd own up to what he did to us. So how did it all go so very, very wrong thereafter?

H. Honour had suggested the matter be finalised today for the benefit of both the complainant and the accused. He explained the options the accused had, basically a plea or proceed to committal. He then stood the matter down briefly for the parties to obtain instructions. The great OPP didn't communicate with me at all – I suspect they didn't dare – but the truth is I was happy with the prospect of a good behaviour bond. It wasn't perfect justice, but it was something tangible for me, the elusive acknowledgement I was desperate for.

Mr Strut-Bittern then said his client wished to exercise his right to go to committal. Of course, what more would I expect from a perpetrator? In other words, King Claudius rejected the offer of pleading guilty to the lesser charge of unlawful assault with conviction, so then the OPP said they'd be reinstating the original charges. Now King Claudius faced the serious charges of rape again. He just couldn't admit that he did it and settle for a good behaviour bond. Like his sister Regan said, 'He will never admit what he did to us because he hasn't got the guts to admit it to Dad,' their father, King Lear.

So, the game plan from there was obviously for 'good' man King Lear, 70 years old, and his 'good' bad-boy son, King Claudius, pushing 50 years old, to lie to each other and for

Aunty, King Lear's wife, to play the good woman and support their deceit, their criminal behaviour and their immaturity. Lying, 'good' bad Catholic Christians, the three of them. Too bad for me, their two abused daughters, and almost certainly more victims. Aunty paints Christian idols, King Lear does the money collection at church, their boys were altar boys at St Michael's and they donate generously to the church in envelopes each week, never mere coins. Aunty and Uncle are the pillars of the Catholic Church in Conservative Town. Baba would be so proud. I am utterly disgusted.

H. Honour told Sir Dodo that it's not for him to tell him how to do his job; however, he recommends that the OPP withdraw the charges and make fresh ones as appropriate. You see, the police had got the original charges wrong. They should not have been charges of rape but rather indecent assault of a minor under 10 years and indecent assault of a minor under 16. Rape was the wrong charge for that period. Rape in the 1980s only referred to forced sexual intercourse and was rather specific in terms of the behaviour it defined. Nowadays, any form of unwanted sexual activity is deemed 'rape' as it's a very broad charge now. This is the inattention to detail that one gets from the police, I'm afraid, or worse still, he may have been deliberately charged incorrectly. Who knows with the Conservative Town Police Station, which is unashamedly Catholic? This is not dissimilar to no cases of child sexual abuse being reported to police by the Special Issues Committee against their alleged paedophile priests or inaction on criminal confessions made via the confessional box. Police mostly take no action on victims' statements made to them and when they do, the law ignores what a victim says in a witness box too and, through cross-examination, allows a new false narrative to be created. This is what pillars of the community do to victims.

The Committal Hearing was adjourned, part heard, to [DATE] 2014 at 9:00 a.m. for Special Mention. The only current charge remaining was now Unlawful Assault and his conditions of bail were extended after some discussions. There was also talk of Goneril and Regan as witnesses now. King Claudius was saying he wants to be able to talk to his sisters as he's very close to them and one is going to be having a baby. What a joke that he's close to them! Since when? Not during my forty-three years of life! Nor Goneril and Regan's! Goneril went to live in Faraway about fifteen years ago to get away from him and the family and now Regan is too. As Goneril said to me in 2014, 'I have a new family now, here in Faraway.'

The OPP and Strut-Bittern, Esq, and H. Honour, Magistrate Woodpigeon, spent a long time having Form 32 discussions including about varying bail. I couldn't really follow it and didn't know if Goneril and Regan would be called as witnesses or not. H. Honour said to be circumspect about it, allowing conversation about everyday things but not about the case or their evidence. In the end, I understood that as they had made statements, they are now police witnesses who can be cross-examined but that King Claudius could talk to them in the interim. I thought to myself, Great, there's further opportunity for the smarmy King Claudius to play with the strings of his puppet sisters, as if in a Shakespearean play.

I passed onto the police the numerous relevant text messages between Regan and I about how King Claudius abused us, the texts dating from July 2013 to November 2013. I also provided the Telstra phone logs of outgoing calls made to Regan's and Goneril's phones and we said we should be subpoenaing Regan's phone records to document her phone calls to me. They take place between some of the text messages, so some of the texts relate to and lead on from telephone conversations we had. I said the other victims should be cross-examined on what those conversations with me were about. They were about our counselling, recovery, appropriate ways to deal with King Claudius, Regan's earlier attempt to confront him two years earlier and what happened to each of us alone and in the group sexual assault. We discussed bed linen and bedroom decor and the years the girls' and boys' bedrooms swapped sides of the hallway at their house in Cambridge Street.

The group sexual assault involved King Claudius, Hamlet and another boy whom Aunty, King Lear's wife, said was someone named O'Bourke, a fellow friend of King Claudius' from St Michael's College. Aunty, King Lear's wife, told me his name was O'Bourke. I cannot remember, but she could, and she told Regan this too. Aunty, King Lear's wife, said to Regan that King Claudius moved on from Goneril and me to my younger cousin Regan. That seems plausible to me as I don't know why he stopped abusing me aside from me quitting ballet, so I would not be there regularly on Saturdays anymore. Regan told me he stopped sexually abusing her when she threatened to tell her mum and dad if he touched her one more time. She also said that she remembers King Claudius being much older when he did things to her, certainly over 18 years old for some of her abuse. Remember, there is an eight-year age gap between Regan and King Claudius. King Claudius lived at home when he was 18 too, while he did a draftsman course in Conservative Town. I understand that King Claudius had left St Michael's at the end of Year 11 in 1985. To the best of my recollection, King Claudius lived at home until he was 20 years old, just before he got married to Tamora Jerkov. Frankly, I don't know how Goneril and Regan could bear being the bridesmaids at his wedding to Tamora, but I suppose they had no real choice.

Lead Up to the Special Mention

On [DATE] 2014, Sr. Det Jacob Rosser of Conservative Town SOCIT called me. He told me that Madam Mallee-fowl of the OPP had called him to discuss calling me about my matter. Rosser said she'd like to speak to me. I told SC Rosser that I was more than happy to call her and thought it strange that she wouldn't just call me herself. I then called her directly after he gave me her direct number. I thought it would be about the anticipated new charges being brought against my cousin, to fix the mistakes the police had made with bringing incorrect charges initially.

When I called Ms Madam Mallee-fowl, she confirmed that the one remaining charge of unlawful assault was being withdrawn. I expected this. However, she then said that there would be no revised charges replacing the four rape charges, that King Claudius would be discharged from bail and nothing further would be happening to him. She recommended that I access support agencies if I needed support. I was utterly devastated.

She confirmed that the OPP had received my formal complaint, that a new barrister would be briefed for the special mention at 9:00 a.m. on [DATE] 2014. She also informed me, condescendingly, that the OPP was not concerned about my threat of going to the media.

When I mentioned that I wanted to make a second statement that would fully particularise all the sexual assaults, she said that any further statement would face the same problems if the offences are in the same period, namely, that the defense of doli incapax would apply. I explained that the offences are all between the years 1981 to 1984 inclusive. That would not change as I don't lie and I'm not about to start now. So doli incapax only applies to the first two years of his offending, not the last two years of his offending, but it's a rebuttable presumption in any event. In my civil case, the County Court Judge Lovebird had no difficulty with this, so why do the OPP?

Ms Madam Mallee-fowl explained that my case had been re-reviewed by Chief Crown Prosecutor Lord Pheasant-feather and he said that the original rape charges were not appropriate; they should have been charges of sexual penetration of a minor under 10 and 16. I told her, 'It's your error, yet I'm made to pay for it by you dropping my case. Why?' I said that someone should lose their job over the way my matter had been handled and Ms Madam Mallee-fowl scoffed at my suggestion, saying, 'Oh, no one will lose their job.' She also said that doli incapax would be a valid defence because of my cousin's age at the time and that if he was just a few years older at the time, they would proceed with the prosecution. This is not fair or right as he was 14 and 15 (nearly 16) years old during the offences I particularised in my first statement. The bulk of the offences he committed when he was 12 and 13 are found in my second statement to police. She said that the problem is that the law can't prosecute cases like mine. I defended myself and said the OPP should be prosecuting it; it's a sexual assault case like any other. I asked why the government is telling victims to go to the police to then be treated like this. She snapped back, 'I'm not paid to sit here and listen to you rant at me about it!'

She continued to say, 'That's what happens with these historic cases,' and that on a scale of sexual offences, 'your matter is minor'. She said the problem is that King Claudius was a child at the time. I said children abusing others when there's nearly a five-year age gap is not innocent child's play. It's sex abuse of a much younger child by an older child who knew what they were doing was wrong. I explained, by way of example, that the group offence was when I was wearing leg warmers, which is in 1984, the last year of ballet. I only ever had one pair of leg warmers; they only came out into ballet fashion then. I was 11, making him 15 and eight months at the time.

On 8 April 2014, after discussing my matter with Dr Mary Smith, I called Conservative Town police and spoke to Superintendent Matthew Dull about my matter and the conduct of the OPP and told him that I had spoken to many other professional people about it too. They are all very concerned about this happening in Victoria today, after so many people working in this sector have worked tirelessly to ensure that victims are prioritised and heard. Dull was shocked and told me that my case sounds reminiscent of sex abuse cases in the 1980s, in the days of the rape squad. I told him it's impossible to navigate the system, yet I am a practising lawyer. What chance do my clients have if I can't understand or use it? He agreed that it was a disgraceful situation.

Yet Superintendent Matthew Dull, a most senior policeman in the Rockies region, encompassing Conservative Town Police Station, who could do something, who could do a lot, said a lot but did nothing. He read from his script, the same one that had seen no prosecutions from Conservative Town for clergy abusers despite Conservative Town's Special Issues Committee (SIC) and no justice for brave survivors. I suspect he was one of the original shredders, like in Teenage Mutant Ninja Turtles, the master of the foot clan from Conservative Town Police Station. I suspect that this is why Dr Mary Smith contacted him about my matter and put me in touch with him – so that my case would go nowhere. For I later learned that she is married to Dr Butts, ex-priest/psychologist who sat on the Special Issues Committee[50], the committee that advised the bishop of allegations of child sexual abuse but did not report any of these cases to the police – a member of Team Shredder. This is not surprising given that three members of the SIC were from Catholic Church Insurance and Dull later became involved in Towards Healing, an in-house Catholic Church compensation scheme for child sexual abuse survivors.

I confirmed that I still wished to make another supplementary statement to further particularise the offences as they alleged that was what was required, further particularisation, and Madam Mallee-fowl told me that she'd have to ask the informant SC Rosser about this and get back to me. She never contacted me again.

Nonetheless, I made my second statement on [DATE] 2014, a week after the Special Mention, without anyone's advice or nod. The words just poured out of me, I couldn't do anything else for days. I sat in the study at home and typed my heart out, making my own statement to right the wrong – I wasn't going to leave it to the police this time. To my knowledge, King Claudius has never been brought in for questioning about my second statement. It sits there on the police file, another serving of truth that no one wants to dish up to him for some strange reason, together with the taped confession.

I wrote to SC Rosser many times, enquiring as to what's happening with my second statement, but he later left SOCIT Conservative Town and advised that SC Jerimiah Codswallop is the person to speak to about it now. I wrote to SC Codswallop numerous times, enquiring as to what's happening with my second statement. I have never received a reply. I have left phone messages with numerous members of SOCIT for Jerimiah Codswallop to return my call. No return call has ever been made to me. Police have done nothing about it. Finally, in August 2017, I received an email from Codswallop saying that he agrees with the decision of the OPP not to proceed with my case. Profound stuff.

I remember a conversation I had with DS Rosser about how I was almost certain there was a Catholic cover-up in the OPP and he assured me I was wrong and that I 'should not let crazy thoughts like that creep into my head'. I was certain then of the Catholic mafia and now I also have reason to believe that there are Catholic conspirators in the Conservative Town SOCIT Unit and in the OPP, I am positively certain.

Years later, in May 2016, the IBAC[51] hearings in Conservative Town unveiled a disturbing level of corruption in the Conservative Town Police Station, confirming my suspicions. It is, without a shadow of a doubt, the worst, most corrupt police station in Australia. So, who's running the show there one might ask? SC Matthew Dull and, before him, SC Paul Fang, two names that surprisingly managed to evade the attention of the Royal Commission into Institutional Responses to Child Sexual Abuse in the Conservative Town Case Study. However were they missed? I wonder. Two most senior officers who disappeared from the ranks, one disappearing the day after the release of Paulina's book Sinful[52]. How coincidental or miraculous – praise be to God again. A reliable source has told me that Paul Fang's son, a policeman like his father, has plans to come to Conservative Town, which concerns me deeply. I think it is now common knowledge that there is a great divide in Conservative Town Police Station: the crooked Catholic cops versus the good cops. From where I'm standing, it's easy to see who's who.

A Very Special Mention with a Surprise Visitor

Surprise! Grand Poobah Lord Pheasant-feather, SC, Chief Crown Prosecutor, appeared at the special mention of my matter held two weeks later, [DATE] 2014. I nearly fell off my chair as he entered the stage, but this was no Gilbert and Sullivan opera.

The OPP dropped all charges against King Claudius, with Chief Crown Prosecutor Lord Pheasant-feather, SC, himself appearing together with a male barrister the OPP briefed and the manager of the sex offences unit of the OPP, Ms Madam Mallee-fowl. They obviously needed three most senior representatives from the OPP that day to withdraw a matter of one lowly charge of unlawful assault; such was my resistance. The lowest offence on the criminal scale needed to be withdrawn by three most senior lawyers in our State of Victoria. To the non-lawyers reading this, it's unheard of, trust me; Lord Pheasant-feather is the most senior government lawyer in the state of Victoria. I was extremely suspicious of why it was so important that Pheasant-feather himself be there with his full legal entourage when a junior lawyer alone for the OPP could have done the same for far less taxpayer's money. The truth is, I could have done this appearance during professional legal training, before being issued with a practising certificate, with leave of the Court, and it would have been granted by the Magistrate. Charges of unlawful assault are withdrawn in courts every day as it's the lowest criminal charge on the spectrum of offences. Pheasant-feather most certainly does not appear – or I should hope he does not appear – at cases like this as the taxpayer is funding this legal overkill. So, what justified his presence? Catholic mafia? Or was it an expensive lesson in exclusive legal training for me, to not mess with sex-abusing men because men at the top and the smirking Madam Mallee-fowl like it that way? Thank you, but I have enough continuing professional development (CPD) points.

I still cannot understand why they were all there to simply withdraw one charge of unlawful assault. No one has explained it to me and I'm still waiting. There must have been someone or something they were trying to protect, and I believe this was someone in the Catholic Church, not little King Claudius. Who else commands the likes of Lord Pheasant-feather, SC, himself to withdraw a case when the whole point of the OPP is to convict successfully and the Magistrate had already given that clear indication at the part-heard committal? Did Lord Pheasant-feather simply have nothing better to do that day than to work against the aim of his own office? The DPP should have been happy that his office was set to have another conviction under their belt. No? Why on earth not?

I am reminded of one of the most famous religious images of all time – or of the twenty-first century, at least: a photograph of Cardinal Campeius accompanying Cardinal Carlisle to court for matters of child sexual abuse. I imagine a most regrettable decision now for Campeius but clearly not at the time. Campeius is not the sort of person to do anything he doesn't want to do. He wanted to be there for Cardinal Carlisle, or he would not have been; it's quite simple. Like Cardinal Carlisle had then Archbishop Campeius by his side, my cousin had Lord Pheasant-feather, SC, the top lawyer of the OPP, accompanying him to court, another paedophile seemingly being protected by the Law and the State, collaborating to cover it all up.

I figured that I must be a secondary victim of clergy sexual abuse. Nothing else explains it and the lack of any alternative explanation, convincing or otherwise, confirms my suspicions.

I'm still waiting for more than three years now for someone to dispel this theory. Good luck with that. To date, I've only received correspondence from government agencies that makes no sense but should make sense. Moreover, I suspect that King Claudius may be a victim of clergy abuse so someone in the OPP may be protecting the Church at all costs, including at my expense as a possible secondary victim of clergy abuse. Time will tell, but if I am correct, I will consider taking legal action against the OPP.

On [DATE] 2014, my matter based on charges against my cousin King Claudius, who had sexually abused me when I was a child, was unceremoniously dropped. The OPP had previously presided over the original charges, four counts of Rape, being downgraded to one charge of Unlawful Assault with a strong submission made by the OPP, not defence counsel, to the Magistrate for Diversion along the way. I would have expected the defence counsel Strut-Bittern, Esq, to have done so, not the OPP. On [DATE] 2014, without so much as a word to me of any kind whilst at Court, the remaining charge was simply withdrawn. What had happened to me didn't matter to anyone. Apparently, what happened to me was not a crime! Lord Pheasant-feather, SC, had executed the shameful Catholic cover-up task. The eternal flame was now snuffed out. 'All rise.'

Aside from the devastating outcome, even more upsetting were the actions and manner of the OPP and its most senior representatives that day. When we arrived at the Magistrates' Court at about 8:50 a.m., we observed Lord Pheasant-feather and Ms Madam Mallee-fowl, manager of the sex offences unit of the OPP, together with another man who turned out to be a barrister briefed by the OPP to represent the Informant, SC Rosser. I knew what Lord Pheasant-feather looked like from the media. I also remember seeing his family reunion reported on television one night and feeling so angry watching him swanning about at a garden party. I saw who appeared to be his children and possibly grandchildren happily frolicking on the lawns of some estate. I thought to myself, What an ostentatious display of hypocrisy. The children looked roughly my age at the time I was sexually abused. I do not wish that man well or his progeny. He is pure evil in my eyes.

Lord Pheasant-feather, Madam Mallee-fowl and the barrister they briefed gathered together with Strut-Bittern, Esq, barrister for the defendant, and the defendant himself, King Claudius Pavlovic, and the defendant's father, King Lear Pavlovic. They were clearly engaged in a happy, jovial discussion in the court foyer for a few minutes, just opposite the cafeteria near the board displaying the daily court lists. They all seemed already familiar with one another. I was also standing close by in the court foyer near the café, watching them all. Without speaking to me or acknowledging me in any way, they all walked past me, got into the same lift together and made their way up to court 10. So, King Claudius, my abuser, and the top dogs of the OPP were all chatting and going in the same lift together. I thought, Top effort, OPP, really independent!They had clearly all met before that day.

Nobody from the OPP took the time or was considerate enough to speak to me or even tell me which court the matter was in. By sheer good luck, we were able to find them in time after speaking to Registry staff. When we entered the court room, still nobody spoke to me, turned to acknowledge me, or looked at me. I went up to the clerk and asked if this was the King Claudius Pavlovic matter and he said it was. I felt like a pariah and completely unrepresented or considered and that's because that was the reality. How can a complainant have no lawyer? I still wonder. It's outrageous.

There was no other matter listed in that court as it was a special mention at 9:00 a.m., so they knew who I was, sitting with my husband and my father right behind them in the front row in courtroom 10, which is quite small. Ms Madam Mallee-fowl was facing me as OPP instructor and constantly smirking with pen poised at her notebook, looking down, deliberately avoiding my gaze from one metre away. I believe that this was a deliberate bullying and intimidation tactic. I would love to know if that is part of OPP training as the manager of the sex offences unit of the OPP. What a fine example of a pathetic woman cleaning up the mess of men!

Pheasant-feather, SC, Madam Mallee-fowl and the barrister they briefed were not speaking to one another, giving only a few discreet nods or knowing looks to each other. The barrister was busy reading a copy of the letter of complaint I had sent to the OPP dated [DATE] 2014. I could easily read it from where I was sitting in the first row of seats, directly behind Lord Pheasant-feather and his exclusive brethren at the bar table.

H. Honour Magistrate Woodpigeon came onto the bench and said, 'Good morning, gentlemen. I note this matter is being withdrawn.' I asked if I could say something and H. Honour said 'no' this time. Woodpigeon then said words to the effect of 'It's not my role to enquire as to the prosecutorial discretion of the OPP. I will mark the file withdrawn. Thank you, gentlemen', and then promptly left the bench.

I was stunned. This was the same magistrate who had done the right thing two weeks earlier and had assured me that new charges should be brought, and the matter should proceed by way of conviction. Someone had got to him too, and Lord Pheasant-feather's presence alone told him not to interfere. In any event, legally, a magistrate can't force a prosecution, so his hands were tied without any charges.

As we were leaving the courtroom, I approached Ms Madam Mallee-fowl and asked her, 'Are you Madam Mallee-fowl?'who told me in no uncertain terms that she was but that she was not interested in speaking to me and said, 'Why would I? You will only abuse me.' I have never abused her before and I imagine this was her way out of it. Or maybe she expected she would be verbally abused after her pathetic, bitchy, schoolgirl bully performance in the courtroom.

Lord Pheasant-feather then walked towards the lifts and while he was waiting, I walked up to him and said to him, 'You should be ashamed of yourself. What an absolute disgrace.' He arrogantly turned his head and sniffed disdainfully at me and entered the lift again in the company of the defendant and his counsel in what can only be described as a blatant display of comradery and of being untouchable and beyond the reach of the law, just like the Catholic Church and just like King Claudius.

No one from the OPP came to speak to me. That was an insult in of itself. Was that meant to be a lesson for me in watching the big guns come down to put me, a female victim who speaks up, back in her box? Well done to the OPP; if that was their mission, they certainly achieved it. I think it's time for the OPP to change their mission statement to reflect this new vision of re-traumatising childhood sexual abuse victims.

I am deeply concerned after looking at the OPP website, including their Strategic Plan 2013–2017. In my case, like many others, they haven't achieved any of the following values they say are part of their strategic plan: to act fairly, to act with integrity, to respect others, to work together, to strive for excellence. Moreover, their stated vision is 'to make a positive

difference to the community through the justice system' and
their purpose is 'to provide an independent prosecution service
to the people of Victoria'. They have certainly not achieved
any of the above in my case and many others. Just look at the
woeful statistics.

The OPP website tells me that the OPP works in up to fifty
courts each day to prosecute serious criminal matters on behalf
of the community. Was mine not a serious matter? It was
serious to me, but as Madam Mallee-fowl said to me, my
matters on a scale are minor. I will never forget how I felt
when she said that to me. I can only hope she doesn't have
children. Moreover, if it was so minor, what was she and
briefed counsel and Lord Pheasant-feather, SC, all doing there?
Is that not the burning question?

The OPP website also states, 'A key aim of the OPP is to
prosecute sex offences in a way that minimises the stress for
victims and enhances their confidence in the justice system.'
Well, in my case, they have failed to achieve this aim dismally.
The statistics reveal that they're failing dismally across the
board, not just in my case but also in most sexual assault cases
bar a few as there's only a 3 per cent conviction rate.

So, what are the OPP lawyers doing there, day in, day out?
It seems it's glorified paper shuffling and phone calls fobbing
off sexual assault complainants with a pro forma letter sent off
confirming, 'Dear John, Sorry, but we have decided not to
pursue your matter any further.' Busy days lawyering there, if
that's what you'd call it. I suspect that the OPP has some other
agenda where my matters are concerned and where all sexual
abuse matters are concerned, unless there's multiple witnesses,
CCTV footage, admissible DNA and the perpetrator is not
connected to senior Catholics or judicial officers. To consider
that the Chief Crown Prosecutor himself, together with a

barrister and an instructor, had to appear before a magistrate to withdraw one charge of Unlawful Assault is indicative of the concerns the Office must have had. When the matter last came before the Court for the Committal Hearing, Magistrate Woodpigeon gave me an opportunity to speak and did not determine the matter as the OPP wanted. On this occasion, the OPP were clearly taking no chances by making sure H. Honour saw who was supportive of the OPP stance.

To see my cousin, the defendant, his father, King Lear Pavlovic, and his defence team clearly so welcomed and so much a part of the OPP group in these circumstances was a total disgrace. If ever the body meant to defend the victim of such a crime made the victim feel further victimised, this was the occasion. Why would a victim of childhood sexual abuse ever feel that she or he could come forward and make a complaint to authorities when clearly, those authorities are not prepared to prosecute the case to the full extent of the law as they are meant to?

I still ask what Lord Pheasant-feather was doing there. He is the State's top lawyer and would be expensive, I imagine – $20,000 per day I estimate. Who approved the budget for him to leave his office for my minor matter, simply to withdraw one remaining charge of unlawful assault? It is mind-boggling. It leads me to believe that my matter isn't so minor after all. Not at all. In fact, I believe King Claudius was sexually abused by Catholic clergy as an altar boy and then used this learnt behaviour to sexually abuse me and his sisters, together with his brother Hamlet and a friend from St Michael's College Conservative Town, the Devil's playground. I suspect that the OPP didn't want me, another trouble-making victim lawyer like John Ellis, this time opening up the unopened can of worms that is secondary victims of clergy abuse.

My Three Complaints to Three Brick Walls

I complained to the OPP, the Attorney General and the Ombudsman, all to no avail. And years later I complained to the Victims of Crime Commissioner but this didn't achieve anything either. I had a compelling case with a fully admissible taped confession. Magistrate Woodpigeon agreed with me that Diversion was not appropriate and gave an indication that there was enough evidence for a trial and for the Committal to proceed and made it clear that they wanted to hear it.

I was far from satisfied with the way the OPP handled my matter. I never in my wildest dreams considered that the organisation whose very reason for being was to carry forward the cases of those victimised by criminal behaviour perpetrated by members of the community would leave me denied, stranded and unrepresented at the courtroom door.

At that time, I wondered what would happen to the taped confession now. I was afraid it would magically disappear like my case had as part of the cover-up of clergy abuse, keeping King Claudius off the hook and secretly paid off as a primary victim and rendering me powerless and invisible as a secondary victim. I wonder whether King Claudius was given money in a secret payout by the Conservative Town Diocese as that would explain a great deal. I had to get a copy of that pretext call urgently before it got 'lost'. I also suspect that King Claudius may have been an OPP witness and they wouldn't want him to become like Cameron Carlisle, a victim and a perpetrator, for then they would have to consider and acknowledge secondary victims of clergy abuse.

Now I had something I would regret for the rest of my life, like my cousin told me his sexual abuse of me is something he has regretted all his life. But for me, it's coming forward to the police and disclosing my abuse. Thank you to the great OPP working very hard for perpetrators. My new meaning for the acronym OPP – Official Perpetrator Protection!

In my opinion, all the various parties supposedly prosecuting this matter for my benefit as a victim of sex abuse were intent on protecting the Catholic Church because there is a strong link between various clergy and my cousin's family. I have reason to believe that both King Claudius and Hamlet were sexually abused while they were altar boys in Conservative Town at St Vincent's Primary, St Michael's College and St Michael's Cathedral and they repeated that behaviour on me and their sisters, Goneril and Regan, for many years.

King Claudius' lawyer always briefed Strut-Bittern, Esq, of counsel in this matter. He is related to Magistrate Lapwing. I believe what happened in my case is all about politics and power and protection of the Catholic Church. The matter is full of big names and important, prominent people – but for what reason? King Claudius is a relative nobody, as am I, but his treatment and the way the matter was conducted, particularly by the body that was meant to be prosecuting without fear or favour, had all the hallmarks of protection of a seriously important individual.

Disturbingly, one current Crown Prosecutor, David Swallow, previously worked at Bates & Fenton Lawyers in Loganville in the mid-1990s, representing convicted paedophile priest the Bishop of Winchester, who abused one of my clients whom I represented in the Royal Commission into Institutional Responses to Child Sexual Abuse. Swallow was previously involved in the protection of priests and their paedophile ring and I suspect that he, still to this day, remains determined to protect the Catholic Church and anyone who has been involved in what went on in Conservative Town, albeit now from the office of the OPP. The Director of the OPP, Edmond Friarbird, was meant to be briefed in the Bishop of Winchester matter when he was a criminal defence barrister but was unable to accept the brief, so it went to another barrister in the end. However, I suspect that Bates & Fenton and David Swallow working in that office intended to brief Friarbird for a reason. It's all about one's political persuasion.

I suspect that Edmond Friarbird was there at the OPP as Director for the same reason and it's not to prosecute crime without fear or favour. It's to send me a smarmy letter full of smug hypocrisy, wishing me well for the future, proffering me to get over it in the face of them dropping my matter. An apologist for the Catholic Church perhaps? I want Mr Friarbird to know that his letter sent to me inspires me to soar above all this Catholic conspiracy until my last breath. Lord Pheasant-feather is another disappointment as Friarbird's number-one henchman and lickspittle, working together to make my case disappear like magic, a power not dissimilar to a religious miracle such as Jesus' touch restoring sight or the ability to walk. A power that has no proof yet can't be questioned. The mystery of the faith and the mystery of the law – together one whopping great mystery!

Silenced by a Suppression Order

In 2014, after the criminal case was withdrawn, I wanted to go to the media about it as I was devastated, angry and completely bewildered with the criminal 'injustice' system, the Catholic Church, King Claudius and my extended family. I had to tell my clients and others to warn them about how complainants of historic sexual assault are treated. I was disgusted with the legal profession and that this could happen in the year 2014! However, when I sought a copy of the taped confession (pretext call) in the process, I was told by Freedom of Information that because there was a Suppression Order in place, I couldn't have a copy. Then I was provided with a redacted copy for my money, so I could only hear my traumatised voice as his calm, monotone responses were all erased. I resented the FOI fee, swore and fumed. I picked up the phone and called my journalist friend, the wonderful Charmion at The Conservative Town Daily Bugle.

It took seven months and numerous court hearings to finally have the Suppression Order revoked as my cousin King Claudius contested my application and wanted it kept in place to protect his crimes and silence me forever, even though the case was over. Surprise, surprise – it's perpetrators who want and need suppression orders and King Claudius fought me for it and lost. When I did win, eventually, I was denied costs for some unknown reason by Magistrate Quail in Loganville. I wonder whether he is also part of the Catholic conspiracy from Loganville, only a short drive from Catholic Conservative Town.

The Suppression Order was finally revoked in March 2015 but only after an unnecessarily lengthy legal battle. I fought for seven months through various court hearings over a legal technicality of applying to revoke it using the new application form under the Open Courts Act (2013)[53] rather than under the Magistrates' Court Act (1989)[54]. I used the only form that exists to make this application, from the Magistrates' Court's own website, but was punished for this unnecessarily and made to reapply using the exact same form but needing to refer to the old Magistrates' Court Act, in the alternative, in my reasons for my application.

This is one of the most ridiculous legal red herrings, particularly in the face of the Open Courts Act and the transitional provisions it contains, intended to assist parties and uphold their freedom of speech, not fetter them. I note that there is still only the one inept and ambiguous form on the website that will continue to trip up the next victim who wants to fight for their freedom of speech in a matter where a Suppression Order was made before 1 December 2013. I predict that there may be many victims in this category whose cases were heard years ago and now, at a time where they might be more inclined to speak up about it or want to name and shame the perpetrator, may well find they can't because of an eternal Suppression Order. This may happen as a perpetrator is released from prison years later and the victim can't say anything. Again, I suspect that many victims would not even know if there was a Suppression Order still in place as a result of a long-finished criminal matter where they were a witness.

On [DATE] 2014, I applied for a review of a Suppression Order (Non-Publication Order) that was made on [DATE] 2013 during the now abandoned criminal case. This application was initially listed before Magistrate Pricklefinch on [DATE] 2014. On this date, Magistrate Pricklefinch recused themselves and made no findings or decisions in the matter other than that they were not able to hear the matter. H. Honour expressed the view in the hearing that as I appeared before them frequently as a legal practitioner in Conservative Town, it was therefore not appropriate for them to hear and determine the matter. I took no issue with this. However, having recused themselves, they then offered their view that the application was not in the correct form.

I then brought a fresh application for Review of a

Suppression Order on [DATE] 2014 which was heard on
[DATE] 2014 by H. Honour Magistrate Starling. The matter
was then adjourned to [DATE] 2015 as H. Honour felt the
magistrate who made the Suppression Order originally should
hear the application to revoke it.

On [DATE] 2015, H. Honour Magistrate Quail heard my
application for the revocation of the Suppression Order made
on [DATE] 2013. Unfortunately, H. Honour sits in Loganville,
so I had to travel there for the matter to be determined, even
though the offending happened in Conservative Town and so
the correct jurisdiction to hear it was Conservative Town.

On [DATE] 2015, H. Honour Magistrate Quail made an
Order to revoke the Suppression Order and handed down their
seventeen-paged Reasons for Decision. My application was
successful, but no order for costs was made about that part of
the revocation application heard before Magistrate Quail.
Their orders were, inter alia, that the issue of costs for the
[DATE] 2014, previously reserved by H. Honour Magistrate
Pricklefinch, be remitted to them for determination. So, it still
wasn't over for me. The Suppression Order was now revoked
but only after one hell of an unnecessarily dramatic, costly and
frustrating journey. I won the return of my right to freedom of
speech, but no costs were granted in my favour. The
magistrate refused to grant me costs, saying in their Reasons
for Decision:

'Given her concerns about being restricted in pursuing her
grievances against the DPP, Ms Jones had no choice but to
apply for the SO [Suppression Order] to be revoked or varied.
Nonetheless, such applications are rare and clearly, in this case,
personal to her personal circumstances. In my view, therefore,
her application ought be at her cost.'[55]

I received a pyrrhic victory, the kind that victims who speak up like me are used to getting. The kind we're advised we'll get – a further encouragement to drop it. Good girls accept pyrrhic victories, apparently; wanting anything more deems you vengeful and a whore. My submission for costs after my Suppression Order matter was humble at most yet still denied. Seeking costs if you're a woman seemingly equates to vengeful bitch, yet it's well-established legal principle that costs follow a win. So why wasn't I granted costs? Because I'm a woman in a man's world and that's not feminist claptrap to the patriarchal prigs reading this. That's the reality.

The fact is that the revocation of the Suppression Order was necessary for me to access the audio recordings of the abortive committal of the defendant before Magistrate Woodpigeon, the OPP's submissions in court concerning the withdrawal of the charges and the evidence led in the criminal proceedings to the stage of withdrawal. None of these were accessible to me or to my counsel advising me as to my legal position in the absence of the criminal prosecution. Equally, I was not at liberty to discuss the legal processes to which I had been subject. Why would a victim want to be gagged after a sexual assault, denied their freedom of speech after they've already been sexually abused and utterly disrespected? Especially once someone has come forward and disclosed to police, they're more likely to want to speak up to other people as well. Has no one thought this through before me?

The only remaining issue for consideration by the court then was the issue of costs reserved [DATE] 2014, when King Claudius' lawyers had wrongly called my application 'incompetent' because of the application form neglecting to have a simple tick box: Suppression Order under the Magistrates' Court Act or under the Open Court's Act. A simple pro forma change such as this, which is obviously much needed, remains wanting despite my correspondence to the court raising this loophole.

After serious delays of some four months to get a court date in the Conservative Town Magistrates' Court, it finally returned to H. Honour Magistrate Pricklefinch, on [DATE] 2015, for determination. H. Honour denied the original cost application made by my cousin for that day. Only now was the matter fully over. It had cost me more than $10,000 to have my freedom of speech restored. A high price for a fundamental freedom when I had no say in it being taken away from me in the first place. Only now could I finally have The Conservative Town Daily Bugle publish my newspaper article[56].

The personal, psychological and financial consequences of reporting the sexual assaults upon myself still leave me in no doubt about whether it is morally and ethically correct for a legal practitioner to advise a victim of sexual abuse to report their abuse to the police given the possible personal consequences incidental to the legal process itself. Under the Suppression Order, I was completely restricted in my capacity as a citizen and as a legal practitioner to make any comment upon these critical issues making any reference to my own experience. I found the Suppression Order particularly egregious in these circumstances where the Order served only to protect the perpetrator of the offences and limit any discussion of or the seeking of any other remedy against him.

My newspaper article about my experience of the legal system at that point was finally published in the Conservative Town Daily Bugle on [DATE] 2015. It received a very positive response and I was stronger because of it. My burden was lighter because others were sharing the legal insanity with me. However, journalist Charmion told me that her bosses' lawyers had decided I was not permitted to even mention that the perpetrator was a family member but rather just someone I knew, which added to my frustration. I wanted to disclose that my matter was a case of very serious family violence, but once again, the truth needed to be hidden to hide the dirty linen and the subterfuge of the powerful.

VOCAT

In 2016, I applied for Victims of Crime Compensation, a relatively easy and accessible form of compensation from the government, which, importantly, would provide the elusive acknowledgement that I was indeed a victim of crime, albeit token. This was very important to me as I still didn't have this acknowledgement from my cousin, my family, or the legal system through the criminal process, which I should have had as the magistrate suggested, in the form of a conviction and good behaviour bond or similar, including an admission in the form of the new agreed statement for diversion.

Initially, I received some interim awards from VOCAT for counselling and the cost of the psychologist's report was covered, the report that is necessary to determine psychological injury. However, VOCAT also advised that they intended on notifying my cousin about my application and for this to not occur, I needed to make written submissions to the Tribunal as to why he should not be notified. Due to an administrative oversight by my office, my submissions weren't sent off but sat as a draft administration email, triggering VOCAT to inform my cousin about my application before I realised. Predictably, King Claudius opted to become involved in my matter quite unnecessarily and when I tried to rectify the situation, it was too late.

The VOCAT hearing was listed about three weeks after I

broke my leg and ankle in three places, not because of a crime but rather because of an unfortunate accident. I slipped on a benign-looking rock in the Rockies and fell awkwardly, crashing down onto my own leg and, lay hyperventilating on a large cold rock in excruciating pain for three hours with four broken bones, waiting to be rescued. I made the national news and had a very slow recovery as I couldn't bear weight for about eight weeks. Just existing was a trial, but I made it to this hearing, a sight in my wheelchair, with my leg outstretched in front on a special extension piece. I was already in pain by the time I arrived at court and keeping my leg elevated in the car, propped up by doonas and pillows, was far from easy, as sitting sideways made me car sick.

Antony parked the car in Court Street, fluking a spot near the corner of Court and Judgement Streets. It was lunchtime, but there was no time for lunch as Antony and my parents transferred me from car to wheelchair. Then I had to go to the toilet, which involved complications beyond anything I could have foreseen. For starters, I couldn't reach the door with my hand, so I opened it with my foot and then just wheeled myself through. Then I had to backtrack to lock the door and then I had to manoeuvre myself onto the toilet seat in a way that I could get back into the wheelchair. It was a mental game as much as a physical challenge as I had to plan each movement carefully. I was exhausted, so I didn't want to drink anything else for fear of needing to go again.

After my spectacular fall in the Rockies, I started noticing other wheelchairs too, just as I noticed prams once I had my first baby, and I developed a bizarre wheelchair envy, seeing fancier ones than the one Omni loaned me. When Antony brought it home, with a collection of other disabled equipment, I noticed the word Karma on the side of it. I couldn't believe the brand name; that was just not funny nor PC! Why was I paying for karma that was not my karma? This sort of karma belonged to King Claudius, so why was I copping it? Clearly, it was delivered to the wrong person, but the karma made itself at home, multiplied and shifted to poor Antony.

When the matter ended that day, Antony went to get the car to collect me from the front entrance, so I'd have less inconvenience and distance to travel. However, he returned shortly after claiming the car had been stolen.

'What?' I said.

'It's gone. It's not where I parked it. Someone's nicked it.'

Antony looked like he'd failed me and felt responsible for it.

'Are you sure?' I enquired.

'Yes, it's not bloody there.'

'What's the time?' I asked, thinking of the peak hour outside.

'It's 4:25 p.m. or thereabouts.'

'It's not a clearway, is it?'

'Oh shit, I don't think so, but –'

'Go, go and check!' I said, cutting him off.

Poor Antony raced off, distressed at my being a damsel in distress that he could not rescue. I started to laugh with my parents as the situation was hilarious, really. I was stuck and needed to go home, but all my parents and I could do was sit and wait.

A few minutes later, we received a call from Antony, who was in a taxi, on his way to collect our car that had been towed away and impounded in Fernvale. He paid the three hundred–odd dollars and collected us about an hour later. While we waited, we drank coffee in the café next to court, the automatic doors letting in icy blasts of wind with each new customer. It was getting dark outside and there was rain streaming down the panes of glass, reminding me of the entrance to the art gallery, and how I used to play with that water as a child. The sounds of the impatient traffic mimicked our impatience. I was desperate for my meds to take the pain away as my leg was throbbing by now and I couldn't seem to get any relief. Why did my days at court always end so badly?

The Karma wheelchair and I were eventually packed into the car and the drama was driven home. In the car, we did a post-mortem on the day as we always did. We recalled how King Claudius' lawyer Barnaby Bustard-Braggart had appeared in his usual undignified fashion. 'Sorry I'm late, Your Honour. The court gave me the bum steer!' bursting out laughing as I mocked him. Barnaby was totally uncooperative and unnecessarily rude towards my barrister, Mr Owl, of counsel, especially when Mr Owl asked him if he could be shown a document but was told abruptly, 'No, get it from your instructor!' He was always entertaining, I'll give him that much. Court days always made me feel like I was queuing up to see the circus.

Down the highway, as we drove through the hills, I closed my eyes and thought about the morning I'd spent at the gallery before court, looking at Degas' ballerinas. What had happened to this little ballerina though? I opined that karma had taken good care of me; I had pirouetted right off the stage, down the mountain, down the courthouse steps and was now a mangled mess. I started to believe in past lives and wondered what the hell I'd done. Maybe I'd pay a visit to one of those shonky crystal shops with dragons and witches in the window and get my palms read.

In any event, the VOCAT matter was subsequently adjourned until after the outcome of the pending civil matter that had kicked off in the meantime, which is understandable, for I agree that the government shouldn't pay where the offender can. However, as a result, my truth and recognition of the crimes was on hold again, with a civil trial now set for [DATE] 2017 and now I had an unpaid legal bill to buy back my freedom of speech as a victim of crime. The government or King Claudius owed me my costs and I wanted my money back, now!

As a result, my status as a victim of crime remained elusive in both real life and on paper, to be determined after [DATE] 2017, the day my civil trial is now due to commence, which is also Gospa Velika 2017. Ironically, this Catholic festive day was the very day I disclosed my abuse to my extended family, four long years ago, in 2013, in my Uncle and Auntie's dining room. Stranger still, Rolf Harris returned to the news almost to the same day too this year, a hung jury, with the judge failing to order a re-trial, setting him free from further sexual abuse allegations. The great adversarial system working its working day again, both locally and abroad. My eyes roll. I started making a mental list of countries I could move to live that have the Inquisitorial System – in my opinion, a model far better suited to crime in the modern day. Ironically, Italy is one of them, the land of the Catholic, the land of the Pope and Cardinal Campeius.

Strangely, my clergy abuse clients were recently denied VOCAT compensation as they were told in writing that they should seek compensation from the Royal Commission or the Church instead. One of my clients needed urgent rehabilitation for chronic long-term alcohol and drug abuse but was refused despite our appeal of their decision. The VOCAT Tribunal deemed that he can simply wait for redress until next year, which is ironic as VOCAT usually grants interim awards to help assist a survivor until the final award is made. I was very disappointed and rather surprised by the outcome, so we appealed it, but disturbingly, VOCAT upheld their original decision. Their reasoning was so offensive and essentially blames my client for his inevitable trajectory and then uses that very trajectory as the reason why they wouldn't grant the interim award.

It is worth quoting from their letter as follows:

'The Tribunal has considered your letter . . . and your request for an interim award in circumstances, which include –

This application being filed almost 40 years after the alleged offending.

Sexual offending not being reported to police prior to 2015 and no prosecution yet proceeding or authorised.

Significant history including drug and alcohol abuse, family suicide and multi-layered ill health issues affecting the applicant almost certainly of mixed aetiology.

The Tribunal will not authorise an interim award here.

The Catholic Church and the Royal Commission have both been involved in considering compensation for victims of institutionalised sexual abuse. Commonwealth funding and/or Catholic Church compensation may well be available. Sourcing those funding entitlements is more direct and more appropriate than interim awards from this Tribunal.

The Tribunal expects an applicant in these circumstances to exhaust alternate compensation entitlements before seeking a final award.'[57]

In the circumstances, I find this correspondence utterly offensive. I am frustrated that VOCAT will not assist my client on an interim basis as I predict that approximately $20,000 would have been adequate to fund his place in a live-in detox clinic for urgent rehabilitation. The correspondence is also very judgmental in that it, in effect, punishes my client for his trajectory. He would, in reality, have to be a 'sleeper'[58] like me, with no symptoms and no negative life events to have happened to him in the interim that could confuse the line of causation for the purposes of VOCAT. Furthermore, they raise the issue of the lengthy time taken to disclose and report to police, as if unaware that a forty-year delay in disclosing abuse is quite normal. Thirty-three years is the average, after all. All this letter suggests to me is that only experts in child sexual abuse should be determining VOCAT awards in these matters. And suicide in his family, there is, yes; his brother was also abused by clergy, but it seems that VOCAT punished him for that too.

If ever there was a victim of crime deserving of an interim award, it would be my amazingly wonderful clergy abuse clients. Again, this matter also shows once again that sexual abuse does not fit into the legal system and at a time when we have maximum awareness and media coverage. It's truly concerning. Predictably, my client then flatly refused to allow us to approach the Catholic Diocese in Conservative Town for urgent funding as that is the last place he wants to accept money from after what has happened to him at a Conservative Town Catholic Primary School.

Although the Royal Commission has made its final recommendations and although things look promising, redress is still a long way off yet, possibly twelve months away, which would have made an interim VOCAT award more than appropriate. In any event, any amount received under VOCAT could be paid back later if other compensation was successfully obtained.

What will my clients live on until then? Centrelink, which we know is inadequate and is less than war veterans get, on the disability support pension (DSP), who also suffer from PTSD, yet their symptoms are well recognised and respected, with badges of honour, to boot and a national public holiday. What's the difference between their PTSD and PTSD of war veterans? There is no difference. My clients and friends John Bates and Gonzalo have worked hard at building awareness and putting pressure on politicians about this very paradox. I can only hope that the government changes its eligibility requirements for survivors of child sexual abuse to receive the DSP.

Sadly, yet predictably, one of my clients who made the allegations against a Catholic prest spent time in prison as, without rehabilitation, his behaviour spiralled out of control. There's nothing surprising about this at all. Now any rehabilitation he might get will be from inside prison walls. I ask, is this the best we can do and provide for a victim of clergy sexual abuse? Wait until their self-destructive demise and then blame them for it? I'm appalled.

And as for my own VOCAT outcome, it can't be finalised as King Claudius' lawyer won't consent to the Settlement Terms being given to VOCAT and VOCAT won't finalise without them. Another legal stalemate for me – the predetermined outcome for a good girl, so it seems.

There are only two mistakes one can make along the road to truth – not going all the way and not starting.

— **Buddha**[59]

Civil Matters (Most Uncivil)

In [DATE] 2015, I issued civil proceedings against my cousin, suing him for common law damages by filing a Statement of Claim in the County Court. Another $1,000 filing fee, my early Christmas present. Lucky me. However, it would take almost four months to serve my cousin as his lawyers decided to continue to be difficult and not accept service of the documents. This is an old trick oft used by the Catholic Church, including in the famous John Ellis matter.

Needless to say, once it was served personally by a process server in March 2016, incurring more unnecessary costs, his lawyers notified us that they acted for him again. How predictable. Then began the next chapter of mindless fun that is civil litigation.

Civil litigation prescribes interlocutory steps that are meant to be non-controversial; dates and a timeline of events are set and agreed to by consent. The Civil Procedure Act (2010)[60] and the Civil Procedure Rules[61] provide for this. Mediation takes place and offers are exchanged, followed by court events only if required, to speed up the process as much as possible. However, my proactive and cooperative approach was met with rudeness and belligerence from my cousin's unprofessional lawyers, almost without fail. Seemingly, King Claudius' lawyer takes great delight in frustrating and misrepresenting others; clearly a happy duo, he and my cousin. With each piece of nasty correspondence, my anger and frustration grew. Though I never dreamed of quitting, not for a minute, I farmed the matter out of my office as my emotional welfare could no longer stand representing myself against his unprofessional lawyer from Court Jester Solicitors.

This lawyer of his was male and a friend of the Pavlovic family for years beforehand. He was also a friend of a student who killed her boyfriend. It didn't surprise me at all that he was friends with her and according to court transcripts, he was a real charmer, just like King Claudius. I had met him before at family celebrations held at the house of Uncle King Lear and Aunty, King Lear's wife. I found him to be slippery slick. Like his greasy hair and the greasy, pale pallor of his skin.

I had problems with my own lawyers too and had to change lawyers three times from when I began the civil matter in [DATE] 2015. My first lawyer was a crook and a disaster who only caused delay. The barrister briefed by him to settle the Statement of Claim we'd already drafted couldn't do so after six months of waiting and subsequently never did. I essentially received a legal bill from him for having briefed a barrister and I had one conference with him. I received no product, just wasted my time and money. My husband, Antony, went and paid him a visit in chambers and on this occasion he lied, telling Antony that the draft Statement of Claim was in the post. He never settled it and we never received anything from him at any time. What a legal eagle, recommended by the Law Institute of Victoria, who, in turn, recommended that I not lodge a complaint about him as there wasn't much that would happen to him and my time would be wasted pursuing it. Hmmm.

My next lawyer was thoroughly incompetent, briefing a barrister who simply denied my experience of the legal system, pathetically defending it as if his career depended on it, which

it does, I suppose. It was laughable that he seemed unfamiliar
with the concept of a legal loophole yet is lauded as one of our
profession's finest. Is that a prerequisite to practise, to deny the
corrupt reality of the legal system to complainants so they stop
complaining but, when defending someone, utilise every legal
loophole there is? Basically, while he and the instructing
solicitor mucked around with my increasingly expensive
document, I paid money for her to pull apart the Statement of
Claim, file a new one, change her mind and then have the male
barrister she briefed put it back together again, almost in its
original form. Costly stuff is legal incompetence and one-
upmanship. I had to pay a lot for his 'distinct style', which the
instructing solicitor tried to justify. I had just paid to be
insulted by the barrister was all.

Disturbingly, this document was made slightly different by
them to my statements to the police, which then formed the
basis for the defence arguing that there were 'inconsistencies'
in my documents. Moreover, counsel then suggested that I
counter this by writing an affidavit as to how the passage of
time had caused my memory to fail me. This advice is possibly
the worst I have encountered and I did not follow it, of course,
as only an amoeba would! Beware, victims of sexual abuse,
he's an expert in personal injuries.

My last lawyers have been amazing, not because of their
fine document preparation and attention to detail but because
they had respected me at every turn and have acknowledged
my obvious and inevitable hurt and frustration. However, the
barrister they briefed turned out to be incompetent and quite
rude and won't be briefed again. With my new instructions,
not to brief him again, the matter proceeded but in the most
protracted and unjust way, including when represented by a
Queen's Counsel who was equally incompetent, ineffective

and plainly rude. I sacked him too and I subsequently asked my lawyers to cease acting as well. After this, I self-represented, bringing the matter to finalisation whilst doing so as I'd had a gut full of these birdbrains and their crap.

At risk of the remainder of this chapter being really boring, I think it's important to trot this frustrating existence out as this is what it feels like to be a victim and stuck in a legal quagmire whilst being denied a basic pair of gumboots to get you through it. When you see the legal eagles robed and wigged and swanning around the court precinct, this is what they're doing – glorified administration. Its pomp and pageantry much of the time, really, with very little substantive content and when there is, they get it wrong.

Dear Diary

The following paragraphs form a diary of sorts, an outpouring of my anger towards the defendant and his reptilian lawyer and my utter disappointment and frustration regarding the County Court and its staff in the way it has mismanaged my matter.

The latest legal shenanigans in my civil case are as follows:

[DATE] 2017

We went to Court for the Summons and the other side didn't show – not the lawyer nor a barrister nor his client, King Claudius. I had my lawyer and my barrister there; legal overkill. As there was no appearance by the defendant and no word from the defendant about it, the matter was simply adjourned by the Judicial Registrar (JR) for seven days despite our Affidavit of Service. H. Honour ordered that we file further affidavits showing the trail of correspondence since the last affidavit was filed by us just a week earlier, which already explained same. This is despite us showing the JR the one-line, curt email was all that had been received by us from his lawyers since the affidavit we filed only a week earlier and, in addition to that, our Affidavit of Service. To think that H. Honour still required that in affidavit form was, in the circumstances, unnecessarily officious and expensive.

[DATE] 2017

We went to court for the return of the matter and once again, King Claudius and his lawyer didn't show. Once again, I had my lawyer and the same barrister they briefed again. The matter was stood down until 10:30 a.m. at the defendant's insistence, for he called the court at 9:10 a.m. and claimed he had a matter in the Supreme Court he had to attend to. Why he didn't brief counsel is beyond me and why he wasn't later told to also defies all logic and legal norms. After that indulgence, the matter was then called at approximately 11:00 a.m. and he still didn't show, but the matter finally proceeded ex parte, to my real surprise.

For the record, the JR didn't make mention of their absence at all though, didn't reprimand them for breach of the Orders, didn't even read the affidavits we had filed in timely fashion as he had ordered a week earlier and simply said there was no paperwork on the court file, as if dissatisfied with us, or trying to put us on the back foot. His clerk or my barrister should have and could have provided them to him in an instant, but I suspect that he didn't want them as then he'd have to acknowledge my ongoing perfect legal servitude in the face of the defendant's blatant disregard for the Orders. Clearly, the JR didn't want to give us credit for what we'd done to comply with his Orders. To put the matter simply, he had another agenda, which was to work for King Claudius in his absence. I was ready to pull my hair out, but then things got even worse!

The JR then referred to case law in defence of King Claudius and said he couldn't strike the matter out for fear of appeal. Adding insult to injury, the JR made orders that King Claudius comply with the original breached orders rather than the more recent ones he'd also breached to file the Further and Better Particulars to the Defence and his Affidavit of Documents. Never mind the many subsequent orders he's breached, fourteen in total; clearly, he's not required to answer why he's not shown up and why he's breached all court Orders to date. Where's his requirement of legal servitude like I'm saddled with? Why wasn't he held in contempt of court and especially his dodgy solicitor? Why was the red carpet rolled out for them every time, even in their absence?

In other words, the JR had let my abuser go right back to the start to get the matter back on track. He had let him breach all subsequent court orders without comment or reprimand. He had ordered us to file affidavits to reveal the precise position of the other side as best we could, costing me more money regardless, when really that should have been asked for from the other side. The JR was intrigued and wanted to know whether King Claudius or his lawyer was responsible for their non-compliance but notably at my expense. And how was I to prove that to the Bench anyway? Then, when we returned to court and complied with the Orders, he didn't even have the decency to read the affidavits that he'd ordered be filed.

King Claudius' lawyer finally turned up to court at 11:25

a.m. after the matter was heard and the courtroom door was closed and locked shut. We were still at court debriefing when we saw him stroll into the court building at a very leisurely pace with no briefcase, no file and no paperwork, unhurried and as cool as a cucumber. Slippery slick as always, with his female assistant trailing after him, calling out his name sweetly. He walked as if he owned the place. I suspect that's the behaviour of someone who has legal immunity.

King Claudius' lawyer wrote a rude and discourteous email to the court later that day, objecting to the matter having been heard in his absence and still claimed that he'd not been served with anything by my lawyers. This is despite our numerous affidavits of service, noting that he'd been served by us three times with the court Orders and indicating the method of service on each occasion. Moreover, a group email sent to him and the court by us received a reply from him, proving his receipt of same in any event. He was just playing more expensive games and I was being sent the fees, while the court pretended not to know. A game called 'Delay and Deny' that the Catholic Church invented.

Yet my barrister's greatest concern that day was that my body language would 'piss off the judge'. Being completely honest with myself, I admit that may have been entirely possible, but I say he had more pressing things to concern himself with – the substantive aspects of the application to strike out King Claudius' defence. His lacklustre performance, with little offered by way of submissions, told me he'd done little or no preparation. He had no idea of the case to which JR referred nor any other case law to support my application yet did not ask for the matter to be stood down for a brief time while he read it, which is the normal course in that event. He simply mumbled and shuffled his way through the mention, head down and submissive like a naughty schoolboy as to a headmaster.

So many clients have the same experience of so-called learned counsel, being that many are far from learned. It's more than fair to say that my barrister that day was more concerned about making easy money and his ongoing relationship with the bench than to present my case solidly and with conviction. I was stuck sitting behind him at court, feeling muzzled and stifled. He needed to have run the JR through the affidavit or at least offered to do so, as is usual practise. He needed to argue why the matter should not proceed past today. I know because I do this as a lawyer; it's called 'fight for your client'. He needed to understand the matter and seek to put the matter to rest. He did none of that and I would have been far better to self-represent. He had no opposing counsel or self-represented other party; open slather. I asked him to call me into the witness box, but he said no way, that will really piss the judge off. Why is it that I am seen as upsetting the judge rather than King Claudius? I am a dream client who has done everything and complied with every order and paid everyone – a really good girl – and aren't I a sucker? Just what the legal profession wants – a girl who wants to be kept in check, hungry for the carrot of justice that will never come. For that's the purpose of the court, so it seems; to make money out of victims like me.

[DATE] 2017

The clock said 4:01 p.m. and my heart leapt. I think I must have hit Refresh on my computer and phone at least fifty times that day, waiting to see if four years of legal bullshit had finally come to an end. It had; he'd missed the deadline. It was over. I literally skipped on the spot in my office, I just didn't know what to do with myself. This was the best birthday present I could give my dad today. We could finally put all this frustration and pain behind us. Peace at last, the bookend that Magistrate Woodpigeon had desired for us more than three years ago, before the matter morphed into a three-headed beast: King Claudius (the Church), the Law and the State.

Notwithstanding the rules about the court accepting documents by e-filing only, my receptionist called the County Court to make sure they hadn't received anything for filing in person by Barnaby Bustard-Braggart that hadn't been uploaded onto the portal yet and they confirmed there wasn't anything. Good! After all, the court only accepts e-filing of documents now, no filing over the counter. My husband ran upstairs to grab his briefcase and came back down the stairs, telling us all, 'He's filed!' It was 4:25 p.m. My heart sank. We checked the online e-filing on Court Connect[62] and there sat three new documents. I stared at the entries in disbelief. Sarah rang registry again to find out how this could happen, and they explained that he'd filed after 4:00 p.m., so it's registered as being filed on [DATE], the next working day after a public holiday. I said we'll be objecting to the late filing and proceeding with our application for default judgement on Tuesday, relying on the fact that the self-executed Orders in my favour had now been actioned and indeed executed. It should be over now, but would the law still be interested in his aborted defence?

I called my lawyers and they said not to panic, and that the documents the defendant filed are totally incompetent as one affidavit is filed unsworn and the other affidavit has been sworn by the wrong person. I thought to myself, yes, that's Barnaby's standard – stuff up the defendant's last chance.Moreover, they are both filed late, out of time. These were documents that should have been filed many months earlier, in [DATE] 2017. Yet the Judicial Registrar had ordered that they could still be filed to hold the Defence together, giving King Claudius another final, undeserved, easy ride at another easy chance. What about the JR ordering his compliance with all previous Orders also, including Costs Orders in my favour, not yet complied with? Strangely, he's not cross about his Orders being breached by King Claudius and his lawyer. Why would the truth 'piss off the judge'? I wonder.

[DATE] 2017

Behold, another new document had been filed by the defendant, another Affidavit of Documents, or perhaps a legally competent one this time that is sworn and has legal standing would be a welcome change. In any event, any further materials wanting to be filed by the defendant should not be accepted by Registry and should be well and truly irrelevant to the court by now, surely. Alas, no.

Watching the law and King Claudius is like watching a father and his son. It's like watching a father indulge his little belligerent boy who wants to stay in the bath and play with his boats, crashing them into one another for fun, long after the bathwater has gone cold, after dinner has gone cold, after bedtime. Way past the time to put your son to bed and pack away his toys. It's time for the law to say, 'Game over, son.' It's time for Uncle King Lear to say, 'You be good boy, King Claudius.' But that father-and-son team are too busy playing charades with each other and now the law has joined in. Don't spoil this little game, Cleopatra.

But I'm still waiting. Waiting endlessly. Now for some strange and unknown reason, I am to wait further, wondering what the JR will do. Where are the Orders I've been waiting so long for? Why hasn't the Order been executed automatically as ordered so that I can end this sorry chapter of my life? I want to get onto the important topic of my damages without any further delay, but it seems that the JR is determined to have me spend more money to win or lose; who knows? Or is his plan even more insidious than that that it lives eternally in the courts like an eternal flame. Well, that's not justice.

I say that psychiatric assessments really should be ordered for King Claudius and his lawyer, never mind me. Whatever are they doing, those two legally unsound and mentally insane boys swanning around in men's shoes? King Claudius can act like a child, the little prince King Claudius grown into a king, King Claudius, all he likes, who is a sociopathic king suffering from Peter Pan complex in my humble, unqualified opinion. He can play hide-and-seek, play charades, play little boys' games with his lawyer, the late-running, dishevelled, venomous, unethical lawyer with his poison pen correspondence, contemptuous conduct and criminal friends.

Why has that lawyer not been held in contempt of Court by this Honourable Court? Why has that lawyer not simply ceased acting, like all lawyers do without client money, client instructions, or whatever the case may be? The law should not allow the other side to be dragged through the courts at the substandard set by this shabby lawyer. If the client doesn't pay or doesn't follow advice, the lawyer ceases acting. Simple. In the event the lawyer is incompetent, the client simply gets new legal representation or fronts the court himself and self-represents. To have neither the lawyer nor the client there at two consecutive hearings and no reasonable excuse makes a mockery of the court and disrespects those that do follow the Orders like good-girl me, seemingly to no advantage. It also tells me that its deliberate game-playing done with the confidence of some sort of safety net. Furthermore, it seems that I have annoyed the court by complying with its Orders, for it clearly makes them nervous to do anything ex parte or to make Orders in my favour.

King Claudius' lawyer behaved appallingly at his convicted criminal friend's trial and was said to be uncooperative and rather peevish when called to give evidence as a witness. That certainly dovetails with my experience of him too. Notably, when I do a Google search of his name, a picture comes up of him in orange prison uniform. It's either a bad joke or telling of a very concerning history.

[DATE]2017

At 10:30 a.m., the court listed my matter for Directions Hearing on [DATE] 2017 and then, approximately ten minutes later, noted that it was a listing error. These events are evident on Court Connect, the County Court website that records the filing of all documents in a matter. This caused a lot of stress as my lawyers tried to brief counsel at extremely short notice for the next day and, because of the strange complexity in the matter, hopefully brief my Queen's Counsel again, Captain Plumage. Captain Plumage, QC, was unavailable though, so I started to panic as I realised that I need someone who can really end this matter rather than have another person who simply stands there politely conversing with the JR, making insulting comments such as 'The court is correct' like my previous counsel Emmanuel Cuckoo had done. The fact is that the court is not correct and far from it. The court is prejudicing me and systemically abusing me by ignoring its own orders. It is ignoring the Civil Procedure Rules for my cousin and his lawyer, yet ordering me to follow them alone. The court and King Claudius are breaching Court Orders and Civil Procedure Rules and abusing the intent of the legislation. Why is this legally permissible?

The law can indulge the little King Claudius and his merry mate-a-lots all it likes. I'm still standing. I'm still here waiting for the game to end – in checkmate. For the time being, all I care about is that the trial date remains fixed for [DATE] 2017, Gospa Velika. The legal feast in the form of the trial will satiate me for life, for I will finally get to question the little boy who's been hiding, the sham that is King Claudius. But the trial should not run at all as King Claudius' defence is already struck out, but in this matter, seemingly, anything goes.

And so, the waiting continued. And continued. My case was in no man's land, outside the sphere of the law. I had won, but no one was prepared to bring it to its conclusion and finalise the Orders already made by the court. It was a simple typing-up exercise by administration that was required by the court, yet when I called Registry numerous times, they advised that the JR still had the file on his desk in chambers and they were waiting for him to make a decision. What decision? I asked. I told them that there is no decision to make anymore. The Orders are self-executing Orders. So, let's see it then. Execute them! Execute him!

[DATE] 2017

On this day, the waiting got to me. I couldn't wait any longer. I'd had enough of waiting and called Registry and was then transferred to the Judge's Associate. I explained that the defendant had filed another document on [DATE] 2017, an Affidavit of Service that should not even be looked at or considered by the JR.

I was told again to wait and that the JR had the file in chambers and would decide soon. What decision is there to make? I asked. I said there's nothing to be determined by him; there only needs to be an administrative typing-up of Orders in my favour. The Judge's Associate, Mr Cormorant, couldn't say any more, which was fair enough but so unbelievably frustrating.

At 3:59 p.m. this same day, further correspondence was filed onto the portal by the defendant. At the time of writing, I was unaware of its content as my lawyers were not copied into it, so I called the court to complain rather than paying my lawyers to chase it up.

I cannot adequately put into words how absolutely frustrated I am. I cannot exist in this space. Should I be preparing for a trial in seven weeks' time, or can I finally rest? Who knows? How can I maintain my sanity, composure and happiness in this space? It's impossible. The delays are unjustified, the departure from civil procedure rules is galling and the breaching of the Orders by King Claudius and by the court itself is very concerning. This is a conspiracy, not a theory. It's a conspiracy to disrespect me and my welfare at every turn.

Sadly, I now absolutely hate lawyers, judges and everything the legal profession stands for, for look at what it does to good people, good girls seeking justice. I've been turned inside out and been put in a never-ending wash cycle called the law. Insert another gold coin in the slot, please - sorry, I should say place another 'gold ingot' on the scales of justice please Cleopatra.

[DATE] 2017

My lawyers called me and said not to speak to the Judge's Associate again as he had called them, complaining about me having called Registry myself when I have lawyers acting. Why is the court concerned about my behaviour, calling my lawyers to complain about my request for Orders instead of focussing on the issue at hand? And yes, I did threaten to call Derryn Hinch about it. Why don't they concern themselves with the defendant and call King Claudius' lawyers instead and ask him about his legally contemptuous behaviour? Why don't they just give me my Orders since I won? And then there would be no need for me to call them or Derryn Hinch. Needless to say, I did call Mr Hinch as I am a huge fan of him and his Justice Party. That man makes complete and utter sense to me; he speaks normally and gets on with it. A good man of action!

[DATE] 2017

Yesterday, I'd been busy in Big Smoke with the unveiling of the painting of Det Sgt Stephen Adams, which had provided a temporary distraction from the unknown status of my matter. It was a huge day, a watershed moment as Chief Commissioner Elbow gave the painting and the tireless work of DS Adams his sincere commendation.

The phone rang and it was my lawyer Jamie Heron. Jamie told me that the JR had just made the self-executing orders. I had won. It was finally over. I could hardly believe it, just when I'd virtually given up all hope. I was now free to make an application for Judgement in Default of Defence. I was now well on the way to getting the acknowledgement I was so desperate for, a piece of paper that would be my tangible proof that something bad had happened to me.

I could then turn to the matter of my damages and his payment of my legal costs. On the question of damages, there are damages in relation to the original offending and then aggravated damages to consider. The fact is that King Claudius did everything he possibly could to aggravate my damages for four years: denied it to all the family; denied it to police, giving a 'no comment' interview; would not settle for a good behaviour bond with conviction at the part-heard committal and opted to put me through a trial instead; fought my suppression order application to keep me silenced so his crimes would be safely hidden; and, finally, fought my VOCAT and civil matter for what will be two years by the time the matter concludes – if it ever does.

Along the way, he has shown flagrant disregard for court orders, has not paid my interim costs orders, has not shown himself at court since [DATE] 2014. This is a man who lives in Richville, works in Wealthy Street and drives a big Mercedes. This is a man who instructs his lawyer not to attend court numerous times for no disclosed reason. This is a man whose lawyer also fails to attend court and does not seek an adjournment nor ceases acting. His lawyer claims his client, King Claudius, was overseas at critical court moments yet does not advise the court of this at any stage. This is a man who has never made an offer to settle at any time. This is a man who is selfish and self-obsessed, who concerns himself with gym workouts, sailing, male manicures and massages, who remains king of the castle to the court and to the Pavlovic family. A tosser. This is a man who has got away with what he did to my cousins, his sisters, and me with no shame, penalty, sacrifice, loss, or opportunity cost. He is surrounded by the extended family and he has their unflinching support. His children also have their connection to the extended family. The fact remains that King Claudius has lost nothing despite him sexually abusing me for four years. He has never made any effort to put things right whatsoever.

I, on the other hand, have lost almost everything just for speaking up. I have lost the Pavlovic family and my favourite cousins, Goneril and Regan. My children have lost their connection to their second cousins, Pavlovic celebrations and all the other relatives' parties and the colourful culture that comes with them. My parents have lost their family and essentially their social life, which was mainly based around family, particularly in the golden years of their retirement. My father has lost all his siblings, living and dead.

What sort of person like King Claudius can call himself a man when he is such a cruel and heartless bastard to cause this much ongoing damage and pain? He couldn't apologise and admit what he's done to the family to put things right. King Claudius is not a man. King Claudius is a sociopath. King Claudius is guilty, not only criminally and civilly but also morally. Put simply, King Claudius should pay for what he did back then and what he's done since I disclosed, causing me so much further pain and suffering. King Claudius should go to my father and apologise for ruining his life through his lies. King Claudius should apologise to me for ruining me.

There's the initial damage he caused in the 1980s and now there's the aggravated damages caused by his responses now, as an adult, at nearly 50 years of age. Will he ever grow up?

In the summer of 2013, only months before I disclosed, King Claudius visited my parents. I hope he feels guilty every time he looks at the series of life drawings he asked my parents for and happily took from them that day but didn't pay for, embarrassing himself by offering my father $50 for them and, worse still, then realising he had no money in his wallet to pay the insulting amount. I rest my case about his character. Moreover, knowing that he sexually abused me, their daughter, it's quite creepy that he wanted their life drawings in any event. He has no right to have nudes on his walls, especially those that my parents drew. King Claudius, if you have the IQ to read this book and learn it's about you, return the drawings to my parents you creep.

[DATE] 2017

'Stop press!' It's still not over. King Claudius' solicitors filed a Summons today, with no Affidavit in Support, which is not allowed by the court and so should not have been accepted for filing by the Court Registry. I understand the document has no legal standing, yet King Claudius' lawyer has managed to file it. He must be Superman, Mum!

Moreover, the court is so concerned about King Claudius and his rights that they have also given him a date within the next two weeks to hear it, [DATE] 2017. A new D-Day for me. A date so soon when the courts are chock-a-block and people are waiting for court dates for many months like me. King Claudius gets one within ten days to have a court hearing to incur further costs to me to discuss a decision that he isn't even allowed to discuss because it's not in the right form. He should have sought a Review of the Orders made by the Judicial Registrar, but he did not do that, flagrantly ignoring the advice of registry. He has simply filed a Summons and the court has just followed suit for him despite him going against protocol in a matter that has already been struck out and final orders have already been made where I won and I am to get costs. All costs in my civil matter since December 2015 and all Orders in my favour in default judgement are finally coming my way.

I have just looked up some statistics in the annual reports of the County Court, and it reveals how many matters have been settled by defences being struck out, by cases being struck out, by non-appearances, and all the statistics are trotted out there for me to see year after year. And it's a wonderful thing to see because in my matter, all those reasons were relevant; each reason could have ended the matter, yet none of them have worked and been applied in my matter to bring it to its finality as the court hasn't allowed it. So, under each column where I see those things have happened in my matter, they have not legitimately been dealt with and finalised according to that reason in my matter as the court would not allow it. So now I am left with some type of weird reasoning as to how he can issue a Summons in a matter where it's already finalised and has already been struck out. Its already over.

I fail to even understand how registry staff could accept his document and if it's filed, there should be a corresponding error message under the next item in the Court Connect portal that says, 'Error: unsworn affidavit incorrectly filed in matter – rejected' or the like. Certainly, they reprimanded my lawyers publicly on that portal for things far more minor, such as putting the incorrect court location on a form and publicly noted this on Court Connect. Yet they allowed the defendant to file wholly incompetent and unfilable documents on numerous occasions, but no errors are listed on Court Connect for them. I am completely unable to understand or process this discrimination and unjust course of action. The wrong form has been used as he needed to seek a Review, not a Summons. He can't seek a Review by Summons in a matter that has already ended by the Defence being struck out.

So now I must find money to attend a court hearing in a matter that is already finished as the great King Claudius has summonsed me back to court. I have got to find it for the barrister and for my lawyer to go there and hear some argument about why we are all standing there again, yet King Claudius hasn't turned up to court since [DATE] 2014, more than three years ago. Nor has he filed a document that's properly filed and sworn by him. He remains silent and his documents remain incompetent, yet he gets supported by the court ad nauseam and gets to keep his money in his pocket, whilst I'm ordered to spend more.

I have never read anything written by King Claudius with his signature on it. Ever. Not until the Judicial Registrar gave him a free pass to play the game again on [DATE] 2017 and so then I had to have lawyers there, barristers there, legal arguments on the ready again after two times where he didn't even come to court when he knows that court is on and he is served with all these expensive documents at my expense that my lawyers have prepared because the court keeps ordering them. It's grossly unjust.

Now that the matter has been finalised, I have got to go back there and find all the money for all the prep to hear from the defendant that the default judgement needs to be set aside. And again, I'm in the same position, playing a game that I don't know the rules to. And no one can solve it. No one can legally solve it for me. No one can financially solve it for me. I'm just expected to live another normal day where I worry about clients and then come home and worry about my children's needs and what to cook for dinner – chicken or mince? But I can't. I feel like someone's ripping out my heart and saying, 'Walk without your raw heart pumping, please – oh, but that's OK because there's the footpath, so you should be able to do it.' That's what's going on here. I'm at a loss.

This is nothing but an expensive legal game and now my cousin has sought advice from a top barrister experienced in interlocutory applications. Is it going to be a case of who you know again? Will it matter to the court so much so that common sense will be thrown out the window? Or will a so-called 'good man' actually be a good man and stop this constant and repeated abuse?

I feel like a yo-yo, now looking over at the amazing vase of flowers from my loveable parents with the florist card marked, 'You won.' I'm jerked around from one day to the next. I can't mentally prepare for what's ahead because it's unknown and unprecedented.

And now the flowers from my parents have since browned. Despite watering them, they have gotten tired, their turgid stems now wilted, their petals dropped. I know how they feel. I look like them: a wreck. I look at pictures of me before and after my disclosure on Facebook and I can hardly recognise myself. What they say is all true – the truth should free you, but it doesn't free you; it virtually kills you.

Being stuck like this impacts on my ability to be my old version of normal, to wake up and feel good like I used to, full of positivity. My children see me with my sails at half-mast; my husband misses the old me and so do I. My parents, friends, family and everyone must deal with this new me and it's not fair on me or them. Being strong for my clients keeps me going and being a devoted mum buoys me, but there's no time for self-care and I'm in crisis, which is inevitable because of the time I've spent feeding three all-consuming things: King Claudius, King Claudius' ego and the law (id, ego and superego). I have reverted to Freudian theory on this rare occasion only because it suits me!

[DATE] 2017

The Chamber of Secrecy

My parents and I arrived at Oh Dickensian Chambers to meet my barrister, Captain Plumage, QC, before the hearing. We were five minutes early and were asked to wait while he drank his coffee. Captain Plumage, QC, was busy on other matters until approximately thirty minutes later, when he ushered us in, just thirty-five minutes before the hearing. I noted that he shared his rooms in chambers with the previous barrister I had asked not to be briefed again, Mr Cuckoo. This was an ominous sign.

As we sat down, Captain Plumage, QC, said confidently and rather abruptly, 'He has a complete defence,' and I was a little taken aback. I asked, 'What are you doing for me today then, given your view?' I also reminded him of his previous brief, whereby he drafted Further and Better Particulars and gave his view that the Defence was weak and not particularised and could be fought using the pretext call. Expensive advice that I had assumed was correct. Yet nine months later, the same Captain Plumage, QC, said, 'His sorrysaid during the pretext call is not specific to your allegations,' and reminded me that his sisters' statements do not corroborate my allegations either. Captain Plumage, QC, then said I haven't even got Orders in my favour yet, so it's hopeless and the judge would be wrong at law to not set the Orders aside.

I immediately corrected him and said I certainly did have final Orders in my favour, but idiotically, he still doubted me. I showed him on Court Connect and then I asked whether he had read my affidavit – as it was obvious that he hadn't – and whether he would tender it today, as discussed with my lawyers. Captain Plumage, QC, then said it was worse than the opposing solicitor's affidavit and he would not be tendering it. He called it garbage and was so rude that he immediately apologised without prompting. I respectfully disagreed with him and said, 'At least use it as a basis for your submissions.' My fill-in solicitor, Luke Hummingbird, then arrived and was able to provide Captain Plumage, QC, with a copy of the final Orders made in my favour to satisfy Captain Plumage, QC, that I was right. Captain Plumage, QC, was unmoved in his arrogant stance, preening his plumage in self-adoration.

What I immediately realised was that he didn't know my case, not at all. I didn't know whether this was due to his lack of preparation or his lack of interest, or maybe my solicitors hadn't briefed him properly. There was little to discuss, according to Captain Plumage, QC. He simply informed us that the judge today would be wrong at law to not set aside the Orders and told my solicitor to take us over to the court, dismissing us in more ways than one. I felt like I was being ordered into the docks! This was the start of the most galling legal day and was a precursor for an outcome far worse than anyone could have expected, including my lawyers or jaded me.

He told us about how he didn't need to be robed today and excused himself while he put on his tie. As if I cared about his stupid dress-ups. I am a supporter of doing away with all that ridiculous legal garb. The point is, where was his substantive comment and strategic advice in support of my case? Captain Plumage, QC, was preoccupied with his obvious disappointment that his peacock's plumage would not be on full display today, full of his own self-importance and I was paying for this preoccupation.

The Court That Should Be Moot

H. Honour Judge Lovebird was presiding. This was a judge with a history of giving light sentences to sex offenders, with successful appeals to the Supreme Court adding years onto their sentences. Not the political persuasion in a judge that I was hoping for but rather the male apologist that I had expected. I was stuck with them, but maybe I'd be pleasantly surprised. Unfortunately, I was not pleasantly surprised nor impressed – far from it, in fact. H. Honour decided against me and set aside the Orders for default judgement and costs found in my favour. I was shattered. That was only a small part of the day though, for the process was far, far worse than the outcome.

First, H. Honour had little control over their courtroom and did not seem too fazed by the outrageously unruly conduct of the other party. The defendant himself was not at court – no surprise there – and was represented by Basil Coxcombe, of counsel, and his solicitor, Barnaby Bustard-Braggart, was present as instructor, or so it initially appeared, judging from his instructor's-seat position. As the hearing unfolded, it became clear that this was a set-up though.

The defendant's solicitor did the following in contempt of court. Whilst at the bar table, from the instructor's chair, he made numerous mobile phone calls and even consistently spoke on his mobile phone whilst H. Honour was on the bench. He consistently spoke over Captain Plumage, QC, muttered, interjected and exclaimed loudly in response to each matter put by Captain Plumage, QC; he even spoke indirectly to me, the smart-arse that he is. He behaved far worse than any angry or drug-fuelled client I have ever seen, as if completely unaware of court protocol and respectful and appropriate demeanour. He deserved to be taken to the naughty corner, but H. Honour did nothing. He continued to thrust papers, bang his hand on the bar table, gesture wildly and smirk and lie whilst eating lollies or pills, whilst at the bar table, from a little box.

At one point, he bizarrely demanded to talk to the judge and was refused, H. Honour referring him to his counsel. However, he ignored H. Honour and, shortly after, pulled this stunt again, moving from the instructor's chair and sitting next to his counsel at the other side of the bar table and speaking out of turn, saying, 'The defendant briefed counsel, not my firm.' Was he on a drug-fuelled high, for in what capacity was he then standing there? Had King Claudius sacked him? No, he's still on the court record. So, what's going on? He can't be acting for him if King Claudius briefed counsel directly.

At this point, H. Honour called him into the witness box to hear evidence from him. He stormed over angrily and was sworn in and his counsel led him through the basics – name, address – at which point he then rudely jumped in, stating, 'Any cost orders need to be made against my firm, not the defendant.' Earlier on, my counsel was asked if he had any questions for him, but to my horror, he declined the opportunity. Here was another opportunity to show his numerous and blatant breaches of the Civil Procedure Rules, but Barnaby Bustard-Braggart left the witness box immediately even before being dismissed, which is rude and unprecedented for a lawyer and, with that, then stood up and immaturely stormed back to the bar table. H. Honour allowed this constant display of hostility and rebellion, in total contempt of the court, yet they did not declare it nor put a stop to it. The tip staff also did nothing, much to my surprise. This is meant to be a superior court, yet I have to say that the Magistrates'

Court in Conservative Town commands far more order and
respect even on its hairiest days like Family Violence and
Children's Court duty list days.

The decision of H. Honour to ignore his outrageous
manner, not even warning him of his contemptuous
behaviour, was so alarming and unjust to me. They afforded
me no respect and allowed the court to be brought down to
the lowest common denominator: Barnaby Bustard-Braggart.
More importantly still, H. Honour allowed a conflict of interest
to arise when King Claudius' solicitor told the court that he
had not briefed the barrister representing King Claudius.
Surprisingly, H. Honour did not then ask the obvious question
as to whether Barnaby Bustard-Braggart still acted for King
Claudius or whether they were simply there to muddy the
waters and attempt to protect themselves from being sued by
their client. H. Honour should have asked whether Barnaby
Bustard-Braggart planned on seeking leave to cease to act and
withdraw from the matter in light of his comments. This is
because one must seek leave to cease acting in the County
Court. In absence of these questions being asked of Barnaby
Bustard-Braggart by H. Honour, even more galling was
Captain Plumage, QC, not asking them. He didn't question
him at all.

Even Captain Plumage, QC, was so obviously shaken by
the solicitor's conduct that he told him to 'Shut up!' not once
but twice and loudly, in a short-tempered fashion. I thought
poorly of him for doing so as unfortunately, he had stooped to
Barnaby Bustard-Braggart's gutter level. Nearly forty years of
advocacy should better equip him with clever and legally
condemning responses to put an imp like Barnaby Bustard-
Braggart back in his place, yet he seemed completely
unprepared. I am no barrister or silk, but as a solicitor

advocate, I would have at least asked H. Honour to consider removing Barnaby Bustard-Braggart from the courtroom if he couldn't conduct himself in a professional manner. Sadly, everyone opted to indulge Barnaby Bustard-Braggart instead of making him answerable. I was livid and rightly so but sat like a good girl with my mouth shut, albeit with a look of serious concern.

The obvious problem was that the court cannot allow a party to be prejudiced because of the misconduct of their solicitor. For that reason, the court separated the behaviour of the defendant from that of his solicitor and the solicitor swore to the same. The solicitor claimed that we had not made discovery, had not served them with the psychologist's reports, had not cooperated with him nor met with our obligations under the Civil Procedure Act, had not arranged mediation; all false and the converse was, in fact, true. My solicitor had filed affidavits of service at every turn and we had complied with every single Order, but this solicitor simply lied, denied and refuted, claiming that he had not received anything. With an absence of prompt protestations from my grey peahen counsel, clearly missing his male plumage and garb, H. Honour gave Barnaby Bustard-Braggart the benefit of the doubt, putting into question an expensive year of legal servitude on my part and ordered everything be done by me again. I was literally ordered to redo a year of legal process and pay another year of lawyer's fees just to get to the same legal stage again – how to lose $55,000 in some careless legal minutes.

Obviously, this was planned by King Claudius' solicitors to create a legal fiction whereby the defendant is prejudiced by the solicitor's behaviour so we all must start over. The aim to delay and bleed me dry was simple to achieve and he did it. It was planned and premeditated, and the court will be blissfully unaware of whether the defendant – or his solicitor, personally – pays the costs ordered to me. It was a carefully contrived denial and delay. The court played dumb or fell for it but, in any event, punished me for it. So desperate was the court not to prejudice King Claudius that they deliberately and wilfully – yet ever so politely – caused significant and irrefutable prejudice to me.

King Claudius' lawyer handed up written submissions; my QC handed up nothing. He would not tender my affidavit; it's as if he wanted me to lose. I was beyond angry, but I was getting close to the earth's core when Captain Plumage, QC, used Barnaby Bustard-Braggart's affidavit to address the court, tactically a very weak and lazy thing to do. An approach taken by someone unprepared or bribed. Non-lawyer clients would not be likely to know this, but of course I knew, as would any lawyer sitting in the client seat. I was so frustrated. It felt like a deliberate fettering of my position at a very high price. I was paying this QC to show his plumage like a peacock, but he appeared as the dull peahen all right, brown and blending into the background. Maybe his robes and wigs are magic and without them, he's rendered useless. Mem Fox, I needed to borrow 'the magic hat'[63] to turn this coy counsel into a tiger.

H. Honour then set aside the orders, my precious, victorious orders, and made new sickening orders, setting a new timetable and creating costly court events for the parties to conduct discovery before H. Honour –'on video', as Judge warned us. As a result of my QC's impolite outburst, H. Honour equalised the parties' behaviour as if we were equally responsible for the protracted nature of the proceedings and the resulting stalemate. I was livid. To add insult to injury, the defendant's barrister then started saying that I, the plaintiff, had wasted time causing these delays instead of getting on with the steps in readiness for trial. In fact, the converse is true. The defendant had breached fourteen orders in a row. Fourteen! I had done everything, complying with all orders to get to trial other than compulsory mediation, which couldn't be done because the defendant wouldn't correspond with my lawyers about dates, to cause delay. I cannot mediate with myself. Captain Plumage, QC, never mentioned the fourteen breaches and justified his clear intention not to raise them by saying, 'Compared to other cases I've done, that's not many breaches, Cleopatra.'

The worst part is that the trial date of [DATE] 2017, set to run for seven days, was vacated by the court the moment that default judgement was made in my favour, on [DATE] 2017. So now the next available trial date is on [DATE] 2018, next year, nine months away. That's certainly prejudicing me, especially in terms of my mental health. It is also financially punishing on me, for I have been ordered to repeat the steps I've already completed in a more expensive way, serving documents by express post now, to ensure the ability to prove service through tracking numbers. Apparently, affidavits of service are not enough in this matter, yet that suffices in all other matters. That's why we have affidavits of service; to satisfy the court as our duty as lawyers is higher to the court than we have to our clients. In this way, the court can be confident of our professional ethical obligations. I don't understand why the court doesn't hold the trial date for the successful applicant until after the appeal period has passed, for this completely avoidable and victim-damaging delay must happen often.

Maybe the court should consider the likelihood of me wanting the trial to go ahead – I'm desperate for it, in fact – versus the wish of the defendant to prolong my agony in any way possible and derail my Gospa Velika trial. It's patently obvious. Perhaps the court should give credit to the party who does everything by the book and not throw the book at them instead by making insulting and prejudicial Orders. Why would a plaintiff cause delay or not comply with Orders? It makes no sense as they are bringing the action at great emotional and financial expense.

H. Honour acknowledged prejudice to me but said it is ameliorated by the trial date being reset, in the shadows of them having just said that sexual assault trials should be expedited wherever possible. What a joke! H. Honour then asked in open court whether that aim applied in this civil jurisdiction as they knew it applied in a criminal case. How insulting to all women to say one thing and do another, like a smiling assassin. My life is on hold, left hanging in anxiety, waiting for the trial. Obviously, causing any delay would be the last thing that I'd want to do. I'm bringing this action, after all. Why would I want a delay? Any and every psychologist could easily explain to the court why I wouldn't want to cause delay of any kind. The defendant has caused delay at every turn because that's the only way he can win. He's hoping that I'll get so frustrated that I'll give up. He has lost once I go in the witness box and he knows that. The only way they can win is if I drop it. Fat chance, I told myself with a confidence that would soon wax and wane because after two years in the County Court I had got nowhere.

H. Honour should also know that causing delay is the number-one aim of the defendant and their Orders enabled him to achieve it. The aim is to frustrate me so much that I give up as they are doing anything to avoid having King Claudius in the witness box to answer questions. To H. Honour, it's merely a timetable change. To me, it's everything.

Normal life is on hold again and that's the killer to all plaintiffs, not just me. If H. Honour doesn't know how many plaintiffs commit suicide during the legal process, how many develop a drug addiction, how many experience a worsening of their psychiatric conditions, I wonder what H. Honour takes away holistically after each working day. What does H. Honour honestly think they are creating up there on high? A fair chance for the defendant who deserves another chance and another chance ad infinitum. That's not a fair chance. That's unfair chances and illegal money making, in my book.

At one point, when Barnaby Bustard-Braggart was speaking rudely to Captain Plumage, QC, whilst waiting for H. Honour to come onto the bench, he said something like 'for you and for our audience here', referring to my parents and me as we were the only other people in the courtroom at that time. I then retorted, 'Barnaby, don't you ever indirectly speak to me again. You are outrageous, I have to say.' He did not respond, at least not verbally.

At the end of the matter, the defendant's barrister and Barnaby Bustard-Braggart left the courtroom and I remained with my parents, having a sad debrief for a while. I was devastated and utterly spent. The quiet and dull Captain Plumage, QC, had picked up his unopened bag of tricks, clearly saved for another more deserving matter on another day, and we left the courtroom after him. He was holding the door open for us, a common politeness missing from him until then, but standing ahead, I could see Barnaby Bustard-Braggart in the distance, at the T-intersection ahead near the lifts. We needed to walk past him to get to the lifts and he could see us coming. Yet he deliberately stood there in the middle of the corridor, creating a bottleneck, with an idiotic smirk on his face like a circus clown, staring at us as we approached. He then said something to Captain Plumage, QC, a passing comment I didn't quite hear, to which I just heard Captain Plumage, QC, politely reply, 'Sir.' I did not look at Barnaby Bustard-Braggart as we passed him. He was obviously there to gloat that he had won. It was obviously so very personal to him, this case, being King Claudius' long-time friend. Who else would risk the reputation of their own law firm, going on affidavit to swear to his office not receiving anything substantive from my lawyers for more than six months? Like my cousin, he has no bottom line. As they say, birds of a feather flock together, Liar birds and that is no spelling error.

In the safety of the lift, I realised I had missed a golden opportunity to say, 'Goodonya, mate!' to Barnaby not for winning but for being a pig! You see, in the late '80s my father found a newspaper article entitled 'Goodonya!' about a winning tennis player. I cut it out at the time and stuck it on our fridge and it became a private family joke. Dad explained that there's an understanding amongst Croatians that the common Aussie saying 'Goodonya' translates into 'pig'. Esprit d'escalier!

Peevish is true. Pathetic is also true. The court was correct that time. Immature, childish, unprofessional, contemptuous is Barnaby Bustard-Braggart – obviously just what the Court likes and condones. The Legal Services Board need to take away his practising certificate. An honest and respectable female is an inconvenience to the legal script, to the legal narrative that is the law. I am an inconvenience to this court, but I won't say to this honourable court, for it would be a misuse of the word honourable in this case.

This is what many plaintiffs bringing an action of sexual assault think about the court and its players. It's certainly what my clients think. Most judges just don't get it, or worse still, they do get it, but they condone it, carefully planning over their eggs benedict and freshly squeezed orange juice how many lives they'll ruin today, under the guise of 'civil' orders, orders reinforcing the misuse of power, re-traumatising victims, most uncivil for a civilised First World society – civil orders most uncivil.

Another Wasted Day in Court

[DATE] 2017

On this day, we were back in court yet again, seeking clarification on the costs order. Sadly, I needed no clarification, but my lawyers did as they seemed to have difficulty believing how poorly the barrister they briefed, Captain Plumage, QC, executed his brief.

As per usual, I entered the court building feeling no respect for it, pushing through the door like someone who clearly has issues, glancing up at Lady Justice with a steely eye. I unloaded my bag, phone and folder into the tub without thinking and walked through security when I heard,

'Excuse me, madam, you have a weapon in your bag.'

'No, I don't,' I said, not in the mood for this rigmarole. 'I've gone through court security thousands of times and I have no weapons, not even a nail file', I said.

'Sorry, madam, step this way, please.'

'I'm a lawyer. I know the drill and I don't have any weapons.' I said with an air of superiority, trying to pull rank. What on earth was I saying – why was I was expecting that being a lawyer would get me somewhere?

'We have found this,' he said, holding a corkscrew I immediately recognised as mine, a gift from my children's school commemorating their 150-year anniversary.

'Oh my god, I'm so sorry. Yes, that's mine!' I said, looking embarrassingly at the offending object.

As I shuffled off, feeling utterly stupid, my next thrill was to see my name in lights on the big board again: Jones v Pavlovic, all my sadness condensed into two surnames; married and maiden. Courtroom 2.5 again. Off I go, my parents by my side. We went up the escalators, past all the artwork and impressive glass panelling, but the visual splendour was shattered as we passed a group of smokers in the courtyard during a break, reminding me of the imperfection of the human condition, addiction to substances bringing us closer to death. My almond croissant I'd eaten earlier in the café next door was no different; sugar I didn't need.

My parents and I camped in the interview room next to the courtroom while we waited for my lawyer to arrive. What would happen in these learned walls today? I was scared to think. Not much, I knew that much.

As expected, H. Honour Judge Lovebird clarified that they had only granted me costs for one day, being [DATE] 2017. What an insult the Order was though. Determined to not cause prejudice to King Claudius, by the behaviour of his lawyer, H. Honour prejudiced me by wasting all the money I'd spent to date to get the matter thus far. I was being made to do it all over again at double the cost. How can the Court possibly sanction this?

Even more annoying, on this day Barnaby Bustard-Braggart turned up again, clearly still acting for King Claudius. So, the whole charade of Barnaby Bustard-Braggart telling the Court that King Claudius had briefed the barrister directly, not he or his firm, was clearly just that; a charade to cause delay. They achieved it without judicial question or otherwise.

I told my lawyers to appeal the decision of [DATE] 2017 forthwith and to obtain the transcript of that day and today. The transcripts would reveal everything and the basis for which I am appealing; H. Honour erring on a number of fronts and incompetent counsel who went against my instructions, did not make an appropriate argument for costs thrown away and did not tender my affidavit.

H. Honour had told my lawyer Jamie Heron a few times that certain matters should have been raised on DATE by our Queens Counsel Captain Plumage, namely costs thrown away and that clarification should have been sought about the Orders by counsel on the day. Exactly what my instructions were to Captain Plumage and my lawyers before, during and after the hearing, and as per my affidavit and written instructions; all of which were ignored. H. Honour reserved costs of [DATE] 2017 so it remains an argument for another day.

Unrepresented Once Again

[DATE] 2017

On this day, I asked my lawyers to cease acting. There were several reasons for this – but most importantly the fact that they lost my case after I had already won by the silk they briefed and his failure and their failure to follow my crystal-clear and repeated instructions. This is when the legal game playing heated up to boiling point and I could see things clearly for the first time now that I was at the helm without the legal subterfuge and sycophants.

However, the transition from legally represented to self-represented was far from smooth. I couldn't file documents on the portal or access Court Connect as everything had to now go through the self-represented litigant coordinator. Rather than assisting me, it became another legal tripwire preventing me from obtaining a transcript in time. I had to wait for my former lawyers to formally withdraw off the court record too, which took weeks. Things became more protracted before there was any sign of improvement.

'I'd like to file these subpoenas, please.'

'What's the matter name?'

'Jones and Pavlovic and I'm the plaintiff.'

'Yes,' she said looking, at my documents. 'You'll have to speak with Amanda, who is currently at lunch, but she's due to return shortly.'

'No problem,' I said as I went to the back of the queue again, sitting on a bench seat.

I waited for more than thirty minutes before I was finally attended to.

'Sorry, my meeting ran overtime. How can I help you?' said a pleasant voice.

'No worries. I'd like to file these subpoenas, please,' I said hopefully. 'I can make the payment for them today. There are six in total.'

'Sorry, but I can't accept these subpoenas, sorry. You need special leave of the court to file them.'

'But the self-represented litigant coordinator told me that I could file them over the counter today as I am unable to file them on the portal now that I'm a self-represented litigant,' I explained. 'Can I leave them on file then, in case H. Honour approves them in chambers?' I asked wearily.

'No, you'd best take them with you. You need to give your reasons in writing to H. Honour for consideration.'

'Sorry, I didn't know. Thanks anyway,' I said, deflated. I

wanted my cousins to have to lie in court to save their brother. I wanted to transfer the pressure onto them and their 'fake' happy family for a change, but the Judge didn't allow it.

County Court Registry never actually assisted me either, not even once. They treated me with contempt, yet they couldn't do enough for Barnaby Bustard-Braggart. They accepted his documents without an affidavit in support. They bent the rules for him at every turn, even commented on by H. Honour. I wondered how he can possibly have friends in high places when he's a gutter dweller. The Registry and the Bench worked in conjunction to get rid of me, regardless.

My first port of call was to obtain a transcript for the fateful hearing where the judgement in my favour, including a full costs order, was set aside. I was required to pay $1,300 for this transcript, yet another unrecoverable legal cost that the law presumes is a fair and just pleasure for me. Yes, with four children, I have nothing better to spend my money on, thank you. Unfortunately, I needed to have the transcript to help me decide whether to appeal the decision to the Supreme Court as one can only do this when the judge has erred at law. However, despite having a strong case, I decided against it as I feared it would amount to another costly exercise in me being right but getting no traction from the law other than further legal bills. To appeal, I'd be looking at a $4,700 filing fee, just to have the application considered. Then there would be extensive legal advice and document preparation, including court books, required at great further expense.

I decided against it in preference for focussing on the matter itself and the upcoming trial. Moreover, the Court of Appeal has been widely criticised in recent times, particularly by the High Court, for giving manifestly unjust sentences for heinous crimes because of a slavish adherence to current sentencing practises, above all other principles of sentencing. I wanted to avoid adding myself to those statistics thank you very much. Anyway, why would the law work for me all of a sudden when it never has up until now? So, I dropped the idea of appealing – but certainly not because there weren't grounds. I had already spent over $50,000 in the last twelve months on legal fees alone. I was sick of working hard for this draining case instead of for my family.

Amongst other things, I later discovered that my previous lawyers had not filed all my documents in readiness for trial. Similarly, King Claudius' lawyer claimed that he hadn't been served with my documents despite there being affidavits of service on file. Moreover, this lawyer would not correspond with me in any way and subsequently claimed that he had not received any emails or mailed correspondence from me or my previous lawyers, the same crap he had made up on [DATE] 2017 that had contributed to the matter going awry. To combat this, I went into overdrive and served him personally at his office and began sending choruses of emails to him and the court and the judge's associates. I was utterly hamstrung, and I needed the court to know and to do something about it.

The response of King Claudius' lawyer was to do more of the same as clearly, this had been working for him to date until he realised that he was about to miss a deadline to request me to attend upon a psychologist of the defendant's choice. Then he sent a late request, which breached all the Orders for adherence to a strict timetable. He was thumbing his nose at the law and at me, but the law finally did something to stop it. Hip, hip, hoo-bloody-ray!

Through numerous hearings in close succession before H. Honour Judge Plover, the costly tomfoolery of King Claudius' lawyer was brought into light. Judge Plover ordered that all correspondence between us be provided to them by his lawyer and I separately, for they were interested to see what game playing had been going on for the past year. I was immensely relieved, for it stopped the rot and caused a tremendous backfire on King Claudius' lawyer that he could never have predicted and was furious about, for all inter partes correspondence suddenly became subject to the scrutiny of the court. For example, King Claudius' lawyer had claimed that my symptoms of PTSD had simply been copied and pasted by me from Wikipedia. He was personally venomous and so unprofessional that he caused the ire of the court and me on numerous occasions. Three different judges made costs orders in my favour against this lawyer personally for tens of thousands of dollars, which is highly unusual, not costs orders against the defendant, which normally happens. But there was nothing normal about my matter though, especially the way his lawyer conducted the matter and conducted himself throughout. He acted as if he had never-ending legal immunity!

I cannot faithfully trot out all the ridiculous legal shenanigans brought to me by the court and Court Jester Solicitors; it really is a case of one having to go through it themselves to truly understand the blatant, deliberate and callous legal abuse. But what took place was so traumatising and all-consuming. You go to bed with it, wake up with it, dream about it and mull over it in the day. It becomes your life at the expense of everything else. I imagine it's like what it must be for a heroin addict to get their next hit and the vicious cycle of needing to feel OK. I never felt settled or at ease and was preoccupied with the need to prove the crime had been done for almost five years. Yet fighting in court for justice, using the truth and the law and being thorough and respectful got me absolutely nowhere. I didn't have the ingredients to win. I still wonder what they are and whether they even exist.

My First Court Day as a Self-Represented Litigant

The cases before mine were made more interesting than they would have otherwise been because they involved self-represented litigants; people who had run out of money or never had any to pay lawyers in the first place. I listened to H. Honour explaining things, clarifying procedural matters and re-adjusting expectations. In the matter immediately before mine, the judge explained to a lady from a non-English speaking background, 'If you've come here to engage in a crusade, I need to warn you that this is not the right forum' and 'Your application is not in the right form.'

I thought about those words 'engage in a crusade' and decided that every case could look like a crusade if it was not decipherable to those more learned, but the substantive merit in the case doesn't change, only the fancy lawyer's words around it. She was missing the lawyer's language to galvanise her experience, missing the formula. Without it, her case was hopeless, the judge was telling her that, but the lady wasn't comprehending, so he tried a new line of attack:

'You can't just come along here and incur costs to the other party like you're doing! Ms Plumridge-Gull here – and I thank you for your patience, counsel – has come along today for nothing as the matter cannot proceed as it's not in the correct form! The Department may seek costs against you, do you understand?'

'Yes, but they shouldn't have done this to me, Your Worship, because Mr Featherstone from the Department told me . . .,' she said, repeating her previous commentary and getting the judicial officer's title wrong.

H. Honour was back to square one, but I wondered why it was that the judge can clearly see a valid costs argument here, where it's an individual versus the government, but when it's me versus a renegade practitioner, the lines become blurred, as if H. Honour is sitting up there with a giant eraser, deliberately smudging everything. If anything, the bench should become more scathing of a practitioner who opts to behave in contempt than a disenfranchised woman who is trying her best to fit into the law, with limited English and a bag full of wrongs.

I filed the following submissions in advance of the hearing:

IN THE COUNTY COURT
OF VICTORIA
AT CONSERVATIVE TOWN

COMMON LAW DIVISION
GENERAL LIST
BETWEEN

CLEOPATRA JONES   **Plaintiff**

And
KING CLAUDIUS   **Defendant**

**PLAINTIFF'S SUBMISSIONS
FOR DIRECTIONS HEARING DATE**

Date of Document: BEYOND BELIEF
Filed on behalf of: The Plaintiff
Telephone: 03 44556677
Prepared by: Cleopatra Jones
Address: 101 Help Street, Conservative Town Vic 3000

Email: Cleopatra@Joneslawyers.com.au

I am the plaintiff in the above matter.

I am now a self-represented litigant.

My Submissions contained herein are to be read in conjunction with the following documents:

Reasons for Seeking Leave to Issue Subpoenas[DATE] 2017; and

Affidavit of Serviceof Cleopatra Jones, affirmed, [DATE] 2017, contemporaneously sent for filing via email on [DATE] to the Self-Represented Litigant Coordinator at the following email address: slr@countycourt.vic.gov.au.

I respectfully raise the following housekeeping matters that I say need the Court's urgent attention and clarification:

Unpaid Costs Orders in the Plaintiff's Favour

Prejudice to the Plaintiff

Mediation/Psychologist Dr Insightful

Affidavits of Service

Communications between the Parties

Vacate the Directions Hearing Ordered for [DATE] before H. Honour Judge Lovebird

Transcript of Hearing - 2017 Received [DATE] after Submissions were submitted to self-rep coordinator for filing

Service of Documents

The Trial Set Down for [DATE] to [DATE] be extended as

necessary On [DATE], H. Honour Judge Lovebird said (and I quote) (Transcript — pg. 69, line 4),

This is the sort of case where a steady hand needs to be kept on the wheel.

All right, so mediation is to take place on or before [DATE]. Mediator is to be appointed jointly by the parties in default of agreement as to the identity of the mediator. Reserve liberty to apply at short notice for appointment of a mediator – or, I should say, on the question of appointment of a mediator.

Since [DATE], now some three months later, there has been no real progress in the matter, no acknowledgement of interlocutory steps done by me or my former lawyers; in fact, at a mention on [DATE] the defendant blatantly denied having been served documents as per [DATE] Orders despite the newly Ordered method of service by registered post.

On [DATE], H. Honour Judge Lovebird goes further about Barnaby Bustard-Braggart and his conduct and says:

SEE ANNEXED PAGE RE. TRANSCRIPT

In relation to Paragraphs 4a to 4i inclusive, I respectfully say as follows:

Unpaid Costs Orders in the Plaintiff's Favour

Contemporaneously with an Order for default judgement against the defendant, Judicial Registrar Partridge-Saxon made Orders for Costs in favour of the Plaintiff on [DATE] 2017 that currently remain wholly unpaid by Court Jester Lawyers (Barnaby Bustard-Braggart), the Defendant's Solicitors.

On [DATE] 2017, Barnaby Bustard-Braggart, the principal

of Court Jester Lawyers, provided sworn evidence from the witness box and said under oath that any Orders for costs need to be made against Court Jester Lawyers and not the defendant. This is because the defendant was not to be prejudiced by the actions – or lack thereof – of Barnaby Bustard-Braggart, as a result of the defendant's failure to comply with the Orders of [DATE] 2016 and [DATE] 2017, including breaches of fourteen (14) Orders made by this Honourable Court as listed in the table below:

[DATE] 2016	Judicial Registrar Partridge-Saxon	Order	Parties must cooperate to ensure compliance with their obligations under the Civil Procedure Act 2010, including the obligation to minimise delay.
[DATE] 2016	Judicial Registrar Partridge-Saxon	Order 4	The parties shall cooperate in completing the interlocutory processes so action is brought to trial as quickly as possible.
		Order 6	Unless the Defendant makes the application contemplated by paragraph 5 by 4:00 p.m. on [DATE] 2017, the defendant is to file and serve any Further and Better Particulars of the Defence.
		Order 7	By 4:00 p.m. on [DATE] 2017, the parties must deliver any request for FBPs of a pleading. Any request must be answered within 28 days.
		Order 8	By 4:00 p.m. on [DATE] 2017, each party must make Discovery.
		Order 9	All other interlocutory processes will be conducted in accordance with the Rules of the Court
		Order 11	By [DATE] 2017, the parties must have completed mediation of the dispute.

[DATE] 2017	Judge Cockatoo	Order 1	By 4:00 p.m. on [DATE] 2017, the Defendant is to file and serve Further and Better Particulars of the Defence to Plaintiff's Amended Statement of Claim in accordance with the Plaintiff's Request served on [DATE] 2017.
		Order 2	By 4:00 p.m. on [DATE] 2017, the Defendant is to file and serve an Affidavit of Documents.
[DATE] 2017	Judicial Registrar Partridge-Saxon	Order 2	Any application by the Defendant to oppose the Plaintiff's application is to be supported by an affidavit, particularising as to why the Orders of [DATE] 2016 and [DATE] 2017, have not been complied with.
[DATE] 2017	Judicial Registrar Partridge-Saxon	Order 1	Unless the Defendant files and serves Further and Better Particulars of the Defence to the Plaintiff's Amended Statement of Claim and files and serves an Affidavit of Documents by [DATE] 2017, the Defendant's Defence will be struck out.
		Order 2	The Defendant is to pay the Plaintiff's costs of the Directions Hearing on [DATE] 2017 and [DATE] 2017. The issue as to whether the Defendant or the Defendant's Solicitor pays these costs is reserved.
[DATE] 2017	Judge Lovebird	Order 10	The Defendant's Solicitors pay the Plaintiff's costs of today thrown away.
		Order 12	The Plaintiff's Solicitors' fees to be paid by the Defendant's Solicitors on an indemnity basis and, in default of agreement, to be determined by the Costs Court.
		Order 11	Certify Senior Counsel's fee fixed at $3,000 for the day.

On [DATE] 2017, H. Honour Judge Lovebird clarified to the parties that the outstanding costs orders in favour of the Plaintiff made by Judicial Registrar Partridge-Saxon on [DATE] 2017 and H. Honour on [DATE] 2017 need to be paid by Barnaby Bustard-Braggart 'forthwith'.

In a letter from Barnaby Bustard-Braggart to the Plaintiff dated [DATE] 2017, Barnaby Bustard-Braggart claims that as per Rule 63A.20.1, 'costs may not be taxed until completion of the proceeding unless the Court orders otherwise'. There is no such Rule 63A.20.1.

If my learned friend means Rule 63A.21.1, then this Rule only applies to costs in proceedings before a Registrar or a

Costs Court. So arguably, this applies to JR Partridge-Saxon's Orders, but there is still the Indemnity Costs Order in the Plaintiff's favour for the hearing of [DATE] 2017, to which that Rule does not apply as it was a proceeding before a Judge.

To date, I have not received any payment from Barnaby Bustard-Braggart despite more than four months having passed since the first Orders were made. I received a payment from Barnaby Bustard-Braggart of $3,000 by cheque dated [DATE] 2017 but received on [DATE] 2017 by express post. The cheque was made out to Jones Lawyers instead of to me personally.

Under r 63 A.13 and O

I respectfully ask this Honourable Court to make an Order that Barnaby Bustard-Braggart has a further seven days to pay these outstanding Costs Orders directly to me, by 5:00 p.m. on [DATE] 2017, after which time retrospective penalty interest will accrue(Penalty Interest as per Section 29 (1)(C)(i) of the Civil Procedure Act) from the date the respective Orders were made, being from [DATE] 2017 and [DATE] 2017, respectively.

Alternatively, I ask that if the Defendant Solicitor fails to make timely and full payment of the Costs Orders as above, I seek liberty to apply at short notice to have the Defendant's defence struck out under r 63A.03 (2) of the Rules.

The sum of the outstanding Costs Orders in favour of the plaintiff is as follows:

[DATE] 2017	Judicial Registrar Partridge-Saxon	Order 2	The Defendant is to pay the Plaintiff's costs of the Directions Hearing on [DATE] 2017 and [DATE] 2017. The issue as to whether the Defendant or the Defendant's Solicitor pays these costs is reserved.	A Bill of Costs was submitted to the Costs Court once the matter was finalised on [DATE] 2017. The Costs Court responded that the matter is now not finalised, so reserves its decision.	~~$ 9,000~~ $9,004.50
[DATE] 2017	Judge Lovebird	Order 10	The Defendant's Solicitors pay the Plaintiff's costs of today thrown away.	Unpaid. I am unsure whether my former lawyers submitted a Bill of Costs to the defendant's solicitors	~~$ 5,000~~ $5,985.50
		Order 12	The Plaintiff's Solicitors' fees are to be paid by the Defendant's Solicitors on an indemnity basis and, in default of agreement, to be determined by the Costs Court.	Order 12 indemnity costs are in relation to plaintiff's costs in Order 10 only	N/A
		Order 11	Certify Senior Counsel's fee fixed at $3,000 for the day.	Unpaid	$ 3,000
				TOTAL	~~$17,000~~ $17,990

Prejudice to the Plaintiff

On [DATE] 2017, the defendant claimed that I would suffer no prejudice by his late filing of his documents; however, I say this is completely false and I have been absolutely prejudiced by H. Honour Judge Lovebird's decision to set aside default judgement in my favour, reinstate his defence and not give costs thrown away from more than one day after a year of one-sided legal servitude by me, the Plaintiff.

I say that the following factors, overlooked by H. Honour Judge Lovebird, are now relevant and a direct result of the Defendant's behaviour and attitude to these proceedings, causing me serious prejudice as follows:

The Defendant's Uncooperative Approach
The matter has dragged on well beyond the timeline consented to and seen as appropriate in the Consent Orders of [DATE] 2016. We have not even had mediation or the promise of same because of the Defendant's belligerence and mediation was previously Ordered to have taken place before [DATE] 2017. This breaches both the Orders and the Civil Procedure Rules and the Overarching Obligations of the Defendant and his lawyer.

Time
The trial dates allocated for one week's trial commencing on [DATE] 2017 have now been vacated by the Court. But for the Defendant's approach, we were ready to proceed. The trajectory of this matter is completely unpredictable and this affects both my mental and physical health as I can't plan or allocate my energies. I am a busy working mum, with four children aged between 7 and 16 years. The conduct of the

Defendant and the mismanagement of the matter by the Court staff have been all-consuming and had a detrimental effect on me. The effect of protracted proceedings on plaintiffs is no secret and if sexual assault is a matter that should be expedited wherever possible, this aim has certainly not been achieved in this matter.

Cost

My ability to afford to go to mediation and to trial has been compromised by the protracted nature of these proceedings, derailed by the Defendant at every opportunity, creating a situation where more and more costs are generated for hearings like the defendant's Summons on [DATE] 2017 and ex parte hearings caused by non-appearance by the Defendant and legal fanfaronade brought by the Defendant. I believe that this is a deliberate tactic used by the Defendant to bleed me dry.

Breaches of Orders

The Defendant claims that I do not suffer any prejudice arising from his documents being filed approximately twenty (20) minutes late. I assert that I have suffered considerable prejudice because what he filed twenty (20) minutes late was legally invalid in any event, such as unsworn affidavits and applications miraculously accepted for filing without affidavits in support without reprimand. The only legally valid documents were filed on [DATE] 2017 instead of [DATE] by 4:00 p.m., in breach of the Orders. The Defendant himself admits this, evidenced by his request for the time to file to be extended to [DATE] 2017 nunc pro tunc as only then were the correct documents filed.

The Defendant successfully asked that the date for filing his documents be extended from [DATE] 2015 to [DATE] 2017 pursuant to r 3.02 of the Rules, six (6) days after the self-executing Order. This was a self-serving request as it conveniently extends the deadline imposed by the Court to a time convenient to the Defendant, notwithstanding the many other opportunities provided previously, all of which were ignored, that he had to file documents within time and participate in these proceedings. For the Defendant's Solicitors to say that he never received Orders or documents from my Solicitors is in my respectful submission both untruthful and, frankly, unbelievable, yet this was the highly questionable basis on which the matter was overturned.

In light of this, I now ask this Honourable Court to extend the time for me to file my Particulars of Special Damages and documents in support to a date subject to the Court's filing of self-represented litigant documents, pursuant to r 3.02 of the Rules, due to the failure of my previous lawyers to file this document as per my instructions and as Ordered, notwithstanding the fact that my former lawyers served it in time on Barnaby Bustard-Braggart on [DATE] 2017.

Location

Although I agree to the necessity of the trial being held in Big Smoke, I have been put to the expense of attending in Court in Big Smoke for two years on interlocutory matters. The Defendant himself has never attended Court in this matter. I ask that all other interlocutory steps take place in Conservative Town as that is the correct location (R 28.01 and 28.02) and it otherwise prejudices me in terms of time and money.

Mediation

Regulations 50.07 (1), (9), and (10) of the County Court Civil

Procedure Rules (2008) state the following:

50.07 Reference to Mediator

(1) The power and discretion of the Court as to mediation under section 47A of the Act shall be exercised subject to and in accordance with this Rule.

(9) The Court may determine the remuneration of the mediator and by what party or parties and in what proportion the remuneration is to be paid, either in the first instance or finally.

(10) The Court may order any party to give security for the remuneration of the mediator.

My ability to participate in mediation is prejudiced by Barnaby Bustard-Braggart's non-payment of these unpaid Costs Orders. In the event that Barnaby Bustard-Braggart does not make full payment by close of business [DATE] 2017, I ask that Barnaby Bustard-Braggart be Ordered to pay for the Plaintiff's costs of mediation, including my half share of the mediator's costs, my counsel's fees and my travel costs to Big Smoke to attend mediation.

I also respectfully ask this Honourable Court to appoint a mediator and set a date and location for mediation as Barnaby Bustard-Braggart have failed to communicate with me about an appropriate mediator, a date suitable to the parties and the costs of same. I cannot unilaterally organise mediation and H. Honour Judge Lovebird provided for such a scenario on [DATE] 2017, when H. Honour Ordered as follows:

Order 9 — On or before [DATE] 2017, the parties attend mediation. The mediator is to be appointed jointly by the parties. If the parties are unable to do so, liberty to apply before H. Honour Judge Lovebird at short notice on the question of the appointment of a mediator.

However, in the circumstances, I ask that Your Honour deal with this matter today to avoid another costly Court event as I anticipate further silence from the Defendant's Solicitors in an attempt to further delay mediation.

My former Solicitors Hawkeye tried to arrange mediation with Barnaby Bustard-Braggart to no avail over the course of one year, where I spent $56,000 on legal costs yet got no further in this matter than prior to them acting because of the Defendant. Mediation was meant to happen by [DATE] 2017 as ordered, but Defendant wouldn't agree with our available dates with the aim to delay again.

Once I was formally self-representing, from [DATE] 2017, I wrote to the Defendant's Solicitors re. mediation as follows:
-

on [DATE], [DATE], [DATE], [DATE] and [DATE] 2017; and
- yesterday, [DATE] 2017

but Barnaby Bustard-Braggart's emails of [DATE] don't take us any further in finalising mediation.

It would be unfair, futile and burdensome to ask the parties to arrange mediation in light of the above and I ask that it be ordered today.

I had sent Barnaby Bustard-Braggart a summary of available mediators on [DATE] 2017 as I hadn't heard from him about it. I received no response.

*HAND UP THE SUMMARY TO H. HONOUR

DEFENDANT'S REQUEST FOR PSYCHOLOGIST REPORT

I will not agree to any further adjournment of mediation, notwithstanding that the Defendant has advised yesterday, [DATE] 2017, that they want me to see a psychiatrist of their choice. Whilst I'm agreeable to attend, I do take issue with the timing of both their request and the appointment, tentatively booked a few days before Christmas on [DATE] 2017 and the second last day of the business year.

I called Dr Insightful's rooms and was told at 9:30 a.m. today the following alternative times:

2 January 2018 at 12:00 p.m.

4 January 2018 at 10:00 a.m.

10 January 2018 at 10:00 a.m.

11 January 2018 at 10:00 a.m.

I am happy to attend in the new year on any of those dates conditional on:

mediation still taking place on or before [DATE] 2017; and

the trial not be postponed under any circumstances.

Affidavit of Service

Regulation 34.01 of the County Court Civil Procedure Rules (2008) state the following:

34.01 Powers of Court

(1) At any stage of a proceeding, the Court may give any direction for the conduct of the proceeding which it thinks conducive to its effective, complete, prompt and economical determination.

I respectfully submit that Affidavits of Service should suffice in this matter like they do ordinarily in all other legal matters. A lawyer's duty to the Court is higher than their duty to their client. For this Honourable Court to not accept Affidavits of Service filed by my former lawyers and ask the parties to go a step further and serve by registered post is unnecessarily expensive, laborious and inconvenient. It also necessitates an Affidavit of Service in any event that attaches all proof of postage. This is tedious, time consuming and unnecessary. I respectfully submit that the Court has the right to form a view of a solicitor when that solicitor claims that they have not been served, despite Affidavits of Service to the contrary, particularly when they are unable to provide an adequate explanation for not having received served materials when evidence of electronic receipt of documents was provided and admitted by that very solicitor.

Furthermore, one would be excused for asking why the Court would accept some Affidavits of Service and not other Affidavits of Service filed by the same party, as in this case.

H. Honour Judge Lovebird said on [DATE]2017:

[Page No.] Blaming things on other people in the office in this day and age is not good enough. If a document has been served in accordance with the rules, it has been served.

Communications between the Parties

To date, communications between the parties have hit a bottleneck again because of Barnaby Bustard-Braggart not replying to any substantive matters that I attempt to communicate with him about. I have recently copied the Directions Group, Judge's Associates and other parties into emails I have sent Barnaby Bustard-Braggart to show a pattern of non-communication where Barnaby Bustard-Braggart is concerned. Court Jester Lawyers have claimed that they have not received communications from me or my lawyers throughout the entirety of this proceeding, yet I have electronic confirmation that they have. The behaviour and conduct of Barnaby Bustard-Braggart is deliberately fettering this matter and is obvious when all other parties and the Court are in receipt of such group emails and transmissions.

On learning of my former lawyer's intention to cease acting, on [DATE] 2017, the Defendant's Solicitors wrote to my former lawyers and sent them a Draft Minutes of Consent that were insulting with the sole intention of being so, seeking the following Orders:

that the proceeding be dismissed;

no order as to Costs; and

all prior Costs Orders in the proceeding are set aside or waived by the plaintiff.

I can assure the Defendant's Solicitor and the Defendant that there is absolutely no chance of me withdrawing or satisfying their wishful thinking. Not ever.

I respectfully ask this Honourable Court to Order that all future communication between the parties go through the self-represented litigant coordinator for sending on to Barnaby Bustard-Braggart on my behalf and to me from Barnaby Bustard-Braggart on their behalf, accordingly. In this way, the Court will be clear about who is stymieing the matter by not complying with their Overarching Obligations and remind them of same.

Vacating the Directions Hearing set for [DATE]2017

H. Honour Judge Lovebird set this date for the sole reason of holding Discovery of Documents in the courtroom, in front of H. Honour. This was in response to them wanting to be sure that discovery had been affected because of Barnaby Bustard-Braggart falsely claiming that he had not received any documents from my lawyers at any time.

I respectfully submit, however, that there is no point in having this Directions Hearing on [DATE] 2017 as mediation is ordered to take place on or before this date, being [DATE]

2017. In the event that mediation takes place, it is essential to ensure that the documents have already been served and therefore, the parties are in a position to mediate, in full knowledge of each other's case.

I do not see reason for another costly Court event after mediation and ask that the Directions Hearing fixed for [DATE] 2017 now be vacated.

Transcript of Hearing on [DATE]2017

My former lawyers sought leave to apply for a Transcript of the Hearing of [DATE] 2017, when H. Honour Judge Lovebird set aside Final Orders of Judicial Registrar Partridge-Saxon for default judgement and costs in my favour. On my instructions to appeal H. Honour's decision, I asked that the Transcript be obtained to assist me in supporting my grounds for appeal to the Supreme Court of Appeal. The Court approved the release of the Transcript to my former lawyers in these circumstances.

Subsequently, I asked my lawyers to cease acting based on the poor performance of Captain Plumage, the QC they briefed and their poor conduct on my file, including the non-filing of important documents as Ordered, putting me in breach of Orders unknowingly.

This change in my representation to becoming a self-represented litigant caused the Transcript to be held in abeyance while the Court considered my request for the Transcript. I was first told by the Court that I had to wait to request the Transcript until my former lawyers had formally ceased acting. This took a few weeks.

Once they filed their Notice of Ceasing to Act, I sought leave to apply for the Transcript myself as a self-represented litigant and paid the Transcript service the quoted $1,300 to transcribe that hearing.

It was only after this that the Judge's Associate confirmed that H. Honour needed to review the Transcript first before releasing it to me so that she could make grammatical changes to it where required. I am still waiting for the Transcript to be released to me. Until that time, I cannot make an informed decision about appealing H. Honour's decision, which is very costly, making a complaint to the Legal Services Board about the unprofessional conduct of Barnaby Bustard-Braggart and also suing my former lawyers Hawkeye Lawyers.

Service of Documents

To date, I have served Court Jester Lawyers twice with the discovery documents as a self-represented litigant, albeit unsealed documents.

I hereby undertake to serve them with the sealed copies of my documents once the Court files and issues them on my behalf, as a self-represented litigant, as I have no other way of filing available to me.

In the event that I receive the sealed documents in time before the 11:00 a.m. hearing on [DATE] 2017, I will seek to serve Barnaby Bustard-Braggart from the bar table as I am concerned about further denials of Barnaby Bustard-Braggart about receipt of served documents based on his past unconscionable conduct.

The Trial

I respectfully submit that the Trial set down for [DATE] 2018 to [DATE] 2018, be extended beyond [DATE] 2017 if possible and/or necessary to allow adequate time to hear evidence from all proposed witnesses, witnesses as identified in my **Reasons for Seeking Leave to Issue Subpoenas** filed contemporaneously.

I am unaware of who the Defendant proposes calling as witnesses, but I respectfully ask that the Court make Orders that the Defendant file and serve his proposed witness list within fourteen (14) days of the date of these Orders for the Court to fix further appropriate number of days for Trial if need be.

However, I am not prepared to vacate the current Trial date to do so as the Trial was vacated immediately by Court staff when I won this matter in [DATE] 2017. When the Defendant successfully appealed, my Trial dates were lost and new Trial dates needed to be fixed for some nine (9) months later. I am not prepared to be further prejudiced in terms of time and mental health to withstand another unnecessary delay that I am not responsible for.

I now seek the following Orders in relation to the above housekeeping matters as follows, in addition to and including those sought in relation to my **Reasons for Seeking Leave to Issue Subpoenas**:

That this Honourable Court appoint a mediator specialised in personal injuries and sets a date and location for mediation to occur on or before [DATE] 2017

That the Defendant's Solicitors Barnaby Bustard-Braggart pay the Plaintiff all outstanding Costs Orders in her favour within seven (7) days of the date of these Orders, to be paid on or before close of business on [DATE] 2017, into the Plaintiff's nominated bank account as follows:

Westpac Bank
Account name: Antony and Cleopatra Jones

BSB: Account Number:

In the event that this payment is not made within time, for the following Orders:

That the Defendant's defence be struck out under <u>Section 51 of the CPA and</u> r 63A.03 (2)<u>(3b)</u> of the Rules <u>or, in the alternative,</u>

That after [DATE] 2017, <u>under Section 29 of the CPA,retrospective</u> penalty interest will accrue from the date the Costs Orders were first made, being [DATE] 2017 and

That Barnaby Bustard-Braggart pay the Plaintiff's costs of mediation, including:

her half share of the mediator's costs;

her counsel's fees; and

her travel costs to Big Smoke – or other appropriate location – to attend mediation.

That Order 9 of [DATE] 2017 be dismissed and that the Court Orders that Affidavits of Service are satisfactory to establish and provide proof of service, without the necessity for service by registered post.

That all future communication between the parties go through the self-represented litigant coordinator

That Order 4 of [DATE] 2017 be dismissed and that the Court Orders that the Directions Hearing fixed for [DATE] 2017 be vacated

That this Honourable Court release to the Plaintiff the Transcript of the Hearing on [DATE] 2017 as a matter of urgency

That the time be extended for the Plaintiff to file <u>Particulars of Special Damages</u> and documents/evidence in support to a date to be fixed subject to the Court's filing of self-represented litigant documents

That the Defendant file and serve his proposed witness list within fourteen (14) days from the date of these Orders and for the Court to fix further appropriate number of days for trial if need be, in chambers, without vacating the existing trial dates or necessity for the parties to attend

That the witnesses not book any overseas travel to be taken in [DATE] 2018–[DATE] 2018 inclusive so that they are present in Australia and available to attend trial

That the witnesses' costs in complying with the subpoena be capped at a reasonable daily rate in an amount that this Honourable Court sees fit, in addition to the $25 conduct money to be given by cheque at point of issue

That Barnaby Bustard-Braggart Lawyers and the Defendant be prevented from disclosing to any potential witnesses that they may be subpoenaed in this matter

That the trial days be extended, given the number of potential and relevant witnesses I wish to call, including, most importantly, the Defendant himself

That the Defendant pay the Costs of this hearing

That the Defendant pay the plaintiff $300 in travel costs and incidental expenses to attend upon Dr Insightful for psychological assessment seven (7) days prior to the Plaintiff's attendance, by direct debit into her bank account:

Westpac Bank
Account name: Antony and Cleopatra Jones
BSB: Account Number:

I humbly ask this Honourable Court to grant the Orders I seek.

Dated:[DATE] 2017

And again, at yet another mention of my matter only six days later, a new set of Submissions, for the judge had given me the option of being heard, meaning giving my submissions orally and I took him up on it. Barnaby Bustard-Braggart, however, did not for obvious reasons. He wanted to avoid H. Honour any way he could, for he knew the game was up!

My Submissions for the Directions Hearings on [DATE]2017

My Position

I strenuously oppose the application of the Defendant's solicitor Mr Barnaby Bustard-Braggart ('Barnaby Bustard-Braggart') to vary the Orders of H. Honour Judge Lovebird made [DATE] 2017 in any way.

This includes in relation to the following matters, which are the subject of the Defendant's application:

to extend the date from [DATE] 2017 to [DATE] 2017 for the defendant to file his Affidavit sworn [DATE] 2017;

to extend the date for the filing of any further expert medical report of Dr Insightful, Dr Clever, or any other psychiatrist of the Defendant's choosing from [DATE] 2017 to any other date after that date; and

to extend the date of mediation past [DATE] 2017.

I have made these written submissions in response to the following:

the Affidavit of Barnaby Bustard-Braggart sworn [DATE] 2017;

the correspondence of H. Honour Judge Plover's Associate Mr Cormorant of [DATE] at 4:07 p.m., which states that the parties can be heard on [DATE] if they so wish; and

the correspondence of Barnaby Bustard-Braggart at 4:18 p.m. and 5:04 p.m. on [DATE] 2017 in response, which addresses the Court in writing as to his views and also states that the Defendant does not want to be heard, subject to what I might say about the matter.

I confirm that I wish to be heard on [DATE] 2017 by video link from Conservative Town, irrespective of whether the Defendant's Solicitor wishes to be heard or not. I am not surprised that Barnaby Bustard-Braggart has opted to put his position by email instead, preferring to avoid any scrutiny.

The Primary Position of H. Honour Judge Plover

In relation to the primary position of H. Honour Judge Plover, I say as follows:

that mediation **should** be conducted within the strict timetable of H. Honour Judge Lovebird's orders made [DATE] 2017; and

that the Defendant **should not** be entitled to proceed with the proposed medical examination of Dr Insightful or any other psychiatrist in the event that mediation does not settle the matter.

I give detailed reasons for my view in my submissions contained herein under the following subheadings:

Affidavit of Barnaby Bustard-Braggart sworn [DATE] 2017

Late filing of Barnaby Bustard-Braggart's Affidavit sworn [DATE] 2017

The reports being served late as a possible basis for requesting their own report

The contemptuous conduct of the Defendant's Solicitor Mr
Bustard-Braggart

Further prejudice to the Plaintiff

Circumstances around the request for a Psychiatrist's
Report by Dr Insightful

My status as a newly self-represented litigant

Mr Bustard-Braggart's personal relationship with the
Defendant

My emotional and physical health

Mediation

Orders I seek

Affidavit of Barnaby Bustard-Braggart sworn [DATE]2017

I have read the affidavit of Barnaby Bustard-Braggart
('Barnaby Bustard-Braggart's Affidavit') sworn on [DATE]
2017, and I now say the following in response:

In relation to Order 3 made on [DATE] 2017 by H. Honour
Judge Plover, I say that Barnaby Bustard-Braggart does not
provide any valid excuse for not having made any adequate
enquiries or arrangements for me to attend upon a psychiatrist
until [DATE] 2017, the day before the Directions Hearing on
[DATE] 2017.

I submit that Barnaby Bustard-Braggart's affidavit was full
of irrelevancies and barely addressed the content that H.
Honour Judge Plover was seeking in Order 3(a), (b), and (c)
inclusive.

Barnaby Bustard-Braggart had fourteen (14) weeks and two
(2) days (or 100 days) from [DATE] 2017 to make an
appointment that would enable the Defendant to comply with
the orders in relation to the appointment, the filing of the
report and mediation. If the Defendant was anxious that I be
assessed by his own choice of psychiatrist, as is commonplace
and to be expected, he would have been equally keen to

instruct Barnaby Bustard-Braggart to do so at the first available opportunity after [DATE] 2017. That he did not do so is, I respectfully submit, indicative of a desire to prolong and draw out this matter at every opportunity. I find it hard to conceive that Barnaby Bustard-Braggart would have only been instructed about this on or about [DATE] 2017.

Barnaby Bustard-Braggart has been in practise for many years, approximately seventeen (17), yet he claims he did not realise how long it would take to book me in to see an appropriate medical expert. This truly defies all sense and understanding. Moreover, it appears that he also failed to consider or understand the time frame required to obtain expert medical reports, which usually have a six- (6) to eight- (8) week turnaround.

Barnaby Bustard-Braggart also claims in his affidavit that he was relying on counsel to recommend an appropriate psychiatrist. By his own admissions, he only briefed counsel on [DATE] 2017, so I say there would not be much choice in terms of available psychiatrists at that stage to even consult counsel in any event.

In relation to Paragraph [] of Barnaby Bustard-Braggart's affidavit, Barnaby Bustard-Braggart says that he tried to book an appointment with another psychiatrist and that he (the psychiatrist) was unavailable. Notably, Barnaby Bustard-Braggart does not disclose who that psychiatrist was, which I say indicates the lack of veracity of his claim. Barnaby Bustard-Braggart knows only too well as a lawyer that any claim like this made by affidavit requires proof and is seldom given any weight where there is no evidence.

The fact that I made repeated contact with his office on 10, 11, 12, 13, 15, 20, and [DATE] 2017 should have alerted him to the outstanding issue of mediation as that was the very subject of those emails. It should have served as a daily reminder to him about needing to ensure that all orders were complied with by the Defendant or that they were in the process of being complied with.

I did not receive a response from Barnaby Bustard-Braggart to any of my correspondence about mediation until [DATE] 2017, yet I was sent read receipts from Barnaby Bustard-Braggart and his other staff that confirmed that he had read and received my emails, despite his lack of response.

The correspondence sent on the dates in Paragraph 3(f) above was all about mediation. There was no mention of a psychiatrist from Barnaby Bustard-Braggart at all until [DATE] 2017 at 2:49 p.m. Furthermore, his promise earlier that day of reverting back to me about an appropriate mediator and his client's available dates was not kept. Rather, as if by last-minute miraculous idea, Barnaby Bustard-Braggart wrote to me about attending upon Dr Insightful, with the veiled threat that the trial dates might be jeopardised if I were unable to make the [DATE] 2017 appointment.

I say that Barnaby Bustard-Braggart's attempts on [DATE] 2017 to secure alternative psychiatrist appointments are nothing but a desperate attempt at making his office appear to this Honourable Court to be complying with the orders when he really seeks not to because of his inflated ego and sense of entitlement.

Late filing of Barnaby Bustard-Braggart's Affidavit

As I anticipated, filing and service of Barnaby Bustard-Braggart's affidavit as ordered by H. Honour Judge Plover was late once again, filed after 4:00 p.m. on [DATE] 2017, causing the date of filing to be correctly recorded as [DATE] 2017. The orders say for the affidavit to be filed and served by 4:00 p.m. on [DATE] 2017. Barnaby Bustard-Braggart served me at 4:18 p.m. and filed at a time unknown to me but after 4:00 p.m. in any event. I say that he does this deliberately as it's all a game to him and his aim is to make me look unreasonable for not being amused. It feels like I'm stuck in a game of cat and mouse with him and I, the mouse, am getting tired.

This issue of late filing by Barnaby Bustard-Braggart was an issue at the Summons Hearing on [DATE] 2017, and the Court allowed the filing of his documents to be extended from 4:19 p.m. [DATE] 2017 (therefore correctly recorded as [DATE] 2017) to [DATE] 2017, with a highly questionable basis. These are the very documents that he was meant to have filed in [DATE] 2017. Considering the point that was made about the importance of complying with Orders by H. Honour Judge Lovebird on [DATE] 2017, it is galling that Barnaby Bustard-Braggart has continued to show flagrant disregard for the Court and to myself by filing and serving ordered documents late once again, just because he can. Ordinarily, I may not take issue with this, but in the circumstances of persistent delays and denials, I certainly do.

Furthermore, I feel that the path forward that Barnaby Bustard-Braggart suggests in his affidavit is put at the last minute to desperately avoid a submissions contest at all costs. He was not present at Court on the last occasion and briefed counsel Ms Penelope Peahen, I suspect, so that he could avoid all anticipated questioning from the bench about his concerning approach.

Barnaby Bustard-Braggart's affidavit tells me that he does things his own way and in his own time and simply expects more of the same latitude from the Court. He is not interested in affording any respect to the process, to the Court, or to me and has learned that he can get away with breaching Orders.

The path forward that Barnaby Bustard-Braggart suggests requires agreement from the Court and myself to breaching the Orders for his benefit. But for the fact that this matter has been listed in the self-represented litigant stream, I respectfully submit that Barnaby Bustard-Braggart would have made no further attempt at suggesting alternative appointments but continue to bully his way to have his way with Dr Insightful's appointment, the expert report to be filed by [DATE] 2018 and mediation delayed to [DATE] 2018 as suggested in his email of [DATE] 2017 at 1:13 p.m., advising that those were the directions he was seeking, just minutes before the Directions Hearing.

I say that unless the Defendant can have me assessed and a report filed and served in time to fully comply with the orders, I am not agreeable to it.

I say further that his affidavit should not even be accepted, for the Rules say that anything filed and served after 4:00 p.m. is taken to be filed the next day, in this case being [DATE] 2017. If the Court is of a view to consider his materials filed late to further accommodate Barnaby Bustard-Braggart and his consistently poor conduct, I still say that the content is of a kind that H. Honour indicated that he would not be impressed with.

Order 3 states that by 4:00 p.m. on [DATE] 2017, the Solicitor for the Defendant is to file and serve an affidavit which sets out:

a. the date upon which Professor Insightful was first approached for the purpose of fixing a medical examination by her of the Plaintiff;

b. the reason for the delay between the date referred to in Paragraph (a) hereof and the date of the order made by H.

Honour Judge Lovebird in this proceeding; and

c. the reason for which a mediation in this proceeding should be delayed so as to allow the Plaintiff to attend a medical examination by Professor Insightful.

Barnaby Bustard-Braggart's affidavit is full of irrelevant material that serves only as a smokescreen for his own failings. He attempts to excuse his failings by appearing to carry out the next step rather than doing as he ought in the first place. His is little more than a tawdry attempt to shift blame.

In the affidavit of Barnaby Bustard-Braggart on [DATE] 2017, he blamed his non-compliance with orders on the administrative failings of his office whilst denying service and, on this basis, changed the entire course of the matter. I say he is attempting to do this again but has been caught out and is now desperately scrabbling at complying, relying on an expected reasonableness from me that he has exhausted a long time ago.

If the Defendant and or the Defendant's Solicitor's aim was to exhaust and frustrate through legal trickery, he won, but now Barnaby Bustard-Braggart cannot expect a kind turn in the Defendant's favour from me.

The reports being served late as a possible basis for requesting their own report

The two reports of Dr Guru aren't markedly different in their content. The amended report has important factual corrections that needed to be made, but the reports are not substantively different.

The two reports of Dr Ian Intelligent were already served on Barnaby Bustard-Braggart in 2016 as part of the VOCAT matter. For Barnaby Bustard-Braggart to now say that he has only just been served with fresh materials is not correct.

Barnaby Bustard-Braggart's affidavit does not suggest that the Defendant wanted to have me examined because of anything arising in the materials served on the Defendant on [DATE] 2017, for there was nothing new that he had not seen before other than the amended report of Dr Guru, which has only minor changes.

Barnaby Bustard-Braggart's claims as to what he thinks is prejudicial to me should be of very little interest to this Court. His disrespect of me has been long-standing in his physical demeanour, including standing where we needed to pass and gloating to Captain Plumage, QC, outside Court on [DATE] 2017, and in his choice of language in his correspondence over four and a half (4.5) years, which is overtly, personally offensive, examples of which are contained in correspondence provided to H. Honour Judge Plover as per the Orders made [DATE] 2017.

The Defendant's Solicitors have had my reports from VOCAT since the 2016 hearing, so their behaviour since then to cause delay at every turn has been in open knowledge of my worsening psychological condition, which is exacerbated by delays. I say that this makes the behaviour of Barnaby Bustard-Braggart and the instructions of the Defendant particularly callous and unforgivable.

I do not want to hear about how the conduct of Barnaby Bustard-Braggart himself must not cause prejudice to the defendant when I say it is the Defendant who is instructing Barnaby Bustard-Braggart to conduct this matter in the way that he has to cause maximum psychological damage and that for some reason, Barnaby Bustard-Braggart is willing to conduct himself in this concerning, unprofessional manner for this client, the Defendant.

The contemptuous conduct of the Defendant's Solicitor Mr Bustard-Braggart

This application is really all about the Defendant's Solicitor Mr Bustard-Braggart and his callous conduct on the Defendant's cruel instructions, to the point where I feel that Barnaby Bustard-Braggart is almost the Defendant or at least is more invested than the Defendant. It's about how much further latitude the Court and I personally ought to extend to Barnaby Bustard-Braggart to serve the wishes of his client.

On [DATE] 2017, H. Honour Judge Lovebird set aside the Orders of Judicial Registrar Partridge-Saxon and set a new interlocutory timetable and made new Orders, including for mediation by [DATE] 2017, accordingly.

This occurred because Mr Bustard-Braggart created a situation whereby he deliberately misled the Court into believing that he had never received correspondence, documents and materials previously served upon him by my former Solicitors. This created a situation where the default judgement occurred because of the false narrative he created that says he had been deceived into not responding and not being at Court on both [DATE] and [DATE] 2017. There is proof of this deception in a group email sent to all the parties to which Barnaby Bustard-Braggart was copied into and Barnaby Bustard-Braggart even replied to, claiming he was unaware of a summons and that they had other things on in any event. Any solicitor, including Barnaby Bustard-Braggart, knows to brief counsel when they are personally unable to appear or to, at the very least, send their client to Court to avoid the risk of the matter being struck out or adverse orders being made in your absence. Why was Barnaby Bustard-

Braggart unperturbed about consecutive non-appearances? Why was he nonplussed about the possible negative outcomes for his client?

On [DATE] 2017, Mr Bustard-Braggart attempted to create a further artifice whereby Counsel for the Defendant, Mr Coxcombe, was made to appear to be directly briefed by the Defendant whilst Mr Bustard-Braggart appeared for himself. Through Barnaby Bustard-Braggart's representations, it was open to the Court to consider that the Defendant, King Claudius, was, from this point forward, no longer represented by Barnaby Bustard-Braggart Solicitors. In fact, Barnaby Bustard-Braggart went into the witness box and, under oath, said that costs orders need to be made against his firm, not the Defendant. Then he went even further and said the Defendant, King Claudius himself, had briefed counsel and stressed that his firm Barnaby Bustard-Braggart did not brief counsel Mr Coxcombe. This matter of who Barnaby Bustard-Braggart was acting for and indeed appearing for was never clarified though and led to H. Honour giving both Mr Bustard-Braggart and the Defendant the benefit of the doubt but at my expense. This is a strategy employed on other occasions by Barnaby Bustard-Braggart Solicitors where a pretence is developed to appear that they no longer act for the Defendant. This was so at the commencement of this civil proceeding where Barnaby Bustard-Braggart Solicitors would neither confirm nor deny that they acted, so I had to serve the writ on the Defendant personally, another successful delaying tactic employed by Barnaby Bustard-Braggart.

I say that Barnaby Bustard-Braggart deliberately briefed counsel on [DATE] 2017 to avoid being questioned directly by the Court about his approach, buying time to invent further excuses at his leisure, subsequently ordered to be provided on affidavit. I say further that his intention to not appear on [DATE] 2017 is further evidence of this.

Further prejudice to the Plaintiff

In my respectful submission on [DATE] 2017, the risk of any prejudice to the Defendant by the conduct of his solicitor was removed from the Defendant and placed onto me instead.

H. Honour Judge Lovebird acknowledged this on [DATE] 2017, when she said at Transcript page 53, line 17 (when she set aside Judicial Registrar Partridge-Saxon's Orders made [DATE] 2017):

(p.) I am satisfied that the grounds are made out to justify setting aside the order as are articulated in the cases referred to. There is some prejudice and I acknowledge that. Such a prejudice can only be mitigated **by a strict timetable for compliance with any further procedural directions** and a prioritised date for trial.

Well, the 'prioritised date' for trial was set for [DATE], and I wouldn't call that prioritised, particularly in the circumstance where the trial date was vacated immediately on me winning the matter by default judgement, before the Defendant was successful in setting aside my Orders in my favour, based on a tissue of lies put to the Court by Barnaby Bustard-Braggart and Counsel for the Defendant, Mr Coxcombe.

I ask this Honourable Court to consider the words of H. Honour Judge Lovebird closely: 'Such a prejudice can only be mitigated **by a strict timetable for compliance with any further procedural directions** and a prioritised date for trial.'

I respectfully submit that strict compliance means denying the Defendant's suggested path forward, which is conditional on a late-served expert report, in the context of a history of non-compliance.

Circumstances around the request for Psychiatrist's Report by Dr Insightful

I have now obtained the Transcript of hearing of [DATE] 2017, and I think it's rather important to note some of H. Honour's comments as they give context and provide the reasons for their Orders and the management path they ultimately chose for the matter to finally progress. Their comments go to the heart of the Defendant's application, in the circumstance where Your Honour is asked to use your discretion about whether to indulge Barnaby Bustard-Braggart again in any way, however seemingly minor.

Further, I wish to stress the following:

H. Honour Judge Lovebird said at Transcript page 69, line 4 in reference to mediation:

This is the sort of case where a steady hand needs to be kept on the wheel.All right, so mediation is to take place on or before [DATE] 2017. Mediator is to be appointed jointly by the parties in default of agreement as to the identity of the mediator. Reserve liberty to apply at short notice for appointment of a mediator – or, I should say, on the question of appointment of a mediator.

Since [DATE] 2017, more than three and a half (3.5) months have elapsed, yet there has been no real progress in these interlocutory matters as follows:

There has been a history of no acknowledgement by the Defendant of the interlocutory steps done by me or my former lawyers by either no correspondence in reply or severely delayed correspondence.

At a mention on [DATE] 2017, the Defendant's Solicitor

Barnaby Bustard-Braggart, miraculously appearing again for King Claudius despite their seemingly severed relationship on [DATE] 2017, blatantly denied having been served with my documents on [DATE] 2017, in accordance with the Orders, being the serving of Particulars of Special Damages and medical reports in support, despite my former lawyers having served him by the newly Ordered method of service, being by registered post.

Of serious concern is the fact that now Mr Bustard-Braggart writes to me on [DATE] 2017 and at paragraph 4 of his document and changes his story, finally admitting, 'On [DATE], we were served with your Particulars of Special Damages dated [DATE] 2017 and an expert medical report of Dr Gilbert dated [DATE] 2017.' (I presume he means Dr Gilbert Guru.)

I respectfully submit that this goes directly to the character of Mr Bustard-Braggart and his willingness to say whatever suits him at the time rather than the truth as an officer of the Court, a duty above that to his client, which I say includes instructions to create delay at all costs.

This is a pattern of behaviour that has been established by the Defendant's Solicitor from the commencement of this matter, right back in early 2016, when we were unable to get any substantive response from him in relation to our draft consent orders and we had to ask for a Directions Hearing to get the matter on some sort of track.

At that time, Mr Chiffchaff of civil registry advised us that in the circumstances of no contact from the Defendant's Solicitors, the matter would simply be listed for a Directions Hearing, but then nothing happened for months until we contacted the Court again and were told we needed to formally apply for a Directions Hearing. I am concerned that

Mr Bustard-Braggart has friends and contacts in the civil
registry that are in a position to bend the rules for him yet
maintain an officious and steely adherence to the Rules for me,
by his own admissions in his affidavit sworn on [DATE] 2017.
For example, on [DATE], H. Honour refers to the confidence
Mr Bustard-Braggart displays by calling up someone called
Robin in registry and expecting to get his own way. I have had
to endure twenty-three (23) months of that approach by Mr
Bustard-Braggart in this matter and in the criminal matter in
2013 to 2014, the suppression order matter in 2014 to 2015, the
VOCAT matter in 2015 and 2016, and now the civil matter,
and it has taken an enormous toll on me both psychologically
and financially as it has contributed to prolonging the matter
and exacerbating my suffering, four and a half (4.5) years of the
Defendant instructing Mr Bustard-Braggart to behave with
contempt of me and this Honourable Court.

It might be argued that the twenty-three-month timeline
for this civil matter, which has not even had mediation, is quite
a normal trajectory, but as Your Honour said on the last
occasion in Court, 'this matter has become legendary, dragged
kicking and screaming by the defendant's solicitor', or words to
that effect. He had a chance to 'get his house in order', and he
has chosen not to heed the warning or respect this last chance.

I do not wish to have the case prolonged any further as any
delay is, without doubt, prejudicial to me in every way.
Barnaby Bustard-Braggart cannot convincingly feign to
ameliorate prejudice whilst causing further delay of any kind.

My status as a newly self-represented litigant

I am now a self-represented litigant because of running out of
money to be legally represented, by the delays deliberately

created by the Defendant's Solicitor, who appears to employ the strategies of delay and obfuscation as a tactic to bleed my financial resources and my mental health, prejudicing my ability to afford to go to trial.

I have also been prejudiced by the conduct of my former Solicitors, both Ibis Legal and Hawkeye Lawyers, and the counsel they briefed and recommended to me.

Mr Bustard-Braggart's personal relationship with the Defendant

It is important to note that the Defendant, King Claudius, is a long-time close personal friend of Mr Bustard-Braggart. I have met Mr Bustard-Braggart at the Defendant's parents' house on a number of occasions prior to my disclosure in 2013. I respectfully submit that it is this personal friendship with the Defendant that is causing Mr Bustard-Braggart to risk his professional reputation in this matter by deliberately mismanaging the case in the following ways:

Going beyond the usual lawyer–client relationship to the extent that he has with the Defendant in this matter.

Being personally offensive to me in correspondence, making derogatory comments about my sexual abuse allegations and my memory.

Not turning up to Court or even briefing counsel to appear on these occasions. He does not even advise the Defendant to appear in the circumstances where Barnaby Bustard-Braggart has advised the Court on the day by email or cursory phone call that he is unavailable. On the occasions when he does appear at Court, he does so late and then makes requests that the matter be stood down while he completes some other task or familiarises himself with the matter at that point. This alone put me to the cost of JR Partridge-Saxon ordering that I provide two affidavits to the Court about the correspondence last received from Barnaby Bustard-Braggart as he was curious as to why he failed to appear on two consecutive occasions on [DATE] and [DATE] 2017, wondering if it was due to Barnaby Bustard-Braggart or the Defendant. Jr Partridge-Saxon wanted to find out, but it was at my further cost.

Barnaby Bustard-Braggart banging his fists at the bar table and literally storming into the witness box on [DATE] 2017, speaking on his mobile telephone whilst Counsel was addressing the Court, and rudely and consistently interjecting loudly no matter who was speaking, H. Honour Judge Lovebird included, whilst matters were being heard on [DATE] 2017.

It is difficult from reading the Transcript to see evidence of all the above criticisms; however, if Your Honour were to watch the video of the hearing, Your Honour would be in no doubt and, I respectfully submit, rather horrified. In fact, I say it is the sort of video that one would play at Leo Cussen Institute to teach young aspiring law students how **not** to behave and as a refresher course in a course on ethics CPD. Why he was not held in contempt of Court, I'll never know.

In these and numerous other similar behaviours, Mr Bustard-Braggart consistently demonstrates contempt for this Honourable Court and an obvious desire to antagonise all parties, particularly myself as the Plaintiff in this child sexual assault matter. He appears to derive some personal pleasure at knowing that he has caused extra distress to me. The matter has clearly become personal to him given his friendship with the Defendant.

On [DATE] 2017, H. Honour summarised the situation quite beautifully, in my respectful submission:

At Transcript pg., line:

H. HONOUR: 'I'm far from impressed by the conduct of your instructing solicitor, even the outbursts today, jumping to your side of the Bar table, interfering with the orderly presentation of your submissions. I was trying to ask you questions. he's barking at you. There's an old saying –'don't buy a dog and bark yourself'. And I thought that it made for a lengthy hearing.

Didn't need to be such a lengthy hearing. Then there's the affidavit that, some circumstances of which are totally inexplicable. The missing details as to why documents that were apparently served went missing. there's the high-handed manner of dealing with the Court by thinking. you just need to make a phone call to somebody called Robin in registry and then you get your wish as to what happens in Court. That is not the way litigation is conducted.

Then there's the most uncivilised manner in which the exchanges between your instructor, speaking over the top of you, and then over the top of Captain Plumage, QC. I can understand why things went awry. But in any event, it's not the plaintiff's fault that Registrar Partridge-Saxon determined to act on a self-executing order. H. Honour was entitled to take account of the full facts, which he did as he's represented in the order that he made. He was fully aware of the time delay, butit was no doubt against a backdrop of non-compliance.

There is no reason why the plaintiff should be out of pocket in the circumstances. She was entitled to have judgement entered in her favour as the order was a self-executing order. The correspondence was late in the day. no doubt Captain Plumage, QC, had already been briefed in any event ready to appear today. So I don't know that such a late service would've

altered the obligation to pay counsel's fees. He's only seeking
half a day and quite frankly, I do not think that it is out of the
ballpark.

It's an indulgence that the defendant is seeking from the
plaintiff and from the Court. And in these circumstances, the
defendant should pay the actual costs that the plaintiff incurred
as a result of the defendant's default. I propose to order that
the defendant pay the Plaintiffs costs' –

MR BUSTARD-BRAGGART: Your Honour, Mr –

H. HONOUR: If you wish to say something, Mr Coxcombe
can call you to give evidence.

MR BUSTARD-BRAGGART: Mr Coxcombe is briefed on
behalf of the defendant.

H. HONOUR: Mr Coxcombe?

MR BUSTARD-BRAGGART: He's not briefed on behalf of
Barnaby Bustard-Braggart Solicitors.

It is my respectful submission that here is an example of
exactly why provisions of legislation addressed by the
Overarching Obligations and Rules of the Civil Procedure Act
(2010) are brought into being. If these rules and obligations are
not applied where the conduct of an Officer of the Court is so
flagrant and disrespectful, one has every right to wonder why
they exist at all. I ask this Honourable Court to consider
S. 9(2)(a), amended by No. 1/2011 s. 6. of the Civil Procedure
Act (2010) as follows:

• the extent to which the parties have complied with any
  mandatory or voluntary pre⊠litigation processes;

• the extent to which the parties have used reasonable
  endeavors to resolve the dispute by agreement or to limit
  the issues in dispute;

- the degree of promptness with which the parties have conducted the proceeding, including the degree to which each party has been timely in undertaking interlocutory steps in relation to the proceeding;

- the degree to which any lack of promptness by a party in undertaking the proceeding has arisen from circumstances beyond the control of that party;

- the degree to which each person to whom the overarching obligations apply has complied with the overarching obligations in relation to the proceeding;

- any prejudice that may be suffered by a party as a consequence of any Order proposed to be made or direction proposed to be given by the Court;

- the public importance of the issues in dispute and the desirability of a judicial determination of those issues;

- the extent to which the parties have had the benefit of legal advice and representation; and the extent to which Barnaby Bustard-Braggart has complied with the overarching obligations, if at all.

On [DATE] 2017, Barnaby Bustard-Braggart instructed Counsel Ms Peahen to tell the Court that he never received the medical reports of Dr Ian Intelligent until [DATE] 2017. This is untruthful in that he was provided with these very reports by me in [DATE] 2016, as part of the VOCAT matter. Ms Peahen then double-checked and acknowledged that she did, in fact, have the Dr Intelligent reports.

Barnaby Bustard-Braggart also wrote to me on [DATE] 2017, saying that I did not serve them with any medical reports on which I seek to rely by [DATE] 2017. This is not true. I understand that my former lawyers Hawkeye Lawyers served these reports on Barnaby Bustard-Braggart Solicitors. I attended the appointment with Dr Gilbert Guru at the earliest opportunity, in February 2017. The report cost me $2,200. Five weeks earlier, I paid the jury set-down fee in the amount of approximately $1,000. It makes no sense for me to comply with all Orders and do all things by the dates required to comply as I have done if I then set about delaying service, correspondence, or anything else. That is illogical for a Plaintiff to do so.

I respectfully ask the Court to consider the likelihood of me wanting to delay or ever instruct my former Solicitors to delay anything if I am the Plaintiff alleging sexual assault. I consider that I'm lucky to be alive and standing here given what we know about the trajectory of sexual assault victims. I am, I suspect, a 'sleeper' victim, as discussed in detail by Prof Carolyn Quadrio in the Royal Commission into Institutional Responses to Child Sexual Abuse; one who appears to not have any symptoms of sexual assault for many years but then does many years later. In my case, it was since I was triggered by my own children, when Kate turned 7, and the smug behaviour of the Defendant just before my disclosure.

I already had the reports of Dr Ian Intelligent provided to the Defendant's Solicitors in July 2016 as part of the VOCAT matter. Notwithstanding the possession of these medical reports, my former lawyers Hawkeye Lawyers recommended Dr Guru as one of the best in Big Smoke, and I attended at his office to be assessed at the earliest opportunity, taking another day off work to do so.

To attend upon Dr Insightful on [DATE] 2017 would have the following effect:

It would seriously impact upon my mental health, having

me relive my childhood sexual assaults soon before Christmas, as I celebrate Christmas, the European Christmas Eve, on 24 December 2017.

It would impact on the last week of business in our firm, which is very busy with family law clients the week before Christmas for obvious reasons.

It would further prejudice the Plaintiff to grant another indulgence to Mr Bustard-Braggart to attend upon another psychiatrist if it requires the orders to be breached or extended for the following reasons:

He tried to bully me into sticking to the date of [DATE] 2017, saying in correspondence of [DATE] 2017 that otherwise, the trial date could be jeopardised.

He expects me to cancel other commitments to accommodate him and last-minute appointments [DATE], only two (2) weeks away, when there is no obligation on me to do so. He is seeking an indulgence, not me.

Further Prejudice to the Plaintiff

As per my Submissions dated [DATE] 2017, I now repeat the following on the basis that they are relevant to the discretion required to decide this application:

On [DATE] 2017, the Defendant claimed that I would suffer no prejudice by his late filing of his documents; however, I say this is completely false and I have been absolutely prejudiced by H. Honour Judge Lovebird's decision to set aside default judgement in my favour, reinstate his defence and not give costs thrown away from more than one day, after a year of one-sided legal servitude by me, the Plaintiff.

I say that the following factors, overlooked by H. Honour Judge Lovebird, are now relevant and a direct result of the

Defendant's behaviour and attitude to these proceedings, causing me serious prejudice as follows:

The Defendant's uncooperative approach

The matter has dragged on well beyond the timeline consented to and seen as appropriate in the Consent Orders of [DATE] 2016. We have not even had mediation or the promise of same because of the Defendant's belligerence and mediation was previously Ordered to have taken place, before [DATE] 2017. This breaches both the Orders and the Civil Procedure Rules and the Overarching Obligations of the Defendant and his lawyer.

Time

The trial dates allocated for one week's trial commencing on [DATE] 2017 have now been vacated by the Court. But for the Defendant's approach, we were ready to proceed. The trajectory of this matter is completely unpredictable and this affects both my mental and physical health as I can't plan or allocate my energies. I am a busy working mum, with four children aged between 7 and 16 years. The conduct of the Defendant and the mismanagement of the matter by the Court staff have been all-consuming and had a detrimental effect on me. The effect of protracted proceedings on plaintiffs is no secret and if sexual assault is a matter that should be expediated wherever possible, this aim has certainly not been achieved in this matter.

Cost

My ability to afford to go to mediation and to trial has been compromised by the protracted nature of these proceedings, derailed by the Defendant at every opportunity, creating a situation where more and more costs are generated for hearings like the defendant's Summons on [DATE] 2017 and ex parte hearings caused by non-appearance by the Defendant and legal fanfaronade brought by the Defendant. I believe that this is a deliberate tactic used by the Defendant to bleed me dry.

Breaches of Orders

The Defendant claims that I do not suffer any prejudice arising from his documents being filed approximately twenty (20) minutes late. I assert that I have suffered considerable prejudice because what he filed twenty (20) minutes late was legally invalid in any event, such as unsworn affidavits and applications miraculously accepted for filing without affidavits in support without reprimand. The only legally valid documents were filed on [DATE] 2017 instead of [DATE] by 4:00 p.m., in breach of the Orders by six (6) days, not nineteen (19) minutes as Mr Bustard-Braggart alleges as he seeks to minimise his misconduct. The Defendant himself admits this, evidenced by his request for the time to file to be extended to [DATE] nunc pro tunc, as only then were the correct documents filed.

The Defendant successfully asked that the date for filing his documents be extended from [DATE] 2015 to [DATE] 2017 pursuant to r 3.02 of the Rules, six (6) days after the self-executing Order. This was a self-serving request as it conveniently extends the deadline imposed by the Court to a time convenient to the Defendant, notwithstanding the many other opportunities provided previously, all of which were ignored, that he had to file documents within time and participate in these proceedings. For the Defendant's Solicitors to say that he never received Orders or documents from my Solicitors is, in my respectful submission, both untruthful and, frankly, unbelievable, yet this was the highly questionable basis on which the matter was overturned.

My Emotional and Physical Health

On [DATE] 2017, I attended upon Dr Gilbert Guru to be psychiatrically assessed. My report has been provided to this Honourable Court and to the Defendant's Solicitors in a timely fashion, as per the Orders, as well as my psychologist's report by Dr Ian Intelligent in relation to my adjourned VOCAT application.

I say that in full knowledge of my fragile state, the Defendant has continued to behave with disrespect to me and to this Honourable Court so as to aggravate my mental health and, in turn, my physical health as follows:

My emotional health has been adversely affected in the following ways:

I have PTSD (nightmares and insomnia).

My social life has suffered (too exhausted to enjoy life, decline invites).

My relationship with my children and husband and my parents has been under enormous strain.

My children have seen me stressed and crying all the time, on my computer at home, working at every opportunity, through the night.

They have witnessed my insomnia.

I have lost my entire extended family, whom I was extremely close to; as have my family, my parents and my brother and his partner.

My physical health has also been adversely affected in the following ways:

Headaches and neck/back strain because of stress

MRI and CT scans because of persistent headaches in [DATE] and [DATE] 2017

Weight gain – comfort eating, stress, less time for exercise as all spare time previously had for recreation has been taken up by this matter, which has been all-consuming in trying to achieve what should be simple and straightforward interlocutory steps

Mediation

Regulations 50.07 (1), (9), and (10) of the County Court Civil Procedure Rules (2008) state the following:

50.07 Reference to mediator

(1) The power and discretion of the Court as to mediation under section 47A of the Act shall be exercised subject to and in accordance with this Rule.

(9) The Court may determine the remuneration of the mediator and by what party or parties and in what proportion the remuneration is to be paid, either in the first instance or finally.

(10) The Court may order any party to give security for the remuneration of the mediator.

A brief history of the issue of mediation

My former Solicitors Hawkeye Lawyers tried to arrange mediation with Barnaby Bustard-Braggart to no avail over the course of one whole year, where I spent more than $56,000 on legal costs from [DATE] 2016 to [DATE] 2017 yet got no further in this matter than prior to them acting. This was entirely due to the behaviour of the Defendant and his solicitor Barnaby Bustard-Braggart.

Mediation was first Ordered to happen by [DATE] 2017, but the Defendant wouldn't agree with our available dates, with the aim to cause delay again wherever possible. Moreover, Barnaby Bustard-Braggart claimed his client was overseas during May, but I ask why his client was overseas at that time for three (3) weeks when he knew that was when mediation was ordered to occur since 2 December 2016 since the Defendant agreed to the consent orders on [DATE] 2016.

Once I was formally self-representing, from [DATE] 2017, I wrote to the Defendant's Solicitors regarding mediation on six (6) occasions in 2017 but Barnaby Bustard-Braggart's emails of [DATE] did not take us any further in finalising mediation.

I had provided Barnaby Bustard-Braggart with a summary of available mediators on [DATE] 2017 as I hadn't heard from him about it despite his promise to revert back with his client's instructions regarding available dates. I received no response about it, and so at 5:00 p.m., I sent them a list of mediators and their available dates, seeking agreement.

On [DATE] 2017, I then received correspondence from Barnaby Bustard-Braggart about an alternative mediator and, on [DATE] 2017, a follow-up email asking me about my availability.

With all due respect, I have never received such a flurry of correspondence from Barnaby Bustard-Braggart as I have in recent days as I am used to receiving limited and aggressive responses to my lawyers and now myself to our correspondence begging for substantive replies.

DEFENDANT'S REQUEST FOR PSYCHOLOGIST REPORT

I will not agree to any further adjournment of mediation, notwithstanding that the Defendant has finally advised, on [DATE] 2017, one day before the Directions Hearing, that they now want me to see a psychiatrist of their choice.

Whist I'm agreeable to attend, I do take issue with the timing of both their request and the appointment, tentatively booked a few days before Christmas on [DATE] 2017 and the second last day of the business year and, importantly, well after the Ordered date for mediation. More likely than not, they would then seek a further delay and mediation would have to occur afterthe Ordered date of [DATE] 2017.

I called Dr Insightful's rooms at 9:30 a.m. on [DATE] 2017 and was told the following alternative times:

2 January 2018 at 12:00 p.m. (not 2:00 p.m. as in Barnaby Bustard-Braggart's affidavit)

4 January 2018 at 10:00 a.m.

10 January 2018 at 10:00 a.m.

11 January 2018 at 10:00 a.m.

I am not agreeable to attending upon a psychiatrist unless the subsequent report and mediation are as per [DATE] 2017 Orders. With all due respect, I say that regardless of the outcome of mediation, there should be no further expert medical report sought and, furthermore, that the trial must not be postponed under any circumstances.

Orders I seek today:

That Order 4 of [DATE] 2017 be dismissed and that the Court Orders that the Directions Hearing fixed for [DATE] 2017 be vacated.

That the Plaintiff will attend upon a psychiatrist of the Defendant's choice, where that psychiatrist can produce a report for this Honourable Court by [DATE] 2017, as ordered by Judge Lovebird on [DATE] 2017. In the event that the Defendant cannot find such a psychiatrist, the Defendant has no further right to request such an appointment and report before trial.

Under Rule 33.05 of the Rules:

That the Defendant pay the Plaintiff $300 in travel costs and other expenses incidental to the medical examination, to attend upon a psychiatrist as directed by the Defendant for psychological assessment as per Paragraph 2 above, at least seven (7) days prior to the Plaintiff's required attendance, by direct debit into her personal bank account:

Westpac Bank
Account name: Antony and Cleopatra Jones
BSB: Account Number:

In the event that the payment in Paragraph 3 above is not received in time and not into the appropriate account in Paragraph 3 above, that the Plaintiff has the right to not attend this appointment and that any appointment cancellation costs of that appointment be borne by the Defendant or by the Defendant's Solicitors if he is again at fault or there is another alleged administrative failing of his office, Barnaby Bustard-Braggart Lawyers.

That the shared costs of mediation be paid upfront to the Court by the parties, as security, prior to any mediation.

That the Defendant pay the Costs of today, for he is seeking the indulgence of the Court to extend the date for Orders to be complied with and only addressed the issue on the death knell.

I humbly ask this Honourable Court to grant the Orders I seek.
Dated:[DATE] 2017

After hearing my Submissions, I will never forget Judge Plover telling me, in a very sombre tone,

'Ms Jones, what these Submissions indicate to me is that they are written by someone very damaged.'

Well, albeit patronising, thank you. I should think so, Your Honour, if this is the sexual assault list. But why then did they ward me off from pursuing it further to trial, with their speech about one party ultimately thinking the bench is so clever and made the best decision and the other thinking they are an idiot and that there's no guarantee which one I'll be? My goodness, scrap the sexual assault list from the court if that's the reality. Why have it at all, seriously?

But that was my inner monologue answering the bench and, in reality, I stood there dumbfounded at the Bar table with tears in my eyes, quietly nodding. I was rendered speechless, staring once again at the courtroom stage in disbelief, crowned a victim yet seemingly in the wrong place to achieve justice. As a lawyer, this was so galling, I nearly vomited.

'Go back. You've come too far. This is not the right way. I warn you now of impending danger. There is great risk to you to continue. I need to dissuade you', is what I really heard him say if I added up his words together with his body language.

'Can't you see this is not the place for "damaged" people?' is what one can read between the lines. My inner monologue told me, You poor naïve girl!

But where exactly is the place for damaged people who dare to seek justice then if it's not the police station, the OPP, the Magistrates' Court, the County Court personal injury (sexual assault) list? Where do I go, and where do all my clients go?

After my Submissions, the judge ruled that I must attend upon Dr Clever despite the late request, and I was to simply clear my calendar to make it happen. I was furious but more so afterwards as King Claudius' lawyer refused to release the report as it was completely unsupportive of his client's case and overwhelmingly supportive of mine. I had to argue that it must be released and thankfully, Judge Plover ordered that it be released. Well, after the great almighty fuss to have it done at such short notice, I should damn well think so.

But what bugged me the most is that Barnaby didn't show up. The court had issued a Summons and he was a no show, a dangerous move professionally, but he always thumbed his nose at the court, so this was nothing new to me, but Judge Plover was far from impressed and adjourned the matter to next week.

Then the judge said to me, 'Ms Jones, I want you to think carefully about proceeding further. If this goes to trial, someone is going to win and think I'm a wonderfully intelligent person who got it right and the other is going to think I'm dumb and got it wrong. And we don't know which one you're going to be, do we?'

When the matter returned, it seemed the circus was in town as Barnaby entered the courtroom in his crumpled suit. This was another day where Barnaby Bustard-Braggart swore at the judge, jumped around rudely at the bar table and went into an absolute meltdown. He'd behaved just as poorly before, but I could swear that today was his audition for NIDA!

The judge asked him why he had not filed his affidavit as ordered and asked that he file another affidavit.

Barnaby rebelled rudely, 'Any affidavit will just have exactly the same in there as my previous affidavit.'

Judge Plover was not amused.

He then demanded that the judge allow him to go into the witness box instead of going on affidavit, but Judge Plover was guarding his Orders as closely as he would his nest of eggs on a spring lawn, aggressively fending him off at every pass with his sharp beak.

'Jesus!' yelled Barnaby at the Judge.

'What did you just say to me?' shouted Judge Plover back at him.

'I said Jesus!' screamed Barnaby. Clearly, he had absolutely lost the plot and his code of ethics as well.

Judge retorted angrily, 'How dare you blaspheme in this courtroom! I'm on the verge of reporting you to the Legal Services Board. You are not a professional lawyer and I may just hold you in contempt of court.'

'But can I just say something, Your Honour?' demanded Barnaby.

'No, absolutely not. I've heard enough from the bar table in this matter. You will have an affidavit for me by lunchtime today, Mr Bustard-Braggart.'

'But my office didn't get the email about the Summons until today, Your Honour!' said Barnaby, to which Judge Plover asked,

'Yes, why is your office the one so out of order? I have to ask myself, is it an accident or so on purpose?'

Barnaby then boldly and fearlessly stated, 'You're ranting, Your Honour!' sitting back lazily in his seat.

Judge Plover yelled back, 'Stand up when you address me!'

'Yes, sorry, Your Honour, but I just wanted to say how good it was of me to put all those costs orders onto me, to save the defendant,' groveled Barnaby, sucking up to the Judge.

But the truth was that it was a carefully constructed narrative of Barnaby's, designed to get both he and his client out of paying anything for this trickery. And this is what ultimately happened. Twenty-three months had passed since I filed the Statement of Claim. In that time, the defendant had breached fourteen orders, simple interlocutory steps had been made into Herculean impasses and we hadn't even had mediation yet. There had already been more than a dozen court hearings too, made so difficult that a QC was sent, including for a Directions Hearing, and all this was just racking up endless expense to me. Barnaby Bustard-Braggart was ordered to pay me more than $22,000 in costs.

A Day Out with Dr Clever

When I attended upon Dr Clever, I was at the point of absolutely spitting the dummy. I was moping about feeling sorry for myself, put out again to see yet another specialist in Big Smoke for King Claudius. Judge Plover explained that it's to my benefit to have another psychological assessment done and I understood what he was saying, but I was angry. Everything goes my cousin's way, it seems, with or without his effort but usually without any whatsoever.

So off I drove to Palm Fronds, my old familiar roads near Buckle Street, where I had gone for regular pregnancy care with my first baby some seventeen years ago, when I still lived in the city. I reflected on where my life had gone since then and sat in the same café window I had sat in years ago, happily people-watching then but now staring out desperately, searching for strength from outside of me for another retell, as if I could somehow borrow it from the souls of passers-by, just to get me through today. I'd give it back, I promise.My coffee arrived, with a heart dusted on the top just in time for me, but caffeine was no longer an effective source and besides, I was tired of telling. Tired of myself and my story. Couldn't Big Brother just connect all my files in all the professional offices that had a file on me now so that I had one story that everyone could feast on rather than everyone in the law feasting on my variations in my retells?

At this point, I'd spent five years telling the truth, being brave, and frankly, I was sick of the story myself. I wanted new horizons and a new existence, a new vista. I was tired of court documents, correspondence and reports and today was to be the making of yet another one. I was going to pour my heart out to yet another stranger, vulnerable and hopeful that they'd believe me and not think I was a basket case. My poor client was going through the same thing in court today across town, but how many others were facing the same sad morning?

The problem is that the law makes everything bigger than it needs to be. That allegedly essential, laborious legal process is crippling. I thought, Here I am, the good girl again, in the right place at the right time – early, in fact, but my clients have been inconvenienced because of Judge Plover ignoring my submissions about my two family law client trials I had this week, including one running today.

Dr Clever was the consummate professional and the staff in his rooms were cheery and helpful, but I was sick of waiting rooms too. Years ago, I used to be happy to use the waiting as an opportunity to quietly read a magazine, but even that reverse psychology had worn thin! I was also sick of filling out client pro formas and questionnaires. It was a shitty existence and it had gone on for far too long. It was too high a price to keep having to tell the truth until it hopefully landed in the right place to gain traction. Regardless, for me, it never did, and my truth drifted into outer space, into another orbit.

Mediation and Meditation — Both a State of Mind

I had known all along what to wear for this day: a black dress as Baba would have liked. I had plenty of them to choose from and besides, I'm sure 'my black' makes me look thin. I'm also sure that Friday, [DATE] 2017, was just another ordinary day out in manic Big Smoke for so many people, but for me, it was the most important day in five years, a funeral of sorts. I would see King Claudius face to face and end my pain on my terms. I would also bury my hope in the law's ability to put this right. There was certainly no justice.

In the days leading up to this day, I made a promise to myself that it was to be the final day out in Big Smoke for my matter. My parents, Antony and I arrived at mediation with a clear mind to settle the matter no matter what. I decided that I had foolishly paid homage to the law and its games for far too long. My children needed to come first again and I needed to give time back to myself in positive ways, not fighting a giant monolith. Christopher has Year 12 next year and I couldn't imagine another year of court, lawyers and judges where my matter was concerned. I wanted this to be over with and I suddenly realised that I could make that happen. I had almost forgotten what autonomous decision making felt like because the law saps that from you too, entirely.

Once I made that decision and promise to myself to let the law go, to let go of any inkling that the law is good, I was free. I made the mental disconnect and it was surprisingly easy to cope with thereafter. I was free and it felt so good. I felt light, albeit twenty-five kilos heavier. I saw the law for what it was and realised I had been on a fool's errand and at a very high price. We were living from pay to pay, juggling school fees and legal fees and for what? For my eternal hope that the law would turn good? That it was there to right the wrongs done to me by King Claudius and acknowledge that bad things had, in fact, happened to me? That way, I could respect my profession once again and happily continue practising, knowing that my love of helping people would not be in vain.

When you are so invested in something, it's hard to let go. When your sense of self is wrapped up in that thing, it's even harder. But my advice has dramatically changed to sex assault victims now and I have nothing good to say about the legal system when it comes to sexual assault. With the end of my case came the end of my hope for the law to redeem itself. I have mostly recovered from the trauma and have begun a new chapter of my life now and it began on this day, the day of mediation, notably and ironically far away from a courtroom.

'And the winner of the Bitch of the Year Award goes to my cousin Desdemona Homemaker!' appearing at mediation like Cardinal Campeius for Cardinal Carlisle. Desdemona was a girl who was addicted to pulp fiction as a child and had every Mills & Boon romance filed neatly in a drawer in her bedroom. A woman who couldn't tell her 'daddy' when she went to a nightclub in her '30s or bought a new dress. A woman who said she couldn't date a man unless he was clad in an Armani suit. A pseudo feminist who was a member of Zonta. A woman I've never seen with a male by her side other than King Claudius or her dogs, Tom and Jerry. What a sad individual in the midst of feminism, equality and the #MeToo movement but especially knowing what I went through. A woman with no children by choice and selfish design, thank goodness, but a woman whose actions and words do everything but support women. Maybe I simply failed to see the '666' on her scalp back when we were children.

My parents literally laughed when they saw her there and wondered how it was possibly in her interests to be there to the point of feeling sorry for her. Undoubtedly, money had exchanged hands, or was it a case of 'keep your enemies closer'? Needless to say, I was not agreeable to having Desdemona present during the mediation and declared this from the outset, so she supported him from a back room, like all true cowards, lurking on the sidelines with her evil aura.

'Hello, you must be Cleopatra,' said Sir Richard Vernon as he entered the room.

'Yes,' I said enthusiastically, immediately noticing his thick gold neck chain set off by his tanned chest. I figured that the unbuttoned shirt was quite deliberate and part of his attempt at a suave gigolo look. I was quite shocked that this was the choice for my mediator, hand-picked by a seemingly conservative judge who had told me, 'I know just the man for the job. Don't you worry, Cleopatra.' But now my gut instinct told me to be very worried, so I made the effort to remind myself that looks can be deceiving but I was never a fan of the '80s Gold Coast' look.

'You know that the other side are here now, so I'm going to go and have a talk with them and see where things are at,' said Vernon laboriously.

I said in staccato, 'OK, but tell them that I do not agree to my cousin Desdemona being present,' to which he replied smarmily, 'I'll see what I can do,' stretching his vowels.

When he next returned to the room, he told me, 'He will agree to her not being there in the room if you don't bring in your parents or your husband,' smiling knowingly.

'No problem,' I said as I thought to myself how King Claudius needs Desdemona one hundred times more than I need anyone.

I turned to my counsel, Mr Warren Warbler, and said, 'How typical that he brought her, the biggest liar in the family, with him, just to try and nark me.'

With a furrowed brow, Warbler said, 'It's not a good idea for you to be in the room,' to which I retorted,

'Whatever do you mean? No! It's vitally important that I'm in there, symbolically and emotionally, as this is the first time he's been face to face with me or conversed with me since the pretext call four and a half years ago.'

Cleopatra is Sexually Harassed

Warbler nervously conceded and at about 2:30 pm we entered the conference room, ready to mediate. I was surprisingly calm and had no intention of losing my cool like my QC had done in court. Warbler and I were the first to enter, as per the mediator's plan, so we chose to sit on the far side of the table, with the spotless glass wall framing other crazy business deals going on behind us, no doubt. Transfers of money, shifts of power and losses and gains of control – what we call the humble working day.

Then we engaged in small talk with the mediator while we waited for my cousin to join us and he did shortly thereafter, sitting directly opposite me, with our opposing counsels also facing each other. He appears after three years – he does exist!And his old faithful friend and court jester Barnaby Bustard-Braggart sat on the other side of King Claudius, casually leaning back on his chair, in jeans and a shirt, like he owned the place. His body language was try-hard and his cavalier attitude did him no favours. He reminded me of men who sit on overcrowded trains, desperate to draw attention to their genitals, with their legs splayed out to the sides and arms outstretched behind their heads, oozing a dicky confidence.

After a brief introduction delivered by the mediator, counsel started summarising our case, during which Barnaby rudely interjected, saying annoying things like, 'When you say event,what eventare we talking about here?' After four and a half years, the event was no mystery. Even his own barrister diplomatically stepped in and right over the top of his instructor and said, 'I think we can safely assume that you're referring to all the events as alleged in her Statement of Claim.'

'Yes,' said Warbler, relieved that opposing counsel was professional with the integrity that his instructor clearly lacked. I looked at Barnaby and thought, He is nothing but a self-important upstart with the same modus operandi – waste time and big note himself wherever possible. He tried to pull a half-intelligent look on his face, but it didn't work.

Warbler went on, stressing the point that the three psychologists' reports about me all concur damage (and Judge Plover had also given that indication from the bench - and in such a complimentary way, I'm sure!). Warbler also said, 'Importantly, no alternative theory has been put by the defence as to my client's damage, quantum now being the only issue.'

At one point, when his barrister was speaking, relaying his instructions that were lies about me, I became slightly teary and I caught King Claudius' eye. We looked at each other momentarily, but then after a few seconds, he made an annoyed face at me, shrugging and bringing his hands to his face, miming 'What?' as if to say, 'What are you looking at me for?' I just thought to myself, What a narcissistic sociopath. He has no conscience.

Opposing counsel then put their case, saying, 'There are problems with the Statement of Claim and we have two witnesses, Hamlet and Grumio, who will show in glorious fashionthat Cleopatra is lying.' He went on, 'In any event, the behaviour alleged is normalised sexual behaviour for children of that age,' and at that, Barnaby recoiled, bouncing up from his chair like a popinjay, briefly leaving the room to fetch something he claimed would be 'rather helpful to everyone'. He returned holding colour photocopies of a chart of sexualised behaviours, that which I had seen when working at the Department of Human Services. As he pushed this piece of minimising paper across the table towards me, he said in a cocky voice, 'It's normal kid behaviour.' I left the page where it landed, refusing to acknowledge it, and turned my head away from him. I was already familiar with that chart and I knew where he was going...the 'child's play' argument was rearing its ugly head.

Then Barnaby boldly brought everyone to attention and said, sliming all over us, 'Anyone for strip chasey, spin the bottle, perhaps?' I looked at him in utter shock as he smirked at me. Had I not just heard him sexually harass me, the only woman in a room full of men? My mind was racing and my heart was thumping in anger when I turned to look to Warbler to fight for my revenge. I could feel my pulse as every fibre of my being was offended and being tested. It was flight or fight from this filth.

Warbler rolled his eyes, clearly appalled, and said to me, 'Don't say anything. It's not worth it,' and looked to the door, indicating we leave. As I stood up to go, I said to Warbler, loud enough for all to hear, 'See what I mean? He's like this at court too!'

When we returned to our waiting room, I told Mum and Dad and Antony that I'd just been sexually harassed in there and I then re-enacted Barnaby's behaviour in my heightened state. They looked at me in disbelief. Warbler did not dispute my rendition but soon left the room.

After this, the offers game began, the first being an offer of payment to me, 'to acknowledge the fracture in the family.' - Vernon said they were the defendant's words. Well, the fracture in the family certainly is one massive thing. 'But what about for the sexual assaults?' I snapped back angrily.

'Now Cleopatra, you have to understand the conditions upon which that offer is made,' Vernon said. 'There will be no admission of the allegations or guilt and there will need to be a confidentiality clause, of course. Oh, and all existing costs orders against Court Jester Solicitors in your favour will need to be dropped too.'

'No way. Are you joking? Why?' I complained.

His eyes cast low.

I went on, 'OK, tell him I reject that and here's my counter offer; damages, a written apology, no confidentiality agreement and I want my costs on top. Barnaby was an utter prick, which is why three separate judges reprimanded him on three separate occasions with orders for costs made against him personally.'

The mediator exited to relay my sentiments to the royal party. He eventually returned and explained, 'Confidentiality is number one to him and this could be a bridge too far. But he is happy to give a confidential apology, but we have a way to go on quantum.'

We discussed various offers and as the financial ping-pong ensued, Vernon returned saying, 'This is as high as he can go. I must say, he seems very genuine as he broke down crying in

front of me, explaining that he'll have to scrape together every
last cent he has to pay me. He even had to call his wife to get
the final approval for his latest upping of his offer to go on his
credit card.' Jesus wept as violins played.

'Bahahaha. That's too much to bear! Don't you understand
that this is a rich guy with no dependent children from a very
rich family? Don't be fooled by his crocodile tears!' I exclaimed,
but it was too late. The game of charades had started, and
there was no end in sight. I was the heartless wench bringing a
man to his knees in front of another man. But I know only too
well that men always support men, and it was clear that
Vernon had taken him under his wing and felt sorry for him.
That's the kind of impartiality that I'm used to from the law,
that right there! 'Oh, and he wants you to know that
he'spaying for this, not his parents.' As if that was meant to
comfort me, another lie somewhere on the Richter scale of
lies.

From this point on, Vernon saw me as the thorn in his side.
He became impatient with me and my barrister, Warbler,
didn't appear to do anything to counter this. Vernon was
annoyed that I kept separating the different costs orders,
maintaining that in agreements, its protocol that previous
orders be dropped. He refused to understand the intricacies of
my matter and seemingly couldn't deviate from the pro forma.
Two types of costs orders clearly threw him.

I then heard a loud whoosh, then a definitive click.

'Folks, we have to finish up for today as the air conditioner
has switched off and it's going to get uncomfortably hot in
here,' Vernon said. I thought to myself, Great, my life is being
determined by a pre-programmed air-conditioner timer. There
were no terms of settlement drawn up yet. There was no
evidence of the day's work. The air pressure was released

throughout the building and with that, the pressure to sign
evaporated through the ducts. My learned counsel had
intermittently read the newspaper throughout the afternoon
instead of drafting something or closing the gap on anything.

The mediator looked at me and said, 'So, do we have a
deal, Cleopatra?'

I retorted, 'No, we don't because the settlement can't be
inclusive of costs. For whose costs are we talking about? The
problem is that in my case, there are two separate costs orders
– those against the defendant and those against the defendant's
solicitor. If I settle with the defendant on the terms he's
seeking, all the costs orders previously made in my favour
against the defendant's solicitor would be lost too.' But
Barnaby and the cost orders made against him personally have
got nothing to do with the settlement between my cousin and
me, but Barnaby was desperate to ride on the coattails of the
settlement to avoid paying the three sets of costs orders against
him.

Vernon said, 'That's the deal, sorry. They're not going to
entertain anything more!'

As always, the substance and outcome of the mediation
must remain confidential, but what I can say is that there were
cross-party negotiations post-mediation, which led to a
resolution of the matter to my satisfaction; however, this
required extraordinary involvement by the mediator of the
likes I've never seen before. But that's not surprising when
everything in my case is unheard of and unprecedented.

Near the end of the day, Warbler attempted to provide a
new narrative about the sexual harassment, which went as
follows, 'Cleopatra, I've spoken to the mediator and you must
have misheard Barnaby as he was merely saying that games
like "strip chasey" and "spin the bottle" are normal childhood

games.' But that was rubbish and those games were not the subject of my matter in any event. I know what I heard thirty minutes ago; they all heard it. The bullshit 'passage of time' argument was not going to work for these lawyers this time! Everyone could remember what happened thirty minutes ago. It was an invitation to play from Barnaby Bustard-Braggart that I automatically declined but one that should not have been made by that wannabe cock in the first place, yet not one of those men in that room admonished him and that's the problem our society has. So-called 'Good' men don't do anything.

Then the landscape changed again when Warbler said to me, 'I want you to sleep on it and I don't want you to sign anything until after he's written his apology to you.' I told him I want to accept their latest offer and be done with it, but there was no lined paper or pen in sight.

Well, let me say that the wait for that apology wasn't worth it. The so-called apology was one of no apology, one that generally says, 'If you feel that I have done anything to you, then I am truly sorry for you feeling this way.' No original dunny paper on offer there. I did not need it anyway; I had the taped confession and that was his only true apology, the one he had made without reservation four and a half years earlier.

Weeks passed by while I waited for his 'apology' and for him to be reasonable about the Terms of Settlement. He sent drafts to me that completely deviated from our agreement on the day of mediation, with ridiculous riders added in by some non-lawyer who thought themselves as one – I suspect that Desdemona must have visited him. The new clauses were laughable. I wrote back with an ultimatum: the original verbal agreement, undrafted because of lazy counsel, or we're off to trial in April 2018! Take your pick!

Predictably, I received a phone call from Vernon and the matter finalised on my terms, but astonishingly, the role of the mediator morphed into one of personal secretary too.

'Cleopatra, would you like me to bank the cheque for you?' Vernon enquired.

'Oh, that would be great,' I said. 'That way, I don't have to worry about it going missing in the mail.'

'OK, who do you bank with?' he enquired.

'Westpac,' I said.

'Very well, I'm going to meet with King Claudius personally at lunchtime today to receive the cheque and then I'll drop by the bank for you. Can you email me your bank account details please?' I wondered why he was dealing with my cousin directly and not through my cousin's lawyer.

'Certainly. I really appreciate this, thank you', I said, utterly surprised.

The same mediator then bent over backwards for my cousin and me again, just six days later, for cheque number two. I've never known that this was the job description of a mediator – to do the parties' personal banking and to meet with the parties to receive settlement money. Had King Claudius and Vernon had a savoury bite together too – or unsavoury? Maybe I could have had him collect my dry cleaning too?

The Consent Orders were eventually signed on [DATE] 2017, and the County Court matter was withdrawn forthwith. Another hush money deal, the usual ending for a proactive victim of sex assault.

Cleopatra's Milk Bath

I began to make peace with my battle-weary self. Clever Cleopatra rested. I quietly sat in the garden. I stared at the sky. I looked at the peaceful clouds drift on by. The pace of my life needed to match nature again. I was so out of sync with everything.

I dashed upstairs and rummaged through Kate's drawers; Body Shop milk bath was the best thing going but even that seemed an indulgence compared to how I'd been living. I drew the line at her strawberry lip balm, but my life had been reduced to raiding a primary school girls beauty stock to feel good. I filled the bath and let the steam relax me. I promised myself that I would visit make up counters and get some quality products again soon, after I shaved my legs.

I threw myself into party mode for Christopher's 17th birthday. Life went on; there was still fun in the world. I wrapped up my legal matters for the Christmas break and started to decelerate. I didn't have the yoga poses or the alternative mantras, but Cleopatra calmed and finally slept deeply.

And then two weeks later after signing . . .

'Twas the night before Christmas when all through the house, not a creature was stirring, not even a mouse. The stockings were hung by the children with care, in hope that Saint Nicholas soon would be there. The children were nestled all snug in their beds, while visions of sugarplums danced in their heads, and Mama in her kerchief and I in my cap had just settled our brains for a long winter's nap when out on the lawn, there arose such a clatter. I sprang from the bed to see what was the matter . . .'[64]

whence came a letter from Barnaby Bastard-Braggart,

threatening to sue me for defamation on 22 December 2017. I wrote back[65] dispelling his claims of imputations to his character, for his character was already well-damaged and, in any event, he was the cause of his own strife.

And so, the Christmas story continued . . .

With a wink of his eye and a twist of his head, I soon gave me to know I had nothing to dread . . . I heard him exclaim ere he drove out of sight, 'Happy Christmas to all and to all a good night!'[66]

Peace at Christmas . . . finally. Cleopatra's battle armour was laid to rest for the last time.

We victims are forced to accept that we will be silenced at every juncture. It is only my fight to revoke the Suppression Order that allows me to even write this book; otherwise, my experiences could never be told. The best way to help my clients and other survivors is to tell my story so they can determine what their own story will be, in an informed way. Albeit forced to do it anonymously, I can assure you, there is no justice in the law.

Part 3

Our Injustice System

Chapter 18

How Does a Sad Story Like Mine Happen Today, in 2017?

During the Royal Commission into Institutional Responses to Child Sexual Abuse hearings in Rome, Cardinal Campeius told us that he was not very interested in Cardinal Carlisle's abuse in the Town of Travesty, in Western Victoria, when he said, 'It was a sad story, and it wasn't of much interest to me.'

My story is like many a story of childhood sexual abuse, a sad story of not much interest to anyone. How can this be so? Are we such an apathetic nation? Or just plain pathetic?

There are many people and processes I'd like to thank for the unjust outcome after four years of sexual abuse and a lifetime of trauma. Yes, I lay blame on the following: King Claudius, my family, the legal profession, the police, and the Catholic Church. One good man skittled early in the process, a fine Magistrate, H. Honour Woodpigeon, but even their hands were tied in the end. The remainder are a sorry bunch of inept individuals who neither have integrity nor take any responsibility for the mess I have found myself in instead of King Claudius, who was thrown a lifeline at every turn. King Claudius created this mess, but neither he nor anyone else is willing to clean it up and give me the apology and the slice of justice I so rightly deserve. Why?

There are such low conviction rates for cases that actually

make it to trial, it hardly appears worth it to report sexual abuse. Remember, only 3 per cent are found proved. How do offenders get away with it so regularly you might ask? The legal system almost seems designed to go off the rails at every step. I have drawn a flow chart[67] of sexual abuse and it has a bottleneck at every point.

It is often suggested that cases that don't proceed to prosecution are made up and, similarly, that men who are acquitted didn't do the crimes as alleged as the law proved they didn't. This is far from the case though and hides the true statistics of sex abusers percolating through our legal system. We know that many sex abusers often have numerous victims, are opportunistic, re-offend and often escape detection because of the significant delays in reporting child sexual abuse and the shame associated with reporting any sexual abuse, historic or otherwise. We also know that the majority of sexual abuse happens away from any institutional context: at home, at your neighbour's house, at your cousin's house, at your grandparents' house. So, whilst I agree that the Royal Commission into Institutional Responses to Child Sexual Abuse has a caused a terrific ripple effect in raising awareness of sexual abuse in the community generally, it is only the tip of the iceberg, in my opinion, and the ripple hasn't even hit the legal system yet in any real or encouraging way. Rather, it's met with a dam wall carefully constructed and maintained by the police and the legal profession daily.

Senator Derryn Hinch has been pushing for a national public database of child sex offenders for years and, since becoming a senator, has introduced legislation to confiscate all passports of registered sex offenders to stop the child sexual abuse holidays so common particularly across South East Asia. Action, swift and effective. In the same way, we need to change all the laws around sexual abuse as they are completely inadequate as they currently stand. Derryn Hinch keeps banging on and I'm certain he will work hard to turn the recommendations made by the Royal Commission into law.

A number of writers have written much about how hopelessly our adversarial system deals with victims of childhood sexual assault and how the evidentiary problems that arise provide fertile ground for character assassination of victims and findings of 'not guilty.' And this is a critical point. We keep letting the offenders get away with it and are far too soft on them on the occasions when they are convicted. This just condones their behaviour and creates a legal culture whereby defendants have a bank of lawyers to choose from, ready to get them off, to secure their legal reputation for being a shrewd lawyer. The truth is that almost any lawyer can get you off. The courts don't want to punish you; there aren't enough jails, and many don't consider sexual assault a crime. Just look at the case law, not from 1850 or 1950 but from the current day, 2018. It's shameful.

When the law works its working day, I suspect that all its legal players are satisfied. They do not feel that any injustice has been done. They proffer comments such as 'That's the best outcome we could have expected' and 'You were never going to get a better decision from that judge'. One barrister even told me, 'Put your lawyer hat on, Cleopatra, 'coz I don't do emotion.' Through tears, I told him, 'Please understand. I'm a client today.' Arrogant, self-important counsel talked on, disturbingly unaffected. I do not believe that to be a good lawyer, one should or needs to emotionally shut down at all. This is a misnomer proffered by legal practitioners regularly. It is also characteristic of sociopaths whose emotional intelligence, I say, is on the same scale as those who kill. I really do question the emotional intelligence of a sizable percentage of the Bar and honestly wonder about their sociopathic tendencies, feeding their often arrogant and offensive behaviour towards clients: clients who talk common sense, an oft-forgotten language to most lawyers; lawyers who walk away from court mocking clients for being normal people with normal emotional responses.

I'll never forget the Committal Hearing in one of my husband's matters, involving intergenerational abuse by a clean-shaven, tanned grandfather who retained his relatively good looks, sitting smug in the dock, after his daughter had given evidence against him. During negotiations outside the courtroom, defence counsel and the prosecutor commented on her attitude and suspected agenda when she said angrily from the witness box to the magistrate, 'I've been waiting for this day for a long time.' Of course, she had been waiting for this day to come, but her confidence, attitude, barbed tongue and young age - illustrative of a brash, fearless young woman - attracted immediate criticism and suspicion from those most learned. Again, female confidence equals vengefulness and the law and its players pounced on it in their usual patronising fashion.

I consider that childhood sexual abuse is the worst crime a victim could endure as with murder, a victim is dead and the suffering shifts to the victim's family. So, the legal system expects a victim to cope with the ongoing effects of child sexual abuse and then cope with a legal process that doesn't work – and only on the rare occasions that the police decide to prosecute.

I walk around on court days in my own matter asking myself, Does anyone care about what happened to me in this place?I look at the coat of arms; I look at the stage that is the courtroom: cold, austere, harsh, just like a church. I'm not in awe of either institution, I'm afraid. Every time I enter and sit in the front row in the client seat, I leave crying, feeling utterly disrespected and devalued. Why is it that other routine matters get so much more court time in comparison? The courts hear lengthy pleas all day long and the bench seems to listen intently, affording the defendant and their lawyer respect at every turn. This doesn't happen for me. I am yet to see a defendant cry like me, the plaintiff, even when they're in the dock or are taken to the cells. Don't they feel the pain of injustice against them? Or is it the cool, calculated calm of justice they feel that stops their tears, for they did the crime alleged?

On 13 April 2017 at the Modern Prosecutor Conference held in Melbourne, the Honourable Justice Peter McClellan, AM, made the following comments about our criminal justice system:

'There are likely to be some, perhaps many, practitioners and judges who are resistant to change . . . It has been suggested that the Commission's work has had such a transformative effect on the mind of the general community that it is now much more difficult to secure an acquittal in relation to child sexual offences. The data tells a different story.'[68]

Furthermore, Justice McClellan refers to statistics that reveal that conviction rates are lower than ever before. Why have they dropped? If more people are coming forward, where's the evidence that the system is finally working for the victims? Why aren't perpetrators being held accountable yet? In my opinion, they remain at liberty as the judiciary and the parole board keep letting them off the hook and so do most police. It's not a question of whether they do; it's a question of why they do.

The much-anticipated Interim Recommendations of the Royal Commission into Institutional Responses to Child Sexual Abuse were released on 14 August 2017 in the form of the Criminal Justice Report.[69] It makes some commendable observations and recommendations, including that the criminal offence of 'failure to report' should apply in relation to knowledge gained or suspicions that are or should have been formed, in whole or in part, on the basis of information disclosed in or in connection with a religious confession. Another is the need for the police and OPP to better inform victims throughout the process and to provide a complaints procedure. Another is that the laws governing the admissibility of tendency and coincidence evidence in prosecutions for child sexual abuse offences should be reformed to facilitate greater admissibility and cross-admissibility of tendency and coincidence evidence and joint trials. Another is that tendency or coincidence evidence about a defendant in a child sexual offence prosecution should not be required to be proved beyond reasonable doubt. All to be applauded.

However, the Commission falls short of recommending a single key factor in the provision of true justice: providing complainants with their own independent lawyer. Stakeholder and individual submissions made to the Royal Commission included the following where sexual assault is concerned: switching to an inquisitorial model, a model based on the International Criminal Court, providing victims with legal representation or creating statutory victims' advocates and giving victims enforceable legal rights. However, the Royal Commission's response to such suggestions was as follows:

'We conclude that while there are aspects of the system that can be improved to better meet the needs of survivors, a major structural change to the role of the victim in the criminal justice system is not required or recommended. Our recommendations throughout this report, if implemented, will significantly improve the criminal justice system's response to victims and survivors of child sexual abuse.'[70]

Whilst I am certainly supportive of the recommendations that it makes, it does not go anywhere near far enough. A 'softly, softly' approach is too slow and denies the basic injustice of having one party completely unrepresented simply for the sake of the status quo. As I have said elsewhere in this book and publicly for years, how can one still justify one party being unrepresented in a legal matter? Their recommending giving all victims an information pack on the criminal justice process, including on trials, tends to suggest that complainants do need legal advice, by their own admissions.

Complainants are certainly a party to the proceeding, just not a recognised party with rights and we pretend to scratch our heads, wondering why so many trials are unsuccessful in securing a conviction. An interested party is not a party to the proceeding; one must first be joined to the proceeding to have any real position. It is manifestly unjust and, frankly, insulting to recommend we maintain the status quo and that the system will work with a few tweaks here and there. It's saying, 'Let's give complainants a show bag, in essence, with information brochures, court stickers, agency referrals, sticky notes, a pen from the OPP and sample tissues from Kleenex.'

The criminal jurisdiction is so suspiciously desperate to defy the current fact that all parties need to be independently legally represented. That old thinking simply must go. Complainants don't need another friendly hand-holder or a dog to pat in the court room provided by the State; they need a lawyer. Anything less is a legal nonsense.

Chapter 19

Fact versus Fiction

Crime dramas from America, the UK and Australia have romanticized criminal law; they have made it look exciting and even sexy. Law remains a top career pick for our bright, aspiring school students. My eyes roll again. Home-grown shows like Rake and Janet King have made lawyering look attractive, entertaining and intellectually challenging. I say being a lawyer attracts unwarranted respect much of the time. It's frustrating, not stimulating. It's archaic, not progressive. Its reactive, not proactive. Your quest for justice and to make the world better day by day, if that were ever one's intent, is completely fettered by the police, the judiciary, opposing counsel and majority solicitors who have simply 'checked out'. I'm afraid to say that I believe that for most of my colleagues, it seems that becoming a lawyer is what they set out to achieve and they'll happily live off the kudos of that, never mind about what the practise of it amounts to and who they become in the process. They'll claw onto the retention of wigs to hide the vacuum between their ears.

The truth is that there are many lawyers who behave just like Rake and the bench tolerates them and they even win favour with the bench for being foppish, unprepared fools – but only if you're male, I might add, with all due respect. I am always concerned when young aspiring law students and work-experience students tell me they are interested in practising in criminal law. If they only knew that it means working for maintaining the status quo, giving a defence to what should often be indefensible crimes, or maybe they know but believe they should be assisted to get away with their crimes and find that stimulating. Or maybe they believe in the old chestnut 'innocent till proven guilty'. My belief in this lasts the length of the movie Shawshank Redemption[71], an all-time favourite of mine. No one wants an innocent man denied his freedom – and especially when it's Morgan Freeman. Is the real-life actor innocent in his real life though? Sadly, news reports since that movie was made, claim he's yet another Hollywood sex offender.

In my opinion, this legal foundation stone 'innocent till proven guilty' is an outdated mantra that should not be used in criminal law today because the standard of proof required, 'beyond all reasonable doubt', makes it virtually impossible to prove. Innocent men aren't going to jail – far from it. Guilty men aren't going to jail much of the time either and when they do, they're out on parole before you know it. Sitting in the County Court for a week will convince you undoubtedly; even a day's observation should do the trick.

I think most matters that make it into a courtroom these days are all cases where the accused is most likely guilty and would be found so if we had a lower standard of proof. There are so many professional and legal sieves that strain out the false reports at the police investigation stage and preliminary court hearings that what remains are the criminals almost certainly guilty of their crimes as alleged and a courtroom full of professionals with a sympathetic ear to the perpetrator instead of the victim. It's almost a case of any plea will do these days because it's a legal game and the best of the profession seemingly love playing it. For there lies their intellectual challenge, so it seems, keeping the bad guys at liberty with a quick plea from the book of 'Any plea will do'. From where I'm sitting, there's not much intellectual rigour in that.

In cases of serious, indictable crime, I say that this is utterly deplorable. I am surprised that there hasn't been a serious vigilante revolt against our legal system. It's so bad right here in Australia, the lucky country, where on average one woman per week is killed by their current or former partner and, allegedly, we don't know how to stop it. It's just ridiculous denial and inaction from those who have the power to change it. I know how to stop it and so do they. If all men treated girls and women and their own daughters like the late Anthony Foster, family violence would eventually be a thing of the past. Bills can be passed and new legislation can be enacted overnight. Unfortunately, the men and women who resist stand to lose money, prestige and votes, so we're left with glorious inaction and a Prime Minister who consistently says nothing about family violence, which is arguably the greatest problem that Australia faces. Solving family violence would also positively impact on the nation's rampant drug abuse and reduce the need to turn to substances for relief from emotional pain. It would undoubtedly help curb our growing suicide rate.

The show Broadchurch[72] was hugely popular here in Australia. David Tennant is fabulous as Detective Inspector Alec Hardy and the character he plays in that show is arguably a better performance than his role as the Doctor in Doctor Who[73]. But let's be clear that both are fictional characters and in real life, detectives like that are so rare they are almost extinct. I can think of two: former Detective Andrew Aguecheek and Detective Stephen Adams of Victoria Police. After that, I draw a blank.

Chapter 20

Relationship between the Police and the OPP:
Official Perpetrator Protection!

For a lawyer to do less than his utmost is, I strongly feel, a betrayal of his client. Though in criminal trials, one tends to focus on the defence attorney and his client, the accused, the prosecutor is also a lawyer and he too has a client: the People. And the People are equally entitled to their day in Court, to a fair and impartial trial, and to justice.[74]
— Vincent Bugliosi, Helter Skelter: The True Story of the
   Manson Murders

Somewhere, lurking in the grey area at the bottom of the swamp, Lake Provincial, found somewhere between your local SOCIT Unit, the OPP and the Vatican, are the statements of truth we're looking for. A victim's statement to the police is the only truth in a courtroom. In the shredder bin of the local Conservative Town cop shop or the OPP office are pages of truth, hidden from view, denied oxygen at all costs. The senior police in Conservative Town certainly have a lot to answer for, as does the Vatican.

But fine Sgt Stephen Adams is fighting the good fight and he observed the link between suicide and clergy sexual abuse long ago in this Conservative Town hotspot for suicide, but he was met with fierce opposition internally and faced social isolation. The invites to police BBQs and dinners stopped. Adams was treated like Det Sgt Aguecheek was in Sunraysia over clergy sexual abuse – completely professionally ostracised.

Copies of the pages of truth of clergy abuse were kept, locked away somewhere in the OPP and the Vatican under files probably labelled 'Special Issues Committee' or 'Cardinal Bourchier — Conservative Town', 'Bishop of Ely — Conservative Town', or even 'Cardinal Campeius — Conservative Town'. I doubt that anyone in the Vatican would need to have looked up Conservative Town on the map. In an organised paedophile ring, the locations are chosen carefully. I suspect that men like Luke Fang and Dr Butts have acted as 'special ministers' for the church in a way, eliminating any impediments to the paedophile operation. Police like Adams are a fly in the ointment.

No one is privy to communication between the OPP and the local police station. What goes on between those offices and officers remains a mystery and in whose interests is that mystery preserved, I ask. When I applied for a copy of the pretext call under Freedom of Information and subpoenaed the police file in my matter, I never received any internal communication from either the OPP or Victoria Police. Their communications, decision making and reasoning for their inaction, delay and withdrawal of all charges remain a mystery. Even the logbook entries are mostly redacted. What privileged information about my matter lies under those numerous lines blacked out in black texter? Nothing honourable, I'm sure. Mistakes covered up under the guise of privilege. Mistakes that one has no forum to question no matter how rich you are.

What's equally disturbing is the current approach of policing when it comes to childhood sexual abuse today. It's as if the Special Issues Committee is still operating here in

Conservative Town, alive and well, hiding and delaying, considering the findings of the IBAC Inquiry in 2016. It seems that despite the spin and the push in the media, the police have been ineffectual in bringing perpetrators of sexual abuse to the court's attention. SANO takes a long time before arresting, interviewing and charging any alleged sex offender compared to other criminals. My clients are always expectedly anxious and fragile and as the days pass, their despair grows. The state of my client complainants against various clergy is testament to this grand plan; one has since died and the other has recently spent time in jail. The church knows that delay works and, unfortunately, delay is condoned by the criminal justice system.

I remember a conversation I had with SANO Sr Det Edward Davy in Feb 2016, where he told one of my clients that a particular priest would be charged in four weeks and I told him that I did not believe him. I asked him if he realised that clients take those dates literally as they need something to hope for. They literally mark it on their calendar and live for the day to come. He shouldn't tell them a date he can't keep to as it's very difficult to manage their expectations, particularly as we're talking about a seriously suicidal client base here. I know.

My client had a female abuser from the clergy too, an evil nun by the name of Sister Sycorax from St Simeon, who has not been charged and whom I understand gave a 'no comment' interview. Again, for what purpose did she avail herself of her right to silence? On church legal advice? Why do the church lawyers give that advice? I wonder whether she goes to confession and whether she's admitted to sexually abusing little boys, my clients, whilst married to Christ. Adulterous old nun. If paedophilia isn't a crime or a sin under canon law, adultery is by the church's own admission and design. Isn't it still one of the Ten Commandments? I no longer have a Bible to check.

I often wonder why that evil nun has still not been charged. Do the police consider her too old to prosecute, or does her habit give her an untouchable status? I say that she needs to be brought to justice no matter how old she is or who she is. If she's fit enough to ride her bike around Conservative Town at liberty, as she's been seen to do, she's fit enough to plead and stand trial! Who in Conservative Town decided that she should get away with her crimes? Someone in the Conservative Town Catholic Boy's Club, no doubt. That's how this town works, after all.

Chapter 21

Legal Conundrums

The famous Mars Bar is a highly valued commodity worldwide and in Conservative Town. Conservative Town police cars arrive at Coles Supermarket in a cavalcade to catch the Mars Bar thief, a hungry man caught red-handed with a few grocery items hidden in her jacket. It happens daily, petty crime. Stealing is wrong, I agree, but this is the crime that's easy to process and police love it. Invariably, they manage to get it right and seemingly always have the resources for it. Coles get their goods returned; the shoplifter is arrested and is taken off to the custody suite and the Conservative Town Magistrates' Court urgently. Daily legal process. The community is kept safe and in check. God forbid Coles were to lose money and not be restored their property.

However, where's the law and order where serious crime to the person is concerned? There isn't any. To say that there is much room for improvement when it comes to the practise of law in the area of serious, indictable crime like rape and murder is a whopping great understatement. For starters, victims are seldom restored to their pre-crime state. Police often don't arrive, or they arrive too late. When police do prosecute, the judiciary find in favour of the defendant and through their ominous and repeated warnings, so does the jury. Society protests at the disparity between the crime and the sentence given. Victims' families lament at perpetrators being let out on parole before they themselves are even at stage two of the grief cycle with their counsellor.

I think it's important to look closely at what goes on in the courts for victims of serious crime in both criminal and civil jurisdictions. I will now outline the legal landmines that keep victims forever victims of the system, albeit survivors of sexual abuse.

In the Case of Criminal Matters

Party to the proceeding

In criminal matters, it is the State or the Crown that prosecutes the matter against the accused. The victim of crime is currently not a party to the proceeding at all and is not mentioned in the case citation. The effect of this is more than literal though, for it has practical consequences that are detrimental to the victim.

I say that the victim should be immediately joined as a party to the criminal proceeding. They should be a party on paper and in practise. They should receive every piece of paper in the matter: the police brief, witness statements, photographs, CCTV footage, court orders, correspondence and copies of all charges. Everything that the defence lawyers are currently entitled to have under the Evidence Act[75] should also be available to the victim and their lawyer, the lawyer I claim they should be allowed to have and should be entitled to now.

In my criminal matter, there was a Suppression Order made of which I was subject to, yet I was never served with or given a copy of it at any time. The first time I saw it was by chance after I won my Application to Revoke a Suppression Order, well after my criminal case had ended. When I applied for the audio recording of my proceeding and was told I could not have it as there was a Suppression Order in place, I was shocked and realised that I needed to apply forthwith to try to have it removed. Under my Freedom of Information application, I was finally given a copy of the Order. If I had not wanted to speak up about my matter to the newspaper, I would never have known what the Order consisted of, nor would I have known that the Suppression Order was still in place, long after the case had been withdrawn by the Crown. In fact, the Order would have gagged me for life without me knowing as it was made 'Until further Order'. It's fair to assume that the chances of me breaching that Order unknowingly would have been extremely high over my lifetime, knowing my mouth and my quest for social justice.

The point is, how can you have an Order made that places conditions on a complainant victim and yet that person is not given a copy of the Order at any stage? My knowledge of the Suppression Order simply rested on my general knowledge; I did not know the specific conditions of it and what it specifically prohibited, and I didn't know that I was specifically named on it. It was only after I saw it, after my case was over, that I realised what type of suppression order it was and what conditions I'd been subjected to and still was subjected to despite the criminal case being well and truly over. I consider this to be legally untenable and bizarre.

The sad reality is that I could have breached it at any time without knowing. Could I say something privately but not publicly about my case or nothing at all? Could I speak of but not print my views? Could I say anything I liked but just not name him? Could I only say something anonymously and not even mention my own name? How can a complainant possibly know this without seeing the Order and the conditions of the Order?

Why has no great legal mind thought of this before? Why does the Open Courts Act (2013) not make provision for the service of the Suppression Order on complainants? This is because the supposed intent of the legislation, to encourage and not fetter freedom of speech, is at cross purposes with the practise and procedures of the Act. Like Intervention Orders, Suppression Orders have now become a tool used to protect the wrongdoer rather than provide protection to the victim. Ignore the politically correct spin and perhaps listen to me or Sen Derryn Hinch when it comes to the truth about Suppression Orders. It's still about gagging the victim under the guise of protecting the victim without the victim knowing. That is paternalistic and patronising and, I say, should be considered legally untenable.

The victim's right to a lawyer

Currently, the victim does not have legal representation, independent or otherwise. There is no one legally advising the victim throughout the criminal process at any point.

The OPP is only instructed by the police informant, not the victim of crime. The victim is merely a police witness in the police case against the defendant, only called upon when and if decided by the police. The victim has no control over the case and their wishes are not paramount and are seldom considered in any decision making. If the police and or OPP want the case dropped but the victim doesn't, it's a case of 'Too bad, victim'. Sometimes the wishes of the police and the victim do dovetail, but most often, they do not.

The truth is that the aim of the office of the OPP and aim of the victim can often be quite different. The police may wish to secure numerous charges against a defendant and there might be multiple complainants, yet the police are often only interested in the more serious charges. This can mean that your complaint is completely ignored, or your charges are dropped during their bargaining process with defence counsel and the allegations of other complainants are still pursued. For example, it's often more important to secure the charge of rape in one matter against a defendant than indecent assault against the same defendant in another matter. In this way, sexual offending is standardised and prioritised according to the police mandate and OPP office policy at the time. The crimes against you will likely be minimised in the process and dropped more often than not. In this way, one victim may be bargained against another victim. The problem is that victims don't grade their abuse against other victims though as all abuse is traumatising and no one is less important or severe, only to the police.

The truth is that the offending against you may not be of police interest beyond you making a statement. I suspect that most victims do not work at gaining the courage to report the crime simply to report it to police for the record, so to speak. I suspect that most like me, expect a response commensurate with the crime. I say that in crimes of sexual assault, this should surely mean police action and court convictions most of the time. After all, its second to murder in terms of serious crime. Yet so many cases that are reported to the SOCIT unit get dropped. So many family law clients who raise and report abuse of their children by a parent or relative complain that the police and courts largely ignore their concerns or investigate, but the sexual abuse goes unpunished and they are left to pick up the pieces.

OPP assistance such as their victim support service does not help victims substantively. Offering court support, essentially hand-holding and passing tissues, masks the reality that victims are on their own at court. Their family may come and the court network ladies are there to sit next to you and offer a cup of tea, but where is that victim legally? Who is advocating for them in that courtroom? No one is the truthful answer.

Most victims do not understand what is said by lawyers and the magistrate or judge in a courtroom, nor the significance of same. Even as a lawyer, I could not follow it at times, nor could my criminal lawyer husband. I verily believe that most victims would want their matter to proceed at court once they'd reported it, so if the police determine not to proceed, which happens at an alarming rate, this can cause real emotional harm to complainants. The victim should have a lawyer of their own who can advocate for them and argue why, for example, the Committal should proceed in the same way that a defence lawyer can argue that charges should be dropped.

In the Royal Commission into Institutional Responses to Child Sexual Abuse, all complainants were funded by the State to be legally represented if they so wished. This representation masks the reality of how the justice system really works though because complainants are always unrepresented, but when the law is on show, it's obviously important to disguise the harsh reality of the position of victims. I suspect that very few cases would succeed in a criminal jurisdiction that were the subject of that Royal Commission, but we will soon see. Those that have succeeded are mostly where the defendant pleaded guilty in any event, like Cardinal Carlisle's matters. Any successful outcome because of the confession of the defendant is far different from the outcomes in the face of a defendant's denial and the legal system should not get a pat on the back when a defendant pleads guilty. After all, 97 per cent of the time, the system works in favour of the defendant.

The fact is that victim complainants know how to survive not telling. They have practised that every day since the abuse. On average, it takes thirty-three years to tell. It's surviving after telling that's the harder thing to do, especially when your expectation of a concerned and appropriate response is met with ignorance and inaction. Being disrespected all over again is a bitter pill to swallow and has you living in an undefined grey area that is worse than the dark hole you were in before. At least then, you knew you were in a hole; you knew the size of the hole and that it was black in there. When you enter the enter the legal arena, it's fifty million shades of grey.

Victim's right to private prosecution

The victim should be entitled to prosecute the matter privately at their own expense if they so wish, especially where the OPP drop the matter at their whim or initially refuse to prosecute. The police dropped my case, but their reasons for doing so are unacceptable to me, which is completely unsatisfactory and reeks of something very fishy. I would have loved the opportunity to instruct a barrister to argue or have myself argue why the committal should proceed. I knew every legal argument, but I was not in a position to say anything other than during the platform I spontaneously created for myself when addressing the court on the issue of diversion.

This is not right and is manifestly unjust. I should be able to fight for my life and truth just as the accused can fight to deny it. No one should be in a begging position, begging for the police to prosecute. The complainant should not be on the back foot at all, ever. Why do we tolerate such injustice in the year 2018? It doesn't have to be this way. We need legislative change.

Victim's right of appeal

The OPP should be answerable to someone, being a government body, but in fact, they are answerable to no one. At the time of writing, and when I gave my Statement to the Royal Commission, they didn't even have a complaints form. That's rather telling in of itself. What other government department doesn't have a complaints form, a complaints officer and a complaints hotline? Isn't that the stuff of government agencies; surveys and consultants presenting agency data each year? Ordinarily, government departments are structured this way to ensure that their policies and procedures are met and that they maintain the perception of same. So why not for the great almighty OPP? I understand that they now have one – after the recommendations were made by the Royal Commission. Bravo!

In my matter, I wrote to the DPP, the Attorney General and the Ombudsman. The Ombudsman couldn't help me as they don't deal with individual cases. The Attorney General at the time, the Honourable Robert Clark, MP, said he does not have the power to enquire into the prosecutorial discretion of the OPP. His Chief of Staff, Ross Rugby, wrote to me on his behalf in July 2014:

It would not be appropriate for the Attorney-General or his office to comment on the DPP's exercise of prosecutorial discretion in relation to your matter. The DPP is an independent statutory office holder, who is not subject to direction by the Attorney-General or executive government.

The Attorney-General does not have the power to effect decisions of the DPP or to investigate complaints relating to the DPP's handling of individual cases.[76]

The DPP Edmond Friarbird said he was satisfied with the OPP's decision to withdraw the initial (rape) charges and the remaining (unlawful assault) charge. The legal term for withdrawing a case is the Latin phrase 'nolle prosequi', meaning 'be unwilling to pursue.' That leaves a victim silenced and with nowhere to go in terms of criminal justice. Interestingly, the entry of a nolle prosequi is not an acquittal and the defendant may still be re-indicted on the same charge. Of greater interest still, the magistrate was willing to pursue it at Committal but not the OPP in full knowledge of the magistrate's views, which is rather confusing.

Moreover, Friarbird's letter does not mention the discretion his office has to re-charge him with the correct charges, as the magistrate had suggested they do. This is quite legally unsound to have an untouchable government office. The politics behind this chasm of a legal loophole is rather telling. Even defendants have a right of appeal, all the way to the High Court, often funded by the taxpayer via legal aid. How is it that Adrian Bayley, killer of Jill Meagher, can fight for his rights, funded by the taxpayer, all the way to the High Court and I can't fight for mine at all, even privately, at the lowest Magistrates' Court level? That utterly offends me as a tax-paying, law-abiding citizen and as a victim and as a lawyer.

The legal concept of doli incapax should be repealed

Today it's fair to say that almost every fully cognisant 14-year-old knows the wrongness of their actions. The Children's Court is clogged with children committing offences knowingly. In any event, it's currently a rebuttable presumption, so there can hardly be a blanket reliance on it other than by lazy lawyers at the OPP, who bend over for the defence counsel at mere mention of it.

Moreover, times have changed since the concept of doli incapax was introduced in the Crimes Act (1914), a time when children were much more naïve, without television, mobile phones, or social media and much less worldly wise.

Section 4N of the <u>Crimes Act</u> (Cth.) 1914 deals with crimes committed by children over 10 but under 14 years as follows:

A child aged 10 years or more but under 14 years old can only be liable for an offence against a law of the Commonwealth if the child knows that his or her conduct is wrong.

The question whether a child knows that his or her conduct is wrong is one of fact. The burden of proving this is on the prosecution.

It is arguable that a great many of today's 14-year-olds are akin to an 18-year-old person, an adult, back then. The law needs to recognise a 14-year-old for who they are today and the general knowledge they have today. The law still says a child is a child until the age of 18, but in the case of committing serious criminal acts against the person, one should not uphold an outdated notion of what a 14-year-old is in either the criminal or family law stream in the Children's Court. Otherwise, it's like saying no to your 14-year-old child who wants to go to a matinee movie with friends because they're unchaperoned.

Furthermore, I say that given that the law has recently changed to recognise the requisite intent behind children committing criminal terrorist acts, which received much publicity and little dissent from legal circles, it should in terms of sexual assault as well. What's the problem? What's the difference in mens rea between a 14-year-old knowingly raping someone in an alley and a 14-year-old knowingly blowing up a pedestrian on a street with his home-made bomb? My cousin Decius blew up a bridge with a home-made bomb as a teenager and he knew what he was doing was wrong, just like King Claudius. The law is unjustifiably inconsistent in its application here.

Doli incapax was abolished in England and Wales in 1998 but persists in other common law jurisdictions, including in Australia. At the time of writing, there is debate about the continuance of doli incapax as a defense in Australia and opinion from stakeholders such as Victoria Legal Aid and private defence lawyers has been sought. In the 1993 shocking UK murder case of James Bulger, the toddler who was murdered by two children, John Venables and Robert Thompson, it was obvious that children can hold the knowledge that what they are doing is wrong, and they were found guilty of murder. Murder is a crime with serious consequences. The cruel and deadly intent of these children made worldwide news. No one can tell me that those evil children didn't intend on killing the little toddler James Bulger, no matter how intelligently and legally one looks at that case. Likewise, no one can convince me that they didn't know that killing was wrong because they were children under 14 years of age.

Looking at those child killers' faces, I am reminded of my discussions in Criminology tutorials, in my days at Traditional University in 1992 and 1993, about varying theories of criminality. I remember laughing at ideas such as criminals having identifiable physical features such as close-set eyes and large protruding foreheads. I remember thinking of The

Omen[77], a popular movie in the 1980s in Australia, and noted that the killer child Robert Thompson looked much like the child actor in Damien: Omen II in his role as Damien, the antichrist. Whilst I maintain my belief in the criminal mind having little to do with inherited physical appearance, I do think the urge to hunt, hurt, stalk and kill is strongly and inherently male. I think it has less to do with environment and upbringing and more to do with genetics. Obviously, women and girls can also hurt and kill, and I acknowledge that they do so but in a very small percentage compared to men and boys. I know I'm probably in a minority on this, but we need to be asking why.

The defendant's right to silence should be repealed

When a defendant has admitted the offending to the police or in a pretext call (taped confession), the defendant should lose their right to silence. They should not be able to revert to saying nothing after they've already recently admitted to it. A common-sense approach suggests that they wouldn't admit it and then deny it, unless the law provided them with that nonsensical option, which it currently does.

Furthermore, I do not think that the defendant should have a right to silence at all. Why don't they give interviews where they immediately profess that they didn't do it if they didn't do it, like I would? I'd be desperate to say, 'No, I never did that!' or the like. What is it about denying a crime that makes everyone so worried legally? No matter how one asks the question, if you didn't commit a crime as alleged, you're never going to admit to it unless you are unfit mentally or you did it. So why the legal advice to remain silent? Why is this played out day after day? Moreover, if he had to deny it every time he was asked and give his reasons why every time, he could then be judged for his 'inconsistencies' between each denial the same way we do for complainants.

The defendant's right to make a 'no comment' interview should be repealed

When a defendant has admitted the offending to the police or in a pretext call (taped confession), the defendant should lose their right to make a 'no comment' interview thereafter. Otherwise, their denial is incongruous with their contemporaneous admissions.

The defendant should have to make a plea

When a defendant has admitted the offending to the police during an interview or in a pretext call (taped confession), the defendant should lose their right to not have to make a plea. They should not have the luxury of deciding this after the committal has run and they have been afforded the luxury of seeing the strength of the case against them. In other words, if they admit to doing it, they should then have to plead guilty and at the earliest opportunity. After all, no one would admit to offending if they didn't commit the crime as alleged. I also think that its farcical that so many plead guilty later along in the criminal proceedings, after complainants have already been put through a committal hearing and even a trial.

A defendant should not have a right to pull the pin by pleading guilty when they choose to so late in a proceeding. All the legal incentives to encourage an early plea of guilt should not be required as it's insulting to complainants. I often see criminals who have no remorse wait until the last minute to change their plea to guilty. Excuses are made such as 'She's just lying', 'That boy's lying – he misbehaves at school and is an attention seeker', or 'The court will believe her, so I'll just plead guilty anyway.' Or excuses like 'I was told I had to plead guilty by that lawyer because he said I wouldn't be able to win it. The court would believe her, so I needed to plead guilty to get a lesser penalty'.

All this tells me is that sociopaths have a beautiful way of turning all fault back on the victim – for the offending and their sentence. There is never any room for self-reflection or anything that would illicit feelings of guilt. They don't feel guilt, ever.

Committal Hearings

The OPP should not have the power to prevent a committal hearing from running when a defendant has admitted the offending to the police or in a pretext call (taped confession). It is the victim's right for the evidence to be tested by a magistrate to determine if there is a case to answer. The OPP should not have the power to override this for their own undisclosed reasons as that's where corruption breeds.

Furthermore, I don't see why in the above circumstances, where there's admissions, the matter should not just proceed straight to a trial. What reason could the OPP have for not allowing the trial to proceed? When the magistrate has already given the sentencing indication that there be a conviction, with a good behaviour bond or community service, fines, etc., there can be no costs argument put that the State is put to the wasted cost of running a matter that's unlikely to win. After all, the magistrate has just declared that there is a case to answer.

Pretext Calls

When a defendant admits to the offending on a pretext call, the admission should be enough for the matter to proceed. This is particularly relevant in historic sexual assault matters, where there is usually little or no supporting evidence other than a confession made during a pretext call.

On the day the OPP withdrew my matter, despite the taped confession obtained during the pretext call, I was told that in my matter, it was not enough that I spoke of him sexually abusing me as a child. I was told that I needed to have gone into the specifics of the offending when I called him rather than keeping it general.

There should be a guide to making pretext calls but there isn't. So, I have made one for people considering making one before they make the same mistakes I did and it's rendered useless. The police told me that they cannot assist in any way; otherwise, the call becomes inadmissible. That's fair enough, but this means many victims will engage in this process by opting to make a pretext call and it will likely bear no fruit as they are unaware of what they are meant to ask and say. If they were legally represented, complainants could be informed about pretext calls by their lawyer without raising inadmissibility issues in that the police are meant to be neutral and cannot assist witnesses in obtaining their evidence. I do not think police should have anything to do with it. The complainant's lawyer, if they had one, could do their job and the police could do theirs without parties being at cross purposes, avoiding all possibility of conflict of interest and vital evidence protected from the risk of being deemed inadmissible.

There is no risk to the defendant in the same way at any stage in the criminal process. They are legally advised at every

point about the best way to do something. This is completely
unjust when one considers the position of the victim in
contrast. In addition, the police then use that pretext call to
question the complainant rather than to question the
defendant, who may opt not to be questioned in any event,
another indulgence given to them. So, the pretext call almost
becomes something to trip up the complainant, whereby
judgements are made about their memory and their reliability
as a witness. The complainant also does not receive a copy of
the call, so their recollection is the only thing they have. This
means the evidence is stacked against them from the
beginning. Who on earth designed this woeful state of affairs?
Men who distrust women who are deemed untrustworthy by
men by virtue of their gender alone? There seems to be an
undercurrent of suspicion towards women and children that
men don't face.

Statements to Police

The issue of not particularising the statement enough was
raised with me by the OPP two days before the committal
hearing (nearly one year after my statement was made) and
was used as a supposed basis for the OPP to want to withdraw
the matter. It was never raised as an issue with me any earlier.
In fact, the police and OPP had told me I have a 'strong case'
with the taped confession, which is great because historic
abuse can be extremely hard to prove. In hindsight, I now say
it's near impossible to prove sexual assault beyond all
reasonable doubt.

If this is even true of my Statement, that it lacked sufficient
detail, I say that the statements made to police should be
checked over thoroughly and close to the time they are made

so that any additions or corrections to the Statement or adjustments to the resulting charges are made in a timely manner. Alternatively, Statements could be made with their lawyer instead, if they had one, on affidavit and then taken to the police station. This would ensure that the Statement is full of particulars such as dates, times, places, is in chronological order and does not miss relevant events through the stressful circumstances of telling a stranger at the police station on the spot, with likely PTSD and memory loss at play.

I do this with my clients now – I never send them to the police station to make their statements, ever. There should be considerable time spent on the Statement with a person they've built a trusted relationship with to ensure it is comprehensive. This will give it the best chance of charges being laid and in turn secure a prosecution and conviction more often.

I was told by the solicitor at the OPP that in my case, a problem arose regarding my statement as there were uncharged acts. This means that the police had failed to make charges regarding some of the offences I alleged and told me that this meant that my statement was problematic. Again, another problem created by the police, not me. Surely, if there are uncharged acts, the police can just bring further charges; it happens in courts every day across the country. My husband deals with this very thing day in day out. To not do so is just further evidence of lazy policing or a political agenda at the OPP at cross purposes with its aim of bringing justice to victims.

Police brief

The victim should be provided with a copy of the police brief and all court documents, including a transcript of the pretext call, just as a defendant has access to all of this through his or her lawyer.

Monthly updates

The police should have to call the victim/s monthly, with an update on the progress of the case. The reality is that police generally do not have the time or capacity to call complainants and this means that complainants are left anxiously waiting and wondering, desperate to hear something. Others make a habit of calling the police regularly, seeking an update, but they are often deemed troublemakers. Often the informant is unavailable, on leave, or not rostered on and a message is left to return the call, which rarely happens. Usually, the complainant must call again and again like a desperado for progress updates. They often take the police informant literally when they say, 'I'll call you,' and wait for an inordinate period, usually in vain.

If complainants were independently legally represented, then they could get updates from their own lawyer instead.

Relationship between the SOCIT Units and the OPP

The relationship between these two separate government offices remains a mystery to the public and to complainants. There is constant duck-shoving, with one blaming the other for delays in charging or lack of information and decision making. One is never sure where the matter is in the pipeline; it's top secret, apparently.

The recent charges brought in relation to Cardinal Campeius illustrated this tension beautifully. The OPP say it was a decision made by Victoria Police to charge Cardinal Campeius, yet the police had sought their advices and the brief had been returned by the OPP without an advice in the first instance. It is clearly a political hot potato and I suspect that the OPP wants to wash their hands of it as much as possible. It seems that the responsibility lies with the police informant rather than the OPP chief crown solicitor, which is rather ironic, for in my matter, the converse was true. In my matter, it was the most senior crown prosecutor who personally appeared and withdrew my case. Surely, the question of whether to proceed in my matter should have been left to the local policeman and in the matter of Cardinal Campeius, the chief should decide.

When receiving a police brief, the OPP should check to ensure that all the paperwork is correct and that the correct charges have, in fact, been brought. In my case, just two days before the committal hearing, I was told that the police had brought the wrong charges and that there were also uncharged acts. If this is the case, it needed to be corrected well before the Committal Hearing. This was the path preferred by Magistrate Woodpigeon; however, the OPP did not follow this as they withdrew the incorrect charges and then didn't bring the correct charges either as the magistrate had suggested that they do.

The police working at SOCIT are meant to be specialised and understand the issues surrounding disclosure for victims. The government and police should not encourage people to come forward about sexual abuse unless they will, in fact, prosecute. The legal system further re-victimises you as it's not user friendly and does not prosecute cases often enough and drops charges all too often, leading to even lower conviction rates.

In the Case of Civil Matters

Costs

The pursuit of justice through the civil jurisdiction, often by suing the offender in the County Court, remains unreachable for most complainants. It is simply far too costly to initiate and maintain proceedings through the various stages, including through the many delays, costly adjournments and wasted court events. It is not unusual to spend a minimum of $100,000 on legal bills alone in a fairly standard matter and then there's the risk of having to pay for the other party's legal costs in the event that you lose, which is entirely probable if you're the plaintiff in a sexual assault trial. The decision to pursue civil redress is certainly a costly one for a complainant to make, whatever their decision.

On another note, victims should not be liable for the costs of the removal of Orders that were made by application of another party; rather, the party that sought the Order should pay. For example, there is often a Suppression Order that remains active and enforceable even once the matter has concluded when it's made 'until further order', which was commonly done prior to 1 December 2013, when the Open Courts Act (2013) came into operation. This is ridiculous to make complainants pay, yet the magistrate decided this in the decision of my matter Jones v King Claudius and DPP(2015), as previously referred to.

Having had to apply for the removal of a Suppression

Order at my own expense is another barrier designed to silence the victim who may wish to come forward and advocate for change like myself. I cannot believe that being a victim of crime in an abandoned criminal matter left me without rights, the same rights that I had before I disclosed that I was a victim of crime. I cannot think of a survivor I know who wants to be permanently muzzled. It is fair to say that some survivors may not want to speak out and have their reasons for this stance, which is entirely legitimate and justified. However, opting not to speak and being forced not to speak by court order, with risks of legal consequences, are two very different things.

Despite the spin, I can see that Suppression Orders are only made to protect the accused and their reputation, especially if they are made 'Until further Order' as most victims wouldn't bother applying for a revocation of the Order, causing the silencing of those victims' experience and thereby protecting the villain ad infinitum. To be denied my legal costs when I won because the magistrate deemed me unusual as a victim to want to speak up is legally unjust. I think the #MeToo movement proves this magistrate to be quite wrong.

New court forms needed on the Magistrates' Court website

The magistrate in my case incorrectly determined that I had applied for the review of the Suppression Order under the wrong legislation, being the Open Courts Act (2013), because the courts application form 'Application to Review a Suppression Order' specifies the Open Courts Act in small print. Rather, all that needs to be done is a new application form pro forma be created by the court that asks the applicant to specify which legislation the Suppression Order was originally made under – the Magistrates Court Act (1989)or the Open Courts Act (2013).

If it is the case that Suppression Orders made under the old Magistrates' Court Act can only be reviewed under an application brought under that same act, then the website should have the old application form (if one ever existed) as well as the new one or change the form. Otherwise, all victims will run into the same problem I did, using the same form as it's still the only one available. In turn, they will be liable for the defendant's costs of that hearing if the defendant (or the magistrate) opposes the application and a new application must be made simply because of the nature of the form. This is a ridiculous loophole that could be resolved overnight with a new form that asks one simple question – the date the Suppression Order was made – thereby determining under which act the order was originally made.

At the time of writing, the Magistrates' Court website had still not heeded my advice and the application form remains unedited. Victim, beware! It's not the defendant who'd ever apply to revoke it obviously, so watch out.

Unnecessary costs

Courts should not hear mentions of matters that it does not need to as this is a waste of taxpayers' money. Administrative adjournments should be sought wherever possible. When a court report is not ready, the party responsible should notify the court and seek an adjournment by consent before the hearing date. Currently, magistrates often require parties to come to court to adjourn regardless as they also need to be in agreement that an adjournment is suitable even if all the parties are already in agreement. This situation is so frustrating for clients and should not happen. If courts are so clogged with cases, surely, it makes sense to only hear and list matters that are ready to proceed in some substantive way. Parties and their lawyers often wait around for hours or the better part of a day just to adjourn or for a five-minute mention. It's such an inefficient system. Clients often need to take days off work and organise babysitters to attend court to find that nothing's going to happen at court today. That's lost income and extra expense that most clients can't afford, often with a parking ticket as the cherry on top for their wasted day out.

The OPP sent a solicitor to the mention of my Suppression Order matter in Loganville as the police were a party to the proceeding in the criminal matter that the Order was borne out of. He simply sat there and told the magistrate that he didn't have a view either way, that he did not support nor oppose my application for revocation. King Claudius was opposing my application.

Strangely, the day before the hearing, the OPP claimed that they had not been served with my application and said they were going to seek an adjournment as a result. This would have resulted in us all attending court for nothing, just for the OPP to claim they hadn't been served and to seek an adjournment accordingly to then not have a view in any event. I called the police informant and had him organise an urgent affidavit of service to satisfy the court that the police had, in fact, served the OPP, as he told me he had done. I had served King Claudius and the police with my application and the police, in turn, had served the OPP, the manager of the sex offences unit, Ms Mallee-fowl herself. No wonder they were playing games again as she was involved, which I suspect meant orders from the top dog again to delay and deny!

Ironically, one magistrate criticised me for having filed too many affidavits and documents in the matter, yet they were all necessitated by King Claudius and his lies. At one point, King Claudius' barrister, Strut-Bittern, Esq, argued that the Suppression Order needed to remain in place because he falsely alleged that I had been spreading nasty rumours around the Catholic schools of King Claudius' children that he was a paedophile. After hearing this, I sought two letters from the headmasters of both schools that proved that I had done no such thing. When you have to defend yourself against lies, you should not be criticised by the bench for having done so as this would defy all concepts of justice.

I think that it was most improper for counsel to raise such allegations against me without any proof from the bar table, almost by stealth, putting us in a position with nothing to counter it. This is deliberately misleading the court, yet he got away with it. Later, we were accused of breaching the Suppression Order by writing to the schools, seeking to dispel their baseless accusations in support of our application to revoke. How ironic. Surely, I have the right to defend the allegations, that went to the heart of whether the continuation of the Suppression Order was justified? Regardless, I was never served with a copy so I would never had known if I had breached it or what would constitute a breach.

The same thing happened when I filed affidavits ordered by the bench as to King Claudius' lawyers' lack of correspondence in the civil matter. After I filed them, on the return date, the Judicial Registrar said there was nothing on the file and didn't ask for copies or anything. I had spent money having my lawyers prepare them for nothing, but if I hadn't, I would have been in breach of H. Honour's Orders. It was clear that they didn't want to give me any credit for having complied and did not want to be brought up to speed because what the affidavits revealed didn't suit their agenda and pre-planned argument. These are the legal hoops we victims shouldn't need to jump through.

Statute of Limitations and Passage of time

The Limitation of Actions Amendment (Child Abuse) Act (2015)[78] was a coup for victims of childhood sexual abuse, for it acknowledges how long it takes for survivors to come forward. However, it does not create an automatic right to proceed and the first thing that a complainant needs to address is the legal question of the 'passage of time' causing prejudice to the defendant.

I see the passage of time argument as just another unnecessary stumbling block for victims. I do not believe for a minute that a person wouldn't remember such offending as sexually abusing a child is so significant that it's arguably not something one would ever forget, despite their age now. Certainly, victims remember what happened forever, so why do we even entertain the idea that it's hard for abusers to remember? The Catholic Church gave a fine example of this hypocrisy when, during the Royal Commission hearings, Cardinal Carlisle continued to claim he couldn't remember why he was suddenly being moved from the Town of Sadness for something as big and as scandalous as sexually abusing children, yet he admitted that he remembered the scones and afternoon tea put on for him by the church ladies on this same occasion. This is incongruous and, I must say, entirely unbelievable.

In the matter of Murphy v Connellan (2017) VSCA 116[79], the Supreme Court of Appeal decided to invoke the court's power under s27R to permanently stay proceedings relating to the alleged sexual assault of a minor in 1968 for the first time. The decision in this important case has dire consequences for sexual assault victims as it flies against the spirit of the legislative amendment, made in light of the Royal Commission. The applicant, Marita Murphy, a victim of child sexual assault, must now pay the 'alleged' perpetrator his legal costs as well as her own.

The use of the term alleged offender or alleged rapist is a term wholly offensive to victims despite the legal justification for its use. I don't use it for that very reason when talking to clients unless I absolutely must. I personally do not believe that allegations are just that, merely alleged, until proved true by the law. For how often are they proved true? 3 per cent of the time. So, if one looks at legal outcomes statistically, one would be reduced to say that most people accused of these sexual crimes are not guilty, but rather, have been wrongfully accused by lying women and children. I will never say that, for in my view that is simply not true.

In terms of addressing the issue of the passage of time in my matter and King Claudius' ability to fairly defend the allegations, he certainly remembered what he did during the pretext call from the get-go, so his memory from that time is obviously still there. He also agrees with me in the pretext call that you can't just block it out after thirty years. King Claudius never once questioned me on what I was talking about when I told him I remember him sexually abusing me as a child. He never got angry and he never disputed my recollections or asked me to clarify them. He knew what I was talking about right from the start. What does that tell you about his memory and whether he did it? I believe that memory when police are involved and memory during an unguarded chat are two very different things. It's only the defense lawyers and the burden of proof that twists a defendant's memory from good to poor or non-existent.

The Wrong Act, all right

The Wrongs Act 1958 (Vic)[80] is the main legislation in Victoria governing claims for damages for personal injury (or resulting death) in Victoria, including sexual assault, particularly in cases not involving transport accidents or work injuries. That's nearly sixty years ago!

It is under this Act that a person can sue someone for damages for sexual assault, classified as a civil wrong, but it's an exceedingly slow and exorbitantly expensive way of approaching remedies for sexual assault. For starters, I say it is not a civil wrong anyway; it's a criminal wrong that is being pursued through the court for damages. Clearly, sexual assault needs its own legislation, a new Act and a new specialised court that encompasses all legal action associated with sexual assault from start to finish.

Currently, damages for non-economic loss (pain and suffering) are limited to a maximum amount, which is usually indexed on 1 July each year. The maximum amount as of 20 September 2017 is $577,050. Currently, a claimant must have suffered a 'significant injury' before being entitled to recover damages for non-economic loss pursuant to this Act. Not dislike work injuries cases, non-psychiatric impairment is assessed pursuant to the American Medical Association Guides to the Evaluation of Permanent Impairment(fourth edition)[81]; in cases of psychiatric impairment, the Clinical Guidelines to the Rating of Psychiatric Impairment[82], prepared by the Medical Panel of Psychiatry, Melbourne (October 1997), was used before GEPIC[83] replaced it in 2006. The minimum level for the recovery of damages in these cases is an impairment of more than 5 per cent for non-psychiatric injury or more than 10 per cent for a psychiatric injury. Such impairment must be assessed by an approved medical practitioner or a medical panel as defined by the Act. In assessing psychiatric impairment, it is necessary to disregard any psychiatric impairment or injury consequential on a physical injury.

Forget about any stress had by me having my psychiatric assessments done, necessitated by the process to determine if I am damaged or 'impaired' by four years of childhood sexual abuse. It's a positive stress. It was an absolute pleasure for me to have the assessments done, other than the expense, as it's another opportunity to tell my story, the chance for a professional, independent, adult stranger to assess the damage done to me as a result of sexual abuse in my childhood. I run from nothing, for I have nothing to hide. I even considered the dramatic idea of publishing my psychologists reports as annexures to this book as they are so damn accurate in their description of me and my trajectory, so typical of a 'sleeper' victim.

There are the non-economic damages from pain and suffering and economic damages from loss of income. It is important that damages be punitive in the case of sexual assault as there needs to be a high level of seriousness and a clear deterrent effect. Aggravated damages are particularly relevant in my case as the defendant has aggravated my pain and suffering as much as he possibly could post my disclosure. What he's doing now is almost worse than the abuse. During the pretext call, he said that it's important to him that I'm OK now, but his actions defy this and show no remorse whatsoever.

In my matter, my Assessment of Damages hearing was due

to be scheduled by the court after my win, just before the defendant filed his summons and the matter went pear-shaped again. These Orders were overturned on [DATE] 2017, so we never had the hearing for the Assessment of Damages, the subject of which is irrelevant now until the outcome of the trial – and only if I win. And winning, as we all know, is a long shot because of the system that morphs the truth into a new narrative to defend the defendant right through to a 'not guilty' verdict care of the judge or jury.

Chapter 22

Learned Counsel: If You Have to Say It, It Ain't!

Like most things in life, if you have to say it, it ain't! In the early days of my civil matter, I remember one supposedly learned counsel, my expert barrister, telling me to write an affidavit as to the alleged inconsistencies in my two statements to the police to state that the passage of time had caused my memory to fail me. That's the best that the expert suggested I do in answer to another red herring sent from my cousin's lawyers.

His lawyer had written to mine and claimed that there were inconsistencies between my first statement to the police and my second statement to the police and my Statement of Claim. I was appalled and offended. There were no inconsistencies in any event and any that were perceived by the defence, in an attempt to create a tissue of lies, could have been clarified by me during cross-examination. It was a matter for evidence, not pleadings. You don't forget the truth – if only victims could forget and wake up with a clean slate!

The lawyer who briefed him, a woman, also gave me a lesson on what a vagina is. I mean, really? Was she joking? No, sadly, she wasn't. On counsel advice, she explained to me that my cousin could not have touched me on the vagina as I had alleged in my police statements as 'the vagina is the canal where the baby comes out.' Really? I didn't know that as a mother of four biological children. Silly me, I thought girls had vaginas and boys had penises. I'm sure that lawyer will tell her children, if girls, not to refer to their vaginas if their private parts are touched. They need to say it was their clitoris or labia depending on where they were touched. Have fun with that, lady. Sorry to say, but girls have vaginas in my book, but you can't refer to the associated parts generally as a 'vagina', according to this lawyer. Same for boys as, according to this lawyer, you don't refer to their private parts generally as a 'penis'. If that's the law working its working day, get me out of here.

If I walked up to a man and grabbed him on the penis, I'm fairly sure that's what he'd say, words to the effect of 'She came up to me and grabbed my dick'. If he was uncircumcised, he certainly would not say that I grabbed him on his pants, near his genital area, touching the foreskin through two layers of clothing, pants and underpants. If he was circumcised in the same scenario, he would not say, 'She grabbed me on my pants, near my genital area, touching the glans through two layers of clothing, pants and underpants.' Lawyers need to quit their crap. Referring to a 'vagina', 'fanny', 'penis', or 'dick' generally does not mean the victim is lying. For if that were true and a man said, 'She grabbed my dick,' as he often might before he said, 'She grabbed my penis,' it wouldn't be legally valid, would it, Ms Lawyer? Would it mean he's lying as men don't have a 'dick' as such? Give me an anatomical lesson on man next time and point to his 'dick', please. It's worrying that she is from a specialty firm of sexual assault experts. What is wrong with people these days? Lawyers are becoming more and more absurd and distorted from reality, like the judges they appear before.

On another occasion, I called a well-known senior barrister

to see if he would represent me in the increasingly complicated Suppression Order matter and he said patronisingly that I didn't need him and told me, 'You'd be better off with a junior female barrister.' Thanks for the compliment, I thought to myself. I had told him that my matter was politically sensitive and had tendrils to clergy childhood sexual abuse, but he was disinterested and probably thought that I was just another seriously deluded female with a conspiracy theory. And to think that he was a colleague briefed by my husband. After that, he was added to our firm's 'Do not brief' list. It certainly concerns me that he is involved in a Royal Commission for our indigenous youth with the attitudes he holds.

It is fair to say that the court events in my civil matter were numerous and mostly unnecessary and all at my expense. The problem is that the law doesn't care who pays and who doesn't, you see. It's a process that runs with blinkers on until someone stops paying. There's nothing else going on in the courtroom or in their heads. Mindless paper shuffling across a bench, albeit mahogany, officious judges, one-dimensional magistrates, counsel with gravitas, counsel without. Someone in that courtroom is afforded respect; the other is treated with the utmost suspicion and disdain. That's never murky. The victim is an inconvenient truth and seemingly needs to be put through their paces over and over.

For me, it has been more than four and a half years of legal hell. I've lost my entire extended family as they pretend to believe my cousin and use the excuse of, and hide behind, the criminal proceeding failing, saying that proves I was lying as the police dropped it! King Claudius nicely hides behind this too and has full acceptance from the extended Pavlovic family. King Claudius has never tried to set the record straight, for he's enjoying the trappings of being king, of course. King Claudius' counsel just continue to put these lies to the court while the defendant laughs on from some remote location, too much of a coward to show his face to my parents and me. King Claudius has not come to court since [DATE] 2014, the day police happily let him walk free and released him from his bail conditions!

Judges and counsel talk about everything in the courtroom but what happened to me. The offending is seemingly passé. The law speaks to me daily and seems to be saying, 'It's the process that you are burdened with now, so we'll make you pay one way or another, you troublesome woman.' Meanwhile, the perpetrator begins to believe his own lies and so does the court that seemingly gets annoyed with the victim for being a surviving victim with a modicum of self-respect, still parched and so thirsty for justice.

Why are judges referred to as justices if they don't give justice in their decisions and sentencing? If they deliver injustice to 97 per cent of sexual assault victims, surely, we need an urgent name change for them and for the oxymoron that is criminal justice. Perhaps it should be called criminals justice; getting away with crime.

Chapter 23

It's Still a Case of Who You Know

Introduction — My childhood sexual abuse and the link to the Conservative Town Catholic clergy

Cardinal Campeius; Baba and Dida's friend and local god, the priest I thanked in my own wedding booklet in 1998. Cardinal Campeius, my clients Sebastian and Prospero's alleged abuser. Cardinal Carlisle, the local paedophile priest, now convicted and Australia's worst paedophile. Cardinal Bourchier, the local Bishop. These men of the cloth I'd watch as a child, mingling outside with the church congregation after mass, socialising warmly with the Pavlovic family for more than 50 years.

All my male cousins were altar boys in Conservative Town at the following churches: St Michael's Cathedral, St Michael's College School Chapel, St George's Church and St Marks during the years that Cardinal Bourchier was bishop of Conservative Town, during the years that Cardinal Campeius was the school priest at St Marks. Cardinal Campeius had officiated at my cousin Hecate's confirmation at St Simeons in 1982, standing in the background of a family photo that day, flanked by golden-haired altar boys. According to another survivor of clergy abuse, Harry Percy, King Claudius was Campeius' favourite altar boy and was given the important altar boy tasks such as carrying the thurible, containing incense to bless the host, and ringing the bell. Hamlet was also an altar boy for these priests.

I had both my Communion and Confirmation classes at St Vincent's Primary School as my school, Conservative Town Grammar, didn't hold them. I went with my other Catholic school friends from Grammar to after-school classes there. I really didn't take in the religious information with any seriousness and had only a basic idea about what it was all about. I was mainly excited about going to the beautiful specialty children's wear shop Calico Lace and Flowers in Main Street to buy the dresses with my mum. I loved wearing the floral headband, with its delicate white rosebuds, angelically setting the veil into place. I was made to look like a mini bride of Christ: pure, white and holy. Beautifully virginal.

When I look at first communions now, I just can't believe how ridiculous it all is. What on earth are we doing, indoctrinating our girls like this – to be passive, pretty adornments, pure and faithful to man and his evil? First, the white christening gown, then a white flower-girl dress if you're lucky, then the white Communion dress and veil, then the white Confirmation dress, then sometimes the white Debutante dress, then the bride in her white gown and veil or, if you're a very, very good girl, a nun, a white habit; and be the purest veiled girl of them all. Quiet, passive, dutiful to the world through the lens of Bible-loving, Catholic men. The sort of girl the Pavlovic family could finally be proud of. Disappointingly, there was no Pavlovic girl willing to marry Christ, but I remember my cousin Witch One of the Three Witches came close. There are a lot of victims to Catholicism, many veiled and dressed in white. In my opinion, Australia should be more concerned about these veils than the Islamic hijab or burka. We all know how many nuns and martyrs have been complicit in the abuse of children by priests and how many nuns abused children themselves, some of whose victims are clients of mine. They have told me that the nuns were particularly cruel and appeared to have no difficulty with sexual abuse or physical punishments.

There was another abuser who abused my cousins in the presence of me who was a friend of King Claudius and Hamlet. My Aunty, King Lear's wife, thought his name was O'Bourke. I have no proof, but this may have been the boy named Andrew O'Bourke who, sadly, had committed suicide before I had a chance to meet him. This man was mentioned in Harry Percy's statement to the Royal Commission. He was also a fellow altar boy with King Claudius, Hamlet and Harry Percy, attending St Michael's College at the time.

The police made enquiries of a Grumio O'Bourke when they were investigating my criminal matter, but I was never sure of his Christian name. I do remember his nickname was Obe, as in Obi-Wan Kenobi from Star Wars. Sr Det Jacob Rosser told me that although Grumio admitted he knew King Claudius and that he had gone to his house many times, he denied knowing me and my allegations. Rosser told me he sounded credible and many boys named O'Bourke had the nickname Obe at that time thanks to Star Wars, so nothing further came of it. I do not know whether he is the same boy who was in King Claudius and Hamlet's bedroom. I remember he was relatively handsome, fair haired, thin and even taller than King Claudius, who was a relatively tall boy anyway.

Without knowing the exact name of this boy, I will never be able to properly join the dots in my matter. This does not mean my theory is wrong though, for I am missing a valid explanation for the legal enigma that is my matter. If my suspicions about the link to Catholic clergy are so far-fetched, why have my legal matters played out this way? Can someone please tell me so I can finally lay the matter to rest? I cannot be expected to live with no answers or unconvincing ones at best. I suspect that others out there have the answers but are keeping them well hidden, hence the bizarre mismanagement of my matter by all the organisations that should be held responsible for hiding that truth: the Conservative Town police, the OPP, the DPP, the Attorney-General, the Ombudsman, the various magistrates and judges. Cold, harsh and unsympathetic towards me – the only consistency. I suspect that my file had a big red flag on it and 'Do not allow to proceed' written on the front cover. 'Why?' is the question that remains unanswered, to my immense frustration.

Relationship between Catholic clergy and my extended family

Cardinal Campeius was Conservative Town born and bred, just like Cardinal Carlisle, just like King Claudius. Cardinal Carlisle went to the same primary school as King Claudius, St Vincent's in Conservative Town and the same senior school, St Michael's College in Conservative Town. Campeius was a rowing coach at St Michael's and was a friend of King Claudius' father and the other Pavlovic brothers. My family thought the world of Campeius; he was as good as God to Conservative Town. Praying to God and talking to Campeius were one and the same thing to my family and to many in Conservative Town.

Importantly, Campeius is a good friend of King Claudius' parents, King Lear and King Lear's wife Pavlovic, and even had dinner at their house. King Lear was a builder and his brothers worked in the following related trades: Macbeth a concreter;

Cassius a carpenter; Petruchio a teacher and a builder/sculptor; the late Iago, his brother-in-law, a brick layer; and my father a casual labourer at times but ordinarily a teacher. The Pavlovic brothers all worked for Campeius over many years, approximately fifty years, renovating Saintly College, including its library and offices and Priestly Palace in Conservative Town and other various jobs as listed below.

My father was the exception in the family of tradies. He was a teacher and the only brother in the family to receive a tertiary education and a degree. He was not active in the Catholic faith, nor was my mum, who was born Lutheran but is an atheist like Dad and me. I was the only female cousin in the Pavlovic family to go to a non-Catholic school, Conservative Town Grammar, aside from Desdemona's off-and-on attendance. I am so thankful for the many sacrifices my parents made to send me to that school. I was a dedicated student and extremely driven and wanted to be a lawyer from a very young age, which, looking back, is no surprise to me now as to why.

Works by the Pavlovic brothers and the Pavlovic families' involvement in the Catholic Church in Conservative Town

The entire family were entrenched in the Catholic faith in every way and made a living engaged in ongoing jobs for the church since coming to Australia from Croatia in 1960. My dad was earmarked by his family to enter the priesthood, but thankfully, he refused and went to art school and Hawthorn Teachers College instead. I don't want to think about what could have happened to Dad at the seminary in Misery, where all the Conservative Town boys went.

The extended family have had ongoing work personally from Cardinal Campeius and the Conservative Town parish for over fifty years, including through now deceased Scott Thompson, who oversaw the building works. The following provides a summary of the Pavlovic connection to the Catholic Parish in Conservative Town, to the best of my knowledge:

The Priestly Palace

The Priestly Palace in Main Street, Conservative Town, was accommodation for the Bishop of Conservative Town until it was privately sold in 1996. It was sold with all its religious content: refectory tables, bishop's chairs, cedar dining table, bookcases and magnificent cedar and mahogany antiques.

My uncles had built a new altar for the Priestly Palace. The bishop at the time, Bishop of Ely, had breathing difficulties and they built a new bedroom onto the veranda to access fresh air overnight for him.

Independent University

Campeius' baby, Saintly College, also known as Independent University in East Street, Conservative Town, occupied the Pavlovic builders for decades. They built a library and renovated the new Campeius Wing and I remember visiting Dad at the worksites there over many years as my uncles would call on him to assist as a labourer in school holidays when he wasn't at work. My dad had inherited the old stairs from Saintly College, which became the stairs to his bluestone studio at our home, built in the 1980s, nestled behind our basic brick veneer house. He also inherited an old crucifix from Saintly College, but it was never hung but rather kept as an historical artefact of sorts. He also assisted in various building jobs there during his retirement until I disclosed my abuse, after which the Pavlovic brothers considered Dad to be 'off' like a bucket of prawns, being my father, the father of an injustice collector.

From 1995 to 1999 or thereabouts, Uncle Petruchio was commissioned by Campeius to create several large sculptures and statues for the grounds of Saintly College, including of St Thomas Aquinas, St Camillus and another bishop I can't remember the name of. They are absolutely stunning and so unique. However, Uncle Petruchio was displeased with the amount paid to him as the materials – including bronze, wood, resin, anodised copper – were expensive and after he paid for the materials, there wasn't much left over for his time, labour and artistic contribution. He thought the church were penny-pinching bastards considering how much money and time the Pavlovic family had given to the Conservative Town Parish and Cathedral for over fifty years. The sculptures stand in the grounds to this day, near the aptly named Campeius Wing.

My cousins Witch One and Witch Two, Uncle Macbeth's daughters, studied nursing and teaching there respectively and my cousin Isabella, Uncle Petruchio's daughter, studied teaching there also.

My husband, Antony Jones, also studied teaching there for two years from 1979 to 1980 when Campeius was the director. Antony was expelled and unable to complete third year there as Campeius told him, 'We don't think you're the kind of person that would make a good teacher.' Antony was forced to finish his degree at Conservative Town College of Advanced Education, now Down Under University, and became a teacher for 20 years.

St Michael's Cathedral, Conservative Town

Uncle Petruchio designed and created a shield above the bishop's chair at St Michael's Cathedral. It is no longer there as the bishop took it with him upon his departure, in line with Catholic tradition. My aunts Cassius' wife, King Lear's wife and Lady Macbeth were on all the church committees there for about forty years. I was christened there, had my first communion and confirmation there, as did the majority of the extended family. It is fair to say that our family had all had our christenings, first communions and confirmations, funerals and weddings there at the cathedral wherever possible. Three of my own children were also christened there. The extended family would attend mass there every Sunday, normally at 10:30 a.m., make cakes for the church fetes and even pay to have a special mass for deceased relatives at the monastery.

My male cousins Banquo, Decius, Cassio, King Claudius, Hamlet, Rodrigo and Brabantio were all altar boys but not my brother Romeo. After one communion preparation class, the priest spoke to Dad and said, 'We're concerned that your son has no idea who Jesus and Mary are?'

My Aunty, King Lear's wife, was the contact point for enquiries and the sponsor for the new parishioners for the Conservative Town parish for many years. She was also commissioned by the Catholic Diocese to create an icon painting for the cathedral and has others hanging in the Catholic Church in Tumbleweed. To think that she was paid by the Conservative Town Catholic Diocese for this religious indulgence, a diocese that at that same time refused my request to pay my abused client an interim sum, sickens me. I paid the diocese a personal visit on that occasion, seeking a relatively paltry amount to register his car and pay his children's school fees, but my maiden name did me no favours. Yet, that diocese paid for another client of ours in similar circumstances, so it certainly could be done. They had a personal set against this client, because he was the face of clergy abuse, consistently agitating for the survivor community. The quieter, introverted victims seem to get the Catholic sympathy.

Uncle King Lear, Uncle Macbeth and Uncle Cassius would carry the collection plates at mass and Uncle Cassius and Uncle Cassius' wife would regularly do the offertory. My aunts Lady Macbeth, King Lear's wife and Uncle Cassius' wife sang in the choir at mass every week but not Aunty Emilia, for her husband, Iago, forbade her to sing because it would make her happy and he sought control at every turn.

St Vincent's Primary School

My cousins King Claudius, Hamlet, Goneril and Regan went to primary school there from approximately 1974 to 1986. I had communion classes at St Vincent's in 1982 in a church building behind the church there with Goneril as my school, Conservative Town Grammar, didn't offer these classes. I had confirmation classes there again in 1985 with my school friend Lizzie.

Uncle Petruchio also made a coat of arms for the front of the building of St Vincent's Primary School. It is still used today. I looked at it the other day through a colourful display of Loud Fence ribbons and thought of him and what he might have said about the church now while I was dropping off my son at deb ball practice.

Mother Teresa College

The Pavlovic brothers built a new section of Mother Teresa College in Conservative Town for accommodation for nuns and students to live in.

Catholic schools my family attended in Conservative Town

King Claudius, Hamlet, Goneril and Regan at St Vincent's PS and St Michael's College and Good Girl College for senior school

King Claudius' children at St Michael's College and Calvary College for senior school

Witch One of the Three Witches, Witch Two of the Three Witches, Banquo (Dec.) at St George's PS and Good Girl College for senior school

Desdemona, Cassio, Rodrigo and Brabantio at St George's PS and St Michael's College and Good Girl College for senior school

Witch Three, Helena, Miranda and Cordelia at All Saints PS and Good Girl College for senior school

Hecate, Celia and Decius at Mary Immaculate PS and St Michael's College and Good Girl College for senior school

Bianca, Isabella, Imogen and Virgilia at Mary Immaculate PS and now Isabella's children at St Vincent's PS and St Michael's College for senior school

All Catholic schools, some of which have now become rather infamous, but the Pavlovic tradition and blind faith continue

Celebration dinner at Saintly College in or about 1990

My parents and my father's siblings, together with their partners, attended a dinner in or about 1990 to celebrate the completion of Saintly College renovations and opening and some local priests and Bishops were in attendance.

At that dinner, both my parents and the other Pavlovic family members were sitting on the same table as the clergymen, diagonally opposite them about three metres away on a long trestle table. They clearly heard Cardinal Campieus distastefully boasting about their mates' and their own sexual prowess in the back seats of cars to those at the table – male sexual boasting. It was completely unacceptable and out of place for the occasion and my parents were thoroughly disgusted with them to talk like that and so loudly on an occasion like that. They felt uncomfortable not knowing where to look after this. My father says the clergymen were alarmingly unguarded and they seemed to be assuming that they wouldn't be offending anyone, holding court in a boastful way and encouraging those around them to join in with their sexually-charged banter. Moreover, for priests to be talking about sexual exploits at all questions their vow of celibacy, which we now know is a common struggle for Catholic priests and the church in general.

The point is that much of the Conservative Town business community is beholden to Catholic money and feels obligated to remain silent about that they know. I am surprised that enrolments at Catholic schools in Conservative Town remain high, moreover that a new Catholic primary school has been built in Developers Dream, an outer suburb of Conservative Town. The people of Conservative Town seem unprepared to act to ensure the safety of their children and grandchildren, holding a blind acceptance that policies and procedures have all changed so it's safer now than ever before. Given that so many so many now convicted paedophiles offended in Conservative Town, the 'quiet' within the greater Conservative Town community is confusing. Of all those in the community, it is really only victims of the church who have come forward, tying Loud Fence ribbons throughout Conservative Town's Catholic institutions but, again, not without resistance.

In a disgusting act of desperation to bury the issue, St Michael's Cathedral in Conservative Town decided to remove all the ribbons from its Loud Fence just days after the Royal Commission released its final report and recommendations before Christmas 2017. This is truly ridiculous and indicative of the church's unwillingness to act on the recommendations, which should really be their primary focus now. Rather, the church has opposed the recommendations to date, with a steely adherence on the sanctity of the confessional remaining privileged under canon law. I say there is simply no room for this in modern day Australia.

Chapter 24

Whose Voice Are We Listening To?

As I listened to tributes to the late Anthony Foster at his funeral on 7 June 2017, something occurred to me. I wondered whether the same state funeral would be held for his daughter Emma had she passed away today and not earlier. The qualities that seemed to make Anthony so palatable to so many – grace, calm, softness, kindness – were qualities coming from the father of the victims, not directly from the victims themselves. I even wondered whether the message would have resonated so well if it was coming from his wife, Chrissie, alone –'herstory'. Chrissie's book, Hell on the Way to Heaven[84], is nothing short of brilliant and absolutely consumed me and a box of Kleenex, but I still wondered. It's as if the powers that be can only handle the sanitised version of things and only when it's coming from a male voice.

Anthony's voice will continue being heard forever in my mind, but I suspect that it was his love and respect for his children and his wife Chrissie that drove him so passionately. I am forever in awe of him and his wife Chrissie. I say Chrissie's book should be added to the literary canon for VCE. It's a book that every adult and child should read, considering the high rate of sexual abuse and substance abuse today. Chrissie and the late Anthony Foster are our unsung heroes of today and should be celebrated for their courage and determination. I fully support their nomination for Australians of the Year.

The small number of women at the Bar is testament to this theory about women's voices. Where are all the confident, outspoken and intelligent female lawyers to represent the voices of women and children in a courtroom? If more women than men are graduating from law schools around Australia, where do all the women go? It has been said that there is sexism at the Bar worse than you'll find at the bar at the pub on a Friday night. How is this possible unless the animal of man is just that, an animal, hiding in legal garb?

The small number of women in politics is also suggestive of a glass ceiling seemingly made of unbreakable glass. If women constitute more than half of the population, then where are those same representative numbers in Parliament House representing their fellow women? Are we to believe that socially motivated women are just not interested in politics as a career choice? Do they simply just wish to vote the best man into power to represent the country and get back to baking their scones?

It is worth quoting our wonderfully tough former Prime Minister Julia Gillard from her famous 'misogyny speech' in October 2012:

I will not be lectured about sexism and misogyny by this man [leader of the opposition Tony Abbott]. I will not. And the government will not . . . Not now, not ever. The leader of the opposition says that people who hold sexist views and who are misogynists are not appropriate for high office. Well, I hope the leader of the opposition has got a piece of paper and he is writing out his resignation because if he wants to know what misogyny looks like in modern Australia, he doesn't need a motion in the House of Representatives. He needs a mirror.[85]

And on losing the Prime Ministership, she said on 26 June 2013,

'I want to just say a few remarks about being the first woman to serve in this position. There's been a lot of analysis about the so-called gender wars, me playing the so-called gender card because heaven knows no one noticed I was a woman until I raised it. But against that background, I do want to say about all these issues the reaction to being the first female prime minister does not explain everything about my prime ministership, nor does it explain nothing about my prime ministership. I have been a little bit bemused by those colleagues in the newspapers who have admitted that I have suffered more pressure as a result of my gender than other prime ministers in the past but then concluded that it had zero effect on my political position or the political position of the Labour Party. It doesn't explain everything. It doesn't explain nothing. It explains some things and it is for the nation to think in a sophisticated way about those shades of grey. What I am absolutely confident of is it will be easier for the next woman and the woman after that and the woman after that, and I'm proud of that.'[86]

When I read the newspaper or turn on the television, the news is still largely about the decisions of men, reported mainly by females. Horrifyingly, Donald Trump is the leader of the United States, a case in point showing just how important it is that women don't undervalue themselves and give up their power. Women should support one another like men do. It works for them. We can't wait for men to support us; to equalise the world a little, we must actively fight for it, for look at what men see us women as, and look at the appalling slow rate of change. What more could Hillary have done? How many times must we burn the bra and bring in another wave of feminism? The current debate on abolishing the tax on female sanitary products is not dissimilar as it seems that we're back to square one. However, the #MeToo movement is bringing change at a faster rate than ever before. This is heartening, for the bleeding obvious cannot and should not be overlooked anymore, but notably, it's women leading the charge.

At a Liberal Party fundraising dinner in 2013, attendees dined upon an overtly sexualised menu, describing our then Prime Minister as follows: 'Julia Gillard Kentucky Fried Quail — Small Breasts, Huge Thighs and a Big Red Box.'[87] This is absolutely disgusting, and every woman should feel utterly offended by it. Liberal women, don't giggle and flick your hair; engage your brain. Former Prime Minister Tony Abbott proudly stood by signs 'Ditch the Witch' and 'A Man's Bitch', referring to then Prime Minister Julia Gillard, yet he has never apologised for it. At the time, Ms Gillard said,

I think the best course for him is to reflect on the standards he's exhibited in public life . . . Leader of the opposition should think seriously about the role of women in public life and in Australian society because we are entitled to a better standard than this.[88]

Similarly, it's not acceptable to have Donald Trump, President of the United States, openly and proudly admit to the easy ability to sexually assault women by grabbing them 'by the pussy'. How so many Americans could stomach voting for him beggars belief. Why would we punish the everyday criminal when the man at the top of the free world practises in and condones sexual assault under the guise of 'locker room talk'? What this suggests is that it's OK to say these things in a locker room but just not publicly, but what's the difference, really?

Somewhere, this talk gets traction and this rape consciousness or rape culture bleeds into groups of men everywhere: at university, in the office, in the staff room, on the footy trip – but perhaps what happens on the footy trip should not stay on the footy trip or should not happen at all! Men need to find a new form of fun and stop sexually assaulting women, no matter the circumstances. And women need to stop making excuses for men's disturbingly bad behaviour.

Chapter 25

Order in the Court! Male Calm, Please!

Rage, anger, hostility, revenge and hatred are seen as counter-productive and will render you unheard in a courtroom generally, but that adrenaline fuelling those reactions is what keeps victims alive. You're branded a screaming harpy, a most uncivilised woman if you have an agenda or take issue with injustice. Well, I take issue with this branding. I imagine that Anthony Foster was only a campaigner for justice for so long because we close our ears and eyes when we hear the words sexual abuse and children.

Sexual abuse is about blood, pain, fear, vaginas, shame, unwanted pregnancy, penises, bodily fluid, sore skin, internal hurt, humiliation, sexually transmitted disease, bruises, embarrassment, dirty underpants, isolation and tears. Naturally, the emotions that come with that are fear, rage, anger, bitterness, sadness, frustration, desperation and despair. There needs to be a place in the law that's respected for victims who present in this very normal, inevitable way. We can't all have the refinement and composure of Anthony Foster, Rosie Batty, or Nelson Mandela. I say, why should the law even require it? When someone loses an arm in an accident, the court doesn't require a prosthetic arm before entering the courtroom. In the same way, the symptoms of PTSD should not have to be covered up or criticised, especially if they have no right to a lawyer who could carry the qualities the law likes instead.

As I described earlier, I was recently told that my body language in court (arms crossed and an angry look on my face) would 'piss off the judge'. Same response when I asked the barrister to call me into the witness box: 'He doesn't care about how you're sick of the delays in this process. He only cares about the process.' The only role for me was to sit in the back of the courtroom behind all these men determining the path of my life through slow and inadequate legal outcomes that I was paying for; all the while, King Claudius and his legal team didn't even show up twice. I think the legal profession prefers us women and children not to be in the courtroom at all, frankly – use the remote witness room or stay outside with your emotions and wait for all these legal eagles who know what's best for you, allegedly better than you do, to determine your fate. They are mostly male, after all. They are calm and unemotional and logical . . . and totally and utterly ineffectual in getting victims a just outcome or one that victims desire. For when you sanitise and reduce the truth, it largely disappears.

But are males always calm in a courtroom? Certainly not. Remember, Captain Plumage, QC, became very emotional and barked, 'Shut up!' at the opposing instructing solicitor, falling into the gutter with him, stooping to his level. I, the victim, oft criticised for being emotional, kept my emotions in check. I stayed calm and watched the carnie folk bicker. Where was my cool, calm, sophisticated Captain Plumage, QC, unflinching under pressure with the right words to say at the right time? Why was he ridiculously reactive to an imp like King Claudius' lawyer? I can only imagine how cross he would have been with me if I'd indulged in an emotional outburst like he did.

I honestly believe that the late Anthony Foster knew there was no proper, rightful place for his daughters Emma and Katie in the legal system, so he stood in what should be their place for more than twenty years. It's calm men who have credibility, for angry women don't as they are seemingly in need of a psychiatric assessment and a good mental institution, a re-wiring to know their place again. A harsh lesson that if you travel too far on the road to justice and autonomy as a woman, you'll be punished and taken backwards, back to the start of the legal labyrinth, so you can slowly lose your mind.

On [DATE] 2017, the County Court at Big Smoke, Victoria, did just that to me, took me right back to the start of the game, but I haven't lost my mind, far from it. I know what's going on in courtrooms daily and my knowledge as to the inner workings of the law gives me power. My greatest asset is my inner strength and unbreakable self-belief. Delay is inevitable in the legal system and once you accept that, it becomes bearable, but no wonder the courts are so clogged as the court is responsible for dragging matters along at a snail's pace wherever possible, to the defendant's delight.

I often wonder why it takes so long to come to deal with the substantive issues rather than a year of housekeeping, which should be done out of court, frankly. Courts should only hear matters ready to proceed. It's ridiculous that all parties need to be assembled for mere adjournments and administrative updates. The truth is that very few matters heard at courts daily are actually ready to proceed and they are the only matters that should get judicial time, not the ones with administrative bottlenecks. The courtroom players need to think honestly about what they actually do in court the majority of the time. Many victims speak of their matters taking four to six years to percolate through the legal system, but I do not believe this time frame is legally justifiable. Time is a killer for many victims as the process is often just as toxic as the offending.

Part 4

My Brilliant Career

Chapter 26

Oma and Opa

Oma and Opa, my maternal German grandparents, always said I could do whatever I imagined if I worked hard enough and set my mind to it. My oma worked in the kitchens at Conservative Town Grammar School and told my mum that was the school for little Cleopatra; she was so impressed with it. When Mum and Dad worked in my preschool years, Oma and I read together, wrote together and learned simple maths, especially when I didn't want to. Opa would take us for country drives to Mount Macedon, Woodend and Daylesford in his canary-yellow V8 Monaro with black GT stripes. I would watch Opa prune his roses, trim his hedges and fill his pipe with cherry tobacco. He also smoked Churchill cigars on special occasions and I'd use the empty cigar boxes to store my stamp collection.

I'd play with their Collie Willy in the backyard and hear the familiar sounds of Uncle Bill starting up his motorbike or the lawn mower. I remember trips to Conders Café in Main Street, a diner of sorts with old-fashioned booths with leather seats. I remember being told off by Opa one day because I stood up on the studded seat with my shiny black painted leather shoes. Opa said sternly in his strong German accent, 'Do zat again, no more Conders!' I never did put my feet up on the seat again and continued to enjoy my milkshakes there.

Oma was only 55 years old when she died from ovarian cancer in October 1985, in my grade six year, the year after my sexual abuse stopped. At her funeral, I played 'Memory' from the musical Catson my recorder, producing a godawful sound despite all my dedicated practice as there was no possibility for measured breathing as I sobbed and my tears flowed down the recorder. Oma had told me not to be sad when she died, for she was just going away for a while to put the kettle on and we'd have that cup of coffee together again, one day soon, in the time it takes for the kettle to boil. Beautiful hope – without the heaven.

Opa always said I'd make a good lawyer and he was very proud of me when I was admitted to the Supreme Court of Victoria as a practising lawyer. He joined me at the celebratory lunch at the 'Snail in the Bottle' restaurant with my parents, my first husband, Gallus, and Constance, the lawyer who moved my admission. Opa loved watching Rumpole of the Baileyon television and thought the law and its players were grand and wise. It was Opa who was grand and wise though, not the law. My wonderful opa, a German paratrooper with a hate of the Nazis and a love of the Australian Labour Party. Like me, he also butted heads with the law . . . and he won.

Opa was an electroplater and worked hard to provide for his wife and five children. It was back-breaking work – literally. One day he hurt his back so badly that he was unable to work anymore. The problem was he was not of an age to receive the pension, so he tested the law and he won. Opa changed the law in Australia and was the first to receive a pension before pension age 65 for workplace injury – Re:Willy Panke and Director-General of Social Services (1981) AATA 65 (23 July 1981)[89].

It was on 24 September 1979 that he sustained a serious

injury to his back whilst lifting one of the tanks of solution used in electroplating. He was only 57 years of age and had not worked since. The condition of his back was such that he could never work again as an electroplater or in any other occupation requiring heavy manual labour. There remained the question, which was at the crux of his application for review, whether he had any capacity for work at all, even of a light nature.

As hearsay would have it, the government spied on my opa to try and catch him out. They caught him, but his injuries were so obvious when he was trying to get into his car that they believed him. In his case, the truth saved him from the lies. I am still hoping that will be my story too, but my hope is fading as the legal insanity continues.

Opa died in 2004 at age 82 from heart failure. In December 2000, I named my first child after him. A lot carries with this name and it's all good. Good men who respect women. Clearly, the world desperately needs more good men like my opa. He set the bar high, where it should be. He'd be so proud of me right now. I carry Oma and Opa with me in my heart and their strength forms part of my battle armour in the legal arena.

Opa was absolutely thrilled when he saw where I first worked as a lawyer in Wealthy Street, in a pink marble palace more than thirty stories high.

'I can't believe it!' he said to me. 'Here? Vell done, little Cleopatra. I'm so proud of you.'

'Opa, it's no big deal, truly. It just feels like I'm fighting for the wrong people.'

'Vot?Come off it!' he said deeply in his thick German accent, slurping another mouthful of strong black coffee.

'Truly, there's a lot of dirty business that goes on in there.

I'm working for the bad guys!'

'Little Cleopatra, do your best. Life is beautiful, if you make it so. Verk hard and don't vorry. You vill do ze right zing. I know it in my heart.'

'I'm working here, where I've always dreamed, but it seems like I'm helping the bad guys get away with stuff, Opa.'

'In Germany . . . oh, you vouldn't believe it. Ze corruption, ze brainvoshing – we had to get out. Sometimes you have to go.'

'Yes, that's what I'm saying. One of the solicitors has gone off to join the circus!'

'Vot?'

'It's true, Alice has gone' I said, and it certainly was true. I went on, moving uncomfortably in my chair. 'Opa, I don't know how to tell you this, but I'm working for a client, a tobacco company, who is claiming they did not know their cigarettes caused cancer. But they did and I'm spending my days covering up the evidence.'

'Vot, isn't that illegal?' he said, filling his pipe with tobacco.

'No, Opa, it's called discovery. Essentially, lawyers and paralegal teams hide the evidence under masking tape.'

The truth was I'd done this many times before, at law firms in Sydney while I was at uni. I worked as a paralegal for four years whilst studying, hiding privileged information under masking tape. In one firm, I worked with lawyers over from England and we called ourselves 'the Maskers' and happily chatted and masked over everything remotely incriminating. One of the maskers has become an MP in England, but I always knew he was destined for greatness, a Liverpudlian with a working-class heart.

Pagination and masking of documents funded my studying full time, together with my part-time job at a fancy patisserie in

The Strand and my weekend shifts at Charcoal Chickens. Every day I'd travel into the city from my unit in West Ryde and open the shop at 7:30 a.m., leaving at 12:30 p.m. to get out to the uni by 2:00 p.m. During university holidays, I cut back those hours and worked as a paralegal as it paid better.

Sue-Ellen and Rob were fabulous bosses and I loved that job at the patisserie so much. Making people coffee, selling cakes and dealing with people in a pleasurable way suited me. I always felt vital and it was fast paced and very busy. All the cool emerging designers upstairs would come down for coffee too and I loved going up and seeing their latest couture and some amazing funky jewellery too that I could never afford. One totally hot guy from the band Bunt gave me his CD one day…dream on Cleopatra. The shoe-shiner, the tearoom, the jeweller; these shops were from another world, another time.

My favourite customer was a lady who always asked for the same thing each day, around elevenses, that I called Mrs Tweed:

"Good morning dear. May I have an iced finger bun?", she politely enquired, sounding very British.

"Certainly, and how are you today?" I asked, grabbing my tongs.

"May I have it buttered…thinly if you don't mind?" she asked, almost apologetically.

"Of course!" I said enthusiastically.

"And if you'd be so kind as to wrap it in "glad" and pop it one of those brown paper bags for me?", each word perfectly enunciated. "And do you have one of those pretty little stickers?" she asked, on repeat from all the previous days.

"Not a problem" I answered, whilst wrapping and sticking the elegant oval sticker on the paper fold. "And what's the weather like out there?", I asked, noticing her frilly umbrella with her today.

"It's rather bleak I'm afraid, frightfully gloomy!" she explained.

"Well you take care of yourself, ok?", I said, meaning it in more ways than the weather.

"Now what do I owe you dear?" she enquired as if completely unaware.

"One dollar and ten cents please."

"Well I'll need some change dear, I don't like to carry coins around you see, far too heavy."

"No problem" I said, gently taking the fifty dollar note from her, ever mindful of the queue growing out the door patiently waiting for this lengthy transaction to finally end.

And with her change she tottered past the waiting customers in her heels, designer trench-coat, cashmere twin-set underneath, and back out into the ornate arcade with her finger bun delicately placed in her Chanel handbag. She was always so stylish, her hair wrapped in a French roll as beautifully as that finger bun. I regret that our conversations never passed beyond pleasantries, but was it her inherent British privacy or the onset of Alzheimer's? Was the bun for her or someone else? She always came alone.

Being a busy little patisserie, I thought about having her finger bun wrapped and ready to go, of course I did, but I was quite sure that she needed that conversation in her day. Who knows, I may have been her only interaction in days and I didn't want to short circuit any human contact. But there was a co-dependency there, for the change of pace was an important reminder for me, that it's about the people who come through the door as much as selling the products. It's how you make a person feel that matters; anyone can sell a cake, and I approach lawyering the same way. It's not about the final product, the sealed Court Orders and your bill. If you don't like hearing people's problems, if you roll your eyes on the inside as one repeats their story, if you thought you could feign concern and get away with it, forget it. You must genuinely love problems and people with a passion and want to get down in the trenches with your clients. Betrayal, pain, loss, drama, tears, insecurity; financial and emotional. That's what mediation, Family Court, Children's Court, Magistrates' Court, Family Violence Court is all about and this patisserie was daily practise in mirroring and matching.

Now, some twenty years post-patisserie, I listen to instructions on repeat as if I'd never heard them before, but clients and customers alike just want to be heard and again and again. The lawyering part is truly only about 10% of what I do and it's the 90% that I love. I indulged that lady in the patisserie and played along, for her need for human interaction and admittedly, to hear the sound of her lovely proper Eton accent, but I suspect that I needed her far more than she needed me.

Chapter 27

You Be Good Avvocato

Dida died in 1998, the year after I graduated from law school. I remember him firmly patting me on the shoulder, saying, 'You be good avvocato!' as he handed me a fistful of dollars. That was his only comment to me as the rest of that conversation was conducted in Croatian between Dida and my father. I did not speak or understand Croatian other than the swear words I'd hear my grandparents Baba and Dida consistently yelling at each other. I almost thought they were terms of endearment, the way they carried on.

I suspect that what Dida didn't understand was that to be the 'good avvocato' or lawyer he wanted me to be would come to mean me setting about lifting the layers of patriarchy in our family and in the world around me at every opportunity. You simply cannot represent and advise clients adequately, particularly women and children, without addressing patriarchy. It's impossible. This has meant me being immensely unpopular at times and often ostracised both personally and professionally. My unflinching determination to make the world a better place and to break the silence surrounding childhood sexual abuse, combined with terrible insomnia from PTSD, has seen my work-a-holism take me as far as Rome with my clients to hear the testimony of Cardinal Campeius. It has me up at night at two o'clock, as if I'm employed as a shift worker or a morning TV host, but I'm not. I keep regular office hours, yet I have no work/life balance as my legal case is all-consuming. I answer to clients around the clock as our practise is crisis driven and crises rarely happen between 9:00 a.m. and 5:00 p.m.

Vicarious trauma is par for the course when legally assisting victims of childhood sexual abuse because our legal system does not respect children and adult survivors as it should. It provides for them in meaningless ways that amount to crumbs at most – certainly no justice and certainly no apology. It's a dead end here and a pyrrhic victory there. It seldom works in securing a conviction. Well, it's not good enough and I want it known that the legal system isn't even trying to redress the situation.

There are less convictions now than before our SOCIT units, Witness Assistance programs and Royal Commissions were established. Why? Why do I return to my office almost daily and want to quit this lawyer gig, like so many do and have done before, and leave this so-called honourable profession? And in due course, the law institute will simply conduct yet another survey on why so many female lawyers leave the profession in droves, but it's no mystery. The lawyers keep happily preserving the mystery of the law just as the clergy preserve the mystery of the faith, and on it goes. Clients stream into our office regularly, broken – broken by the law, by the courts, by the police dropping charges or deciding not to prosecute and by judges and magistrates letting sexual offenders off the hook. They want justice and Antony and I desperately try in vain to pick up the pieces, completing a VOCAT application when all else fails, but what victims of sexual assault really need is their own lawyer. This is the type of lawyering that desperately needs doing and I want to do it.

Chapter 28

Family Violence and Feminism

The law still treats men and women differently, though it pretends to try not to. There are some brilliant magistrates who really understand family violence, one brilliant one in Conservative Town, Magistrate Dove, but the majority don't or at least don't want to. Many Federal Circuit Court (FCC) judges certainly don't. The obligatory 'Notice of Risk'[90] is often mocked by judges in the FCC day after day. Orders are made that cannot possibly protect women and children and of course, they don't.

I say let us move on and leave behind the industry built around 'She's lying!' Let's stop asking our girls to be good little girls and good women born to please. That's not how we will save our women and children from suffering and dying to family violence. For that's not how we will save our men from jail, depression and suicide.

The law has made an absolute mockery of women's and children's experience, especially in family law, child protection and intervention orders, where women need the law's assistance the most. It's ironic but no coincidence as violence is most certainly gendered. It's also no coincidence that I chose to work in these areas. Let us hear the voices of children and their reality. Let us jail child abusers and stop giving them time with their children when it's clearly not safe to do so. Let us enforce equal pay. Let us embrace affirmative action as we obviously need it. Let's stop creating another stolen generation of indigenous Australians through our failing child protection system. It's one thing to have finally said we are sorry but another thing entirely to demonstrate that we are sorry. The first pressing thing is to create a redress scheme for victims of the stolen generation without further delay and grandstanding. But getting organisations to sign up to it is another thing altogether, as evidenced by the Royal Commission into Institutional Responses to Child Sexual Abuse.

If we were to believe the claims from many women in power, if we just work a little harder, we can get there too. How insulting. Women must not want it badly enough if we are to believe the likes of Julie Bishop. Does she think she's rare in how hard she's worked and that's why there are so few women in politics? Look what we did to a top lady, the then first female Prime Minister of Australia, Julia Gillard. We blatantly sexualised her on a Liberal Party menu and promptly got rid of her. She was a gutsy lady who went where others turn a blind eye: into the hidden lives of abused children. I thank her for the Royal Commission – a feminist, an atheist, an unmarried, red-headed hero of mine. Australia was threatened by your intelligence, Ms Gillard; it's not ready for intelligent women, I'm sorry to say, the land of the convict and the larrikin. If you had blonde hair and blue eyes, men may have been more willing to listen to you, for women are respected not for their intelligence but for their sexual attractiveness and availability to men, commonly typified by a Barbie-doll-like image. The way we treat women in Australia is far from civilised; that much, I know.

Let us develop scientifically and look at testosterone, male DNA, look to the real reasons why so many men choose to inflict violence on women day after day and why men in power support this. Yes, it's power and control absolutely. But why? Why do good men support and elevate bad men? I'm sick of political correctness too; they are bad men, not good men who just behave badly. With a little more love and guidance, they don't come good again. That's psycho-babble, in my opinion. Until we can admit this to ourselves, violence will remain gendered. For power and control does not live on an island; it's culturally assigned.

For far too long, women have been desperately seeking respect, autonomy, equal pay and affordable childcare. But instead, women have continued to be disrespected, injured, killed, controlled and sexually assaulted. One might ask, why don't women just start being as violent and sexually abusive towards men to force their way in turn? While I obviously don't condone women doing this, I suspect genetics has much to do with it and the answer lies locked in male DNA. That's why women are always at the mercy of men and their laws, pretending they're not battered, behind their white picket fences, praying that if they cook and clean a little better or get a boob job or other surgery to look younger, they'll stop being abused, hoping they won't be noticed or asked about their bruises by neighbours. That's why the news has the same stories nightly, same-fact scenarios with very little variation, more than a change of names. When a man leaves a woman, however, why doesn't that woman plot and kill him and the children?

Certainly, I see that the family unit is the most toxic unit of society. The worst crimes happen there; it's scary and mostly hidden. Sexual assault, financial control and emotional abuse – the price of romance, so it seems. Until we ascribe equality to the sexes, it will remain a toxic mess, the family home. I see it every day. Family law orders, child protection orders and intervention orders, followed by blood on the court steps, blood on the suburban driveway and blood-curdling photos on the police file. The courtroom remains sanitised from the blood and the truth (conveniently called feminist claptrap) and that's all that matters to the privileged on the bench.

In Rome, Cameron Carlisle wasted a perfect opportunity to open the discussion on sexual abuse: do the sexually abused go on to abuse? We now know in his case it's true, proved by his own admissions years before that, but unbeknown to us at the time, he quickly became the public face and spokesperson of the survivors. His uncle, Cardinal Carlisle, testified that he had been sexually abused as a child also, but it's rare, as are female victims who go on to abuse others. So, I suspect that it's less environmental and more genetic. That's why the problem doesn't go away. For the same reason, you can't take the paedophile out of the paedophile. I suspect that it's just on the sexual spectrum, along with every other sexual identity.

The 2007 movie Little Children,[91] directed by Todd Field, is particularly poignant in its depiction of the issue of paedophiles. In one storyline, a convicted paedophile has done his time and returns home to live with his elderly mother. Yet the local community don't want him living there and he feels ostracised under societal pressures. In one grippingly horrific scene, he cuts off his own penis whilst sitting on a swing, just as he's tempted to reoffend by some young children playing in the park. I was getting increasingly distressed about the possibility that he might reoffend and could hardly bear to watch.

The film suggests that paedophilia is something inherently genetic, that a person can't fight it no matter how hard they might try. Similarly, Louis Theroux's 2009 documentary, A

Place for Paedophiles[92], suggests the same thing and is highly recommended viewing, for it interviews many paedophiles about their sexual offending, sexual desire and about the latest treatment programs. I maintain my belief that you can't take the paedophile out of the paedophile, no matter how revolutionary, well-designed and expensive the rehabilitative program.

So, let's fight sexual abuse like we fight cancer: with money, research and dedication, not denial. Let's find the anti-male-violence vaccine. Sorry to be blunt, but dogs calm down and remain so after de-sexing, don't they? Let's face it; we are apes, not Adams and Eves. We are animals, animalistic in our actions and in our thoughts.

I have one daughter, Kate, one stepdaughter, Susan, three sons – Christopher, Declan and Alexander – and one stepson, William. The trajectory doesn't look good where their personal lives are concerned when I look at the statistics, unless I pretend my boys are different from the majority of men. How can they be though? Can their upbringing really fend off their genetics? I'm doubtful and it's certainly worrying. What will their experience be as men and my daughters as women? Will they too hurt and take advantage of those they love like so many do for male ego? Where do those alarming statistics come from? Why aren't we alarmed enough to invest research dollars into the male psyche? I can predict that my book may be branded another exercise in male bashing, but I will continue to fight against male bashing of women until it stops. For my daughters, for everyone's daughter.

I have given much thought to the concept of sexuality today. I believe that we are all on a sliding scale; no one is fully female or fully male, nor have they ever been. I believe that no one is a true male or female but rather a number of traits that together make up a unique person. Their genitalia they are born with is but one body part in a multitude of cells that make up a unique person and it can be changed, fixed, altered or beautified just like any other body part.

The current debate on gay marriage is testament to society forcing our rethink about gender, sexuality and the role of men and women. At the time of writing the final chapter of this book, the law changed in Australia to allow gay couples to marry. What a fantastic coup for all Australians, for without diversity and acceptance, we are a toxic backwater!

Many Australians have now embraced transgender, accepted test-tube babies, gay adoptive parents, gay foster parents, LGBT (Lesbian, Gay, Bi and Transgender), DSG (Diverse Sexuality and Gender), QUILTBAG (Queer/Questioning, Undecided, Intersex, Lesbian, Transgender/Transsexual, Bisexual, Allied/Asexual, Gay/Genderqueer). It is now accepted that one's gender is not necessarily defined by one's genitals they are born with. With gender-reassignment surgery and hormone-replacement therapy, one can alter their parts in the same way one can change their nose if they so wish. It's all about your identity and self-image, not necessarily the body parts you're born with.

Thankfully, since the Full Court of the Family Court decision in Re: Jamie (2013)[93], it is now more widely accepted that if your brain and your body don't match, you are free to change it. But once again, the law in Australia unnecessarily stymied that process with children wanting gender reassignment, needing to obtain an expensive court order to do so, as the advice of their doctor and psychologist was previously not enough. As that brave girl Jamie explained to the media[94], we don't need a court to determine our right to our innate sexuality and allow medication like puberty blockers. In her case, because of inevitable costs and court delays, she nearly missed her crucial hormone and medication timeline to set her body into its desired metamorphosis.

All this legal process, delay and stress over medicine that the child and her parents, in consultation with her doctors, could decide if she was mature enough to consent to taking. It takes brave people like Jamie and her parents to force the law to keep abreast of societal change. If transgender children and their parents cannot afford to use the law to help them to assist their children, there is no point having such laws. We need to be proactive and respectful to the LGBT and other minority sexual groups as they hold particularly high rates of suicide.

Chapter 29

Questioning the Way Forward for
My Clients and Me

I'm proud of being a bad Croatian girl – if that's what I am in my extended family's eyes.

I won't be judged on the cleanliness of my house by the small-minded Croatian housewives, checking for whether there's dust on my furniture. Dust is a sign that other things are flourishing, ladies, like my children and my career. 'I must go and cook dinner before my husband gets home!' I'd regularly hear my Croatian aunts complain to my mum. What even is that? As Mum would say, can't these men boil an egg? When I think of my Croatian aunties I think of the song 'Luka' by Susan Vega, and the shame and denial that comes with family violence. I think of my Auntie Emilia's perfect house, beautiful garden and her big black eye.

I won't be judged in the witness box either, but rather, I'll hold a mirror up to the players around me instead, for they are the ones lying to themselves and each other. Judges, magistrates, defence lawyers and OPP lawyers all lie enough through the use of false narratives to justify any of the following conclusions: 'There are problems with your case', 'There wasn't enough evidence', 'No other witnesses corroborated your evidence', 'You had a weak case' and the perpetual favourite, 'We need to adjourn'. It's mostly poppycock, to tell you the truth. This is the legal lunacy that plays out in courts daily. The truth is that the truth isn't enough for our legal system and is absolutely beside the point – but very few are prepared tell you that. I am. I can assure you that the truth is beside the point to these experts, for it fetters the indoctrinated, sexist criminal narratives that criminal process is structured around.

Apparently, there are more important things for the experts to attend to, like giving directions to juries so they find a degree of doubt when they otherwise wouldn't have, defying all common sense. Or giving cautions to defendants, diversion to defendants, adjournments to defendants and appeals to defendants. Why is the defendant so damn important and in need of so much assistance compared to the complainant? They chose to break the law. Those who want to 'fix' them should do so on their own clock, not on the victims. Punish the crime. Full stop. Rehabilitation doesn't work when it comes to serious crime against the person. Face facts.

Don't worry, the truth enters the courtroom eventually, in the victim impact statement at the end, irrelevant until sentencing and only slightly relevant at best, depending on the magistrate or judge and their personal point of view. Obviously, not much of life's struggle and pain reaches their ivory towers! These cases are often followed by a sad news story finally starring the victim or the deceased victim's family, with the headline like 'Denied Justice Once Again' or 'Monster Escapes Jail'. Is it any wonder the conviction rates aren't rising? Yet we keep advertising for more sexual abuse victims to report to police. It beggars belief. It's just plain ridiculous that our legal system still re-traumatises victims, guilt free, through abusive legal process, but no one in the legal fraternity wants to admit it.

This is what's discussed at our dinner table most nights. With our children, our parents, our siblings, our friends and the small number of family members we still see, notably none from the Pavlovic family. They're too busy mixing up another batch of cement to keep the foundations of the church and our legal system strong, knowing full well the toxicity of the recipe, ironically, the same foundations at Saintly College that my father helped reinforce in the 1990s, with Dad literally crawling under the building to do so, not dissimilar to the French peasants who built the great Notre-Dame Cathedral.

There's no dissent for the need to change the status quo in our household. So where does the resistance come from I ask? From whose household?

From the family man secretly looking up underage girls in school uniform on the internet?

From the man who has a secret life sexually abusing girls?

From males sexually harassing women at work?

From male school and university students date-raping women and sharing on Instagram and other social media?

From male bosses sexualising their office with young blonde office girls?

From politicians in Canberra rejecting thoroughly decent bills about tougher laws on sexual offenders?

From gutless local politicians staying politically safe?

From males in high places nipping into the Men's Gallery in King Street for a lunchtime thrill?

From male judges and magistrates who see sexual assault and other family violence matters as a sport?

It's high time that men started taking a good, hard look at themselves and doing something about their abusing brothers or themselves – or not and the world will stay the same until one day, when you may see your own daughter or granddaughter on the underage sex ads on Backpage.com and finally care.

I certainly won't be fooled by the lies of the Catholic Church and its promotion of so-called good men of the Conservative Town Parish. My family's steadfast support for Catholic clergymen is disturbing in the circumstances and their unflinching support of the Catholic Church in Conservative Town, despite the lying late Cardinal Bourchier and his paedophilic brethren, is shameful.

The year 2017 saw the passing of another good Conservative Town man, Christophero Sly. The late Christophero Sly may have been a respected solicitor and parishioner of the Conservative Town Parish; however, I do have some concerns about his possible role in the Catholic cover-up. After all, you don't get knighted by the Vatican for nothing. What did he do that was so critical for the Catholic Church that it deserved a knighthood? I wonder. Helping a local priest establish a university is one thing, but did he also help in the great Conservative Town paedophilic clergy cover-up?

Mr Sly was a trusted friend of the cathedral and, to the best of my knowledge, a large painting of him by Conservative

Town renowned artist Richard Paintbrush still hangs in the meeting room of Saintly College today. This great friendship between the local clergymen and Sly blossomed during the years of clergy abuse. As the church lawyers, Shylock, Puck & Sly would have been well aware of the allegations against the clergy members at that time and I suspect that they would have sought legal advice from Sly about this almost certainly. Statements to police would likely have been seen by Sly, no doubt, reports about the paedophile priests in the Conservative Town Diocese, of which there were so many as evidenced by the statements made to the Royal Commission. As a devoted member of the Conservative Town Diocese, I suspect that Sly would have been loath to admit the criminality of the priests' conduct, for they were men of God and men of his beloved parish. Moreover, Sly's sister was a nun, Sister Franscisca. Amongst the obituaries of Sly included a message from the Butts family in Baptista. Is it fair to assume that Dr Butts was also friends with the late Mr Sly? That would be logical and answer a great many unanswered questions thanks to the Royal Commission who refused my request to ask them on behalf of my clients.

Mr Sly came to my baba's funeral; such was their mutual admiration for each other, Catholicism and the Conservative Town Parish. I fondly remember Baba, in her broken English, calling her lawyer, Mr Christophero Sly, 'Mr Shy Sly' in error, in her strong Croatian accent and speaking about him with unquestioning admiration. I wonder if Mr Sly ever had the heart to correct her on his name. More importantly, I wonder if Mr Sly knew about the paedophile priests in his parish. I also wonder whether his love of the parish kept him silent too. Certainly, the statements of Brian Shylock and David Shylock in relation to their time as students at St Michael's College, made to the Royal Commission, are also telling of the same Catholic narrative relied upon by church lawyers everywhere, including at SPS (formerly known as Shylock, Puck & Sly), a firm that Mr Sly himself helped establish.

I am often told by men I know that most men are good, particularly by my husband and father. So where are most of these good men? I ask you to show your faces and let us hear your voices loudly. Let bad men hear your voices loudly too, for societal change will happen much more quickly when men want it too and actively demand it from one another. It would be a welcome change to see some besuited business men of Conservative Town tie some loud ribbons on the fence at St Michael's Cathedral.

Chapter 30

Church, Law and State: Independence Lost

The Royal Commission into Institutional Responses to Child Sexual Abuse, the Royal Commission into Family Violence and other Royal Commissions have shown that there seems to be very little independence between the Law, Church and State. Clearly, where big money can be made, corruption breeds. The current calling for so many Royal Commissions is testament to this in law, in politics and in the world of finance.

I participated in the community consultations (as complainant in a criminal matter) and stakeholder consultations (as lawyer) in the Family Violence Royal Commission and gave frank input into the troubles with the current legal system when it comes to family violence, violence in an institutional setting and child sexual abuse generally. I highlighted the various problems for survivors of family violence and child sexual abuse, ignored by the institutions responsible for the abuse.

A good example of the corruption that we are now lifting the lid on is illustrated in the much-discussed 'Ellis Defence'[95]; the Church is not a legal entity and so cannot be sued and it also can't be taxed. How convenient that the Catholic Church retains its charity status in this current climate. Surely, it's time the government ends the charade and declares it a criminal organisation, making a lot of money tax free and is legally responsible for the sexual abuse of children by its intricate web of deception and denial with a whopping tax debt to the Australian Taxation Office. John Ellis should be declared a national hero, brave enough to take his fight to the High Court. It is fair to say that the court's decision protected the church's assets and what they put this brave, intelligent man through should be considered criminal.

Disappointingly, the Royal Commission did not investigate the Conservative Town Police Station and its response to child sexual abuse, for it ran out of time. It originally planned to spend one entire hearing week on the Conservative Town Police Station alone, including the Special-Issues Committee set up by the church in response to the growing number of child sexual abuse reports against clergy and the impending scandal. To the best of my knowledge, the now retired police officer Luke Fang was not even called to give evidence, yet he was the senior policeman at that time on the Special-Issues Committee. One would think that he would have been called as a most crucial witness. I say he certainly should have been called to give evidence. Where was the testimony of any police officers at the time the paedophile operation was in full swing? Where was Supt Matthew Dull and what did he have to say about all this abuse in his Rockies region? Where is Dull now? More silence from the senior ranks of the Conservative Town Police Station.

Another living member of that infamous committee, Dr Butts, had a convenient car accident the night before he was due to give evidence, allegedly a suicide attempt. The sixty-nine questions we submitted to the Commission to be asked of Dr Butts, on behalf of our clients, were redacted and branded outside the scope of the Commission's Terms of Reference.

The Terms of Reference was qualified as follows:

And noting that, without diminishing its criminality or seriousness, your inquiry will not specifically examine the issue of child sexual abuse and related matters outside institutional contexts but that any recommendations you make are likely to improve the response to all forms of child sexual abuse in all contexts.[96]

and

k). the need to ensure that evidence that may be received by you that identifies particular individuals as having been involved in child sexual abuse or related matters is dealt with in a way that does not prejudice current or future criminal or civil proceedings or other contemporaneous inquiries[97].

My clients and I say the questions were precisely on point but simply too close to the truth for public viewing. Since this incident, Dr Butts has been charged and convicted with dangerous driving in relation to his car accident, coincidentally the night before he was due to give evidence in the Royal Commission.

Some of my clients were left wondering when their statements to the Royal Commission would be made public and why they weren't called as witnesses. Why is it difficult and so complicated if all people are equal in the eyes of the law? I suspect that the State is controlled by the church to a large extent and is fearful of applying the law over Canon law. The Royal Commission also tread with utmost caution and accepted Cardinal Campeius was too unwell to attend the Royal Commission in Australia. The seemingly special treatment of Campeius in these circumstances, compared to what the victims had to go though, is rather telling of the control the Catholic Church has over the law and the state.

I started the first day of the week of Royal Commission hearings in Laurent Patisserie with my clients. I was just getting a table when I heard a vaguely familiar voice behind me.

'Hello . . . Cleopatra, how are you? God, it's been years!'

'Yes, good, thanks. Busy but good!' I replied as my brain raced, trying to remember his name and where I knew him from. Of course, it was Ben from Truscotts, Mulberry & Wise.

'You still at the old firm?'

'Nah, I left years ago. And you? Where are you working now?'

'My husband and I have a firm in Conservative Town, but this week, I'm in town for the Royal Commission hearings.'

'Oh yes, I know all about it,' he said with a sad, knowing look. 'I used to work for Catholic Church Insurances, much to the chagrin of my partner, who's a social worker. She hated that I worked there as she worked with abused people.'

'Wow, I can imagine. It's all we talk about at home too.'

'Yeah, they all knew but covered it up, the bastards. It's all about avoiding liability.'

'Yes. It's rather obvious to everyone now, I think.'

'I've been following the Royal Commission closely. Good luck with it all.'

'Thanks, Ben. Good to see you again after all these years.'

'You too.' And off he went onto the footpath, re-joining the conveyor belt of commuters, like a California roll on a sushi train.

Watching him walk away, I immediately remembered the tobacco case and how sick I felt when I had been in his shoes.

That's the law working its working day. Those with the biggest wallet win the game and the Catholic Church is arguably the richest organisation in the world. We had our work cut out for us, but I remained optimistic. There is more than one way to catch a rabbit and I was sure that we were just going to hear the same old thing again today from the clergymen: 'I can't quite recall'and 'I don't remember, sorry'from a creepy voice, not sorry at all.

I asked myself, does common sense, gut instinct and emotional intelligence ever come into the sphere of the law?

I answered myself too, Of course not; that 'namby-pamby' stuff leads to the truth and we learned people can't have that, Ms Jones. We deal with facts, facts covered up by lawyers, new narratives we call the truth. Lies we call 'instructions'. For what would lawyers spend their time doing otherwise?

Become writers of fiction, I answered myself.

Chapter 31

Pinocchio in Rome

When I hurriedly packed my suitcase for Rome to hear the testimony of Campeius, it was a mixture of both excitement and frustration. As lawyers for some of the survivors, including John Bates and Jack Cade, we had argued that Campeius should come to Australia like most parties had. Flimsy medical evidence was accepted by the Royal Commission, so in Rome, Campeius sat and the proverbial mountain came to Mohammed.

I had argued with the Royal Commission about the costs of me going to Rome, which were ultimately borne by me privately. I had argued that if they were paying the lawyers (barristers and solicitors) flights, accommodation and meal allowance to be at the hearings in Sydney, they should do the same for me whilst attending by video link from Rome, albeit capped at the Sydney reimbursement levels. However, my request was refused, probably to dissuade me from going. To the best of my knowledge, I was the only lawyer in Rome and the only one to have made the request to be with my clients in Rome. I wacked it onto the credit card without a second thought. My clients needed me there with them to support them and so that I could instruct our barrister back in Sydney as instructions came to hand.

The Pope led me right to the Quirinale Hotel. He was

sitting with us in the taxi, welcoming us to Campeius' turf, his picture seemingly more important to Italians than the Mona Lisa. Rosary beads hung from the rear-view mirror and the holy laminated picture of the Pope was attached to the sun visor, quite faded. Very Catholic and very devout was my destination, for I was being taxied into the epicentre of paedophilic deceit. It wasn't the welcome to Rome I had wanted, with fashion and gelato, but the one I should have expected, I suppose. I was annoyed by my obvious lack of preparedness for this tidal wave of Catholic culture. Were this many people blindly faithful? The view was so blinding that I bought some sunglasses over there, and the shop had framed every papal visit to its store; he was everywhere I looked. I ate a cannoli in Piazza del Popolo to help soak up the religious insanity around me.

As we were alighting from the taxi, the driver accused us of not having paid. It was a scam that I didn't fall for though as I argued loudly that I'm a lawyer and will call the police. I had paid the taxi fare in advance to a lady at the airport spruiking for the taxi company. It was all legitimate; I bought the tickets from the ticket box, they were printed and we followed the lady as she led the way to the maxi taxi, shared with others. I noticed though that partway through the journey, we stopped at some commission flats and the dodgy lady got off. She was our proof that we had paid and the driver pretended not to know who we were talking about when he tried to scam us. Moments later, outside the entrance to the Quirinale Hotel, Chrissie Foster had her handbag stolen as we were greeted by her and our other friends who had arrived earlier. We suspect it was theft by that same taxi driver who was wrongfully accusing us and making a commotion!

The Quirinale Hotel was a grand old lady of a place, the

elements of yesteryear's lavish design and decor with the chips and imperfections of time yet retaining its architectural splendour. There were velvet curtains, antique wardrobes, parquetry flooring, grand staircases and original oil paintings on the wall akin to that found in the galleries. But in late February 2016, it housed some rather angry international guests, including me.

In the grand old ballroom, Hero and I sat on a large antique chaise like two excited little children, playing with our toys; our souvenirs for our children and friends. Wooden puppets of Pinocchio, top spinners, t-shirts and pencil sharpeners. Hero madly wrote out a letter to Cardinal Campieus, such was Hero's anger for her brother's death, Balthasar, one of the first victims of clergy abuse in the town of Sadness, where Cardinal Carlisle left a tsunami-like trail of suffering. Hero had come to Rome for her late brother, his voice never heard as he drank himself to death to block his pain. Balthasar was one of the first victims of Cardinal Carlisle in the town of Sadness who went to the police before the Victorian Inquiry. Balthasar's prep school photo came to Rome with Hero. The link between clergy sexual abuse and suicide is now indisputable thanks to Det Sgt Stephen Adams of Conservative Town and his tireless work. Stephen knew Balthasar and had spoken to him before his premature death.

While we were waiting for the survivors meeting to begin with Campieus, we were toying with the idea of presenting Campeius with a Pinocchio pencil, symbolic of Campieus' lies. Thankfully our adult brains won the day and the meeting went ahead without our grey-lead Pinocchio,but he was still there in that room alright and that pencil etched his lies forever in our minds.

Like Hero, I too was angry with Campeius and entered that

meeting with a clear agenda, carrying my own history and that of my clients, including Prospero, with me in my heart. Prospero had disclosed to me Cardinal Campeius' abuse of him just a few weeks before the trip to Rome. I also knew Campeius through my long-time family association and suspected that my cousin King Claudius was abused by Campeius or a member of his brethren. Campeius' favourite altar boy was my abuser. In that way, I consider myself a possible secondary victim of clergy abuse. Regardless, I was ready to talk and ready to listen to "Big Campeius" as he was known to many. A dear friend of mine, passionately devoted to survivors, had loaded me up with loud fence ribbons for Rome, some designed with "Campeius", the children's cartoon character. And curious Cardinal Campeius certainly was.

When I spoke to Campeius that day I was not in awe of him or overwhelmed by him. He may be a local God to some, including in Rome and back in Conservative Town, but not to atheist me. I was angry with the Catholic narrative at the hearings but the meetings with Cardinal Campeius provided a glimmer of hope. I urged Campeius to use his profound influence to change Conservative Town and to make it a world model for healing. I told him, 'Conservative Town hangs on your every word. Families are turning away from their family members who have been hurt by the church and its clergy. If you openly supported victims, parishioners would too, in turn, following your lead.'

Curiously, he told me I'm exaggerating his abilities and said I should seek someone in Conservative Town who has 'real gravitas to further the cause.' I answered, 'That's you. You have the necessary gravitas.' He told me it's very difficult for him to do things now from so far away. I said it's quite simple with technology – the world is such a small place now – but he seemed unconvinced yet flattered.

I then said to Campeius, 'I remember you as a child.' He asked me my maiden name and I said, 'Pavlovic,' which he immediately recognised, asking me who my father was –'Which Pavlovic brother?'– and I answered, 'Julius.' At the time Campeius lived in Conservative Town, my father was known as Stephano or Steph. Stephano was his second name, which was used as his Christian name when the old Yugoslavia (now Croatia) was under Italian occupation by Mussolini. I forgot about Dad's name change and so Campeius seemingly drew a blank as his name did not ring a bell.

However, Campeius knew my dad and all the Pavlovic brothers very well. My Uncle Cassius' three children went to the Catholic primary school known as Mary Immaculate (St Marks Primary School in Conservative Town) during the years he was parish priest there. My cousin Decius received a scholarship to St Michael's College from Mary Immaculate and was keen on becoming a priest. He thanked God for his VCE mark and told me his relationship with Jesus was responsible for his academic achievement. My uncle King Lear's children, including King Claudius, who sexually abused me, went to St Vincent's Primary School, Conservative Town, the same school that Cardinal Carlisle went to, the same school I had communion and confirmation preparation classes at. The boys went on to St Michael's College for senior school after that and the girls to Good Girl College, like all the Pavlovic girls. My Uncle Macbeth's children went to St George's Primary School in Conservative Town North, as did Aunty Emilia's children. Witch One of the Three Witches wanted to become a Nun and seriously considered joining a convent during her studies at Saintly College. What an aspiring good girl for Dida, but something changed her mind.

Uncle Petruchio had been commissioned by Campeius to create sculptures for the grounds of Saintly College amongst other artistic jobs for the parish and King Lear's wife paid by the Conservative Town Diocese to paint icons.

Despite my overwhelming passion for the cause, it was extremely difficult for me to stay awake for the late-night hearings in Rome, with contemporaneous jetlag and my usual eight-thirty bedtime, in line with my children's bedtime for many years. The weight of vicarious trauma hung heavily in that room and on my eyelids. There were tears, sighs, alarmed gasps, guffaws, mutterings under breath, notes passed and hands held. This was a vital process for victims of clergy abuse, to hopefully hear the long-awaited acknowledgement from the Catholic Church through Campeius in person. My wonderful friend Gonzalo was drawing mind maps next to me, trying hard to process what Campeius was saying. It was a tough time and my client John Bates was absent one night after the hearings because of his anger and frustration at having his instructions ignored by his counsel back in Sydney. It was a tough time for all of us, away from our own support people; we were quite vulnerable despite the wonderful CASA counsellors who came with us.

Buying some fruit from the market stall on Via Nazionale the next morning, I saw the Pope again, secured to the awning, flapping in the breeze. He was everywhere I looked, as if giving his blessing, but his physical presence, grace and charity were certainly missing at the hearings. The local media feasted on the survivor's stories, but the Pope went into hiding while we sat at his doorstep, waiting for his leadership. The song 'Come Home, Cardinal Pell'[98] by Tim Minchin played in my head throughout the trip, a guiding light in the form of a cheeky, upbeat tune, getting us through our challenging existence there on Campieus' Catholic turf. The best margherita pizza and strong Italian coffee kept us physically fuelled, but mentally, we duelled. We battled to cope and Campeius seemed almost flawless in his delivery until his ill-fated speech about sexual abuse of children not being of much interest to him and dead birds, an absolutely moot point.

I found it rather amusing when Campeius admitted to Kurt Pressman, after the meeting with the survivor group, 'I am not wooden inside,' when discussing his notably cold demeanour, like Pinocchio, the wooden puppet who turns into a real boy – but only after he shows courage and bravery. Where was the courageous leadership from Campeius that we were all so desperate for and where was the Pope in all this mess? Unlike Campeius, the Pope reneged on his promise to meet the survivors. Campeius met with us and he promised action for victims but ultimately gave nothing. His empty words were rendered meaningless. He only helped Conservative Town cover up, not heal.

Prior to the trip to Rome, a local artist painted survivor Cameron Carlisle for an Australian Art Award 2015. The painting did not make the top fifty selection, but I suspect that it was considered too dicey politically. In passing, Cameron had said that his past is available for public view, but he didn't say what it was that he had done. Jacques DeBoys later filled in the gaps by going public about Cameron sexually abusing him. I cannot get over Cameron's cowardly omission, particularly as child sexual abuse was the topic we shared night and day, including in our nightmares. We were united in our cause, a new family of growing strength, yet unbeknown to us, our spokesperson hid a dark secret that he too was an abuser.

Cameron Carlisle did not ruin our credibility but rather revealed the complex nature of childhood sexual abuse. This is a conversation that is begging to be had and needs to be had, but we still seem to be preoccupied with the question 'Are the survivors telling the truth?' We have done little more than clarify that there is a difference between homosexuality and paedophilia and childhood sexual abuse and that alone took many hearing days, for it was clear that the Catholic Church seemed to not know there was a difference. Paedophilia translated into homosexuality under Canon Law, something that could be either silenced, ignored, denied, or fixed in America in places like Fantasy Wells.

Since Cameron was shunned by many in the survivor group, other people have also admitted to me that they sexually abused others after their own childhood sexual abuse. Horrifyingly, they do not see themselves as sex abusers or paedophiles. There seems to be an unwritten assumption that if you were abused, your responding abuse of others should not be judged in the same way. Again, this is not how many victims see it. Sexual abuse is sexual abuse, regardless of the reasons why the abuse happened or how old the perpetrator is.

The Wikipedia definition of a paedophile is as follows:

Paedophilia is a psychiatric disorder in which an adult or older adolescent experiences a primary or exclusive sexual attraction to prepubescent children.[99]

Older children abusing younger children is also paedophilia in my book obviously, as that's my story. It happens at schools between children in the playground, in homes between siblings, in the State's residential care units for children between children. This is child sexual abuse too; it's not anything else in my book just because the perpetrator is a child.

It always worried me how King Claudius, as an adult, would lie down with the children at family functions, watching

Disney movies with them. He'd socialise with the children rather than the adults, which was notably weird. Lying on the carpet, King Claudius would have to bend his long legs just to fit alongside his younger cousins, his own children and his second cousins too. He stuck out like a sore thumb in the rumpus room as normally, young children are the last people you want to hang out with when you're an adult with children of your own and you're in the company of adults.

I suspect other family members were also abused by King Claudius, more than just his sisters and me. It was certainly creepy seeing him appear as the Pied Piper, surrounded by children at most family occasions. I really feel guilty that I didn't disclose his sexual abuse of us earlier than I did as there were other easy pickings for King Claudius in our big family; King Claudius had six siblings, eighteen first cousins, his own three children, his four nieces and nephews (now six at least) and thirteen second cousins (now seventeen at least). Needless to say, I didn't allow my children to be anywhere near him, with his special interest in children like all paedophiles have. However, my children socialised with his children a lot years ago as they lived in Conservative Town with their mother, Tamora, the daughter of my parents' former best friends, Brutus and Portia.

Chapter 32

Putti and Catamites in Rome

At Traditional University, I majored in fine art history and my studies included works of the Baroque and Rococo Periods; powerful, lavish and somewhat disturbing were the images to me. Marble cherubs and fecund children adorning adults in subject matter with overt sexual overtones. The Louvre, the Uffizi, the Sistine Chapel, St Peter's Basilica – the ceilings and walls are crammed full of sexualised imagery and representations of abused children throughout history. Objectified and beautified for the voyeuristic gaze, children appear to be very much a part of an adult's sexual world and interest. Certainly, sexual abuse of children is common to all nations.

Tourists queue up for hours to see paintings of the great masters worldwide. When I went overseas in 1981, I went to St Peters Basilica and a photo was taken of me with the cherubs. Upon looking at paintings over the centuries, particularly ones typical of the Rococo Period, it's obvious to me that the sexualisation of children has been around for centuries, likely from the beginning of time. In more recent years, I have looked at works by the great masters with fresh eyes, full of a new-found concern.

Caravaggio, the great Italian painter, with a preoccupation with a subject matter of homosexual boys, obviously analogous with his own homosexuality. His painting Boy with a Basket of Fruit[100] is suggestive of offering more than fruit to the viewer – also his sexual services. The expression on the young boy of weary yet clear sexual invitation is typical of the homosexual relationships at that time, a right for free men to have their way with young servant boys whilst retaining their own married status without question.

The Warren Cup[101], estimated dated from the first century AD, is an even clearer display of sexuality in ancient times. It depicts two males engaging in anal sex, one a very young boy and the other a much older male. It was perfectly normal to satisfy man's sexual urges in this way in ancient times, using whatever was within arm's reach that took his fancy.

A priest and his young catamite or altar boy is well documented and a practise remaining today, albeit now replaced with the new politically correct term altar servers. Regardless, priests have always had young male accompaniments at their service, religious or otherwise. In its modern usage, the term catamite refers to a boy as the passive or receiving partner in anal intercourse with a man. In its ancient usage, a catamite (Latin catamitus) was a pubescent boy who was the intimate companion of a young man in ancient Greece and Rome, usually in a paederastic relationship. The survivors of clergy abuse would certainly attest to the fact that priests thought it was their God-given right to have sex with them as young boys under Canon Law. Sadly, my friend and brave survivor Boyet was Cardinal Carlisle's live-in catamite at the presbytery in Clearstream and the people of Clearstream and the church, who knew what was going on, simply let it happen.

In the year 2008, the famous photographer Bill Henson stirred up the photography-versus-pornography debate when he was set to exhibit twenty nude photographs of children, some 12 and 13 years old, in Sydney. These works were considered criminal by police and the works were seized and he was charged with the offence of 'publish an indecent article' under the Crimes Act 1900 NSW (Section 578C). His photographs became the subject of another scandal in 2011 when he held another exhibition of nude photographs in Melbourne, again of teenaged girls.

From the sexual relations between young boys and men commonly found in the Roman baths to the incest between family members in the modern day, sex between adults and children continues with no sign of stopping or slowing down. Children are being sold as sex slaves worldwide on the Dark Web and through seemingly legitimate websites such as Backpage.com, where emoticons are used by paedophiles as Morse code for underage sex trade. Children are sold on this website and there's current litigation in the United States trying to close the website down with much difficulty as the page is sponsored by Google and Facebook. Clearly, where there's money, there's power and corruption.

The fashion and modelling industry are also responsible for the sexualisation of children, with young girls wearing clothes like Britney Spears and other teen pop idols – cropped tops exposing belly buttons, short shirts and short shorts, as if ready for a nightclub at 5 years of age, leaving nothing to the imagination. To the best of my knowledge, the department store Target was made to change the clothing designs for young girls because of public criticism and the huge economic backlash.

As a society, we need to ultimately decide whether we condone the sexualisation of children or not. We can hardly criticise some religions allowing multiple young wives, mail-order brides, or overseas sex shopping when our own laws in Australia fail our own sexually abused children so dismally. Why be enraged about the treatment of women in India, for example, when I have had acid poured on me by so-called civilised men here in this country? Legal acid and familial acid, albeit in the form of polite legal conversation, toxic court orders and family banishment.

In a family law matter involving child sexual abuse, my client, the mother, alleged her child was being sexually abused by the father after the child made disclosures to her. The way that SOCIT Conservative Town dealt with the matter was appalling. Initially, the child did their VARE interview with the police, but the inexperienced policewoman formed a view that the mother was lying and threatened her to stay away and to stop reporting her concerns to the police station. Moreover, the DHHS formed a view that the mother was hurting her own child, despite the injuries happening in the father's care, and placed the child with the father.

The timeline on this matter, more than six years now, is quite typical and it has certainly been a tumultuous time legally. The child is seriously traumatised and has disclosed to the mother that the father is still sexually abusing him. The father has never been charged and remains the primary carer.

When children disclose sexual abuse they are almost certainly telling the truth, but are they really believed by anyone other than the mother? Does the truth fit into the adult world somewhere? At the police station? Does it gain traction in that courtroom anywhere against the judicial warnings, disclaimers, presumptions, inferences, biases, prejudices and procedures all designed to protect paedophiles?

If you are unfamiliar with judicial warnings, you should watch a trial one day and see how stacked the law is. The judge explains and stresses the words 'beyond all reasonable doubt', as does the prosecutor, who goes to great lengths to explain they have the burden of proving beyond all reasonable doubt. They explain how the accused is innocent unless the evidence proves otherwise beyond all reasonable doubt. I suspect that most jurors by this stage would be feeling the weight of jury duty, questioning if their suspicions of doubt are even real after hearing the defendant is innocent. This is a crazy starting point and those directions should not be given, in my opinion. I have to say, it's absolutely ludicrous hearing it be said and then looking at the faces of the jury members. Don't wait until your own trial to learn how hopeless the situation is for victims of sexual assault.

Clearly, the law is designed to keep the criminals at liberty, albeit after a corrupt legal game is played. A criminal's liberty is only important as the jails are full and defendants routinely appealing decisions just keep the barristers briefed and the game of law plays on. But someone is the loser – almost always the victim – but no one in that courtroom cares. The victim isn't there anyway, so the job is made easier. Victims are a name at best. They have no power in that courtroom, no place in that courtroom, no legal representative in that court room and no control over what happens in that courtroom.

When statements are taken by police at SOCIT, of child or adult victims of sexual crime, any subsequent statements obtained may well have differences, particularly if some time has passed. This often leads to police dropping the charges due to "inconsistencies" or anomalies in the chronology. The problem is that this can happen to evidence of any complainant, but particularly children, but it doesn't mean that they were lying in their first statement. Every re-tell will be different, hence 'inconsistencies', but the parties invariably pounce on it and out goes another case, just like that. 'Another child telling lies', concludes defence counsel and police just routinely file the discontinuance paperwork. And apparently, that's still a job well done. And all the defendant ever had to say was 'No comment'. Consistent – no memory required for that. So profound. So powerful. So very learned is the laws test of guilt – not! The defendant should have to put his defence into words from the outset and each time thereafter and be questioned again and again and the versions compared for 'inconsistencies', just as happens for victims.

Sexual predators keep getting away with their crimes. Derryn Hinch's Justice Party was born out of this legal reality and public outrage. Derryn Hinch went to jail for naming and shaming paedophiles, it beggars belief. Derryn is criticised for much, for pushing the boundaries, but to jail him for this shows just how unjust our injustice system is and how intent it is on shutting down the whistle-blower. The Law, like the Church, seeks to protect its image at all costs. I say the image of the law is so very tarnished, it isn't worth protecting as I think society well and truly gets the picture by now. Why doesn't the law reflect society and common sense and stop jailing the people who are trying to stop children from being sexually abused? Jail the abusers instead, surely?

I find myself asking the much-vexed question 'Do we really want the sexual abuse of children to stop?' In theory, people are quick to say yes, of course, but in practise, I seriously doubt it; otherwise, we'd be stopping it. Why oh why is there only one good man with some clout, Derryn Hinch, publicly and unashamedly doing so much to stop it? There should be streams of men in power doing this for most change happens top down, not bottom up. Why are good men mostly silent?

My good friend John Bates is my friend before he is my

client. I get him and he gets me. He has turned his personal pain into action and has advocated strongly for survivors, exerting pressure on politicians at local, State and Federal level. But for too many years, the good men pushing this issue have been the victims themselves: exhausted, stressed, unpaid and running on empty around the clock. They formed a support group, were the contact people for that and have talked many men and women out of suicide. Some, they could not save. Their phone numbers had become a 24-hour lifeline of sorts, but the pressure on their own relationships and families was enormous, carrying the welfare of so many others. John Bates and Gonzalo turned to each other for respite and now describe how together, they make a whole person. When one of them can't get out of bed, dealing with depression and PTSD, the other takes over. This is how the survivor community survives. Whilst generous and amazing, this is not acceptable. Where are the strong, unhurt and stable men and women in leadership to take up the cudgels?

Chapter 33

R v Campieus (2017)

The day before the filing hearing on [DATE] 2017, I was contacted by the Sunrise[102] program to do an interview as I was the lawyer for some of the complainants against Campieus. I had to explain, 'I'm their lawyer but just not in the police case against Campieus.' The Senior Producer immediately asked, 'Who's their lawyer for that then?' and I answered, 'They don't have one!' She was rather stumped and I had to explain further as conceptually, it certainly is difficult to get one's head around the fact that they, victims of crime, never have one. That's because the public perception is that the police represent them, but this is a massive misconception.

The truth is no one represents them as, alarmingly, they are not even a party in the case, their case. If the public only understood this, I'm sure they would be far from accepting. I suspect it's only public ignorance that keeps the vulnerable legal status of victims under the radar and it seems that the government and the legal profession are relieved that the public remains deceived. Why do I feel like a whistle-blower about something so obvious that intelligent politicians and lawyers all know already? Why has not one person in power raised this utter injustice to victims and done something about it? Politics aside, you can't have an adversarial system where one adversary is missing.

On [DATE] 2018, I received a Summons regarding my client's documents. My unrepresented client's documents were the new hot property, a chance for the defendant's solicitors to get the 'motherlode' and use it to discredit my clients through character assassination. That's the way it works. So indirectly, the legal system flicks the On-switch on to victims being represented all of a sudden – but only for that specific purpose. In all other aspects of the case, they remain unrepresented.

Then something most concerning happened. I lost my two clients the day before the Summons hearing. After being their lawyer for two years, I was essentially sacked. I had a call from a CASA worker at lunch time the day before saying "Prospero wanted me to tell you that he doesn't need you anymore as I'm advocating for him now." In the case of my other client Sebastian who had recently died, I never heard from his next of kin again. Prospero had told my husband and I that police told him to stay away from us and to let them know whenever he hears from us. I told him that we needed to obtain his instructions and that the police had no right to do this to him, and that he shouldn't feel guilty for seeing us. It felt like he had to sneak into our office when no one was looking.

I suspect that the legal system was ensuring that nothing would alter the old unquestioned false narrative: that the police are there for the victims. The victims' chance at any representation and protecting those documents was now lost. He was on his own.

Having faith in the police and the legal system is virtual suicide. When the police, social workers and/or family members seek to keep complainants away from their very own lawyers, something is very wrong, for they are taking away their strength and keeping them vulnerable to societal pressures to stay the victim, with no legal standing and a puppet to the police, easily manipulated. Sadly victims only realise this once their case is dropped.

On [DATE] 2018, police confirmed they were dropping the charges where allegations by Sebastian are concerned. No surprise there as he had passed away, but two questions spring to mind: why didn't they tell me this when I asked them and why did they wait until after the defendant's solicitors already had a chance to get hold of some of his documents? That way I could have argued that the documents weren't relevant, as the charges were being dropped in relation to his allegations, and the entirety of his documents could have been protected. The answer is twofold; first, police do not represent complainants and are independent of them; and second, police do not care about the individual complainants, only that some of the police charges stick. They do not care which complainants they drop or what happens to them in that process, so long as some charges are secured, the public confidence in the police can be maintained.

The same thing could happen to any other complainant and he or she will not be able to do anything about it. That is not the best we can do for complainants but pressuring them to stay away from me, their lawyer, is unforgivable. If police are so independent as they claim to be, why did they make it their business to direct the complainants, my clients, and their next of kin to stay away from me, to the complainants' detriment?

I am currently waiting on a response from Martin Pakula, Daniel Andrews and Derryn Hinch as there clearly needs to be legislative change to give victims in the criminal justice system the right to a lawyer. It will be the proudest day for me when I can be that lawyer. I will keep renewing my practising certificate each year in the hope that this will happen. Defence lawyers must be wondering when they'll finally have a true adversary. In the mean time I sit with the media in the gallery, when I should really be at the bar table for victims.

The SBS program Insight aired a show on 28 February 2018, 'Rape on Trial'[103] and one defence lawyer on the panel raised concerns when an officer from SOCIT on that panel said police believe complainants are telling the truth, for they are meant to be 'independent investigators'. He went on to say that if the defendant is presumed 'innocent until proved guilty', how can the police possibly adopt this approach? And herein lies the problem, the very real conflict of interest I have spoken about throughout this book.

After the hearing, the players from inside the courtroom came outside and gathered around chatting, but the physical layout outside was just as interesting as inside the courtroom. The OPP lawyers and defence lawyers were assembled in a large group of about ten people and I sat alone on the other side, with only the media. There were no complainants, of course, as it's not their case and they're told by police not to come to court as there's no need to be there, apparently, as if that's doing victims a favour when its actually doing them a huge disservice. Everyone who was usually there was there, but everyone who should be there wasn't; I was butted out, stubbed out and stamped on, crushed with a dirty boot, so the game could continue without question. I had not spoken to my client, only his CASA worker. I had no idea as to his welfare and I was very worried for him.

The great OPP had worked its working day again and it was time for everyone to go home when Virginia Raven approached me and said if I wanted to contact her, I could. I shouted, 'What's happened to my client? Have you heard from him? Is he OK?' She said, 'Yes, I have,' but did not elaborate. I said, 'You should be ashamed of yourselves. I expected you to object when the defence called my client a "bad domino", but you and your colleague let it continue. It's disgusting.'

Needless to say, Prospero's new "advocate" from CASA was not at court advocating for him and his documents. No one was advocating for him. The Magistrate asked me what I wished to do with the documents, but I was in the Magistrate's hands without client instructions. The OPP didn't care about the documents, as the considerable correspondence between the OPP office and my office before that day proved. When I told the court that it was bizarre that all of a sudden after two years of representation I now have no instructions from two clients, the Magistrate objected to my use of the word "bizarre" but then had a convivial discussion with defence counsel about whether it mattered whether my ex-client was the first bad domino in a line of bad dominoes. No one objected to him being called "a bad domino" but the Magistrate and defence counsel would have been furious if the OPP had called the accused such a name. So why didn't the great OPP object to Sebastian's character being slurred so casually? Because he is not their client, no police witness ever is. I sat there gobsmacked while the OPP sat mute without the pressure of victims watching.

Victims of crime need independent legal representation, and the cheap political stunt of giving them a dog to pat in the court room, when giving evidence, is just that. Frankly, I fail to understand how a dog in a courtroom is considered kosher for victims but a lawyer for victims is considered inconceivable by our government. Where is the 'Victims' Lawyer Bill' I'm so desperate for? We need gutsy politicians to make this happen and lawyers willing to admit to the 'justice charade' that goes on that really the media are only there to see, and who are stopped by endless suppression orders.

Part 5

My New Family

Chapter 34

Me, the Weirdo

As I reflect on my time in Rome, I reflect on my own childhood memories again. I realise that the survivor group in Rome was not the first male survivor group I had known personally. When I was a child in the 1980s, my dad formed his own support group, unbeknown to me at the time. The harsh and immature teenager in me called them losers, sussos, deadbeats and druggos who smoked pot. Some were unemployed and some wore strange clothes. Alternatives and outcasts who were into strange music and ideas. There was an eternal university student who had a scary laugh and drove an old recycled postal van, there was another man who was gay (noteworthy at that time in consistently conservative Conservative Town), there was another man who was a masseur and the others included a social worker and a teacher. They were not my cup of tea nor my Mum's.

Dad always had his wacky friends visiting and one day the famous artist Stelarc[104] came to our house with his bionic arm and explanations about safely suspending his body around the world by fish hooks planted directly into his flesh, as he showed me his photographs of various performance art suspensions from famous buildings.

I often wondered why Dad didn't have 'normal' friends who wore beige pants and checked shirts, who drove shiny

new European cars, the ones I would see collect my friends at
Grammar School. Dad spent so much time with these
'weirdos' as if he were dependent on them somehow. I never
knew why until 2013, when Dad disclosed his own abuse. One
of Dad's 'weirdo' friends came to Rome with us; I was quite
shocked when I first saw his name in the Royal Commission
witness list. Of course, it all makes sense to me now. Of course,
Nym is not a weirdo at all, nor has he ever been. Nym had
been sexually abused like my dad, like me. Nym had hosted a
radio show with my dad called Travelling Blind[105] in the 1980s
in Conservative Town and had been part of what I see as Dad's
original survivor group. I now saw the beauty in all those men
I previously branded 'weirdo'. I now desperately wanted to
join that weirdo gang, where you're accepted, believed, never
judged and treated with respect. Being surrounded by like-
minded people is so comforting. You don't have to explain
yourself; they just get you. Dad survived this way; they were
his lifeline.

I am proud to say that I am now part of the survivor family
that has re-formed and grown in number. My friends include
John Bates, Jack Cade, Gonzalo, Philo, Prospero, Nym, Moth,
Matthew Carlisle, Jacques DeBoys, Ajax, Eros, Boyet and the
late Sebastian and they have become my new family now.
They are part of my life far beyond the lawyer–client
relationship I have with some of them. Many are locals living
in Conservative Town and surviving in the aftermath, just like
me. It doesn't matter to me or them that I am a secondary
victim, for it's all the same to us, sexual abuse, whether it's
taught by or orchestrated by the Catholic Clergy in
Conservative Town or in cases where a family member is the
perpetrator with a link to institutional abuse or not. Child
sexual abuse is just that, regardless of the parameters set by a

Royal Commission, the law, or otherwise. The definition of sexual abuse should be set by victims, not politicians in Canberra nor privileged white men on the bench.

Chapter 35

Vale Pavlovic Family

Good riddance, old family; I've shed you like a snake sheds its skin. I've outgrown you all, but I do miss the culture that I was a part of – the piano accordions, the guitars, the din, the fun, the drama, the many celebrations and events, that sense of belonging to an extended clan. My right to my cultural heritage.

However, I do not for a single minute miss the actual individual members within that family, not one of you. I pity you all, the mindless, gutless hypocrites you cousins all are, tucking your children into bed safely at night. Nowhere is safe, people, but one's home is the most dangerous of places. You will turn from your own children in times of adversity as you have turned from me, as Uncle King Lear and Aunty, King Lear's wife, have turned from their abused daughters to support their abusing sons and carried on with the pantomime that is their family. And you think you are any different do you, that real life won't happen to you and yours? What position do you think you will take when something happens to your own children? Think again.

Decius, my allegedly super-clever contemporary, my former cousin. Your emotional intelligence is critically below par. Your telephone call to me on 27 November 2015 was rather telling. You first told me you were in Australia visiting from the United States and wanted to catch up with me and said, 'I hope you're doing OK.' Initially, I was so heartened by your call that you had me in tears. I thanked you for reaching out to me as you were the first cousin to do so. I hadn't spoken to anyone in the family for two years, almost to the day.

You then asked if we could meet up for the sake of your daughter knowing who my parents and I were in the future, but this was in vain. You told me that you were concerned about her, a 1-year-old, not knowing who my parents and I were when she looked at family photographs in the future. But your attempt at contact had a huge rider: that we not discuss King Claudius and the situation at all. Moreover, you then declared that you had just held a birthday party a few days earlier for your daughter and had invited everyone in the family, including King Claudius, but not my parents and I. You had clearly taken sides, Decius; you wanted to barrack for the winning team and then come and see me and take a few photos when no one was looking, behind closed doors. That's called 'having your cake and eating it too'. Don't worry about ever crawling back and changing camps because the door is forever shut on you and your father. Mark my words.

Gallingly, you tried to tell me that I saw the family through rose-coloured glasses and that in your view, we really only remain in contact with a few close relatives each anyway and so you claimed the families' treatment of me should be of no great loss to me. This was coming from you, a man who went all the way to America to live, and then you came all the way back to Australia to have a massive family birthday party for your daughter, who won't even remember it. Newsflash: the party was for you, Decius; that's how important the family is to you. Maybe it is you, not me, as you claim, who is seeing the family through rose-coloured glasses. Maybe take them off

and look at King Claudius and our sick family in the cold light
of day and not when you're homesick.

When I refused contact on your shoddy terms, you asked
whether it would be OK if you called me again in a few years
to see if I would be ready for contact with you then. I told you
that the question wasn't whether I would be ready but
whether you would be ready. I told you that to know you
would mean me going backwards, having to undo all the hard
work I'd done on myself to get me thus far, and would betray
all my current work in the Royal Commission. That's when
you were quick to announce that you were now an atheist –
the most religious cousin I had, now an atheist. Well, blow me
down. Was that your attempt at separating yourself from the
behaviour of the vile Catholic clergy who abused children in
our hometown and covered it up? If it was, you failed, for your
position in the family mirrors and matches the clergy's
behaviour. The Pavlovic family, including you, is treating me
just like the Catholic Church treats its abused parishioners. I
suggest you tell your daughter the truth about who I am in
photos and why I'm absent from the family photos post 2013.
Yeah, that old thing, the truth. I suggest that she Google my
name and work out my absence from there. It won't be hard,
Mr Google.

Quite strange, the holier-than-thou cousin now denouncing
your religion. Interesting. Decius, I suspect something severed
your special relationship with Jesus, whom you claimed was
responsible for your VCE score. Yes, that's what you proudly
told me back in 1991; I remember it well. I wonder – perhaps it
was your days at Mary Immaculate that destroyed your faith.
Or your days at St Michael's College when it was full of now
convicted paedophiles. Or cousin King Claudius, the family sex
offender and family hero.

My cousins Witches One and Two of the Three Witches, you were snookered in Laurent Patisserie in Big Smoke, in December 2015. There I was with our mutual friend John Bates and my dad, your Uncle Julius Caesar, during a break in the Royal Commission hearings, when we bumped into you. How fortuitous for us to see you and your parents there. I cannot believe you passed onto John Bates to tell me how proud you were of me representing him. Oh please, you were supporting him but not me, yet John Bates and I are fighting for the same cause. His family also deserted him when he disclosed his abuse, and your only explanation for your identical treatment of me was 'You know it's hard with family'. Witch Two of the Three Witches, how could you say that to him? What an absolutely pathetic 'good Croatian girl' stance, your good-girl upbringing at home, Good Girl School and Saintly College shining through brightly there. How dim of you. You declare on Facebook that you have a strong-willed daughter. May Hermione always speak up and not follow the model you have set – smile on, drink on, pretend on and follow the crowd.

Witch One of the Three Witches, your position is the same as Decius'. You only come up to me when no one is watching. If John Bates wasn't with me that day, I suspect that you never would have come up to Dad and I like you did. You say one thing and do another. You told King Claudius on Facebook how handsome he is in full knowledge of what he did to his sisters and I. Can't you see how creepy that is? I nearly vomited when I read it. I noticed that the Pope changed his views on divorce, just in time for you. That allowed your dad to support you that day at court, I'm sure; otherwise, I suspect that he would have forbidden it and you would have had to stay a Croatian good girl; a doormat.

Uncle Cassius, I saw you supporting Cardinal Campeius in the Conservative Town Daily Bugle newspaper recently. Not surprisingly, you are helping pay for his legal bills for a top QC, just as King Lear has paid for King Claudius' five-year legal defence, no doubt.

King Claudius, you are the most ridiculous poor excuse of a man. You have brought so much pain to me and to my family, it's unquantifiable. I will never forgive you for the position you have adopted and now maintain. I would have forgiven you for what you did then if you didn't deny what you did then now. You need to own the hurt and loss that you have caused. I will never let you off the hook nor anyone who lies for you. Let your confessions be heard in this book so all can see the great chasm between your words and your actions. Court process and the predicted and likely trajectory is the only thing stopping me from seeking justice to the end of a trial; never mind how ironic that is for me as a lawyer. You know what you did. I pity sociopathic you and your pathetic parents and family.

Chapter 36

Our Fair-Weathered Friends Called Jerkov

What a sad effort at trying to silence me. Right from the beginning, soon after I disclosed, we went to visit you to tell you what had happened, being our best friends. But you already knew, didn't you, Portia? Mum and I have never seen you dance an avoidance jig like that before – nervously bumbling words, bustling plastic bags, raving on about Wilsons fruit and veg over the top of me so I couldn't speak. Shame on you. Then when I finally managed to tell you, you went into a spiel about how your uncle 'felt you up' as a child, but you would never tell your poor Aunty as it would break her heart. What a clear message you were sending me, Portia, you self-interested, spineless latter-day Catholic. And then you went on to ask why I hadn't been to see a counsellor yet in all these years, in an accusatory tone, as if I should have processed and dealt with it all years ago so I could have saved you from it all. I would have thought you'd have more insight, but I was sadly mistaken.

Yet, your story about your satisfaction at seeing the dead man floating down the river in New Guinea, the man who sexually abused your children, tells me justice only matters to you when it relates to your own children, not others.

You are the same woman who has relied on my parents' support for more than forty years, particularly when your son

Sampson died as a pilot in a plane crash in Sky. My wonderful parents who both took weeks off work to physically search for him in South Australia with you. You, the woman whose daughter accused me of being a liar about King Claudius' abuse. The same mother/daughter team who made up rumours about me and spread them over Conservative Town, from St Michael's College and Calvary College to Bethlehem House. The same woman who ditched my parents' lifelong friendship, so you could play pretend and hobnob with the landed gentry of Conservative Town on a tissue of lies. Quite sad. I have nothing but scorn and pity for you and Brutus.

Brutus, the new Australian friend of my dad since you were little children at St Ignatius Primary School, Birdville. Roughly fifty-seven years of friendship with my wonderful father, my family and I, now buried by you to sustain the deception of a sociopathic paedophile. Your daughter Tamora married and divorced a paedophile; face facts.

I will never forget the day I bumped into you and your work colleagues in the beautiful Castle Café, where you sprang to your feet in a show of deep friendship, firmly and ostentatiously patting me on the back the way you do, in a demonstrative display of affection. This was long after my disclosure though, when you no longer associated with me or my family. Never approach me again, Brutus. I don't know who you are.

It's funny how family works, isn't it Brutus? Your own sister Alexas claimed your father sexually abused her, but your family didn't want to believe her either. I saw her several times again in more recent years as an adult and I remember her strong new-aged religious bent – a way to cope with the pain, I imagine. Why didn't you believe her? Why is the truth too hard for you?

I also remember your father affectionately calling me 'Alexas' in his strong Russian accent (my middle name like his daughter's) and his odd Easter card greeting one year: 'Life is a daily risk.' He was certainly right about that. I'm just glad that my parents didn't leave me alone with him and his borscht soup in Urquhart Street.

Chapter 37

The Handshake

In early September 2017, St George's Church in Church Street North, Conservative Town filled with family and friends to honour and pay respect to the late Jakov Zipic. It was a bitterly cold Conservative Town day, but that didn't keep the crowds away. Jakov was a warm and kind man who emigrated to Australia from Croatia in 1956, from the same humble village, Dracevac, where Dad's family came from. In fact, his mother, Baba Pava Zipic (née Pavlovic) and my grandfather, Dida Bruno Pavlovic, were brother and sister. So Jakov Zipic is my dida's nephew, my dad's cousin, and my second cousin. His mother, Baba Pava, is the lady who taught me how to pluck feathers from a chicken when I was in Dracevac as a child in 1981. Pava also visited my parents' house during her trip to Australia in 1976, when I was just 3 years old.

Jakov Zipic was generous and loving like his mother. He had helped my grandparents Baba and Dida when they too emigrated to Australia from Croatia in 1960 with eight children. He and my dida were not dissimilar in appearance, both with pale blue eyes, fair skin and fair hair. He had been present at many celebrations in my childhood and thereafter, along with his brother Slavco Zipic and their families. We were part of the same clan. We had an extended family picnic with them each year in Windsor Gardens in Big Smoke or Lake

Provincial, Conservative Town. Needless to say, I haven't gone since my disclosure and banishment in 2013.

Mum, Dad and I considered that we must go to his funeral no matter the Pavlovic family scission. We had not seen any Pavlovic or extended family for about four years, not since King Lear and King Lear's wife had visited us in September 2013 and after that, their presence at court on [DATE] 2014, but we weren't talking to each other anymore by then. We expected members of our Pavlovic family would attend Jakov's funeral but determined that we had no reason not to be there.

We had no idea what King Claudius, King Lear and King Lear's wife and family loudmouths like Desdemona had told the extended family and what people believed, but we didn't care. People can make up their own minds and I would stand tall regardless of any small-minded conclusions. When we arrived, by chance, we were parked next to my Aunty Emilia and my cousins as we did not recognise their new car. My first cousin Cassio came over on his own to greet us warmly, which we thought was big of him. We signed the funeral attendance book, grabbed a funeral service booklet and took our seats. During the service, we heard the pain of loss from his children and grandchildren and the celebration of happy, beautiful memories. I looked at his friendly face on the cover and could hear the sound of his voice again easily. I watched pictures scrolling of happy family times. I watched the full mass, respectfully remembering the times I had also said the Lord's Prayer, sung the hymns, crossed myself hearing the gospel and knelt in prayer. Now there was only silence and stillness from the three of us despite the active religious ritual around us. We watched our family take holy communion. We watched the priest bless the coffin and Tetka Mary coughed from the incense. We heard Jakov's favourite prayer recited in Croatian by Mercutio for his uncle, the same man who would later become he and his sister Iris Reynaldo's surrogate father.

Mercutio was Jakov's nephew, but in or about 1974, Mercutio's father, Robin Reynaldo, stabbed and killed his own wife, Diana Reynaldo, Mercutio's mother, and Mercutio's younger brother, Solanio, in an horrific act of family violence and later hung himself whilst in jail. As a result, Mercutio and his sister, Iris Reynaldo, were raised by their Uncle Jakov and his then wife Lucetta Zipic. In that way, Jakov's own children, Octavia and Oswald, grew up with their cousins Iris Reynaldo and Mercutio Reynaldo as a brother and sister. When Mum and Dad married on 26 August 1972, Robin Reynaldo and Diana Reynaldo were guests at their wedding. Three-and-a-half-year-old King Claudius was their page boy and Hecate was their flower girl.

After Jakov's funeral service, we happily milled around, talking to people, including family members we had not seen for years. Many seemed surprisingly unaware as to the reason for our considerable absence from family events and were genuinely delighted to see us, asking 'Where have you been?' We were a little unsure of ourselves, having lost our rightful space in such a familial setting, though through no fault of our own. We answered diplomatically but were welcomed and hugged and kissed on both cheeks in that familiar Croatian way. It felt fantastic to be back in our fold again, surrounded by all the familiar faces that had celebrated me throughout my life since birth. I realised just how much King Claudius had taken from me and from my parents, then and there, right at that moment, and my stomach knotted in anger. Familial connection holds you together like glue. No wonder we had been falling apart.

The reaction of those around me suggested that King Lear

and King Lear's wife had not told them what their son King
Claudius had done to me. Perhaps they are unaware of my
plight since that time. What lies had they been told? I
wondered. Where do they think my parents and I went for
four years when previously, we'd been at every event with
bells on? Then I remembered that Malvolio Pavlovic had been
at Gospa Velika the night I disclosed and had heard the whole
thing. He was a Croatian bigwig and knew every Croatian in
Conservative Town. Then I remembered that Snezna Daric
had told me years ago that rumours were flying around
Conservative Town that I had made up lies to go after the
'Pavlovic millions'. I also caught glimpses of my cousin
Desdemona hiding in the wings in the church vestibule with
her Croatian cronies, keeping a low profile for the first time in
her life. She barely made it past the back of the crowd, and she
certainly did not mingle further than with those to whom I
suspect she has told lies about me to. Startlingly, I could not
hear her ordinarily dominating voice. Desdemona had turned
into a church mouse and was hiding together with her mother,
Emilia, Uncle Macbeth and Uncle Cassius. Why were they all
hiding? I wonder. Hiding from the truth again?

I concluded that there is no way that the extended family
could not know what had happened between King Claudius
and I. So, what was going on then?

Then out of nowhere, Uncle King Lear came up to Dad and
I and shook Dad's hand and then mine. I had no time to think;
my body was on autopilot as I reached out my hand to his in
return so as not to create a scene. He said, 'Dobro' (hello), or
some similar cordial greeting to me and I looked him in the eye
and said something equally benign and unmemorable back.
The surprise of his action caught me off guard, but I remember
looking at his face, as if trying to take a mental snapshot in the

second that our eyes locked. I was in shock, as if needing to check his face to see if this was for real. Then I turned and kept going to another circle of people to escape the situation. The last thing I wanted to do was to shake his hand as we were certainly not at peace.

The sign of peace given at church is an interesting thing to me. One is prompted to turn and shake the hands of those in adjacent pews, including strangers, and say, 'Peace be with you.' What lovely symbolic action for a Christian community. To me, it's a little contrived though as it denies the power differential that can exist between those engaged in the handshake. It's like going to a psychologist who suggests ways of improving communication by role playing, instructing that once you get used to relating to each other in new patterns of healthy communication, albeit staged and mechanical initially, after time, your brain believes your body and your words. I suspect that King Lear had tried to replicate the sign of peace he'd given to others in the pews around him just minutes earlier during the service in the hope that his handshake could bring peace between us, to make him appear Christian in action. It didn't. However, could it in the circumstances? It couldn't even display the illusion of same convincingly.

Has he forgotten that I am having a costly court battle with his son King Claudius for more than four and a half years now over his sexual assaults on me?

Has he forgotten that he has failed to tell his son King Claudius, 'You be good boy'?

Has he forgotten his other son Hamlet's involvement in the sexual assaults too?

Has he forgotten that his own position in the family as 'top dog alpha male' is King Claudius' strength?

Has he forgotten what King Claudius did to me and to at least two of his own daughters, Goneril and Regan?

Has he forgotten my isolated dad, Julius Caesar, his younger brother?

Perhaps King Lear had listened to the wise words of Jakov Zipic, referred to in the funeral service that day:
   'Always shake hands, including with your enemy!'
   I was in the thick of the war with his son. However, in truth, I was not really his enemy but to see that King Lear would have to be a leader, not a coward. He would have to support me and his daughters above his abusing sons.
   And so, the stalemate remained, despite the handshake.

Chapter 38

A Chance at Peace

'Ok, we'll leave your ticket at the front desk. See you soon!', I said to Christopher.

'Is Chris coming with us to Dali next week too?', asked Dad.

'Yes, he loves Surrealism. Remember his graffiti art days?"

'Oh yes, he was addicted. I remember his tag,' said Mum.

Anyway, he's on his way,' I replied.

'You know, your lake of waterlilies is far better than Monet's at Giverny. Maybe it's time for a new series?' I said, and I meant it.

'True-true', said Dad.

As I turned into High Street to park at the art gallery, I was delighted to get an untimed spot, right out the front, for I learned as a child how long my Dad spends at art exhibitions; studying each painting up close, then from a few strides back, and then Bump!, straight into someone else who happily joins his art critique, extending my childish whining. We would be a while today.

I opened the grand old door and was talking to Mum about how we'd have afternoon tea in the gallery café at the end, when bang, coming straight towards us were my Aunty and Uncle King Lear and King Lear's wife as they were in the same small two metre space, leaving by the only entry/exit point. As

I looked away to the side, in my ingrained automated response, I heard an exchange of familiar yet brief hellos behind me. And as I turned around, they were gone, the closing door the only evidence of the fleeting reminder of my family lost.

I turned to Mum and Dad and said, "This is really sad. That's your brother dad, we should have a coffee at least, just to break the ice. The fight is over now, maybe it's time for peace."

'Well, I could call him,' said Dad.

'That's a great idea,' I said. 'I think it's time.'

'Do you think today?', asked Mum.

'Yes, why wait?' I wondered, looking at Dad.

"It would be good to have a cuppa with Lady Macbeth too Mum", I said. Next time you see her in Aldi, invite her."

Seven months had passed since the matter finalised between King Claudius and I. The past is the past and everyone knew the score. Moving forward meant wiping the slate clean and meeting up despite what had happened, using the familial history and shared experience before I disclosed to come together again. There were so many happy memories to draw on, and I believe it's never too late. You only need two parties willing to move forward to bury the hatchet. After all, I had done nothing wrong, nor had my parents.

But I expected no apology nor needed any from any of them. I told Dad to tell them we are meeting not to talk about my sexual assaults nor to do a post mortem, but to forge a way forward together, no matter how uncomfortable initially.

Like John Lennon, all we are saying is give peace a chance.

Chapter 39

Calling Home

Dad was notably excited by our renewed hope of mended Pavlovic family; we all were. He took on the task of calling his siblings with a renewed gusto and together we thought how wonderful it would be to go to a family party again. What would that party look like? Would people even talk to me or would I be ignored, eating alone with my family in a corner?

My Dad's rendition of the calls he made is as follows:

Call 1 - Call to King Lear's House

King Lear's Wife answers the phone

Julius–'Hello, this is Julio'
King Lear's Wife –'Oh hello', she said with voice that went from a certain volume petering down to zero.
Julius–'I'm calling you with Cleopatra's suggestion to call you after seeing you today, as we are not getting any younger. We would like to see if we can put it all behind us and see if we can resume our normal human relationships to which we've been accustomed.'

Then there was silence and no response from her, so I kept padding for familiarity to try to strike a response, finding myself gushing with further warmth and enthusiasm for the idea. She did not reciprocate and due to her silence, I proffered a meeting point at BH's at 2pm on Sunday, including with Cleopatra and Antony.

King Lear's Wife –'Oh, it's too much to overcome. I have to consult the family.'

Julius–'Do you mean the Pavlovic brothers?'

King Lear's Wife–'No, I mean myfamily. There's been some wild accusations to get over and it's been pretty damning. And what we had is a home invasion.'

Julius–'Of course you have to consult family', I said, not wanting to antagonise her. 'I say it's been a harrowing experience for everybody and we have all been traumatised by this long drawn out event.'

King Lear's Wife–'It's not just you that's been traumatised during this period, what about us?'

I tried to interject and correct but she kept talking, and I heard some inaudible sounds. I tried to concur with her about the widespread hurt, but she was obsessed with her own side's hurt.

King Lear's Wife–'I'll have to discuss it with my family, so let's leave it at that, alright?'

Julius– Ok, that's fine by me and I'll await your response.

She had poured cold water on my suggestion and turned it into an opportunity to deny the original accusations. There was no mention of the outcome or of her son's admission, but rather an outrage over the invasion of privacy and counter accusations.

Call 2 - to Macbeth & Lady Macbeth

Julius–'Hello Lady Macbeth, how are you?

Lady Macbeth–'Good, thank you very much.'

Julius–'I just wanted to contact you about us meeting up to get things back to normal with our family. We see each other without connecting and its so terribly sad.'

Lady Macbeth–'I am for everything like that, for sure. Let's have Macbeth make the arrangements so I'll let you speak to him."

Julius–'Hello Macbeth, it's been a long time and I wish to meet up with King Lear and you too. We have just seen King Lear and his wife briefly at the gallery, and we were wondering if you'd like to meet with us at BH's next Sunday at 2pm.

Macbeth–'You always welcome to my house. Come see me any, anytime. I am sorry for what I said. I didn't mean no offend nobody. I just said [at Gospa Velika] if somebody not die, it's not as important. I didn't want hurt no-body'

He was emotional and so glad to get back on taking terms, as was I.

Julius–'So I'll see you at BH's at 2pm on Sunday.'

Macbeth –'We go to mass - on Sundays - and we usually go to La Porchetta for lunch, so let's eat at 12 o'clock at La Porchetta. Ok?'

Julius–'Well, we will come there with Cleopatra and Antony at 12pm then.'

Macbeth–'We have been missing not seeing you.'

Julius–'We look forward to seeing you on Sunday and we will be there.'

We ended our conversation in agreement about the importance of family and the priority of getting back together.

Call 3- to my sister Emilia

Emilia – answer service msg left

I called my sister next, but she didn't answer as her phone went to voicemail.

I left the following message:

Julius–'Hi Emilia, we have just seen King Lear and his wife at the art gallery and Macbeth has suggested that we meet at la Porchetta at 12pm after mass as you normally do. It's a definite date for those who wish to make a new start, to forgive and forget the past and be there for the future, without the fighting we've been doing. You are welcome to be there if you are free on this day to open up again the talks and visits we once enjoyed.'

Call 4 – Call to my brother Cassius.

Julius–'Hi Cassius, its Julius, how are you?'

Cassius–'How are you?'

Julius–'Good. I'm ringing because I just talked to King Lear's wife on the phone. Look, we are trying to organise a get together, she said she'll get back to me about meeting us at La Porchetta. We are doing the rounds for Sunday lunch next week. Macbeth invited us for 12pm, as it suited them to have it after mass, and Emilia has been invited on message bank. Cleopatra suggested it and wishes for it to go ahead.'

Cassius –'Oh, that's fantastic, I will be there. I thought it would never happen. It's the best news I've had in years. You can cut short the conversation at any time, but I just want to keep talking to you, I'm so appi. I just want to talk to you and hear your voice. I am looking forward to getting back to what it used to be. We are missing you and only last night we caught up with Brutus and were singing "Lord it's hard to be humble" and we commented that someone is missing from this song – you. It's never been the same without you. Brutus said there's a missing link too and we both missed your antics.'

Julius –'Yes, wonderful, and we are looking forward to catching up and seeing you a La Porchetta. See you then.'

Call 5- My second call to my sister Emilia

Julius - Hello Emilia, this is Julius, how are you?

Emilia- Oh Julio, how are you? I got your message last night and I'm very, very appi that you called. You don't know how much this means to me. I am so appi that you have contacted me, and I'm coming to the meeting. I am supposed to come to Big Smoke but I'm coming to La Porchetta because it's more important. Oh, I'm so appi and it was my birthday last week. Everyone was over here, but if I'd known I would have invited you. My real birthday is three weeks before, but I celebrate the day father registered my birth.

Julius– I know, my birthday has the same problem. But its great news that you can come.

Emilia – Is Calpurnia coming?

Julius– of course.

Emilia- 'I'm so sorry for what I said – you know how you are angry at yourself sometimes? How you can't make people do what you want them to do.'

Julius–'Yes. I'm so looking forward to seeing you on Sunday.'

I could hear the relief in her voice to the opportunity of going back to old times and she broke down, crying in happiness.

Call 6 - Phone call to King Lear

Julius –'Hi King Lear, this is Julio.'

King Lear –'errrrr' (as if saying 'Oh' in a disappointed tone)

Julius –'Look, a lot of time has passed by, and we thought of meeting up. I've called your wife and talked to her, but the time has since changed to 12pm at La Porchetta. What has happened in the past, we can't change but now we want to try to start a new.

King Lear – you mean what's happened or what hasn't happened?

I wasn't going to bite. I was seeking a resolution.

Julius–'Look, I have called the other brothers and Macbeth said because he goes to mass, for us all to meet at La Porchetta, not BH's as I had said to your wife.'

King Lear –'I have to talk to my wife first.'

Julius–'Cassius is coming, and Emilia is coming, and Macbeth and his wife; they are all coming on Sunday.'

King Lear–'I'll get back to you. I don't know, I could be there.'

Julius–'No need to get back to me. It's only an invite for family wising to come. But how's your health by the way?'

King Lear–'I could be better.'

I picked up on his tone of concern about needing to consult his wife, despite the positive family consensus. I also suspected that his wife had not told him of my call to them on Sunday, because he didn't seem to know about it when I spoke to him. Yet, I didn't quiz him on it out of respect to his ill composure, however I knew that something was amiss.

Call 7 - To Brutus

Julius–'Hi Brutus, this is Julio.'

Brutus –'Oh hi Julio', he said in a glum tone.

Julius- We are trying to make amends for the past, for lost

time, and we are meeting at La Porchetta at 12pm on Sunday if you'd like to come. I've discussed it with all the family members and they are all coming but King Lear and his wife are still consulting each other.

Brutus–'I think it's too late to make up. I commend you trying to get us together again, but too much has happened. I think this is better dealt with between your brothers and sister as I am not family. I think the matter will be better dealt with on a one-to-one basis. But I fear it's too late as the differences between Portia and Calpurnia are too vast. Our friendship goes beyond family and is greater and able to withstand all adversity. But not the others. And besides, Cleopatra hates me for some reason, so I can't see how we can make up.'

I take on his pessimism with a sense of disappointment.

Brutus- Too much time spent apart and too much water has gone under the bridge. The way we are speaking now, this is how it couldn't be in mixed company. Its best you do it without us.

Julius –'You are family, even as a joke or general acceptance.' I thought to myself, after all, his grandchildren are King Claudius' kids.

Brutus– No, I'm not family and best not to be involved in this scheme.

Julius– To dismiss this as not family is impossible, since King Claudius and Tamora are more involved then you can dismiss or talk off.

Brutus– so it's this Sunday at your place at 12?

Julius– No, its Sunday at La Porchetta at 12pm. It's good to meet without it being too full on. We are not looking to confront all demons, we just want to find a way forward.

Brutus - I don't want to play 'happy families'

Julius- I accept that that's the case, unless you want to say anything further?

Brutus– No, I don't want to say anything further.

I realised that he was saying any future contact would be on his terms, but he had already been playing happy families for the last five years, based on a lie. He was a walking contradiction as he chose to believe his own daughter's outrageous claims, made to my daughter in my daughter's home, that my daughter was lying.

Call 8 - Cassius' voice message

On Saturday at 10 am I received a voice message on my home phone saying,

Cassius- "Sorry, I decline the invitation for Sunday lunch."

Call 9 - 2nd Call to Cassius

– the rsvp 'yes' that turns to 'no', in 6 days.

Julius– Hi Cassius, its Julio. Sorry to have missed your call – I've just been walking the dogs. Sorry to hear your change of heart too, as I was so looking forward to seeing you. I chatted to King Lear and to Brutus.

Cassius – Did you talk to King Lear's wife today?

Julius – No, two days ago to King Lear and Brutus to see if they are coming.

Cassius- I don't see the point of meeting up. It is too late. So much time has passed and too much water under the bridge.

But I recognised that those were Brutus' words. So much for Brutus not wanting to be involved.

Julius- Why? I acknowledge a time you gave an olive branch, in the past, and I thought you were approaching this with a genuine heart and prospect of reconciliation.

Cassius- Yes, yes, years ago I made a big effort and asked a family friend for advice, and frankly I'd given up. I thought this was never going to happen. It's fucked and ruined forever. The effect has been total, point of no return reached and this stuff cannot be undertaken.

Julius– Who has spoken to, who changed your mind?

Cassius- I have been working at Brabantio's place, renovating, and I saw Emilia, the poor thing. She is so distraught, confused and upset by it all. The sing- a-longs and the get-togethers we used to have can never happen ever again. The loss of faith and the wrecked relationships due to the uncaring way we dealt with this. The way we kept the fight going, under horrendous circumstances, is unforgivable.

I thought to myself, strange that he thinks we kept the fight going when it was King Claudius' continued denial and defence of the allegations, despite his confession, that kept the fight going. That was what was unforgivable.

Julius–'Why do you back King Claudius and King Lear? King Claudius did it. Go ahead, deny the truth, and I hope that all that you stand for goes down in a heap.'

Cassius–'You go ahead with what you got to do', repeating my words like a sulking little boy that doesn't get his own way.

Julius- Christian teachings of forgiveness go unnoticed by you, you should practise what you preach! What we are presented with, what you are doing, is appalling; you should be ashamed of yourself. It's on your conscience what you back, and you are backing someone who has admitted to the crime and we have a taped confession. Yet you back him after all this.

Cassius–'All this rubbish, this pretext call – I don't believe in it.'

He was speaking as if he believes the evidence doesn't exist. Can he really be that stupid, I thought to myself? I might go and play the confession to him.

Julius- All you are doing is blindly following the older brother in opposition to me, the younger brother. You are clinging onto ridiculous and hateful ideas and I can't stand your attitude.

Cassius– There's nothing wrong with my ideas and my conscience is clear.

Julius- you understand that you are asking us to be strangers, and so if I see you down the street, we will pass by each other as total strangers.

Cassius– Yes, that's right.

Julius– So if you hang up now, then that's it. I point out when you see King Claudius next, you'll be able to see him and say he's caused it all by denying what has been captured on tape, admitting to what he did.

Cassius– Yes, that's right. I'm not coming, but there is some decency in me to tell you I'm not coming.

Julius– Well, you stick to everything you stand for, on your bible.'

And with that, I hung up the phone. All hope was gone. His decency was limited to calling me and his comments implied that the rest of his position was far from decent. He had forgotten a time after the Eulogy when he said we will talk again after the court case. Clearly, unbeknown to me at the time, that was conditional on the result being one that supported King Claudius and when this didn't happen, he reneged.

Chapter 40

La Porchetta

We waited and waited. We waited to order too, not wanting to be rude, so the waitress waited as well. Then I heard a familiar Croatian voice and relief rippled through me; I thought to myself this is the first stepping stone to reconciliation. It's happening. I turned and was warmly greeted by a relative, but it was the wrong one; one from another Croatian family who had married into ours. We caught up on the latest and Mr Horvat said to Dad, "I just saw your brothers at Church" but Dad didn't reveal that we were waiting for his brothers to arrive to be with us, as planned with them. It was a reduced list of those coming now though; Macbeth, Lady Macbeth and Emilia; our hope for peace was in their hands. It was also possible that King Lear and his wife were coming too, although Cassius' dramatic change in position suggested otherwise.

I looked at the clock and it was 12.30 so we caved and ordered a garlic focaccia to finally justify our place at the table. We had hope that they were still on their way. They were only half an hour late now, surely they'd still turn up?

It was a bitingly cold day and it looked like snow through the window, but the sleet failed to settle, like my anxiety. The angle of the wind was harsh, directing the weather like the family absence, landing on us and shattering all our hope. Dad said, 'We may as well break the bread' and we all laughed as the reality set in.

I don't know why, but not one Pavlovic showed. Not one person was willing to say 'peace be with you' to me like they had done an hour before at mass to strangers. Like King Lear did in September last year. No Pavlovic ever came through the door. Was it pride, resentment, hatred, bitterness, misguided loyalty, patriarchy or all of the above? Or just plain living the lie to its fullest at all costs. Why could not one of them afford to come in peace to love and serve their Lord? Why was peace too costly for them? What lie had they propagated all these years that kept needing to be propped up and nourished, and that needed to fed by the entire family? What would happen to the lie if someone stopped feeding it, even for a day, just for an hour, over a bite of pizza?

We figured that they had decided that the tiniest crack in the family's rejection of me could crack open their lies and smash King Claudius' carapace like a hammer to an eggshell. I remember the lines of Reg Livermore in Betty Block Buster Follies, learned when I was a child, 'Smashed his skull like an eggshell.'[106] And finally, I could use the analogy in my own life. I had smashed his lies and they didn't like it.

'How very fragile must their lie be Dad?', I asked, knowing the answer.

'Exceedingly', said Dad. 'Fragile is an understatement.'

Oh well, it's another sad chapter for my book.

"Quite!", said Mum.

'It's a crime matriarch stunt, but how can the mother of a sex offender do this? If one of my boys did this, I'd support them too, sure I would, I understand; I'd visit them in jail, pay for their psychiatrist, pay to have lab-rat tests done on them to remove the "mongrel gene", sure', I quipped. But I would not create an alibi, lie for him or hide and protect a grown 50-year-old adult in his criminality, NEVER!', I angrily exclaimed.

My brother's theories about the silent majority supporting me were utterly disproved now. Clearly, he had been flying his peace flag in the wrong house.

'What more do I have to do? Give them my right arm as a peace offering?', I asked Romeo. 'Sacrifice a virgin?' The look on his face said it all.

'Please don't speak of them again', I said adamantly.

Asking more from the victim is never the answer, but I knew this already. Seeking peace from the victim should not be the starting point, but sometimes you have to be the bigger person and lead by example. I had provided the easiest path to reconciliation for them; no questions would be asked of them, no apologies required from them, no recriminations. Just box it up, pack it away and move forward. I was willing to do this for family peace, but I was rejected again. I'd bounce back. Bounce back!

Chapter 41

Forgiveness

To help my Church-loving Pavlovic family and atheist me reconcile, I think it's best to turn to the bible, to get some guidance, so I can get some true Christian perspective here to help me work this out. The bible tells us that before forgiveness, a sin must be admitted and acknowledged. But seemingly, the Pavlovic family is stuck, like society, on the no-brainer issue of the confessional. Had he confessed what he did to me to the extended family? I knew the answer, for King Lear's wife's words to Dad days earlier - 'Cleopatra's wild allegations' - were on repeat in my brain. What a sad, sad, sad, pitiful woman my Aunty is. She knows the truth – her daughters Goneril and Regan told her it happened to them for years too. She is the worst woman I know.

The Pavlovic lie was obviously far too big for the truth now. What had they said? What did their lie look like now that they'd clearly beefed it up again as the threatening opportunity for peace faced them?

Antony came to the rescue saying,

'I hear it every day – excuses like 'Yes, I gave my granddaughter a vibrator for Christmas and I taught her where to put it and I watched her use it, but I didn't touch her' or 'She told me she wanted to suck my dick' or 'She told me she loved it when I touched her' or 'I did it coz my wife had stopped having sex with me.' None are ever original or believable. It'll be a combo of that; something where he admits it, but with a big BUT on the end!', he said looking thoroughly disgusted.

But if that's the case, that meant the same must apply where Goneril and Regan are concerned. And what about Hamlet living in his remote little hamlet? How did King Lear's wife reconstruct her family – with her knitting needles making a new pattern where the back (truth) and the front (lie) don't match? How did she sew it together with the back missing or did she spin an evil web of lies on her spinning wheel? Well, one day Aurora will wake up and prick her finger on that spinning wheel, and the power of the curse will cause the truth to come to life Aunty. Do you think your children and grandchildren will remember you for your trifle recipe?

To truly and fully ingratiate myself, my parents and my children back into the Pavlovic family, I needed to forgive King Claudius, of course I did. But I had done that already years ago; I forgave him for his many sexual assaults of me the minute he told me he was sorry in 2013. But what about their Christian belief in forgiveness of me; if it was true that their lie had flipped me into being the villain, or the sex-hungry primary school girl (whatever!), didn't I deserve their forgiveness, for making up lies about their god-like Pavlovic patriarch, like a naughty little girl. Couldn't I be punished in a lighter way, like sex-offenders are. A promise to be a 'good girl' like a good behaviour bond?

Why was my 'sin', albeit a lie carefully crafted by them, unforgivable? There had been other disasters, accidents and serious dramas in our family, so why was my disclosure different to their disclosures, affairs, arguments, deaths, betrayals, accidents and stinkingly-bad business deals? Am I to believe that the sexual assaults of me are worse than all of that,

70 years of Pavlovic family life and death, put together?

Come on, there are related families who have fought and have even been to court about far less and far more, but that's never been insurmountable.

Looking incredibly hurt, Dad said, 'Cassius told me years ago, We will wait till the court case is over and then we'll talk." but even he has forgotten his own good intention to right the wrongs and support us, even now when it's so easy to do.

They say never live with regrets, but this was the first time I regretted not taking that bastard to trial. That was what Buddha had warned of – not taking the truth to the very end! King Claudius didn't deserve my mercy, nor did the Pavlovic family. They were rotten to the core and they all knew it. Like a house with white ants, there was nothing left behind their sad and ugly façade. They were so vulnerable to the truth that a gentle tap could have toppled the lot of them over. There was serious brick rot in all of their foundations and they were not willing to rebuild, despite being a family of builders, so instead they'd run to the church while the truth crumbles their world around them wall by wall.

Let them be. We get to have the last laugh. I was more powerful than the lot of them; Dida's little good girl with freckles.

Pavlovic family, you may not want to hear the truth from me and I can see your sad limitations. Seeing me, the truth, is clearly too painful for you. But I will continue to talk to you daily through the television and the newspaper:

- Royal Commission into Institutional Responses to Child Sexual Abuse

- Abolishment of Statute of Limitations to bring actions for sexual assault

- #MeToo
- Changes to rape laws and the issue of 'consent'
- Ellis Defence abolished
- National Redress Scheme
- "Pope Accepts Resignation of Archbishop Wilson"
- Numerous trials of historic sexual abuse by clergymen
- Pope accepting clergy resignations world-wide
- National Apology to Survivors - 22 October 2018, which I am attending.

And you can't avoid the tidal wave of truth; these are the articles in your Catholic newsletters too. And your local cathedral is covered in Loud Fence ribbons. And you have to look at your own abused daughters.

Silence and absence are all you can ever give me in reply. I rest my case.

Chapter 42

The Last Calls To Home

Dad made two more calls to ask after the absent attendees; his eldest brother and wife, and his eldest sister. He needed to hear from them as to why they didn't show, for his own sanity. Had some great tragedy befallen them, he wondered? Did they need to do more penance at church first, he asked, bouncing his ideas off me.

Dad said, "I think when I broke the bread at La Porchetta, and we came to share a meal in peace with them, we ended up simply making peace with ourselves."

This is my father's immediate recollection of the calls he made:

First call to Macbeth

Lady Macbeth- hello
    Julius- hello Lady Macbeth, this is Julio. How are you?
    Lady Macbeth- how are you?
    Julius- I wanted to speak to Macbeth, but I hear his voice. Is he busy?
    Lady Macbeth- No, he's not talking, it's the television.
    Julius- oh, sorry I thought he was with people.
    Lady Macbeth- ok.
    Then there was a lengthy silence, while I assumed she was

getting him to come to the phone to speak to me, but then I hear her make an inaudible sound.

Julius– Oh, are you still there? I thought you were getting Macbeth for me. Oh, but I should speak to you too, because you're just as important.

Lady Macbeth- I can speak to you but Macbeth is too ashamed to speak to you.

And next I heard a 'click' as the phone call was hung up by either Lady Macbeth or Macbeth, though I expect it was by Macbeth. Lady Macbeth was like a robot, so controlled, as if they've been overpowered by another and have another voice speaking for them.

Second Call to Emilia

Julio- 'Hello Emilia, its Julio.'

Emilia–'Cacusi me (how are you feeling to me) Julio', she said in a measured controlled tone, nothing like our previous call.

Julio–'Where were you yesterday? We went to La Porchetta and you didn't show up?', I said in an annoyed voice.

Emilia–'I was in Big Smoke for my grandchild's party.'

Julius–'Well, you could have called me to say you're not coming, as we all agreed to come there, but you didn't come; nobody came to meet us, do you know?'

Emilia–'You know I'm not well and there are certain problems with me like my memory, my mind, and I'm not normal anymore. I'm very unwell.'

Julius–'Well, we are all dying in little ways, our Pavlovic family dies at average 84.'

Emilia–'Well, I didn't want to come because of your wife and daughter, and what happened at my house years ago.'

Julius –'I thought you said you had no memory. Who has been talking to you to pressure you to say these things?'

Emilia–'Nobody, I'm just not myself.'

Julius–'But you should have let me know.'

Emilia–'You have a right to be angry, but I rang your son on the phone'

Julius–'But my son has no message bank.'

Emilia–'Well, you can check with Telstra.'

Julius–'I don't know what's wrong with you. Calpurnia and I supported you and your husband Iago when no one else did for more than 50 years, and King Claudius hurt Cleopatra, but you don't care.'

Emilia–'What do you mean? Who hurt her?'

Julius–'Emilia, come on, as you well know, King Claudius sexually abused her, and we've been suffering for years. What do you mean you don't know?'

Emilia–'It's the first I've heard of it'– a truly untenable position.

Julius–'How can that be? You were at Gospa Velika, you heard it. This is what the whole issue is over, and you were there when she disclosed it. Now you say you don't know of this? I'd believe you if you were under duress like someone was going to kill you if you saw us, but what's your excuse? What can you say to me?'

Emilia–'I'm not very well.'

Julius–'That's it? Cleopatra's a woman like you, and you've had your face blackened with bruises, yet you don't support her, my daughter. You're not under Iago's thumb anymore, you need to think of the girls in our family and think of the bad men and what they do to girls and our women. You told me you read the story of Eleni, who is a Greek freedom fighter, yet you pour scorn on my daughter, and pretend you don't know what happened to her.'

Emilia– I talked to my daughter Desdemona and she said be careful of Cleopatra.

Julius – You don't need to be careful, Cleopatra and Calpurnia come with an open heart is all. And they are like you, women – we are no threat to you. If you would have come but for your pre-engagement, what about meeting up another day instead?

Emilia- Oh yes, that would be alright if they want to come and see me.

Julius- how about tomorrow?

Emilia– I have Brabantio over tomorrow, he is for the family, he is good.

Julius- 'I think another day is best'– thinking it should not have interference from the younger generation.

Emilia – ok.

Julius- Well the next day, Wednesday. We will come over then.

Emilia– ok, see you then, in the morning is best.

Julius – 10 o'clock?

Emilia – ok

Julius – See you then.

As I discussed the calls with Dad, I became immediately concerned about the disingenuous nature of the planned meeting with Aunty Emilia. For I felt that the hang-up on him from Uncle Macbeth was closer to the lie and the true family position than the allegedly welcome Wednesday meeting that I was to attend. The chance for a new start in the family for me has passed and now it felt like we were cast as the black sheep, not worthy of a chance that we may resume our previous place in the family, or any place for that matter. We posed a threat too great to get too close to anything and we were being fobbed off rudely and without any care.

I figured that their reactions were a result of just how ridiculous and far-fetched their lie had become. I would not live inside their lie.

Part 6

My Conservative Town Today

Chapter 43

Stuff the Snapdragons

Conservative Town – famous for its Tourist Hill, Floral Festival, beautiful historic streets, brilliant schools and a most evil paedophile ring – is where I remain living. I'm the only abused cousin still living here – funny that. I left for a while, but I came back to raise my family away from gangs and violence of inner city life. Funny that too.

The Loud Fence ribbons remind me of just how unsafe this city was then and still is now. Sexual abuse is not an historic concept in this place or anywhere. It's a recurring scourge. Some days I have a 'Thelma and Louise' moment and just want to hit the highway, keep going and never come back to Conservative Town. Then I rethink things and admit that I must have subconsciously returned to Conservative Town to fix my past and that I shouldn't leave until it's fixed. Until Conservative Town is fixed.

This largely Catholic town, my hometown, was the epicentre of clergy sexual abuse, abuse that leaked out of the church and presbytery walls and into our homes and our child psyches, stealing the innocence from so many children, including me. Stealing their families from them, their church from them, their childhood happiness from them.

I'd like to be easy-going, light of spirit, seeing things at face value and enjoying home-grown events such as the Floral

Festival, but instead, I find my mind wandering off at the
parade, posing silent rhetorical questions to myself, such as
'How many children have been assaulted in this toilet block?'
and at school pick-up, 'How many children here today are
being sexually abused by their family members or by other
fellow children at school today?' I don't think of stranger
danger as that risk is only very small in comparison.

I am astonished by the rising enrolments at Catholic
schools in Conservative Town, particularly post the Royal
Commission. Conservative Town's apparent ability to
overlook horror is galling to me. The communities'
comfortable reliance on the supposed changed culture and
attitude towards clergy sexual abuse is confusing, for I feel that
greater Conservative Town is apathetic and is too quick to
forgive and forget. Particularly in the absence of an admission
and apology from Cardinal Campeius in Rome, for it should be
quite unbelievable to the parishioners of Conservative Town
that their intelligent and revered homespun hero Campeius did
not know what was right under his nose, his nose like
Pinocchio's. Certainly, The Royal Commission held each and
every clergyman who gave evidence to be 'not credible.'

I have almost forgotten how to think lightly and now I
consider it an indulgence to do so. I am trying to teach myself
to live in the moment, but I'm really bad at it. I have spent a
lifetime of attempting to ignore my senses to successfully get
on with life: my gut instinct, my stomach aches from anxiety,
my flashbacks of abuse that I see when my brain 'takes a peek'
as if looking through my fingers when playing hide-and-seek or
through the venetian blinds in Cambridge Street. I'm tired of
doing this. I know what I know, and I won't run away from it.
My senses have guided me full circle. They are right every
time. They were right when I was a child too. My body was

telling me things weren't right. And my beloved momentary happiness of coffee and cake doesn't block out anything; it just makes me fat.

So here I sit in the eye of the storm, facing my past whilst fighting for a better future. If I can't do that using the law because the law doesn't provide justice for victims, then I'll turn my degree into a paper airplane and throw it out the office window. I'll leave the practise of law to the liars and conmen who are satisfied with the status quo. I fear that day is drawing nigh, but then who will fight for my clients and advocate for change? I should not be in a minority, fighting for change, exhausted and at my wit's end. The fact that I am is an indictment on our society, not on me. I consider that I am as strong as they come, but I am crumbing like rubble at the base of a statue that once stood tall and proud. How things would change for me and all victims if they were given the right to a lawyer.

Chapter 44

Lake Provincial

Lake Provincial, Conservative Town, the beautiful backdrop of my life in all its chapters: Dad zooming around it to get us to school on time, the school lap of the lake, running around it later in life, walking my children around it in prams, going on bike rides, feeding the ducks and swans with my toddlers, the scene of huge extended family picnics at the rotunda and, at stressful times, staring at it through tears and a fogged-up windscreen. The same lake Cardinal Bourchier had views of from Bethlehem House in his final months of life. Campeius' view from the Priestly Palace, the same lake he coached rowing crews on and rowed on himself, the same lake my boys now row on.

Many victims, including me, have looked out on and run around that same lake for years, searching for peace, healing and meaning. If only those trees could talk and give us the answers we're looking for here in this town. If only there was a safe legal path to the end of this mess. Unlike the path around Lake Provincial, with encouraging markers at each kilometre, my legal path is undefined; it's as long as a piece of string with legal landmines along the way, camouflage and subterfuge, the tactics of war thrust at me by his lawyer.

I wonder how many people have hung themselves from the trees around the lake, cut down before Conservative Town wakes up. I wonder how many people have fatally overdosed around the lake. I wonder how many people have been sexually assaulted around the lake. The beautiful lake has been witness to it all.

At one stage, the lake dried up completely and became little more than a dust bowl. There was a drought, water was scarce, and the Conservative Town City Council refused to use storm water to fill it. Storm water was diverted back to a housing estate nearby instead to fill its ornamental lakes and to green its golf course. Regardless, the people of Conservative Town kept walking around the giant dust bowl, the willows, plane trees and oaks delineating what once was. My children and I walked into the middle many times as it was such a rare thing to have happen. My young boys dug with gusto in the hope for treasure.

Conservative Town had lost its iconic waterhole, the 'water cooler', where everyone caught up, but surprisingly, people still gathered there out of habit. In the same way, at a time when the integrity of the Catholic Church has been shattered and lost, people have still gathered there at St Michael's Cathedral out of habit. Why can't people more easily embrace change when the evidence is staring them right in the face? Why don't the remaining parishioners question their church leaders and why don't they support Loud Fence and the survivors in real and meaningful ways?

Conservative Town holds one of the highest rates of youth suicide. My dear friend Jo lost her brother to suicide in 2008. Robert had hung himself from a tree in the Mount View pine plantation forest on the outskirts of Conservative Town. It was a well-thought-through plan as he bought the rope from a hardware store just days before, family finding the receipt in his pocket. My friend was utterly heartbroken when she found out as she was very close to him. He was just 27 years old. Although no one can ever be sure with suicide, Jo suspects that her parents' religious fanaticism may have had something to do with it as they were convinced that he was possessed by demons. Certainly, he pinned his baptism certificate up and circled the date before he committed suicide: the sixteenth of the month.

The rate of youth suicide in Conservative Town is very worrying. Det Stephen Adams had made the important connection between clergy abuse and suicide – so many single-vehicle accidents, colliding with a tree, dead instantly. Is it a case of careless driving or a deliberate plan? Families are losing loved ones to drug abuse and the drugs are getting more lethal. The drug ice has changed our community dramatically for the worse and in such a short period, but what is fuelling the unprecedented demand to escape from life's troubles?

We need to tackle suicide head on and the first step in solving the problem is to find out why. I suspect that sexual abuse is one of the top reasons for suicide as it's one of the hardest things to live with. I can vouch for that. What saddens me is that there is no sign of suicide or sexual abuse stopping or even slowing down. Having sex with children is still so prevalent but not only in the known paedophile community. It's often disguised and well hidden by the family man, the sporting coach, the illegal sex trade in underage children, evidenced by the alarming number of missing children. Are they really 'missing', or have they been kidnapped, drugged and beaten into sexual submission? Illegal traffickers of children for sex know only too well that they can make money over many, many years from the one child, whereas with drugs, it's a pay-once-only transaction.

On 5 August 2017, The Courier Mail newspaper reported a

story: 'Online child sex reports increasing'[107]. The article claimed that Australian police are experiencing a spike in reports of online child sex exploitation, with eight thousand reports in 2016, but that sentencing is not commensurate with the crimes. The Australian Federal police claimed that under Commonwealth laws, paedophiles only get two to three years in jail despite the maximum sentence available being fifteen years. Police report that the images are getting worse and now reveal a trend featuring the pain and even death of babies and toddlers.

A Conservative Town Magistrate, H. Honour Kingfisher, who was a Conservative Town solicitor for many years beforehand, gave a slap on the wrist, a Community Corrections Order (CCO), to a man named Toby Belch, who had downloaded thousands of images onto his computer that included sexual activities with toddlers and pre-pubescent children. He was also placed on the sex offender register for just eight years, saying:

'Not only you but the community will benefit from the Court implementing treatment and rehabilitation rather than placing you in prison, which could be unproductive,'[108] *Magistrate Kingfisher said, and following from that, 'Were there to be any form of repeat, it is likely you will receive a substantial term of imprisonment.'*[109]

Belch's lawyer said her client understood he was at a point in time where he could benefit from conditions on a CCO order. How exactly will he benefit when it is so obvious that rehabilitation doesn't work? Moreover, he should be on the sex offenders register for life, as should all sex offenders. I believe that their sexual inclinations will never fade away, go away, or be rehabilitated away. In my view, it's who they are; it's imprinted in their DNA.

I am sick and tired of reading stories like this about sexual predators in my hometown newspaper, The Conservative Town Daily Bugle, as I drink my coffee around Lake Provincial. Where is the social responsibility of town leaders who are meant to care about what happens to Conservative Town? I consider sentences like this to be outrageous, but am I in a minority? Why did Magistrate Kingfisher simply not jail him? As Hinch says, 'Jail, not bail.'

Chapter 45

A New Confetti

The new confetti littering the church grounds, the colourful Loud Fence ribbons, remind me of 7-year-old me when I couldn't find my voice. St Michael's Cathedral, my family church, is now covered in my truth, reminding my belligerent Conservative Town family in spectacular glory. The truth has spread to homes, parks, schools and businesses across Australia as far as remote outback communities. It's gone viral. Glory be to Maureen Hatcher's Loud Fence[110]! It even made its way to the Vatican.

Little did I know that my own personal story would be magnified and mirrored within a year of my disclosure by the experience of so many at the Royal Commission into Institutional Responses to Child Sexual Abuse, including my clients John Bates, Jack Cade, Prospero, Sebastian and Adam Black. I met so many beautiful people during those hearings. Wounded people, some also abandoned by their family, so deep was the church in their familial bones. People abandoned by their church. People who lost their faith in the process. Members of my new family of friends now – we weirdos, we rejects.

It absolutely staggers me how many people seem to be living in total denial about this enormous festering problem, yet it's one of the most serious problems we face.

Notwithstanding Canon Law, on a scale of crimes, murder and sexual assault, particularly childhood sexual assault, are considered the most serious. I'd like to think that's non-controversial. So, the pertinent question begging to be asked is 'Why are these the most inept and unsatisfactory areas of Australian criminal law?' If they deserve the most justice and cause the most physical and emotional harm long term, why does the law simply shrug and refer to legal antiquities designed to let the perpetrator get away with it or inflict a very light punishment at best? I say, why criticise Canon Law when the practise of Australian criminal law is only marginally better?

I am concerned that Conservative Town considers it's now time to remove the ribbons, make memorials to hide away sexual abuse from the public eye and move on. If only it were that simple – an historic problem we've already grappled with and can now lay to rest. Have we really changed our behaviour though? Have families supported their abused family members? Not often. In Conservative Town, families are still putting the Church before their own family members. Can the SOCIT Unit really justify its existence? How does it, for I know the survivors' experiences are far from positive? Are the suicides in Conservative Town dropping? Sadly, no. Are prosecutions rising? No, they're dropping instead.

In 2015, ten members of the Conservative Town survivor group ended their lives. We know that in survivor Moth's class in 1974, one third of the children in grade four at St Simeon's are dead to suicide. Twelve students out of thirty-three lost to premature death as a result of clergy sexual abuse. As my client survivor Jack Cade said in 2015, 'Thoughts of suicide are often there, every day.'[111]

Currently, it's completely irresponsible to talk about

childhood sexual abuse and criminal justice in the same sentence. It's just not possible with our current system. It's, in fact, laughable to talk about childhood sexual abuse and criminal justice. Accessible civil redress is just beginning, with a national redress scheme likely to commence next year, a new phenomenon and what a slow and painful start with a severe handicap of church denial and no interim VOCAT awards. No justice yet. Years of Royal Commissions, Inquiries and court process. A twenty-year sentence of legal servitude for the Fosters to get some semblance of justice for their precious girls. One can hardly describe their win as a true win. I know what's involved legally and it should be deemed too toxic to enter the legal labyrinth. That's why the child abuse complainant's statements will not be put through the legal system to gain redress, for they'd likely lose against the church lawyers and the legal system would be shown up for what it is publicly, for we've all heard their testimony, and there'd be mass public outrage.

When one speaks of a fair trial, all attention is directed at the defendant, but the true concern should be for complainants going in there without lawyers against the best that money, power and connection can obtain. Remember, the prosecutor doesn't care about the complainants and does not represent them; he's playing a legal game with his learned friends. He's not invested in it and has different instructions from the police than the complainants might have given him were they his client.

What really concerns me is when police apply to the court for a Suppression Order to ensure a fair trial for the defendant. However, at the filing hearing or Committal Mention, which are the occasion when one usually applies for the order, there are no lawyers for the complainants there. That's because complainants in criminal law don't have lawyers.

Did the complainants even want a Suppression Order because it's made for them only as it can't be made for the protection of reputation or embarrassment of the defendant? Did they want to be gagged? And under what conditions specifically have they had their freedom of speech curtailed? The fact is they won't know. They could quite easily breach the Suppression Order and not even know it. They will never see the Order or be served with a copy, remember, for they are not a party to the proceeding. It's crazy! They will be subject to an Order that they don't know the conditions of. That is just not legally right or sound.

The truth is that the Open Courts Act (2013)does not make provision for defendants to make application for a Suppression Order. Section 10 states that a Notice of Applications for Suppression Orders must be made to the Court and to all parties to the proceeding. As complainants are not parties to the proceeding, they are not notified about the application. However, under Section 15, Complainants can seek a Review of the Order as 'any other person with a sufficient interest'. Suppression Orders are often put in place under the guise of protecting complainants and saving them from embarrassment of being identified. If that's truly the concern, then surely, someone should ask the complainants their view on this, seeing as the Order affects them.

Under Section 18 of the Open Courts Act 2013[112], the grounds of seeking a Suppression Order are as follows:

A Court or tribunal other than the Coroners Court may make a proceeding suppression order if satisfied as to one or more of the following grounds:

'the order is necessary to prevent a real and substantial risk of prejudice to the proper administration of justice that cannot be prevented by other reasonably available means;

Example:

Another reasonably available means may be directions to the jury.

the order is necessary to prevent prejudice to the interests of the Commonwealth or a State or Territory in relation to national or international security;

the order is necessary to protect the safety of any person;

the order is necessary to avoid causing undue distress or embarrassment to a complainant or witness in any criminal proceeding involving a sexual offence or a family violence offence;

the order is necessary to avoid causing undue distress or embarrassment to a child who is a witness in any criminal proceeding; and

in the case of VCAT, the order is necessary

to avoid the publication of confidential information or information the subject of a certificate under Section 53 or 54 of the Victorian Civil and Administrative Tribunal Act 1998; and

for any other reason in the interests of justice.

The Coroners Court may make a proceeding suppression order in the case of an investigation or inquest into a death or fire if the coroner constituting the Coroners Court reasonably believes that an order is necessary because disclosure would

be likely to prejudice the fair trial of a person; or

be contrary to the public interest.'

The grounds for an Order are quite limited, as you can see, so that freedom of speech is promoted as much as possible. However, real justice would come from provision for complainants being joined as a party in a criminal proceeding and having independent legal representation.

But what does one do when there's no forum left to seek justice if the OPP don't prosecute? My friend the media is one answer. Lobbying politicians is another. Writing this book is another. Demystifying the law and all its bullshit is another. Civil redress shouldn't just be available to the rich. Is the legal profession willing to look at itself in the mirror though? Or will the players simply declare themselves the most beautiful of them all when doing so and forget why they were even looking?

I know I'm on the right track, but there's no yellow brick road leading to justice; it's more like I'm stuck in a legal labyrinth where the truth merely leads to endless dead ends. I suspect that this is why the Fosters continued their fight well after their daughter's matter ended. Why Chrissie continues the fight today, with her daughter Katie and late husband Anthony and late daughter Emma still very much with her, enmeshed in her fighting spirit. Until there are clearly defined and worthwhile processes, we must campaign for an end to this systemic abuse of children and adult victims and survivors. The Catholic Church must be declared a criminal organisation and pay its dues. Lawyers and judges need to realise their legally condoned behaviour is clearly systemic abuse. Politicians need to be bravely enacting new sexual assault legislation.

For the same reasons, the late Katrina Woods' family members are calling for an Inquiry into the decision making of the senior police in the Lindt Café siege in Sydney. Likewise, Mersina Halvagis' father hurts, Rosie Batty battles, Sarah Cafferkey's mum fights, William Terrill's family searches, Daniel Morcombe's family mourns, Madeleine McCann's family wonders. Derryn Hinch and Daniel Andrews are fighting together with families like these for the justice they deserve. For when you lose yourself or a loved one to a criminal or to bumbling legal incompetence or obvious corruption, it's hard to look past it and admire the snapdragons.

Chapter 46

Men of Colours

One good Conservative Town man, my artist father, Julius Caesar, is listening and watching closely, busily using the artist's language of paint on canvas to illustrate Conservative Town's response to clergy sexual abuse. When I think of my Dad, I think of the song "Man of Colours" by Icehouse[113].

Stephen Adams is a good man. Julius Caesar is a good man. These men make their children proud. It's not about money, power, control, assets, or prestige. It's about integrity, humility, honesty and passion for what's right. And what an inheritance I've been given, as have Stephen's children.

These are the real men of colours: without badges, without accolades, without a ticker tape parade, respecting people and the pain that life often brings. In my view, the real Christians are men like these, without their church, without their religion, being kind and respectful to others and setting a fine example for future generations. We need to re-think the alpha male and the true ugliness of the traits that commonly come with that personality type, hence the ugly statistics around family violence and the paedophilic sociopaths that the law unashamedly protects. We need to stop listening to men ordering from the bench and proselytising from the pulpit.

Campeius has been quoted as saying it was his 'Christian duty' to escort Cardinal Carlisle to court. He also said that paedophilia in Conservative Town was a 'shocking coincidence'. Is this the behaviour and sentiment of a Christian though?

On Sunday, 2 July 2017, I nearly spilt my orange juice over the newspaper as I read the front page: 'Exclusive — Chief Prosecutor says crims get off easy and he can't stop it'[114]. Chief Crown Prosecutor Lord Pheasant-feather, SC, is a highly esteemed man in legal circles. He's the State's top prosecutor. He makes the television and represents the Crown in serious, high-profile cases in the High Court. Today he was proffering to be outraged about light sentencing from the courts and appealing for increased sentencing and calling for tougher minimum sentencing. Apparently, he's upset with criminals merely getting slaps on the wrist.

Yet don't forget that this same man, Lord Pheasant-feather, appeared as Chief Crown Prosecutor for the OPP in my matter to withdraw my matter, one charge of unlawful assault against my cousin, after he dropped the rape charges and wanted to agree to Diversion. This grand red-carpet appearance in the Magistrates' Court was to stop a slap on the wrist, to prevent a good behaviour bond for my cousin for four years of sexual assault. Why did the matter command his presence? Why did Lord Pheasant-feather want to stop King Claudius from being punished, albeit in the mildest way possible?

This is also the same man who gave an impressive character reference for convicted paedophile and disgraced ex-Magistrate Sextus Pompeious. That tells you about the man Lord Pheasant-feather truly is. Men who proudly and enthusiastically volunteer to minimise the bad behaviour of other men and conclude that a man can still be good, other than a few misdemeanours here and there like sexual assault apparently. Maybe for petty theft, an affair, perhaps – but surely not for sexual assault, the second most serious crime to murder. The reasons for sentence reveal that other 'good' men also rallied around Pompeious; a serving judge of the County Court, a magistrate and a senior barrister chimed in with Lord Pheasant-feather, SC. For Pompeious had been a criminal barrister, a Crown Prosecutor, a Mayor of a Melbourne suburb, after all. He was a part of the men's club. I suspect that none of them wanted him raped in prison, facing men he'd help put behind bars. What about the victim's trajectory though? Why be concerned about the possibility of a rapist being raped? Seriously, why care? Rape is clearly Pompeiouis' hobby after all.

The judge convicted Pompeious but gave him a three-year sentence, wholly suspended for three years. Draw your own conclusions about who the good men are. Just look at who sits behind those mahogany benches and bar tables, engaging in very costly legal banter – very costly to victims in every way.

But I feel that change is slowly coming and from within the legal profession itself, finally. The Honourable Justice Launcelot Gobbo is standing tall. He is risking his comfort zone, criticism and ostracisation from the legal fraternity. He is a good man, rare but good. I wonder what level of support he is receiving from his legal contemporaries as he gives voice to the multitudes of complainants who have unhappily experienced the court system.

Chapter 47

Women of Truth

'I'm also very proud of having commenced the Royal Commission into child sexual abuse in institutional settings. This Royal Commission is now working its way around the country. I believe it will have many years of work in front of it, but it will change the nation. It will change individual lives as people get to come forward and tell their story. It will change the nation because we will learn how to better protect our children for the future.'[115]
— **Prime Minister Julia Gillard, 26 June 2013**

I am heartened by good women, women of truth who take the hard road, where there's little proof, where proof is hard to find, who listen to children, who listen to women, who act on what they hear with integrity and without denial. Hats off to the following people:

• Former Prime Minister and first female Prime Minister Julia Gillard

• Mothers providing good role models for their daughters and sons

• Women fighting for equality any way they can

• Women brave enough to leave the cycle of violence they're living in

- Wives supporting their abused husbands through their ongoing trauma

- Sisters standing for their siblings lost to substance abuse and suicide

- The women abused when girls at Bethlehem House in Conservative Town by evil paedophile priest Cardinal Carlisle

- Girls coming forward against their teachers and leaders in institutions – films like 'Don't Tell'[116], indicative of children's and women's voices finally being heard

- Women coming forward telling of sexual harassment and abuse in the #MeToo movement

- Mothers supporting their abused children, mostly female, when incest happens, rather than the abuser, who is mostly male

- Mothers believing their children, battling the family law and child protection system, desperate to keep their children safe from harm, safe from their abusive parent, who overwhelmingly is the father

- Female journalists reporting the truth (my friends and fellow warriors Paulina, Nerissa, Charmion and Valeria inspire me)

- Female doctors and teachers reporting abuse to DHHS

- Female counsellors at CASA, nurturing and re-building lives

- Female counsellors at WRISC, Berry Street and like agencies, assisting women and children trapped in the cycle of violence

- Female police working at SOCIT, believing women and children

- Female lawyers devoted to seeking justice for abused clients and sharing their journey with them every step of the way, not just when the law switches on its working day in business hours, like Gloria Allred in the United States and Viv Waller, Judy Courtin and I in Victoria.

- Feminist authors, old and new – my mentor, Simone de Beauvoir, and my modern-day hero, Clementine Ford, who says it as it is which is so refreshing.

I can hear people reeling at this, saying, 'What about the men doing the same dedicated work? Crazy feminist!' I fully commend the men doing the same thing throughout our community, but I feel that too many men deny the epidemic and dynamic that is family violence and the men in power are mostly misogynists worldwide. Men like Barack Obama, Bill Shorten and Derryn Hinch are the exception as men sharing their philosophy on violence against women and children are few in number and are certainly not yet straining to be vocal.

I'll start with our previous Prime Minister Malcom Turnbull. I seldom heard him speak about family violence. Second, we need to sack several magistrates and judges who make a mockery of women seemingly as a sport and cause female lawyers and their clients to cry, literally. This workplace bullying in the courtroom must stop. Female barristers and solicitors everywhere will know what I'm talking about. If we ever have a royal commission into the family law system, the terms of reference need to include this. Third, women need equal pay and equal opportunity now; it's long overdue. Finally, the courts need to get tough on sporting heroes who abuse their partners behind closed doors. Too often, the courts make an arbitrary distinction between the sporting legend on field and off field. Moreover, I am sick and tired of hearing about another woman miraculously dropping to her death from a balcony and the male who pushed her denying it. Same with the Valentine's Day shooting of Reeva Steenkamp. It's so blatantly obvious, family violence, but the law doesn't seem to 'get it'.

Until I see these important and vital changes, I will remain highly critical of good men who do nothing. I absolutely believe that men need to step up, step aside and lose the testosterone. Behave civilly and with respect at home like you do in your day jobs, or your home will break, your women and children will leave you, and then, predictably and reliably, you'll plot revenge, and another death will be added to the worsening statistics on female homicide. Women in the legal profession, when you rise to the bench or senior counsel, don't join the little men's club. Remember, you're a woman and should not morph into a male apologist. You can't be that desperate for approval, can you? And if so, work on your self-esteem before you make another insulting decision, please! Remember the reason you wanted to practise law. If it was to show off or earn lots of money, herein lies the problem.

Men, when facing relationship breakdown, the answer isn't to bash your ex-partner to death and kill the children. Women are free to leave a relationship for any reason they wish, whether you consider it to be valid or not. If it bruises your ego, too bad. You just can't have a good public face and a bad private face anymore, for that is surely a sign of certain mental illness, a schizophrenia of sorts, having such contrasting multiple personalities: the enigmatic footy star by day and the wife basher by night. What was the famous book Dr Jekyll and

Mr Hyde[117] based on again? That's right, the morally duplicitous nature of man. I think Robert Louis Stevenson was onto something there.

Men need to be critical of one another and stop the disrespect of the women in their lives. Speaking the truth about what it is to be a man is the only answer. Questioning the alpha male is a good start. Accepting and loving your gay son or daughter is another. Respecting your female partner, if you have one, is essential to the health of them, you and your children. Stay home with your baby and let your wife have her career for a change and yes, unless you help fight for women to have equal pay, your family will likely live on less on your wife's income. So change it, but don't use her lower pay to keep her out of the workforce. And when you're in Bunnings next buying a statue of Buddha for your house and garden, think about it. Think about what you stand for and what your daughter sees in you as her father or what your sister sees in you as her brother or what your wife sees in you as her partner. Perhaps take some time out to listen to the lyrics of the song by Joe Jackson 'Real Men'[118] and challenge yourself.

In the movie Spotlight, an excellent film about the epidemic of child sexual abuse by Catholic clergy in Boston in the United States, my favourite line is when Michael Keaton, playing Walter 'Robby' Robinson, says to Pete Connelly, Board Member of Catholic Charities:

'That's how it happens, isn't it, Pete? A guy leans on a guy and suddenly, the whole town just looks the other way.'[119]

The point is men allow what they shouldn't. Why? When men gather together in freedom of association, it needs to be in a way that doesn't cause disrespect to women. Men-only clubs, Freemasons' Lodges, men's galleries, men's sheds and men's sporting and recreation clubs are all well and good so long as they don't promote and foster the devaluing of women. Re-think your buck's night activities perhaps, especially if they involve the gang rape of a woman, or the paid re-creation of same.

The indisputable fact remains that children are most often abused by males just as women are. Interestingly, we have been most responsive to the male children who have been abused as most children abused in an institutional setting, particularly a religious and sporting setting, are male because of the history of women's place in society. But in a familial setting, girls are abused far more than boys because the domestic front was always deemed a private domain, with men legally owning their wives and their children, hence the tradition of women changing their names into their husbands' surnames. Girls are often physically weaker than boys too, so they're easier to dominate physically.

Again, there's an undervaluing of girls' voices as opposed to boy's voices, like we listen to men but seldom women. Just like when my relative Tomi dropped the bucket down the well in Croatia and I got blamed for it at age 7. Just like my entire extended family believing King Claudius, not me at age 39, when I disclosed. I ask you, what do you think when you read my statements to the police and this book? If it was about money and lies, wouldn't I have just thrown a penis or two into my statement, claimed he was over 18 when he sexually assaulted me, made sure there was legally defined 'penetration', or just said we had full-on sex for four years? Why would I make it harder for myself to say there are five witnesses during one of the assaults as that requires them all to corroborate my story for me to be successful? Why would I fabricate a story that's not watertight in terms of the elements required for the law to consider it serious? My husband's an experienced criminal lawyer. If it was a lie, it would have been a perfect, well-formulated one, I can assure you. I am telling the truth, albeit without a penis in the story. For who would continue to go through this if they were lying? I have other beautiful, wonderful things in my life that have suffered and been neglected because of my persistence in this matter. I would love to turn my energies to my children again and my husband and I and desert the farce that is the law in this area once and for all. But it would be socially irresponsible, and I couldn't live with myself for keeping the insider information I have secret from victims of sexual abuse. Until I can be a lawyer for victims, I'll keep fighting.

One day in mid 2017, I spoke to Ally Moore on ABC 774[120] talkback radio on the topic of sexual assault. I called in on my phone while driving my son to the gym after hearing the experience of a poor lady who had been stuck in the legal labyrinth since 2014 and was at her wit's end, feeling completely disenfranchised and disheartened. She told listeners that she had been sexually assaulted by a work colleague but went on to make truthful and disparaging comments about the legal process. She complained that the police had taken a year to investigate her complaint and how she's been stuck since then, signing documents, getting psychiatrists reports, constantly having to see her lawyer, etc. I called in to concur and said that the problem is that a complainant in a criminal matter has no lawyer and the process is all-consuming in such negative ways.

The high rate of sexual assault on Victorian university campuses had prompted the discussion as it had been reported in the news that there's been a severe under-reporting by students because of the poor responses to their disclosures. The results do not surprise me but rather serve as evidence to how big a problem sexual assault is and how inadequate our responses are in 2017, despite the institutions established to process these matters. Clearly, the educated, new-aged males of the first world whom we are raising have returned to the caves of history and are thumping their chests in triumph at the latest sexing pics of their latest conquest, uploaded on Instagram and YouTube. Sorry, but from where I'm looking, the animal of man clearly remains just that. An animal albeit with a school bag, a university degree, a successful business, or even a lawyer's wig on.

Part 7

Sad Conclusions

Chapter 48

Secondary Victims of Clergy Abuse

On 16 September 2006, convicted paedophile priest Cardinal Carlisle wrote a letter to his victims from Western Paedophile Prison. The letter included the following passage:

I am now well aware of the far-reaching effects of my disgraceful behaviour, not only to you who would be considered to be my primary victims but to so many other people and communities who have been affected. To parents and families of those I have abused, to their partners, to their extended families, to the communities in which they live, to the Church communities, clergy and religious and teachers, to police who have had to investigate and deal with complaints, to social workers to counsellors and not least of all to my own family and friends, you are all victims of my acts.[121]

We have now learned that there are many hundreds of primary victims of Cardinal Carlisle as he admits in this letter, where he also refers to his many other victims, all secondary victims of sorts. I classify myself as a secondary victim of clergy abuse, but there are many sub-categories: those sexually abused by primary victims of clergy abuse; the ostracised support people to those sexually abused; the family fractured by sexual abuse disclosure; and the primary victim, who doesn't tell, causing injustice to the denied secondary victim.

I know that Jacques DeBoys and I are not the only secondary victims of clergy sexual abuse in Conservative Town. There are many, many people, siblings and schoolmates and cousins who have been sexually abused by those children who were sexually abused by priests. Many are still living here in Conservative Town and the surrounding suburbs, including Dale, Birdville, Silo, Finsbury Park and Provincial. Others left Conservative Town as soon as they could, never to return. Some have gone to the police; the vast majority haven't and who would blame them? Some pretend to themselves to protect themselves from the pain; some block the pain with substances. If the legal system responded fairly and adequately to our claims, I suspect that there would be an avalanche of complainants coming forward in Conservative Town alone, not to mention Australia wide. The Catholics and the cynics might suggest that this would just be an attempt at money grabbing by liars simply trying their luck. I say that it's unlikely but worth the risk in any event as only then would we start to see the true scale of the ripple effect of clergy abuse. It looks to me like the powers that be are desperately trying not to open that can of worms. That's criminal, in my book. I'm doing everything to lift the lid, I can assure you.

Conservative Town has much to lose from not telling the truth, greater community fracture and more lives lost to premature death, including suicide. Conservative Town has one of the highest rates of suicide in Australia, but it's no mystery why. Many victims have not come forward because the legal system re-traumatises them and they don't have the stomach or stamina for further abuse. Frankly, why should they? Why do we ask so much of victims? Why do we expect them to go into the courtroom without a lawyer, against the best lawyer the defendant can buy?

Until the legal system acknowledges secondary victims, all one can do is join the dots. However, I suspect that the Royal Commission received many statements from secondary victims. This matter does not end with the Crown case against Campeius and whether he is found innocent or guilty. This is not about him or any other individual case. It's about the multitudes of offenders and the church's response to the abusers within their parishes world-wide. It's also about our legal system's response to sexual assault here in Australia every day. It's about how quickly new laws can be enacted to give sexual assault a revised path without the legal landmines and enacting the right to a lawyer for victims to fight for justice properly.

Chapter 49

Join the Dots: Conspiracy Theory or Conspiracy?

I cannot prove that there is a link between what King Claudius did to me and clergy abuse. I can easily join the dots though, and so could the court, if it wanted to, but I'll let you be the judge and complete the dot-to-dot picture below. Please consider what I call the 'tendency and coincidence evidence' below and draw your own conclusions:

- Cardinal Carlisle, arguably Australia's worst paedophile, went to St Vincent Primary School in Dale, Conservative Town. King Claudius went to the same primary school approximately thirty years later.

- King Claudius lived a few streets away from the Cardinal Carlisle family home in King Street South, where Cardinal Carlisle would have stayed and visited many times over the period of fifty years that his family lived there in that house, over the road from the primary school.

- King Claudius went to same senior school as the paedophile priests at St Michael's College.

- There are numerous victims of clergy abuse in King Claudius' year level at school (or years around his year level) including John Bates, Gonzalo, Jack Cade, Adam Black and Harry Percy.

- King Claudius was Campeius' favourite altar boy, from the same group of altar boys as Harry Percy, a fellow altar boy and victim of clergy abuse.

- King Claudius did rowing at the time Campeius was coaching rowing.

- King Claudius abused his sisters and I, with two other willing abusers from St Michael's College: his brother Hamlet and another boy, likely named O'Bourke.

- A boy named O'Bourke from St Michael's committed suicide. Could this be the same boy O'Bourke who was in King Claudius and Hamlet's room and who also took part in the sexual abuse of us?

- Police informant Jacob Rosser interviewed a boy named O'Bourke who admitted that he knew King Claudius and went to his house many times, but he told Rosser that he never abused me or anyone and he seemed credible to Rosser, so the police didn't take it any further.

- Aunty, King Lear's wife, said, 'One thousand sorrys a day won't make up for what he's done.' She also told me that she sent the boys to the worksites with King Lear to 'keep them out of mischief'. If she had no idea, what did she mean by 'mischief'? I wonder.

- Rosser never interviewed my cousin Hamlet – no authority for flights to Remote Island from their manager (but they were going to go originally).

- Goneril and Regan supported me initially and concur with their own abuse disclosures.

- Goneril and Regan gave statements after compulsory examination. If they are telling the truth in their statements, why didn't they make them at the start and how do you explain the content of the texts and phone calls between us?

- The Eulogy I sent to my extended family members on 25 November 2013 was not sent to King Lear and Aunty, King Lear's wife, Brutus and Portia, or Goneril and Regan because they all believed me then. Then they did a backflip and supported King Claudius once they knew police were involved.

- Ophelia, Hamlet's partner, sent me text messages that admit what they did to us as older children too, although she attempted to minimise it.

- Campeius was a family friend and knew the Pavlovic brothers very well.

- Campeius was the school priest at Mary Immaculate, while my cousins Hecate, Celia and Decius went to school there.

- The Pavlovic families' involvement in the Conservative Town Catholic Church for fifty years was significant – buildings, renovations, sculptures, coats of arms, bishop's chairs and all church events.

- King Claudius confessed to the abuse during the pretext call.

- King Claudius' lawyer consistently briefed Strut-Bittern, Esq, a relative of Chief Magistrate Alex Lapwing.

- Chief Crown Prosecutor Lord Pheasant-feather, SC (for OPP), attended at court with King Claudius to withdraw charges against him to save him from the lowest form of punishment – a Good Behaviour Bond. Why?

- The DPP sent me a letter that made no sense as to the reasons why they dropped my matter.

- The Conservative Town Police Station refused to interview King Claudius in relation to my second statement and assured me that there's no Catholic cover-up in the OPP and the Conservative Town Police Station as I had alleged. Det Sgt Jerimiah Codswallop, who took over my case after Rosser, seldom returned my calls or emails and when he finally did, he concurred with the OPP decision not to prosecute my case but for reasons unknown.

- The IBAC enquiry in 2016 found Conservative Town to be one of the most corrupt police stations in Australia.

- The Loganville Magistrates' Court denied me costs when I won the Suppression Order revocation despite the well-established legal principle that costs follow a win.

- The Royal Commission did not allow my questions of Dr Butts, member of the Special-Issues Committee, as I suspect it would get too close to the truth.

- Luke Fang evaded all questioning for his role in the Special-Issues Committee despite him being the serving police member on the committee at the time, whose purpose was to bring complaints of sexual abuse to the attention of the bishop. It was his SIC role to do so but above that he was mandated to report to the police (or even make arrests himself in his role as a senior policeman) which carries duties and obligations that cannot simply be turned off when carrying out other roles.

- The County Court initially refused to strike out King Claudius' defence despite two consecutive non-appearances from King Claudius and his lawyers.

- The JR argued case law in support of King Claudius despite no appearance, no compliance with the consent orders or orders of the Court and total failure to comply in any way with the consent orders or court's orders.

- The JR allowed the contemptuous behaviour, didn't even mention their absence, didn't reprimand them for being on the court record, yet not appearing, and then allowed the defence to get back on track, going back to the start, and ordered that the original further and better particulars and discovery be complied with. Moreover, he didn't order that his previous orders imposing obligations on the defence be complied with and didn't comment on how they'd been contravened.

- The JR ordered that I file affidavits as to correspondence between the defendant and us despite me already having done so.

- The JR then ordered that I file another affidavit regarding correspondence again and then he didn't have the courtesy to read the documents he ordered, and he claimed they were not on the file but didn't ask for them from his clerk or from my counsel.

- The County Court also initially hesitated to strike out King Claudius' defence despite its own order, a self-executing order.

- The court refused to hold King Claudius and his lawyer in contempt of court for some unknown reason regarding King Claudius' breaches of orders and persistent failure to comply with the Civil Procedure Rules by both King Claudius and his lawyer.

- We called the court registry every few days, asking after the self-executing orders and were told the file was with JR Partridge-Saxon. The registry staff agreed that King

Claudius' defence should be struck out. We left a message for the JR's associate, who didn't return our calls.

- I called the JR's Associate and he advised that the file was with JR Partridge-Saxon and a decision would be made this week. 'What decision? There isn't one for him to make!' I exclaimed. All that was required was an administrative person in registry to type up the self-executing order.

- The superintendent of Rockies Region Matthew Dull took indefinite leave and essentially retired from the Conservative Town Police Station in a cloud of silence.

- On [DATE] 2017, JR Partridge-Saxon made the self-executing orders in my favour.

- On [DATE] 2017, judgement was entered against the defendant in default, including full costs orders in my favour.

- On [DATE], the defendant filed a summons.

- On [DATE], the Summons Hearing was heard and the judge set aside all the Orders made in my favour, notwithstanding the jester-like performance from the defendant's lawyer, in absolute contempt of court, yet the judge condoned it. The judge put me back to square one, which was unwarranted and completely unjust.

- H. Honour also caused me great prejudice by re-setting a new interlocutory timetable, essentially ordering me to redo the tasks I'd already done. This included creating a court event just for discovery based on the defendant's lies that he had received very little if anything from my lawyers. To combat this, expensive forms of service were ordered as H. Honour determined that the usual Affidavit of Service would not suffice in my case. Likewise, arranging mediation would involve liberty to apply, no doubt, as the defendant refused to respond to our suggested dates for mediation. Captain Plumage, QC, did not argue against this course at all. He didn't raise the fourteen breaches by the defendant and barely spoke of the prejudice issue. He also refused to make a compelling costs argument beyond costs for that day despite my protestations and pleadings.

- On [DATE] 2017, H. Honour clarified the costs order: one day of costs only instead of giving me costs thrown away for a year of wasted legal costs, as is ordinarily commonplace.

- I ultimately self-represented hereafter and became an inconvenient truth to the court.

- The matter was finally resolved at mediation but in utterly bizarre, unprecedented circumstances.

- In DATE the R v Campieus(2017) matter begins with two trials set for mid-late 2018.

- In July 2018, the Pope accepts the resignation of Archbishop Wilson of Adelaide, South Australia, who was convicted in May 2018 of concealing child sexual abuse.

- On 27 February 2019, the suppression order was lifted and the news was made public about Cardinal Campieus being found guilty of five counts of historical sexual abuse.

Chapter 50

Sexual Abuse and the Legal System: Cinderella's Glass Slipper

As a family lawyer and survivor of childhood sexual abuse, in my experience, the legal system simply doesn't work at all well for victims of childhood sexual abuse. It didn't for me in the four years from 2013 to the end of 2017, and my husband and I are both lawyers. If I couldn't get it to work so recently, how will my children, friends, or neighbours without experience or law degrees or from a non-English-speaking background?

Day after day, I see brilliant legal minds working tirelessly to ensure that the perpetrator remains protected by outdated laws and legal loopholes. Day after day, I see the most dedicated social workers tirelessly bolstering the metamorphosis of victims into survivors, encouraging or supporting engagement with the system to seek redress or helping with recovery after re-victimisation by the legal system itself.

Similarly, the local police and SOCIT units are meant to be actively following police protocols and striving for continuous improvement in their dealings with victims when they come forward. At a time of Royal Commissions into child sexual abuse and family violence, the institutional responses to childhood sexual abuse should be working relatively well at least most of the time. We have million-dollar advertising campaigns encouraging people to speak up about recent and historic sexual abuse and specially trained police. Same for family violence. Accordingly, conviction rates should be at their highest in this seemingly progressive society of ours. More and more people are coming forward and going to their local SOCIT unit and disclosing childhood sexual abuse, so why aren't the conviction rates rising? I say we can mostly blame the legal system, which often allows itself to become a puppet for the Catholic Church, and we can partly blame our conservative patriarchal society.

Sadly, I've come to learn that the thickest layer of protection for the perpetrator comes from the family. We as individuals are quick to publicly show our support at white-ribbon events, be openly outraged at high-profile cases like Oscar Pistorius' killing of Reeva Steenkamp in South Africa, Adrian Bayley, Jill Meagher's rapist and killer in Melbourne, and Masa Vukotic, killed in a Melbourne park by Sean Price. However, what do we do when the victim is a member of our own family, especially with links to the Catholic Church? Are we steadfast and fearless in our support, or does our tune change? It's easier to be angry and rally against the institution such as the Catholic Church, the armed forces, or hardened criminals, but what about against our own brothers, fathers, uncles, or grandfathers - seemingly respectable citizens?

On White Ribbon Day in November 2013, I said goodbye to my entire extended Catholic family, a family that pretended it didn't believe me yet knows it's all true. I died the same social death as so many victims who speak up do.

It is now widely accepted that it takes years to find the courage to come forward about childhood sexual abuse. Like me, the men of BoysTown, Queensland, and the men who endured years of sexual abuse by Catholic clergy, survivors may be in their 30s and 40s before they tell someone what happened to them twenty, thirty, or even forty years ago. My own children couldn't believe this had happened to me and that I hadn't done anything about it all these years. 'You're so confident,' they said. 'It couldn't have happened to you.' I decided to tell them because this is when it mostly happens, when you're a vulnerable child, mostly in primary school. No point telling them when they're older; they need to know now in case it happens to them. No child is immune.

We have amended the Limitation of Actions Amendment (Child Abuse) Act (2015) in Victoria so that victims are no longer statute barred by time. This acknowledges the time that it takes to be able to tell. Yet there are still difficulties as one must first establish that the defendant is not prejudiced by the passage of time. For the defendant can claim that because of the offences happening so long ago, they can no longer remember the events, so it's too unfair on them to have to defend the action. They commonly claim that they are prejudiced in their ability to fairly defend it because of the passage of time, which is largely at cross purposes with the abolishment of the Statute of Limitations for child sexual abuse.

Oddly, my clergy abuse clients were even refused a VOCAT application, with VOCAT referring us to the Catholic Church or the Royal Commission to seek redress for them. So, in other words, keep waiting despite the urgent drug-rehabilitation program you need, and you might get some money down the track – but only if the organisation opts in and only if you don't commit suicide or die a premature death in the meantime. Where's the sense in this approach? I ask. Predictably, one of those clients is now in jail for criminal matters, just as I foresaw. For without help, the trajectory of sexual assault victims doesn't change much.

Since 2007, we have significantly widened our definition of family violence to include physical, verbal, or economic abuse. We have smartened up to the subtler forms of abuse and thankfully have dropped our prerequisite for a defined criminal act to have happened, as seen with the rise of intervention orders for acts not actually defined as criminal, such as harassment. Yet women and children seem to be more vulnerable than ever before, regardless of legal pieces of paper titled 'Court Orders' in their handbag or on the school file. I remember my children's school needing to go into lockdown one morning as the father of the children was fresh out of prison and wanted revenge. The first place a man looks to get that revenge is to the children, and so it went. And on it goes . .
.

It's mind-boggling and totally unacceptable that the truth and a victim's story, no matter how compelling, is most often not enough for the OPP to pursue your childhood sexual assault case criminally. Why? Why isn't the truth enough? There are many reasons, as I painfully discovered, and the amendments to the Limitations of Actions Act will not assist with the following stumbling blocks.

First, the legal concept of doli incapax says you can't know the wrongness of your actions if you are under 14 years of age. Honestly, what fully cognisant 13-year-old today doesn't know the wrongness of their actions? I am particularly concerned as recently, there have been studies and discussions around how common intra-familial sexual abuse is between siblings and between children in residential care units. Teachers in schools are calling police when children have been sexually abusing other children at school, only to be told there's nothing police can do. It's a growing problem currently without a working solution. The laws need to be changed urgently in this area.

We can't live in denial; we must accept where sex abuse happens and when it happens and not sweep it under the carpet with all the other inconvenient truths. Sexual abuse is sexual abuse no matter what age it happens to you and no matter how old the offender is. The law says age matters but victims don't. Children are having sex, sexting, watching porn and even experiencing peer group pressure to rape their school friends. How can we still pretend that a child doing this at age 14 or a child even younger still does not know the wrongness of their actions?

The system is not at all ready for victims, speaking from experience. The worst thing I ever did was to go to the police whilst I was in crisis. Sounds crazy, I know. I too thought that's what you do. Well, my advice speaking from experience and as a lawyer has changed. Your statement and your case will suffer for it otherwise. If one must go to the police, write a chronology and take that with you to the police station. Even better, write your statement yourself and have a lawyer check over it first before swearing it as an affidavit. Brainstorm your ideas and write out dates, times, places, ages, witnesses and evidence in date order until you're 100 per cent happy with it.

This is the antithesis of what the victim is really thinking about when considering going to the police station: whether you'll get a nice policeman; whether you'll be believed; the enormity of telling police as there are consequences compared to telling a friend; family and friends changing forever once you disclose; fearing the responsibility for the family fracture and the embarrassment; fearing small town gossip; fearing people judging you negatively as if you're somehow damaged goods; and fearing judgement of you as a parent who might abuse your own children because you've been abused. That's why they need to be represented and assisted by a lawyer.

The problem with the theory that those who are sexually abused go on to sexually abuse others is this. If vast numbers of women and children are abused and if the behaviour is learned, why aren't there vast numbers of female perpetrators? Why do most young female victims not speak about it to anyone and not abuse other children or younger siblings? Again, it does happen but nowhere near in the same numbers as male offenders engaging in this behaviour. We need to be asking why instead of wasting time arguing about whether it's true or not and dragging victims through the courts in the process.

I am glad that the anticipated Redress scheme will not require further evidence from survivors as they have clearly been through enough. Moreover, I suspect that the Commissioners know that the victims would lose in court, for their frailty would unlikely withstand the church lawyers and the truth does not get traction in a courtroom. These matters would have been hidden from public view in private civil cases, but with the Commission, however, everything is on public record, so I suspect that there would be mass public outcry if one of the survivors lost in a court of law. There is a reason why the church chose not to cross-examine the victims and it wasn't to save them from the torment. It's because the rules in a Royal Commission aren't weighed so heavily in the defence's favour there, so the usual legal bag of tricks is rendered useless there. The church didn't want to appear heartless, but it had an ulterior motive.

Pretext calls – a great idea in theory for victims of historic abuse: catch the perpetrator off guard and see if they'll confess unknowingly on tape. Here's what the police don't tell you – it's not enough just to get a confession. For example, saying 'I remember you sexually abusing me as a child' and them confessing and saying sorry and that they've regretted it all their life is not enough for a committal to proceed. Imagine that. One must elicit a confession linked to specific incidents, or so the OPP told me. The police never told me this though. So, the conversation needs to go something like this: 'I remember you putting your penis into my vagina when I was six in the lounge room in Station Street on the green couch.'

Now who speaks like that? And who speaks like that to a perpetrator you've hardly got the guts to speak to and may not have spoken to since the abuse? And who speaks like that when they're trying to catch someone off guard? Wouldn't they be automatically more suspicious and less likely to confess? I remember asking police for a cheat sheet showing the top five questions that elicit a confession and was told they can't help me as it would make it inadmissible. I had to work out what to say on my own, no easy task, with no help. Seriously though, no matter how the question is framed, no one is going to confess to any vague or specific allegations of sexual abuse unless they did it. If perpetrators know the system so well and can use it to their advantage, as they do, why can't victims be equally wise? Why can we only go in on the back foot with a departmental hack? I acknowledge 'innocent until proven guilty', but once they've confessed, they should lose their right to give a 'no comment' interview and to plead 'not guilty'. Furthermore, the level of proof should be lowered from beyond all reasonable doubt so that more cases end in convictions.

I was told by a barrister briefed by the OPP that what's sexual abuse to the perpetrator and you, the victim, are two different things and that's why they're agreeing to diversion. How offensive. That's the whole point. They think they've done nothing wrong. That's nothing new; perpetrators and their lawyers have been minimising their actions for years, but I didn't expect the barrister briefed by the OPP, who was there to prosecute the crime, to say such things! So, is all childhood sex abuse simply child's play, curiosity and experimentation? I don't agree, and I don't think the Department of Human Services would agree either. I know I wouldn't dream of admitting to allegations of sex abuse if someone accused me unless I'd done it or had a mental impairment; it's hardly something you'd admit to lightly. Yet the wife of one of them sent me a text saying just that – 'experimental and curiosity play is not insest (sic)'.[122]

The foundation of our legal system: 'innocent until proved guilty'. In sex abuse cases, this means the accused can give a 'no comment' interview and they don't need to give any evidence in court either. They can just sit there silently, listening to their advantage. Well, this needs to change. They should be compelled to give evidence in all cases. Why is it that they don't want to simply say, 'I didn't do it'? It's insulting that they don't have to. Watching Bill Cosby or Rolf Harris given an armchair ride by the law, not having to say a thing, irks me. If I was wrongly accused, I'd be desperate for the opportunity to say that and opt to be called as a witness in defence of myself. Why can they sit there silent and smug, like Bill Cosby in the recent sexual assault cases in the United States? Because they can. We continue to support that nonsense at great cost to victims. Lawyers advise them not to comment and we watch the legal charade time after time.

The OPP need to listen closely to victims, for it wouldn't even exist without brave survivors coming forward. The problem is it's their case, the police case; you are merely their witness. You have zero control over the case and if they do a bad job, it's a case of 'too bad'. You can't pay for your own barrister like the perpetrator can. Imagine a defendant being stuck using the duty lawyer to represent them in serious cases such as sex abuse. Why can they pay for top representation, but the victim can't?

One thing I noticed was that there was no one advising me along the way; I was left on my own and only occasionally was I told about what was going to happen, regardless of my wishes. My husband and I have many clients who come to us complaining that they don't know what's happening in their criminal matter; they haven't heard from police and are given no sufficient explanation as to what to expect at the committal or trial. We are disgusted by this and assist in any way we can. Being able to represent them is the only just and fair answer.

If this is the way the system is, then there should be allowances to privately prosecute if the victim has the money and the inclination. That's preferable to having a sexist barrister like I copped, who reminded me that the police are his client, not me. Imagine being stuck with the intern for your open-heart surgery if you could afford the specialist. But I did eventually get the specialist. The Chief Crown Prosecutor, Lord Pheasant-feather, SC, came down from on high to ensure my matter would not proceed. In the same time he took to do that he could have rightly prosecuted my matter instead. It remains a mystery at my expense. Why was he there, together with Madam Mallee-fowl and a barrister? Why was it so important that my case be dropped?

One only has to look at the cases of Luke Lazarus, Adrian Bayley, Ben Cousins, Stephen Milne, or Oscar Pistorius to ask, has the world gone mad? I believe they are good examples of really bad decisions. The OPP decides if they'll drop certain charges, not the victim, for reasons best known to the OPP. Or wrong charges may be brought by the police from the start –

for example, 'rape' instead of 'indecent act'; there's bargaining over certain charges being dropped, accepting offers of diversion, all causing the real incidents to be watered down. This is the dirty politics of real criminal law that a brave sexual assault victim faces. Again, without a victim coming forward, the great OPP wouldn't exist and the courts wouldn't be so clogged. Then police could get on with real policing, catching the Mars Bar thief, the easy stuff they all love.

So where does that leave us today, in 2017? No matter how advanced society becomes and how many legal protections are afforded to us, I believe people are still motivated by the three essentials – love, food and shelter – and will do just about anything to survive, survive abusive relationships, survive abusive family life whilst still living in the family and once they've left the family unit. However, adults have different resources and options open to them than a child does. They are older and wiser and have the ability to speak up for themselves when and if they are ready. Moreover, their child brain isn't mal-wired, as in the case of child sexual abuse victims.

So, what do children today do when they are being abused? I'm here to say, not much. They generally don't tell anyone. They let things happen to them repeatedly. They keep the secret often out of fear, misguided loyalty and even love for their abuser or to protect other loved ones. Learned helplessness and Stockholm syndrome commonly play out. Children will only tell if they think they'll be believed and if they won't be in trouble for telling. And even then, they still don't tell. My children scoffed at me and said, 'If that happened to us, of course, we'd tell you, Mum,' but I seriously doubt that. Childhood sexual abuse seems to be in a category all of its own and has a unique disabling quality. The persistent denial of the Catholic Church simply compounds the problem. The persistent attitude of the families to turn away from their abused loved ones is utterly tragic.

In my honest opinion, I say regrettably that we shouldn't be asking brave adults and children to have faith in the system and to come forward unless we can support them in using it in meaningful ways. We need many more successful convictions for our courageous disclosures and the process needs to be completely revamped to enable this to happen. The system needs to change to serve the needs of victims; there's nothing new in that conclusion. Otherwise, what's it all for? I hate to think people out there are still under the illusion that children simply make it all up as they go along, and that good Catholic priests and other clergy are being wrongfully accused by lying, naughty children and therefore need their innocence and freedom protected by learned barristers. This is largely a fiction that feeds the business model that is our criminal injustice system.

So how do we stop the abuse and how do we better support survivors? Education is claimed to be a great panacea, but what's the point unless people are willing to embrace the changes and change their attitude? The problem is we've been educated for generations now and more women than men are graduating from universities, but the current statistics paint a gloomier picture than ever before about child sexual abuse and family violence. What's going on? We need to stop the sexism and treat women and children as equals of men overnight. Not by the year dot. Why else does one women die each week to their current or former partner? Change the law now – no more spin, no more delay. Or expect the same, for what do the news headlines tell us day after day as another wife, mother, girlfriend, or child dies at the hands of man?

My message, albeit perhaps, controversial is simple: unless there are changes in the law, I don't advocate using the legal system at all as I think it sets one up for failure and frustration. It's far better to invest your time and energy into sexual assault counselling or other forms of strengthening and healing to get on with your life. Currently, the law seldom provides any justice at all. Being a lawyer myself, I'm professionally so very ashamed to say so, but personally, I have no shame in saying so.

I understand that the system itself has never been for the faint-hearted, but it seems it's not for the robust either, and re-victimisation is certainly still the order of the day! So, who is the system really working for? Let's not kid ourselves. The positive public message and the reality are worlds apart, I'm afraid to say.

More must be done. Good people who know better must do better and must leave their comfort zones and actively seek the changes that sexually abused children so rightly deserve. We need new legislation that covers all forms of sexual abuse and covers all legal redress, both criminal and civil. There should be private prosecutions available and an urgent new legislation enacted, specific to sexual abuse. Currently, we sue sexual abusers under the Wrongs Act, a civil remedy for 'wrongful act'– again, completely inappropriate wording. What happened to me was not a civil wrong. It was sexual abuse, a criminal act. Because my criminal case was suspiciously pulled, I could not get criminal compensation under the Sentencing Act. Because I sued him for damages, I could not get a final award of compensation under VOCAT. The jumping between different jurisdictions is unnecessarily exhausting. There should be a way of processing sexual assault that's a one-stop shop and there could be if victims were afforded a lawyer in the criminal justice system!

The steps to seek redress don't dovetail, sap years of your life, dragging you from one jurisdiction to another. We need to establish specialist courts for sexual assault from start to finish, where there's no need to double up on applications and affidavits for the same thing and worry about the admissibility of evidence from one jurisdiction to another. For example, there was some concern that my pretext call was inadmissible in the civil proceeding as it was obtained during the criminal proceeding. This is insane. As civil matters are decided on the balance of probabilities, the pretext call would cause my matter to pass the legal test easily. Balance of probabilities means it's more likely than not that the allegations are correct. It means fifty-one to a hundred or more likely. The criminal matter and the civil matter are in relation to the same offending and the same defendant. To maintain it's admissible in one jurisdiction but not the next related jurisdiction only seeks to serve an evil purpose, which is to undermine the changes in the Evidence Act to allow pretext calls in sexual assault matters.

To have more than four and a half years of my life wasted on legal servitude and only finally winning by default is insane. To have then had that judgement then set aside is even crazier. If I had won at trial, I would have had the rocky road of enforcement ahead of me. It remains to be seen whether I will receive any compensation at all, for that is another legal game of cat and mouse: enforcement proceedings, which can be very costly. So, with that known trajectory, I stopped the legal insanity at mediation. It was the only sane option. I stuck my finger up to the law and signed.

Unless we revamp this entire area, it sends a clear message to survivors of sexual abuse that we don't care. 'Suck it up and shut up.' I certainly received that message loud and clear. I feel

I owe it to my children, my family, my friends and my hometown of beautiful Conservative Town to spread the word. This is the only way forward for me; to do anything less would be to deny my own self and betray my children, my family, my friends and my clients. It's most important that we address these issues for future generations, but the resistance is still strong. My own Aunty Emilia applied for an intervention order against me to stop me from telling my story, the truth. My entire extended family – and it's a big one – have completely shunned my family and I. Why aren't they shunning the perpetrator? There's a taped confession; they are educated individuals with children of their own. Why?

And why oh bloody why are people in Conservative Town still trying to take down Loud Fence ribbons in this town? It's not over. It's just the beginning. I'm sure that school teachers and doctors in general practise and hospital emergency rooms are making referrals and CASA and family violence agencies are stretched past breaking point. SOCIT must be the largest police unit in the country, overflowing with statements of truth sent for prosecution. So where is this trend reflected in the statistics? What happens with the referrals and the statements of truth? I wonder. Master Shredder's lurking somewhere and has seemingly cloned himself in SOCIT in the Conservative Town Police Station and in the office of the OPP in Big Smoke.

So, what do we do about this? Sexual abuse still happens today, every day. I don't think education will stop abusers from abusing, especially if the daily court reports show how they continually get away with it so lightly. Education can only help victims after the abuse, so they know where to go to seek help after the fact. Do violent men really see themselves in the family violence ad campaigns? I wonder. I really do believe that the hunger to hurt and dominate in many men is genetically imprinted in male DNA, just as sexual attraction to children is.

Is the answer to become a helicopter parent? What do we tell our children? 'Stranger danger' should not be the message. The deranged stranger rapist down the dark alley like Adrian Bayley and the good girl from the good side of the tracks in the wrong place at the wrong time like the ABC reporter Jill Meagher is the stereotype we must move away from. Whilst these cases make the media, ask yourself why they make the media. They are shocking and sickening, but they don't ruffle anyone's feathers as I don't think Adrian Bayley or Sean Price, killers of Jill Meagher and Masa Vukotic, would have too many fans in high places. They are, in some ways, counter-productive to our cause as they keep the illusion alive that we're tough on crime and have zero tolerance for violence. I only wish that were so.

It is so heart-warming to see a new breed of journalists like Charmion, Valeria, Nerissa and Paulina reporting the truth so accurately, spending so much time on the road to get the real story, not just a story. This means vicarious trauma and hours and hours with 'Conservative Townians', at least the ones willing to talk. It means joining the survivor family in its ups and downs, for that is their reality. It's quite unethical to report anything else but in a topic so critical and life-threatening to so many. In these women, I and many have found an ally, a friend: fearless women of integrity who uphold the quest for truth. It is very disappointing that I find such people in the media but seldom in my own profession as well as they are too busy hiding under their wigs, grandstanding.

Frankly, I wouldn't recommend going anywhere near a courtroom if you're a victim of childhood or adult sexual abuse. Here I stand today as a mother, daughter, wife, friend, feminist and lawyer with a Women's Studies major, on the Board of a Family Violence Support agency for many years, who couldn't get the legal system to work for me. I like to think of myself as positive and proactive, but at the same time, I must admit that the law in this area simply doesn't work. Not for my clients and not for me.

The point is I'm angry about why. Why doesn't it work in this area? Why not after all this time? What's the point of educating children, teaching them to stand up for themselves, only to put them down when they do? What's my journey been for if we're back to square one and in reality, I'm no better off than my great-grandmother, who lived in a patriarchal stone farm on the Dalmatian Coast? She knew her place and didn't dare challenge it. I'm told that's not my place in this country, sitting on a stone step in a small village, plucking chicken feathers with limited options, but the reality of our legal system betrays this message. It has me sitting back on that same stone farm step, feeling undervalued, denied and wronged by the police, the OPP and the courts. Trust me, I don't want to be a victim, but it's difficult to be anything but when you use the legal system. You are typecast a victim by the legal system and remain a victim by and to the legal system. The word survivor can assist psychologically, but I see myself as a victim undoubtedly despite the negative connotation.

I do not want anyone else to go through what I have been through. I've changed and my advice, especially as a lawyer, has changed. My point is, trying to fit childhood sexual abuse into the existing legal framework is like Cinderella's ugly stepsister trying to fit her foot into Cinderella's shoe; it just doesn't fit no matter how hard you try! But it should fit – and easily by now. It should be everyone's priority to ensure that it fits. It should be a 'one size fits all'! But if the shoe is designed so that it only fits one woman called Cinderella, a fiction in any event, herein lies the problem.

After more than four years of battling to break the silence, I'm no better off but rather in a much worse position. The perpetrator walked free with little consequence, I'm financially worse off, I've had to fight and pay to have my freedom of speech restored to its pre-police disclosure state, I've lost my entire extended paternal family and my physical and mental health have really suffered, as anyone's would.

If that's the best that the system can do for me, a child sexual abuse victim, in the year 2017, we have a massive problem that we have not even begun to solve in any real, meaningful way. I decided from the outset of issuing civil proceedings that I'll happily go to jail before I pay my cousin a cent if I lost. I told everyone that I'll pack my toothbrush in case the law wants to punish me for speaking up again. I'll walk Derryn Hinch's path if that's what it takes. My going to jail would make a mockery of the law and give a newsworthy profile to the ineptitude of the law. In the end though, I settled the matter at mediation, so I can't add jail time to my life's journey yet, but I was certainly prepared to have a forced rest!

The sad truth is sexual abuse and other forms of family violence are going on everywhere at an alarming rate, sometimes in the very next room in our own house. It's in all families from all walks of life, rich and poor and in most organisations who have children as members. We must open our eyes, our ears and our minds. I say change the system urgently or don't use it at all. Don't ask victims to come forward if the legal system doesn't respect them when they do. The OPP Victims Charter and services like the Witness Assistance Program are good if they were adhered to, but the real help we need is having a system that works from start to end. It's the substantive stuff that needs the work; anything less is just paying lip service to victims.

Victims can bring their own tissues to court; it's their right to an independent lawyer that they need urgently! If the government can pay witness-assistance workers at the OPP, they can pay victim's lawyers with that money instead. In the Campeius case, witnesses were allowed a support dog to be with them in the witness box when they gave their evidence, but victims don't need a dog in the courtroom; they need a lawyer! This was nothing more than a public relations stunt by the police and sadly, it worked. I know that when I go into hospital for surgery, I want a top surgeon, not a dog to pat in there. How would Campeius go in the trials with a dog instead of learned counsel?

I refuse to be part of the silence and the illusion that it's a more victim-friendly system. SOCIT units only hold any value when the OPP prosecutes matters and they end in a conviction more than 3 per cent of the time. Victims don't want to be baring their souls to simply add to statistics to justify the SOCIT units being there. They do it because they want the perpetrator to finally be made accountable. It is cruel to give victims false hope. Having the guts to finally tell and gaining action and closure from telling are two separate things entirely and currently, they seem to be mutually exclusive.

I successfully fought to have a Suppression Order removed, which is yet another layer of silencing the victim. Now that I have my right to freedom of speech restored, I feel it is my responsibility to do all I can to protect the vulnerable adults and children in our legal system, in our home, in our neighbourhood and in our world. I feel compelled to speak out without shame or fear for what's right. Currently, telling victims to come forward and tell police is far from right.

The Royal Commission into Institutional Responses to Child Sexual Abuse heard from many people, but many people from Conservative Town did not make a statement that could have and should have. The Conservative Town Case Study was one of the most significant, but many Conservative Town people kept quiet. I suspect that the Conservative Town fat cats and prominent families were more interested in protecting their own reputation and financial interest, but it's such a sad indictment on our society that they do. After all, they too have children and hold family secrets that could and should also be the subject of the Royal Commission. I know.

I also know that money alone can't fix the damage created by sexual abuse. My uncle King Lear and Aunty, King Lear's wife, were upstanding Catholic Conservative Town parishioners who are most un-Christian indeed. For many years now, Aunty, King Lear's wife, has painted icons of the Madonna and Child, another example of her Catholic dogma which is so strong that she puts the welfare of the church before her own children, both her abusing sons (and likely victim sons) and her victim daughters. Why doesn't Aunty support her daughters and I and uphold the Christian values of the church by holding her sons accountable for what they did? Moreover, if my suspicions are right and her sons were abused by Catholic clergy, why don't my Aunty and Uncle stand up and help to change the face of the church for the better?

At the start of the Royal Commission hearings in Conservative Town, I watched my Aunty, King Lear's wife, tie a ribbon onto the gates of St Michael's Cathedral right in front of me as I was speaking to a fellow parishioner who had just disclosed her sexual abuse after the Conservative Town Royal Commission hearings had commenced, but her actions are rendered meaningless by her actions towards me and my disclosure and to that of her own daughters. Uncle King Lear is one of the most cowardly men I know, and his big strong hands and the many houses built by them are a disguise for a very weak man building houses on a crumbling foundation. His son King Claudius is just the same as him, a weakling. The sick apple doesn't fall far from the sick tree. Aunty was right back in 2013 when she told me, 'One thousand sorrys a day won't make up for what he's done.' What has King Claudius done to at least try to make things right? Nothing.

I had hoped that the recommendations made by the Royal Commission in December 2017 would be adequate for the lifetime of suffering for so many people in Conservative Town and beyond. However, it stops far short of satisfactory, for it precludes victims who have been to jail and secondary victims and those who have lost loved ones to suicide. It puts a cap on counselling at $5,000. On average, it provides no better than VOCAT or no more than the maximum available under Towards Healing and Kooyoora. It uses a matrix to grade abuse, but it's the after effects of abuse that Redress should be focussing on. It also says victims in the criminal justice system don't need a lawyer, which is truly ridiculous after the government paid for them to have one in the Royal Commission.

I had also hoped that the recommendations are adopted fearlessly by the government as it's what we do with it that matters; otherwise, we're still leaving it up to the victims to be fearless. If we are such a civilised society, let's see it, please, or the child sexual abuse orgy worldwide will surely continue. Or will we all adopt the attitude of Cardinal Campeius and simply say, 'It was a sad story of not much interest to me,' until it happens to our own child?

With a very critical eye, as sharply focussed as Madame Gulbis' ballet eye, I will judge the Law, the State and the Church for what it does from hereon. I will be the new woman in black in my life and if I don't like what I see, especially here in Conservative Town, I will gnaw on that bone until there's nothing left. I will smash Cinderella's glass slipper, make a new one, buy a shoehorn, stretch the leather, cut off the heel and cut off the ends of my shoes so my toes can stick out and get blisters and bleed, just to wear that Cinderella shoe. Until sexual abuse fits in the law, I will squeeze my foot into that shoe awkwardly and wear it in until it fits properly. Until all victims of child sexual abuse fit into the law properly. Until I can represent them as their lawyer in a criminal courtroom, even if I have to say, 'I withdraw that, Your Honour,' after I've already said what needs to be said and achieved the desired effect. That's the way it works, isn't it?

As Simone de Beauvoir said famously, 'One is not born a woman. One becomes one.'[123] How we treat women and children now is telling of the level of respect we afford them today. When we look at the skyrocketing level of family violence today in this so-called civilised country of Australia, we must admit that not much has changed. Whatever are we doing? Where are we all going? What sort of world are we making for our children to live in?

★★★

'Song in the Blood'
A Poem by Jacques Prevert
Translated by Lawrence Ferlinghetti[124]

*Note — I listened to this poem as a child, as recited by Joan Baez on her album Baptism(1968)[125]. Mum and Dad played this vinyl record often and I'd get even more scared when Baez's song 'Magic Wood'[126] came on.

Acronyms:

WRISC — Women's Resource Information Support Centre (family violence support agency)
VOCAT — Victims of Crime Assistance Tribunal (government awards compensation for being a victim of crime)
CASA — Centre Against Sexual Assault (specialised sex-assault counselling)
SOCIT — Sexual Offences and Child Abuse Investigation Team (Victoria Police)
DPP — Director of Public Prosecutions
OPP — Office of Public Prosecutions
SO — Suppression Order (an order prohibiting the publication or discussion of anything to do with the case to ensure a fair trial)
Redress Scheme — the national scheme to compensate victims of clergy abuse
RCFV — Royal Commission into Family Violence
RCCSA — Royal Commission into Institutional Responses to Child Sexual Abuse
PTSD — post-traumatic stress disorder
JR — Judicial Registrar
Doli incapax — a child 14 years and under can't know the wrongness of their actions

MC — Magistrates' Court

FCC — Federal Circuit Court

CC — County Court

SC — Supreme Court

DHHS — Department of Health and Human Services

IBAC — Independent Broad-based Anti-Corruption Commission

OCD — obsessive-compulsive disorder

DSP — Disability-Support Pension

VARE — child interview by police on video recording

APPENDIX

Document A — Cleopatra's Guide
To Pre-text Calls

Cleopatra's Guide for Victims in Criminal Justice System

<u>**Moral to the story:**</u>

Don't enter the CJS, but if you are already in there:

Victims in CJS need their own lawyer:

Sex assault victims have a lawyer paid by government (Attorney Generals Department) when the Royal Commission comes to town, but that hides the reality that victims don't have one in the courts, day after day. They are not even a party to the proceeding.

Police, SOCIT, OPP, lawyers, barristers, judges and court staff feed off the beast that is the CJS and the victim becomes an inconvenient truth in the legal system and often to their family too once they disclose sexual abuse.

They need their own lawyer to advise on the vital aspects of their matter:

Has their <u>statement to police</u> has been sufficiently particularised?

<u>Pretext calls</u> – how to, what you need to say, the level of admission required

<u>Suppression Orders</u> – negotiate the terms or argue against it

etc. Currently victims are not served with it yet are subject to its terms which is legally untenable.

The criminal process/court events trajectory

Check that charges brought by police are all correct and complete (no uncharged acts).

Advocate for victim in courtroom – currently no one does as police instructions to OPP are often different to the victim's wishes

Check all docs in police brief are correct

Because the victim has no legal advice, no legal standing and no legal representation, there's currently a 97% chance that the matter will fail.

Main issues:

Victims of sexual abuse are not told what they should say in the pretext call but the content is everything!

In my case when I asked the police, DSC Rosser, what questions usually elicit a confession, I was told that they can't help me at all as that would make it inadmissible. I told them they should provide a cheat sheet to help victims – the top five questions that get a perpetrator talking and confessing please –Rosser laughed and said no, there's no such thing.

My father and I thought about reverse psychology – you really do need a psychology degree, nerves of steel and the ability to think many steps ahead behind that seemingly casual conversation that the pretext call needs to be. I was so stressed out. You need to almost take in scripts of conversations including varied responses to hypothetical answers.

The discussions must elicit a confession to each allegation:

So saying, "I remember you sexually abusing me when we

were kids" and him saying sorry and that he's regretted it all of his life is not enough to have the OPP proceed. It's too general.

V's

"I remember you putting your penis into my vagina on the green couch in the loungeroom of your grandfather's house in station street at 4 pm after school in November 1992."

On the day of the Committal Hearing when I was distressed about them dropping the charges of rape and accepting an offer of diversion, the OPP's barrister told me that, "what's **sexual abuse** to you and the defendant are two different things." So, when I used the words "sexual abuse" to the defendant, apparently that wasn't not enough.

If it doesn't, there will be "uncharged acts" which can cause your matter to be discontinued so you must cover each allegation (or the ones you do cover won't stick due to the others.)

Stress of it is too much.

Emotional stress You are alone when you make the call, in a room all by yourself in the police station. They give you a microcassette recorder and a blurb to read out before and after the call. This seemed like a major deal to me to remember to do this at the time, as I was already stressed to the max and couldn't seem to easily manage such an ordinarily simple task. It was a scary thing to do and in a foreign place of police station/unfamiliar, sterile place.

Physical stress I was sweating during it and after it I started shaking uncontrollably. My body was in a state of shock – I didn't know what to do with myself in that room. I was on auto pilot and walked out to see the policeman and my father and said, "he's confessed and apologised." Rosser said I was so lucky as it's so rare for perpetrators to do so. I walked out of the police station but I didn't feel a sense of relief like I did when I made my statement to police. This was different. It was like going right back to being a child again, exposed to the power imbalance of being with the perpetrator again albeit over the phone, there doesn't seem to be a distance so there's no layer of protection...I could hear the piano accordion playing again.

Sensory overload Hearing his voice, the cool calm with which he spoke and the concern for the preservation of his own image above all else

"I don't want you to think this is reflective of who I am or what I am now"

He minimised the abuse

"it was silly kids"

I was upset with myself that I started crying during the call whilst he could maintain his unwavering disposition despite my pain, the sociopath he is. I felt like I was back in the mid '80s when it all happened. You have no control over the call, despite thinking you will, as the original power dynamic you had with them is the same – he had to go and wanted to call back later that night. It was on his terms. This is disempowering and distressing as it's disingenuous and so the thought of a further call with an ulterior motive is even more distressing.

Legal Issues

Abolishment of statute of limitations

Now no limit on bringing an action for sexual abuse, regardless of the passage of time

The police ask you whether you have ever confronted the abuser before

Most will say no as most won't have, they've lived the lie and remained silent so this is perfect. But you don't want to waste or wreck your best chance at a confession through misinformation.

Corroborating evidence

The police asked me to ask my cousin Regan to do a pretext call too about what King Claudius did to her. This caused:

Pressure on my relationship with her

A non-corroborative statement from her

She never made a pretext call – she never went to police

Conflict of Interest

Police are mandated to protect society and bring actions against criminals on behalf of the state just as the DHHS bring child protection applications on behalf of the state for the child deemed "at risk" by the protective worker. But what the worker wants and what the child wants are often different and the law affords the child their own lawyer based on the premise that the child and the worker are different parties with different interests. In all jurisdictions each individual party has the right to be independently legally represented, but not in criminal law. This needs urgent change.

The OPP's power is unfetteredand they are unanswerable to the Attorney General, the Ombudsman, the politicians or the judiciary. In my case, even though the OPP originally wanted the case to proceed, the OPP then dropped it, using the Chief Crown Prosecutor to do so. Why? Surely, they wouldn't do that; protect the accused from a good behaviour bond when their whole purpose is to prosecute crime. So, why was Chief Crown Prosecutor, now acting DPP, Lord Pheasant-feather there I ask?

The word vagina

My lawyers from an expert personal injuries firm told me there were problems in my statement to police as I said he had touched me on the vagina when according to them, he didn't as they explained, "that's the canal where the baby comes out of. "This was confirmed by their counsel, which is indeed laughable. In the recent allegations of sexual assault against Craig McLachlan, the complainants also speak of being touched on the vagina, so will they too be deemed wrong by the law if the assault is over clothing? More legal lunacy.

Police got the charges wrong in my matter

They brought charges of "Rape"

Instead of "indecent act with a child under 16."

This caused:

My cousin Goneril to think I was lying to police as I never said he penetrated me and she thought I had told police this to secure a rape charge. I never said that though at any time.

My case was dropped because wrong charges were brought

and also because there were uncharged acts, allegedly.

Level of evidence

My abuser said he'd call me back later. Police said there is no need to answer his anticipated call as they had all they need in first pretext call. So this was a wasted opportunity for further and more detailed disclosures that were still needed, unbeknown to me at the time.

Paid FOI for pretext call

Infuriatingly, I only received a redacted copy with his voice edited out- only my voice was left. Once I issued civil proceedings, I subpoenaed the file and got the unredacted copy.

Victims of historic abuse don't realise the pretext call will be used as something to test the victim's credibility, not to trip up the defendant.

Questions are asked about the pretext call, what they the victim remember they said, what the perpetrator said.

Defendant has the right to silence full stop, so if they opt to remain silent they are not asked about the pretext call at all.

Pretext call becomes counter-productive because by the time of the trial, the victim has a number of documents that re-tell what happened as follows:

Criminal matters –

Has original Statement to Police

Any Supplementary Statement to Police

Pretext call

Civil –

Statement of Claim

Any Chronologies

Affidavit of Documents

By then you've become an inconvenient truth. The defence look for what they call inconsistencies between each re-tell or representation of the story, so the pretext call can be used to discredit the victim in this way. This is very easy to do as each retell will have their variations, but this doesn't mean that each one is not the truth. Sometimes you have time to tell all, other times you don't and summarise, or the focus is on the more traumatic event rather than each and every event etc.

If the victim's aim is acknowledgment, you won't get that through courts or police. Justice Marcia Naeve, Commissioner in the Royal Commission into Family Violence and Judge in the Court of Appeal agrees with this, proposing a new model of dealing with sexual assault as used in South Africa.

Tell your truth to: CASA, family, friends, doctor. Forget courts, lawyers, SOCIT, judges. Once you tell, you think justice and relief (emotional and/or financial) will flow. A victim thinks the big thing is being brave enough to tell but then you expect a response in line with Royal Commission but that's not what you get, far from it.

Document B — Cleopatra's First Statement to Police

Revised 08/12   VP Form 287A

STATEMENT

Name:

_____

STATES:

1.   My full name is   ⌐   ⌐ My date of birth is the ⌐   ⌐1973.

2.   I come from a large Croatian family. The older members of my extended
        family are involved and practice in the beliefs of the Catholic Church. My
        immediate family which includes my father _____ my mother _____ and my
        brother _____ are not actively Catholic.

3.   My father has a number of siblings which are older and younger than him,
        and they have many children. Especially in my younger years as a child we would
        associate with these family members very often for family gatherings. We would
        generally meet at my grandparents' house at ⌐   ⌐ My
        fathers' brother   ⌐ lived directly behind his parents house in ⌐   Street
        South. The two houses were backed onto each other via their fences and as children
        we would run and play between both houses.

4.   _____ is my fathers' _____. He is married to _____ and they
        lived in _____ They have   children. _____
        ⌐ who drowned at Portarlington when he was a child, and

5.   ⌐   ⌐, who is my fathers _____ is married to _____
        They have ⌐ iildren ⌐
        _____

        _____ and _____ and his children always lived
        at the ⌐   Street South house when I was young. ⌐

Revised 08/12   VP Form 287A

_____ It was a big two storey house and it backed onto my grandparents house in ____ Street.

6.   My father had a brother named ____ who died in 1966 in cycling accident.

7.   ____ is the ____ father. He was married to ____ who is now deceased. They have ____ children and lived in ____ who was close in age to ____ and ____

8.   ____ is my fathers ____ She was married to ____ who is now deceased. They also lived in ____ and have ____ children ____ who is about ____ age, then ____ They also had ____ who died at a young age.

9.   ____ is my fathers ____ who is now deceased and he was married to ____ They have ____ children who are ____ and ____ These children are ____

10.   My father's ____ who lives in America and has named ____

11.   All of the brothers, except for my father and ____ were then involved in the building industry. They constructed houses and have different expertise to provide such as carpentry, concreting, bricklaying, building and excavation to name a few. The family dynamic is very much the stereotypical Croatian family in the sense that there is a defined hierarchy present within the structure of the family which gives greater weight to the older members. The males are encouraged to be leaders and provided with opportunity and support, whereas the females have little say on family matters and provide the male members of the family with their opportunity to succeed. As I got older I noticed that my father being one of the younger brothers never seemed to get as much of a say when it came to family matters.

Revised 08/12   VP Form 287A

12.   My father was not in the family business and as such neither of my parents fit
the mould of this stereotype, however my immediate family we were still close with
our extended relatives and would always celebrate occasions or attend functions
such as church as if we were. All of my cousins and their parents were involved in
the church. The families attended ' ___ ___ Cathedral where the children were
alter boys and their mothers worked with the church choir and committees. My
family were always the ones that showed up late to church. My parents never
pushed me to be involved in the church like my cousins were, but I think we went
just to keep the family happy. My cousins all went to the local Catholic Primary
Schools being either'   !   )'   * and'
I went to'   Grammar.

13.   We would always have these family gatherings for any reason you could
imagine. Birthdays, Christmas', visitors from overseas, communions, and feasts of
our lady celebrations. I remember when visitors arrived from overseas we would
travel to and gather at the airport as an entire family to welcome them.

14.   From the age of three years I started doing ballet and violin. The ballet school
that I attended was the'   'School of Ballet. It was in,   Street,
____at the old '   ' My cousins'   and '   also did
ballet with me. I would go to Ballet after school on Tuesdays and then Saturday
mornings also. After ballet on Saturdays I would often go and play at'___ 'and
____house. This wasn't every Saturday and often my Mum would ask me if I
wanted to go, but I liked playing with ____and'   'I was basically an only
child at that time as my brother was either not born or still very young and I enjoyed
playing with kids my own age.

15.   It was on one of these occasions that I was at ____'and   'place
playing. Also at the house were my cousins'   'and'   '. There was a third boy but
I can't remember who that was. The first thing that I remember is going into the
boys room with____and'   'and the three boys.'   'old us girls that each
one of us would have a spot in the room. We laid down in the spots that   'old us
to and we were told to take off our clothes. I remember feeling cold and exposed as I

Revised 08/12

VP Form 287A

was laying the closest to the door of the bedroom. The bedroom itself had two singles sized beds within it but they weren't pushed up against the walls of the bedroom. They were both in from the wall. This created a gap between each bed and the wall, and also a gap in between the two beds. I was made to lay in the gap closest to the door. I was thinking that I wanted to be in a gap further from the door in case someone came in and saw me. I was anxious about the door being opened and I was lying there exposed.   and   also were given one of the gaps each, but I'm not sure where they were allocated in these gaps   and the other boy then stayed with   or

16.   The three of us girls got undressed as we stood in the spots we were told to. I was wearing my outfit from ballet which included leg warmers, stockings and leotard. I laid down on my back with my head facing away from the door and towards the wall. The three boys were together and were talking to each other about what they were going to do.   then said "What we're going to do is feel parts of you and you've got to tell us how it feels."   then came and was with me where I was laying down. I remember seeing a long dark coloured feather in   hand. Politely he said "Now I'm going to use this feather and tell me how it feels?" He started to move the feather up and down the side of my body around my hips and waist. I was cold and feeling rigid and it felt awful for me because I am so ticklish even now. He kept asking "How does that feel?" and I kept saying it tickled. I think I was laughing but it was because of the tickling sensation. I was not enjoying it.   then started to move the feather across my vagina. I remember he was moving it all over my vagina and around my clitoris. It moved it all across the different parts of my vagina. This lasted for about two to three minutes. I was putting up with the feeling of it. It was almost unbearable and I stiffened up in response to the feather touching me there. There was something said to one of the other boys by   and he handed the feather to someone else.

17.   then got a long piece of material or a scarf was shown to me by   I think it was lighter in colour. He again said to me that he wanted me to tell him how it felt. He used this and swirled it along my body. I don't ever remember my breasts being a focus of any of this. With this he was more general in where he moved it across my body. He was asking lots of questions like "Does it feel prickly?", and

Revised 08/12   VP Form 287A

"Does it feel like a snake?" as he moved it along my body. This material was moved across my vagina but he didn't concentrate on this area like with the feather, again finished with this after he was satisfied with the affect it had on me and either passed the material to one of the other boys or put it to the side.

18.   (then said "Now tell me how this feels?" I didn't see what this was, but it was harder than the other things. It was solid and he was able to roll it across my body. He was saying "Does this feel better or worse than the other?"   used this on the top of my vagina. I remember the pressure of this and the feeling it gave me. I felt like I needed to go to the toilet whilst he did this.   rolled this object across the top of my vagina. My legs were open and he was kneeling down. He moved the object from one side of my vagina and rolled it across to the other side of my vagina touching my clitoris as he did it. This rolling happened a number of times back and forth. Whatever this object was he put it to the side or passed it on to one of the other boys. I could hear the other boys in the room speaking to   and and I assumed the same thing was happening to them. Every now and then would get up and leave me and speak to the other boys. I could also hear and   speaking in reply to the boys questions.

19.   then said "I'm going to touch you in different places and tell me how it feels." Using his fingers this time he began to touch my vagina again. He started by separating the lips of my vagina. He put his finger on my clitoris and started to outline shapes on the outside of my vagina. I thought he was drawing shapes and thinking in my head that he was drawing shapes like diamonds and triangles. He was doing a circle around my clitoris with his finger. I felt like was looking at my vagina and was opening my vagina to see what it was. I was thinking that he had a girlfriend and why wasn't he doing this with her. I remember looking at the paint work on the wall while he was doing this. I don't know why but I was focused on small things like marks on the walls and things directly near me. This ended after a number of minutes. Looking back it didn't seem like it was rushed at the time, but I'm not sure if anyone else was home. I remember getting dressed and sitting up looking at my cousins   and   I don't remember   ever saying "don't tell anybody" or anything similar.

Revised 08/12

VP Form 287A

20.   The incident that I've described above wasn't the first or the last time that something happened with [ ] but this was the only time that something happened that involved others. That's why I have the best memory of this occasion.

21.   This type of thing occurred over approximately four years between the years of 1981 to 1984 when I was in Grade 2 to Grade 5. I was about eight years of age when I started. I remember [ ] touching me on the outside of my clothing in the earlier occasions. He would touch me on the vagina on the outside of my clothing. This occurred numerous times. I don't recall ever saying anything to [ ] when this first happened, but I'm sure I would've at least asked him what he was doing. I don't remember him ever saying anything when this happened. This touching moved to touching me underneath my clothing. He would undo my pants or get me to lift up my dress and he would use his hand to touch me directly on my vagina.

22.   These occasions would be opportunistic during visits at his house. It would generally happen while we were playing hide and seek or chase. Hide and seek would almost always be played in the dark and outside. When we played there would be ten to fifteen of us kids playing sometimes across both my grandparents house and [ ] backyard. As [ ] behaviour progressed I remember playing hide and seek and really wanting to hide well so I wasn't found. [ ] was always "it". This never rotated. I wouldn't hide in the normal places. I would go past the boundaries of their yard, down near their chook yard or in the neighbours backyard. My mother would always dress me very nicely and I would be cautious about getting my clothes dirty while playing hide and seek. But I was still prepared to get dirty and get in trouble just so I was well hidden. I remember hearing my heart beating while I was hiding. I didn't want him to find me. I used to hold my breath to try and stop my heart beating. There were numerous occasions where [ ] would find me while we were playing hide and seek. On these occasions [ ] would touch me in the way I've described above by placing his hand inside my pants or up my skirt and touching my vagina with his hand and fingers.

23.   After the incident involving the other boys, and during the later years of this happening [ ] became more opportunistic and more brazen. I remember feeling

Revised 08/12   VP Form 287A

anxious about being caught while he did these things. I thought I'd get in trouble also and I knew it was the wrong thing to do. Myself and the other cousins would all sit around and tell ghost stories. This was more apparent after [ ] had died. [ ] and [ ] and some of the older cousins had organised a séance in the cellar of [ ] house one time. [ ] and I would sometimes be left alone while we were doing these ghost stories. [ ] would take this opportunity to briefly touch me when there was no-one else around or after they'd left a room. They didn't seem planned but I always thought it was probably going to happen if he got the opportunity.

24.   For an unknown reason [ ] stopped doing these things to me. I didn't say anything to anyone at that time. I don't know why he stopped. I first told my ex husband [ ] in the early 1990's, and then my husband [ ] in late 2008. On Thursday the 6th of June, 2013, at lunchtime when I was shopping with my mother in Melbourne I blurted it out. I started crying and told her all of this. After speaking to Mum and Dad I decided to report this.

25.   These experiences have defiantly shaped who I am. I am able to emphasise with victims during my work. It made we want to study law. I don't have much trust in others and feel women need to be independent and stand up for themselves. I feel that I need to act as a voice for women as they are valued less than men. I've always felt venerable in my work life and personal life. I am still exposed to seeing [ ] at family functions. It was initially a feeling fear in the earlier years, and then angry when I was at University and being exposed to these ideas, but now I just think "why?" When I look at my own children I realise it wasn't innocent child play. It makes me angry to know that others don't know about it and I've been living with it. I'm disappointed with myself for not speaking about it earlier. I'm sorry about what this may cause for my cousins [ ] and [ ] and if they are ready to speak about what may have happened to them also.

Document C — Cleopatra's Second Statement to Police

<u>SUPPLEMENTARY STATEMENT OF</u>, _____ ⟶

21st <u>MAY 2014</u>

COPY

Reasons for this 2nd statement:

1. I am making this statement after the OPP withdrew all charges against my cousin
    ____ The OPP told Senior Constable _____ that I could make another statement
    if I so wished.

2. In my opinion ___ is a sociopath and needs therapeutic counselling urgently like
    other sex offenders. He has admitted to offending in the following ways:

    a. In ___ 2013 during a pretext call he admits to sexually abusing me
        and says he's sorry and that he's regretted it all his life.

    b. On ___ 2014, day of the committal, ___ offered diversion with a
        revised statement "I pulled down her pants and touched her on the
        public bone once." That shows his preparedness to admit to some
        offending, with a sexual overtone. On the same day he then retracts
        that offer because he was only prepared to admit if there was no
        conviction. In other words, only if there's no consequence.

    I remember ___ also said something like we were kids, all kids muck around like
    that. I wonder why he's regretted it all his life if he thinks it's simply something all
    kids do. I also wonder why ___ confronted him about it 3 years ago, if it's
    something all kids do. Why do we think it's wrong and that he knew it was wrong?
    The truth is that this behaviour is not the stuff of a normal childhood. I don't think
    we should take ___ minimisation - approach as the healthy way forward. Would
    ___ condone his boys ___ and ___ doing this to his daughter ___ ?

    My sons ___ (13) in year 8 and ___ (11) in year 6 think it's completely wrong
    and couldn't imagine doing this to my daughter ___ (8) and her cousin
    (9) unless they were "sick in the head" were their words. I can guarantee what any
    child in Year 8 at school would say about doing this to some girls in Year 2 at school.
    If one of us had spoken up as children the Department of Human Services would
    have been around in a jiffy. What would a school counsellor say about it?

3. In my first statement I did not particularise all of the offending. I did not know I had
    not done this, not until the OPP told me on Monday ___ 2014, nearly a year
    after I made my statement, just a few days before the Committal on ___ . I

went to the police when I was very upset. I had only just told my parents and it was a big deal to tell the police. It was a really emotional time. I knew that once the secret was out the family would change forever.

4.   I felt the weight of the world on my shoulders. I had had no counselling. I poured it all out with no structure. I had no notes or chronology, repeating some things and leaving other important things out. ___ was reading things back to me whilst typing for my approval which was fine. However, it was all in my head but I couldn't keep track of what I had said and what I still had to cover. I was overwhelmed by the process. Now I know my statement suffered for it. I had no time for clear thought, chronology, and details of all the offending. I was at the stage of wow; I'm actually telling the police and not holding onto this baggage anymore. I was crying and shaking, physically dishevelled as well. I did it all on the one day; I wanted it to be over so I wouldn't have to think about it anymore. It was done; the cat was out of the bag. The sheer relief was immense.

PARTICULARISATION OF OFFENDING 1984 -1981 INCLUSIVE:

5.   In my first statement I say I don't know why ___ stopped doing things to me. Since I disclosed, Aunty, ___ told ___ that she thought ___ may have moved on to ___ after ___ and I. This seems logical.

6.   In any event, at the end of 1984 I quit ballet. Quitting ballet was my way of stopping the abuse. ___ and I had completed our grade 5 Borovonski ballet exams. My Mum and Dad tried to encourage me to keep up with ballet but I was determined to quit. I never told anyone why I really quit, to stay away from ___ and ___ Street. I had been quite good at ballet, in grade 3 I won the Borovonski gold medallion out of all my year level.

7.   I deliberately begged my Mum to get my hair cut short in the summer holidays and refused to re-enrol at ballet in January 1985. Looking back now I realise it was symbolic for me because the end of having long ballet hair meant the end of ___ abusing me. It was at the start of 1985, the start of Grade 6. ___ was going into ___ at St ___

8.   I really missed ballet and I missed seeing ___ and ___ too as previously I saw them quite regularly. They were my favourite cousins. I still invited ___ and ___ but not the other cousins) to my birthdays thereafter. They would always be on my guest list, along with my Grammar school friends.

To clarify the abuse in [____] bedroom in my previous statement:

a). Mid October to December 1984

9.   This group sexual assault happened in late 1984, when I was wearing leg warmers. I
      only wore leg warmers during my last year of ballet; I only ever had 1 pair. They were
      black. This fashion only came out then, they weren't fashionable prior to that time.
      This means I know this happened in 1984.

10.   It happened sometime after October[?] (my birthday), when I was 11 as I'd just had
      my birthday party not long before this incident. I had a birthday picnic in the
      [____] pine plantation forest with my girlfriends from school and [____] and [____]
      of course. My brother [____] was about to turn 3 at the end of December. I was in
      grade 5 at [____] Grammar and Mr [____] was my teacher! [____]ad turned 15 in
      February 1984 so he was 15 and 8 months at least and in [____] was
      13 and in [____]

11.   I was always the tallest child at school in my year, back row and centre in most
      school photos, even taller than the boys. I was also an early developer and started
      getting embarrassed about my breasts starting to grow earlier than my friends,
      which was obvious in my leotards and tutus. When I was sexually assaulted that day
      I remember wondering why [____] didn't even touch my breasts as I was self conscious
      about them already starting to develop.

12.   I started wearing a bra several months later at the start of grade 6! Only a few of us
      wore a bra in grade 6. I remember it well as it was a big deal when I changed for PE
      or swimming lessons at school.

13.   It was a Saturday afternoon and [____] and I had been playing in the
      downstairs rumpus room, dancing around still in our ballet gear. This was normal for
      me as after ballet I would spend the rest of the day in my ballet gear to do the
      shopping or run errands with my parents. I would leave ballet by putting on a
      tracksuit top and replacing my ballet slippers with runners.

14.   Dad would often pick [____] and I up from ballet and stop at the health food
            shop, [____] a few doors down from ballet to buy bags of nuts, apricot
            delight and a yoghurt cone. Dad would play tennis with Uncle [____] at St
            [____] courts and pick me up later Saturday afternoon from [____]
            after tennis. Sometimes after ballet Dad would take [____] and I to the [____]
            [____] behind the [____] Train station. This is where he hosted life drawing

classes. One of his life models [   ] ended up marrying Dad's brother
[   ]. I was the flower girl at their wedding in November 1982.

15. [   ] and his school friend and [   ] were in the billiard room/second lounge
room playing the Atari. [   ] was really into Arnold Schwartsnegger and the
movie Terminator and would always impersonate him in his voice saying "I'll
be back". He thought he was really cool saying this. I remember the other boy
was quite handsome, had sandy blonde hair and was as tall as, if not taller
than, [   ] He had a slim build. I can't remember what his name was, Aunty
[   ] thinks its [   ] but I really have no idea [   ] came over into the
adjoining rumpus room where we were playing and said to come upstairs
with them (the boys) for a minute, so we did. That's when he told us what we
had to do, as I explained in my first statement.

16. It was daytime when it happened but the venetian blinds were shut. The light
wasn't on but there was enough natural light in the room to see everything.

17. My Mum came to collect me from [   ] house later in the day. She had
my brother [   ] with her. He was nearly 3 years old and [   ] nick named
him "little Leroy" from the character Leroy out of Fame, a cool male dancer.
We were dancing around my brother while singing the theme song "Fame"
and [   ] and I were all doing this together. Everyone
loved [   ] and thought he was such a cute little boy. We loved Fame and
Flashdance because they were about dance.

18. We were singing "What a feeling…it's a Flashdance" and the younger ones
were in some dress ups dancing too. I was redressed in my ballet gear from
when [   ] and the others had abused us upstairs. [   ] and I made up
some dance moves for all the kids, including my brother. We did this till my
Mum said its time to go home. She had been having coffee with Aunty
upstairs while we were dancing around.

19. At school we were about to have the end of year concert. I was still trying to
learn to do some break dancing moves as my class was rehearsing to do a
break dancing concert. I remember it well because I couldn't do backspins or
any of the moves very well, so I ended up being the narrator. My school
friends, especially the boys, thought it was funny that a ballet dancer couldn't
break-dance!

20. When I think back on it now, I am struck by how well organised [   ] was, so
premeditated to have all of the equipment ready in the room and also willing
co-offenders on the ready. I believe he was 90% sure I would be there being a
Saturday. He was ready for the scenario to play itself out. After speaking to

_____ about it last year I suspect this was a common weekend activity at their house. I was surprised that I only remembered the group offending happening once, as she told me it happened at least 20 times.

b). 25 December 1980 – December 1984

21. During these years of visiting Baba's and Aunties my cousins and I nearly always played hide and seek or chasey around the backyards of Babas and Aunties. I remember it was often dark when we played as the celebrations would often kick on all night. I could sometimes hear the distant piano accordion playing and the singing from where I was hiding. It was almost comforting until he found me. Then he would touch me on the vagina either on top of my undies or inside them.

22. (___) always organised the games and always seemed to put himself in a position where he could create an opportunity to sexually abuse me. This went on for about 4 years whenever our families got together for any of the many celebrations at Aunties and Baba's house where we children amused ourselves by playing outside games in the garden.

23. As I got older I had to really think of original places to hide so that ___ couldn't find me. I started moving hiding spots, going behind neighbours' fences, going right into the garden beds down low lying directly on the grass or dirt, even if the ground was damp.

24. There were at least 15 occasions per year where the families congregated at either of these houses, bringing all the children together. I ___ never did anything to me during these years at our family beach house in Portarlington, Uncle's caravan or at any other of my Aunty and Uncle's houses. Only at his house, my house and Baba and Dida's house. Please see **Timeline of Events 1980 - 1984** and ___ **Family Tree** attached.

c). Spring 1984

25. One Saturday after ballet in Spring of 1984 I had gone to ( ) house after ballet. We had been at her house when we decided to go to the park in ___ Street. It used to have a maternal Health Nurse Centre there too. I was happy to go and get away from ___ We left ___ behind as ___ would sometimes complain to her Mum that she was sick of ___ lways hanging around her and following us. I didn't mind, I would have done anything for a sister and was a little

disappointed I had a little brother instead of a sister. I thought they were really lucky having each other to play with all the time.

26. Anyway, we didn't stay at the park for long because not long after we got there some older teen-aged girls about [ ] age threatened us. They asked us how old we were and I said 11, [ ] said 10. Then they asked if we wanted to fight and we started getting scared saying "what?, no!!!" Then one girl said "fists or blades?" and [ ] and I immediately ran for our lives straight back to her house to tell her mum what just happened. We were really scared as the girls were dressed in tough street wear, denim and black boots, real "westies" in today's terms. There were 2 of them.

27. Anyway, I remember that [ ] had felt me earlier that day too, on top of my leotard, rubbing me between my legs for about 5 minutes, asking me how do you feel? This was in the girls' downstairs rumpus room. I don't think anyone saw him do this to me. [ ] had gone upstairs briefly, I think to the toilet. I just said quietly " I don't know".

28. The stairs were wooden and creaked as you stepped on them so [ ] would have been confident to quickly do this to me because he could hear the stairs creaking as [ ] came back.

d). In winter (August) 1984

29. In August 1984 Aunty [ ] came to Australia from America. She had moved over there to live when she was 18. She previously visited in 1979 with her daughter [ ] who is the same age as me. This was a big event in our family as we would all gather at the airport to greet her and farewell her in the same way. Then we'd go back to Baba and Dida's to celebrate with a feast including fritola (Croatian doughnuts), help unpack and welcome her back with singing and the piano accordian and guitars. It was exciting as we'd wait to see what we got as presents like sun catchers, Florida tourist souvenirs, jewellery etc. She had long fake fingernails and 2-tone hair, it was really radical to us at the time half blonde and half brown in 2 blocks, a bit like Salt n Peppa, the 80s rap group. Being a hair dresser she was always ahead of Aussie hair trends and we'd always be excited to see how she'd look the next time. She'd even offer to cut, perm or dye our hair, bringing all the solutions and tonics with her.

30. During this visit we went to Baba and Dida's to see her many times. She was staying in the bedroom next to the toilet that looks out onto the back yard.

On one of these occasions while all the adults were talking in Baba's kitchen, ⸏ ⸏touched me in the left hand side bedroom at the end of the passage, next to the sewing room. I was told by⸏ to come with him and he took me down to one of the back bedrooms, the one on the left hand side. He told me to quickly lie down on the ground alongside the bed between the window and the bed and to lift up my dress up. I said I don't want to but he said it won't take long. I knew that he was going to play with my vagina but I was way too scared to stop him.

31.   I was wearing my maroon velvet dress with hand sewn rosebuds on the collar. It was my favourite dress that Mum bought me from Calico Lace and Flowers and was very expensive. I was wearing stockings and had to lift my bottom up off the floor so he could pull down my undies and stockings. I was lying right next to the bed and the coverlet was pale, ice blue nylon with a frill going round the bottom edge. All the beds in the bedrooms had the exact same covers. I remember hiding my face under the frill in an attempt to hide in case someone walked in. I was also worried that someone could see me in the reflection of the dressing table mirror if they walked in.

32.   I remember feeling scared because there were lots of people at the house and I could hear kids running up and down the hallway and the door was opening and closing and there was knocking on the door at one stage and I heard ⸏ ⸏ say go away to some kids. I thought ⸏ must be guarding the door for ⸏ ⸏ There were also kids running past the window, I could see them through the thin gaps in the venetian blinds. I was really scared and anxious and felt sick in the stomach. I asked when can we be finished and he said in a little while. He was rubbing my clitoris and pushing down on it with pressure and asking does this feel good? I said no it doesn't and he just kept saying yes it does, it feels good doesn't it. I just didn't answer after a while because I knew he wasn't going to stop no matter what I said. I was used to him doing this to me.

33.   After about 10 minutes of that he said we will do this again next time ok. I said I don't want you to and he said you'll be with ⸏ it's ok. I was busting to go to the toilet after this and when I did a wee I felt sore and tender there. I went straight to the lounge room after this and sat on the couch feeling sad. I asked mum when we would be going home and she said you know your dad, we could be here for ages. I didn't move out of that lounge till we left.

e). March – April 1984

34.   ⸏ also assaulted me when we came to Babas to crush the grapes for the families' traditional, annual, making of wine. This was between March and April 1984. Even we kids would get to have a turn, jumping in with our bare feet. This would happen

in Babas 2nd garage and would take hours to do. This was in 1984 when I was in grade 5 because I remember giving a report to my teacher Mr _____ and my classmates about the wine making process. They all thought it was fascinating as it was a very Anglo Saxon school and I was one of only a few with an unusual "wog" surname. There were lots of adults and kids around and I'd had my turn at getting my feet into it. A few hours later when we were down near the chook shed, looking at the special Bantams, _____ came up to us and started talking to us. He said to come and play with the others so we followed him and did as we were told like normal. We walked back into Babas with him and went into the sewing room, where the cousins were telling ghost stories. We would listen intently, I loved hearing them. There were silly ones like the husbands head banging on the roof of the stranded ladies car. There were really scary ones too told by the older kids.

35. I was also scared because Baba always said that "Stari" (meaning bad man) was watching. Baba showed us kids Stari's silhouette at the beach house, which was really just a cypress tree that looked like the profile of a man. There were also sculptures my Uncle _____ had made of some heads, black torsos on the internal fence between Babas and Aunties. It was always scary to go past them, especially at night during our family celebrations. _____ and I would hold hands and run past with our eyes closed, daring ourselves. All the cousins had to constantly pluck up the courage to run past them, especially at night when we were playing chasey. Sometimes we were too scared and opted to get to Aunties or back to Baba's going the long way part round the block, past Mr _____ house on the corner of _____ and _____ Streets.

36. After all the kids got up to leave the room he whispered to me stay here a bit. I stayed seated while he closed the door and he immediately started touching me on my vagina. I had on white shorts and a yellow and white striped t-shirt. He put his fingers through the leg of my shorts and into my undies to play with my vagina. This happened for a few minutes. After we left the room, _____ acted like nothing had happened. He always did this.

f). October 1983

37. My 10th Birthday party was held at my house and, _____ and my other cousins were there. This was on or about Saturday, 15th October 1983, 3 days after my actual birthday. I have photos of my party. I was wearing my navy blue velvet dress with the white lace collar that Baba had made for me. I received lots of Strawberry Shortcake dolls and mini figurines as presents as I was collecting them. I was really into them and loved the smell of them.

38. _____ touched me when we were all playing hide and seek outside. My Dad had built a really long and high bluestone wall down the side of the property as we lived on a

corner. He also built a studio out of bluestone to paint in as he was an art teacher and an artist. I had hidden on the outside of the bluestone wall, in an attempt for [   ] to not be able to find me. I thought he wouldn't think to look there, beyond the gate. But he did, probably watched me go there instead of closing his eyes when counting like you are meant to. He found me and touched me on the vagina over my dress, grabbing me there in a firm grip and pushing onto me with his hand as I was leaning against the wall. It wasn't for very long and my dress was bunched up there. I remember the dress tightening around my collar as it was tugged as it had a tight neck anyway. He ran off to find where others were hiding and I fixed my dress nicely and went back inside the garden. The velvet was a bit crushed there where he'd been grabbing.

39.   On this occasion [   ] and [   ] had a birthday sleep over at my house. I had a big antique "princess-sized" bed, in between a double and a queen size. It had a beautiful wooden carved bed-head and bed-end. They both slept in the same bed with me. I woke up in the morning and the bed was all wet, including my nightie. I never wet the bed so I immediately knew that either [   ] or [   ] had as I knew they always wet the bed at their house, it was a constant problem for them. [   ] also sucked her thumb for ages, till she was in the older primary school years.

g). Winter 1983

40.   [   ] also assaulted me the day I was measured by my grandmother for the blue velvet dress. She had promised to make one for every grand-daughter, quite a job as there were at least 9 of us in 1983 to make a dress for. I remember it was winter because it was cold and raining outside when I was measured. She used a soft tape measure and took all my measurements. After this, I went straight to [   ] to play with her, out the gate of Babas. I used the back external stairs to get to her room but she wasn't in there, none of the girls were. Mutchka (Croatian for cat), their big black cat, was curled up asleep on the bed.

41.   [   ] was in his room though and came in to talk to me. He asked me when I got here and I explained. I said I'd better go back because he didn't know where [   ] was. He came with me and led me to their outside toilet block. He led me inside it. I was wearing blue jeans which he unzipped and then slipped his hand into my undies and played with my vagina for about 10 minutes, saying isn't this nice repeatedly. I said I'm freezing cold and he said you'll warm up soon. After this I went straight back to Babas house and [   ] went back up the stairs to his bedroom I assume. I didn't see him again that day. When I got back to Babas my Dad was talking to Baba and Dida in Croatian as usual. I said let's go, this is boring, [   ] not home. I waited in the

lounge sitting in front of the heater for a while; my clothes were lightly damp from running through the rain from house to house, including my desert boots. I remember driving home in my Dad's white panel van.

42. Aunty and Uncle's house also had internal stairs leading to the downstairs billiard/2nd lounge room and a rumpus room on the other side of the stairs, full of the girls toys, dolls, prams, games, dress ups etc. I remember ___ flying down those stairs using the stair rail to slide down. He'd jump over the board at the top using his arms.

43. The billiard room was huge and open plan and included a set up with a TV and Atari system that ___ and ___ would play space invaders and pacman etc on. The room also had a Pianola on the back wall with music scrolls lying around. The lounge furniture there that we would sit on was made of rattan. It was a 3 piece lounge with rusty brown/burnt orange coloured velour cushions. Sometimes we'd sit and watch Dad and Uncle playing billiards there. ___ would have other friends over from St.___ ollege on Saturdays to play when I was also there on Saturdays.

h). Winter 1983 continued

44. I never wanted to have a turn on the Atari in case I'd be left alone playing there with ___ I never played on the Atari, not even once. I remember he touched me under a blanket on that lounge one time when ___ and ___ were there too. He was sitting next to me and he slid his hand into my undies and was playing with my vagina. He wasn't looking at me; he was looking at the screen, pretending to watch the Atari game being played by the others. I was really embarrassed and uncomfortable but too scared to say anything.

45. There were also their friends from their street who would be over at the same time as me including ___ who was pretty with blonde hair. Aunty ___ would sometimes cut up oranges for us and we'd all eat them out the front of the house, sitting along the gutter together.

46. ___ had a friend too named ___ who loved horses and would come to pat ___ brown horse. I never liked horses and was scared of ___ especially after he kicked ___ one time when it was in the back yard when I was there visiting. We would go down the back yard to pat, feed or brush ___ The ___ chool friends, were also into horses. All the girls would look at the chooks in the chook shed, see if there were any eggs, we'd go to the park or the local milk bar to get lollies on occasion. I remember ___ eaching me how to eat some sort of sweet tasting grass in her yard.

i). MY COMMUNION October - December 1982

47. My Mum bought me a beautiful communion dress, complete with veil from Calico Lace and Flowers, a specialist children's boutique in ⬛ Street. It had a pink ribbon v design on the front. It wasn't one of those typically tasteless, tizzy looking ones, it was very expensive. ⬛ Mum, My Aunty ⬛ was my sponsor and I remember my communion present from her, my first missal with a white pearl cover. My Aunty ⬛ gave me a large statue of the Virgin Mary. For my confirmation my Aunty ⬛ gave me a small statue of Mary and baby Jesus on a round marble-type base.

48. We had a big celebration at my house in ⬛ Street, ⬛ or my communion. We had a spit roast in the back yard and all of my extended ⬛ family came, ⬛ included. It was warm weather and we had all the tables set up outside. I remember Mum and I walking home from the farm where Dad selected the live lamb for the feast. They had a big argument and I was crying because Mum did not want us to kill a lamb once she'd seen it. She was too distressed and thought we'd be collecting one that had already been killed.

49. ⬛ touched me on the vagina on this occasion, in my bedroom by lifting up my dress and putting his hand into my undies and playing with my vagina. No one else was in my room at the time. We were standing behind my bedroom door.

50. I went to communion preparation lessons at ⬛ school, ⬛ Primary School because the school I went to, ⬛ Grammar, didn't offer communion or confirmation in those days. My friend ⬛ came too as she was also at my school and wanted to do her communion as she was also Catholic. During this time I also remember going to a fete at ⬛ Primary School one Saturday after ballet with Aunty and the girls.

51. Around this time the song "⬛ started playing on the radio, by ⬛ and I talked about how cool it was to have a song with your parents names in it! This song always reminds me of the ⬛ Street days and how ⬛ made me feel because of what he did to me. I think of him, not ⬛ and ⬛ my Aunty and Uncle. There's another song by Renee Gayer called "Say that you love me one more time" that also reminds me of ⬛

j). Oct 17 1982

52. Aunty ⬛ and Uncle ⬛ id a celebration in their garage down stairs for ⬛ first communion. My mum was ⬛ godmother.

53. Their garage was directly under their lounge room. During the celebration I was crying and Mum and Dad asked me what was wrong but I wouldn't tell them. I was crying because ⬛ had touched me on the vagina on the outside of my clothing. He

did this along the side of the house, along the left side wall. Their boat was usually stored on the front left hand side if you are facing their front stairs.

k). On or about December 1982

54. The house directly next to my grandparents house at [   ] St was also owned by Uncle [   ] as was the house at the back of their property in [   ] Street South. I remember Uncle [   ] and his other brothers renovating these houses. I knew this house as "Mr _____ house."

55. On one occasion in December 1982 while [   ] was renovating this house [   ] had touched me on the vagina inside my undies at Baba's in the back right hand side bedroom. I was wearing a summer dress with ties on the shoulders. It was a light blue floral cotton material. It was a hot day and I remember all the windows of Babas house were open and the thin curtains were all blowing in the breeze.

56. I remember going to the house afterwards with [   ] as my Dad was there checking out the renovation with Uncle. [   ] came there a bit later too and I remember feeling nervous about him in my stomach. He was standing at the back of the house near a large piece of corrugated iron.

l). Christmas Day 1980

57. On 25 December 1980 we went to Baba and Dida's for Christmas like we always did each year. Baba's niece [   ] and family were visiting from Bundaberg, Queensland. [   ] daughter [   ] and son [   ] were there and I remember [   ] telling ghost stories to my cousins and I in the sewing room. She was a lot older than me, older than [   ] I think. [   ] was there too, he died about a month later. We were all squashed into that room but that's where and how we always assembled for ghost stories. We didn't do this anywhere else. That's my first memory of [   ] touching me between my legs on my vagina over my undies, putting his hand up my dress to do this. He didn't say anything to me, he just did it while [   ] was telling a ghost story. I didn't say anything either. I remember it was dark outside and the room was quite dark too as we always kept the light off when telling these ghost stories. There was only a little street light coming through.

58. Later, the same evening, we played games of chasey and hide and seek around the backyard of Babas and Aunties. When [   ] caught me or found me he used this as an opportunity to touch me again under my dress. I remember hiding in all the obvious places like behind a bush, down the side of the house, on the front stairs, behind the outdoor toilet. It never took him long to find me and I always remember him being "it". I think he just made himself " it" all the time. [   ] no one questioned him.

HISTORY OF MUM AND AUNTY'S FRIENDSHIP

59.   ___ was Mum and Dad's page boy when they were married in August 26th 1972 at
         St.___ Church,'_____ He was 3 years and 6 months old; ___ was their 3
         year old flower-girl.

60.   Mum was(___)god-mother; Aunty(___ was my sponsor at my Communion
         and Confirmation. Aunty was my sponsor for the Christening of my own children
         too.

61.   Aunty' ___ and my Mum each made a gingerbread house at Auntie's house in
         December 1980. They were good friends as well as in-laws. Mum really liked her and
         had a closer connection with her than with the Croatian, more traditional in-laws.
         Auntie's background(___)was German, like my Mums. Also, Aunty had been a
         teacher before being a stay at home Mum and Mum was a teacher so they had a few
         things in common. They shared recipes and I was close to her daughters.

62.   Being Australian she wasn't as stuck in gender roles as the others, or so Mum initially
         thought. Aunty never had much autonomy when it came to spending money. Uncle
         ___ ever believed in the girls doing ballet, openly said it's a waste of time and
         money so much so that one year my parents offered to pay for ___ ballet fees.
         Mum gave(___)all my clothes for(___ ● ___)and(___ o wear up as I always
         had beautiful expensive clothes that I'd outgrow, barely worn.

63.   Aunty used to help make the ballet costumes for our ballet recitals but my Mum
         didn't as she didn't have a sewing machine nor did she want one. My Dad helped
         make many sets for the ballet concerts though. One time he made(___ and I
         beautiful fairy wings with tinsel edges, mine was sprayed hot pink, and(___
         was white. We were about 5.

64.   Aunty constantly had washing spilling out of her laundry in a humungous ever
         growing pile on the floor. She was always pregnant, feeding a baby, attending to a
         toddler and all at the same time, having 6 children at the time,(___)was her 7th, a
         surprise born 21 years after(___)I know this because it was funny that when(___
         first son(___ was born in May 1992 or 1993, he had a 5 month old Aunty ___)|

65.   Baba always criticised Aunty for having a messy house and would go over first thing
         in the morning complaining about it. Mum always felt sorry for(___ about this,
         living in such close proximity to Baba, Mum didn't know how Aunty coped! Baba
         was a really traditional housewife into cleaning so much so that she would clean out
         the fish pond with Domestos causing the fish to die with great regularity. Baba told
         my Mum "Better luck next time to have a boy" when I was born. Baba openly said

that to have a girl was a misfortune. She told off my Dad for changing my nappies and doing the dishes as he considered that was my Mums job.

THE YEARS AFTER THE ABUSE BEFORE MY DISCLOSURE

1985 – June 2013

66.   ▇ and I would still be in touch whenever we could and it's fair to say we have always been each other's closest cousin. At family celebrations I would continue to hang out with ▇ and ▇

67.   I went to ▇ College ▇ University residential college) in 1992 and 1993, along with ▇ and ▇ I knew ▇ was there already but I still applied to get in there because I thought I'd have a better chance getting into on campus accommodation at ▇ because he was there. It wasn't because I was a Catholic. I only used this fact to help my application because it's fiercely competitive to get into a residential college. I had no other family ties to the other colleges. I really wanted to go to ▇ College with my Grammar friends. Anyway, ▇ was there too in 1992 with me, studying at ▇ doing dance.

68.   Also, ▇ never abused me; I always suspected that ▇ was the mastermind behind ▇ involvement. ▇ was academically brilliant, ▇ was street smart like the proverbial shithouse rat.

69.   In 1991 ▇ married my parents' best friend's eldest daughter ▇ They had their first child ▇ in May 1992 or 1993, ▇ in about December 20 1995 and ▇ n October 1999. During family celebrations ▇ would always gravitate towards the children, watching Disney movies in the rumpus room rather than socialising with adults. It was weird, my parents have always thought it strange as have ▇ parents' ▇ and ▇

70.   ▇ left ▇ and the kids in around 2001. It was sometime after his brother in law ▇ died in a plane crash in ▇ 2000.

71.   I remember at ▇ funeral ▇ sister) ▇ wasn't happy about ▇ possibly bringing ▇ his new partner, to the funeral. I went with ▇ and the kids to the funeral to support her as I was her friend more than a relative.

72.   ▇ parents and ▇ sed the kids together in ▇ the absence of ▇ who moved to ▇ He never paid child support and being our best friends we heard everything from ▇ and ▇ they were really concerned about ▇ including wetting herself at school because she was so distressed about her parents separation and ▇ response to the breakup. ▇ barely saw his children and when He did he'd often take them to ▇ and ▇ He didn't play an active

hands-on role.' ___ always complained to me about how ___ never paid any child support or school fees and that she was left to carry the load alone, with her parents help. Even ___ and ___ have been sympathetic towards her.

73.　___ and ___ have never been close and all the family are aware of this rift. ___ was the quiet, introverted brother, who barely ever said a word to anyone. ___ was the confident one with charisma and personality. ___ was super smart, dux of St. ___ n yr 12. ___ was far from it.

74.　___ ended up in a de facto relationship with ___ sister ___ so two brothers in one family married 2 sisters in another. They live in ___ island and have 3 kids together. They moved there in 2005 I think, when their eldest child ___ was around 4 or 5. I used to see them when they lived in ___

75.　___ married ___ someone without children who doesn't want any either. Hardly the family man with children as described by his defence lawyer ___ Yes, he is married and yes he does have children but he hasn't raised them. He's never been a family man. ___ cares about ___

76.　I have followed ___ dancing career whenever I could and was always keen to hear her latest dance world news. She later moved to ___ and has her own dance school now. She married ___ who is lovely and have one child together ___ who is about 9 or 10. When she came back to ___ as a guest performer at ___ Dance School Recital I went to watch her. Aunty ___ always calls me when ___ is due to visit so I'd never miss her. Everyone in the family would easily say how close we always were. I have told her many times how proud I am of her and her achievements because I am.

77.　At Uncle ___ funeral in May 2013 ___ youngest sister, disclosed to me that she'd just left an abusive relationship. I suppose she confided in me because I have taken an interest in her over the years and Aunty had asked me to help her with some uni course and career guidance a few years ago. I spoke to ___ about her in the pretext call.

DEVELOPMENTS SINCE MY FIRST STATEMENT MADE IN JUNE 2013:

Aunty ___

78.　In **September 2013** Aunty told ___ that she thinks the other boys name was ___ and that she told ___ at the time that he's not to hang out with him anymore as she thought he was a bad influence on him. I know this because ___ told me herself. She also told me that her parents were very supportive of her.

79. In August 2013 Aunty told me that she sent the boys, ___ and (___ off to the work sites with Uncle, to keep them out of mischief. I believe her when she says she had no idea this was going on. Aunty has always been lovely to me. Even in the face of this she came to my house in September 2013 to thank me for disclosing so that her "family can finally begin to heal". She said it's taken me to be 70 years old to know about my own children and thanked me repeatedly. She said she always knew something was wrong, like an elephant in the room, no one could see or hear it, but still knew it was there. She asked me where I found the courage to come to her house and tell her. She said if I hadn't said anything she'd probably never know as her children had never said anything. She said "1000 sorrys a day wouldn't make up for what he's done." Where has **that** Aunty! ___ gone now?

Uncle',

80. In August 2013 Uncle said that if he'd known at the time he would have killed them ___ and ___ and said "whether it's Rolf Harris or my son, they have to face the consequences". Where has **that** Uncle ___ gone now?

_____ and|_____

81. My conversations with| ___ |and| _____ have confirmed why they and(___ |have moved so far away from family. When they do come to gatherings they spend as little time as possible there and they admitted to me that this is quite deliberate to protect themselves from| ___ . I'm sure; ___ has never babysat their kids either.

82. I feel utterly betrayed by them for the statements they've made to the police. The police told me their statements don't support my statement. This is truly unbelievable, especially after| ___ |voluntarily disclosed to me all of the abuse she suffered from| (___ herself also confided in me about the abuse and told me those group abuse sessions happened often, at least 20 times. I told her I only remember that happening once but since then I wonder if I've blocked some out. All the memories came flooding back when I talked to both of them. It was a cathartic experience for all of us.

83. I have text messages documenting all of these communications between myself and ' ___ |and| ___ , My husband| ___ also heard one conversation with(___ |as it was on speakerphone, at night.

84. When I disclosed this to the family, ___ and I were hoping' ___ |would support us in coming forward. | ___ |was seriously considering making her own pretext call too. Unfortunately when she returned from. ___ |in September 2013, ' ___ |said she'd dealt with it ages ago and didn't want to go back into the past. She wanted to mediate with(\ |and I said for me that's not realistic. In my

experience, work etc, mediation between a predator and his victims is not advisable due to the unequal power relationship and I told her so. [   ] agreed that it's not appropriate and we both talked about there being no mediator for such a situation.

85. [   ] didn't get the validation from her sister and hit flight mode again. All understandable but leaving me alone to fight is one thing, lying in a statement to save your brother is another. I hope they are very happy and can live with what they've done. **They need to remember they are not the only victims.** As [   ] told her brother 3 years ago, go to all your victims and apologise. That's why when her Mum and Dad rang [   ] and told her what I'd disclosed to the family, she rang me soon after and said she's sorry for not having called me 2 years ago, when she herself had confronted [   ] about all the abuse. Now she does an unbelievable backflip because she's probably been paid hush money by the family/the Catholic Church. That theory would go a long way in explaining the re-victimising behaviour of the OPP!!!

86. [   ] and I have often laughed about "fists or blades" our entire adult lives but never spoken about the other nightmare of that day for me about [   ] and being abused by him for years. I wish we had before now. Endless cups of tea, late night catch ups including with [   ] covering all the ups and downs of our lives, except for this. Crazy to think we could have supported each other sooner! But for the families' expected response I imagine we would have.

87. [   ] and [   ] made their statements after they were compelled to by police after a request for compulsory examination. They resisted for a long time, despite police attempts and attempts from me. If [   ] didn't abuse us, why didn't they say so and make their statements voluntarily right from the start? What were all our discussions and texts about? What was stopping them? If they are telling the truth now, couldn't they have told the truth then?

88. [   ] knew exactly what was in my statement because I told her the exact contents over the phone. They both had the benefit of knowing what was in mine before they made theirs. So did [   ] and the entire family. I wrote a letter to all family members on White Ribbon Day last year, November 2013, in reply to all the lies they were spreading about me. In this letter I told them about the abuse so that everyone would be clear. It was my reply and good bye to the family.

89. After seeing the family response to me, [   ], and [   ] have had the benefit of being able to say whatever suits them. I imagine their parents have put enormous pressure on them not to say anything or told them to lie about it, threatening to take them out of the will? I know how the family works and what's important to them! Who knows what the girls motives are?

90. In **March 2013** I was contacted by‗_____ ₫about a photo opportunity. Her friend needed someone with freckles so⌐_____₁thought of me. I was happy to be glammed up (with makeup by⌐_____ for a change and the photos were beautiful. After this in May and June of 2013 I also started getting beauty treatments by⌐_____ called ‗_____‗ which is eyebrow shaping. She would come to see clients in‗_____₁I think monthly, using her parent's garage in₍_____₎Drive, _____₋as a workspace set up as a beauty studio of sorts. I remember chatting away to her and wondering how and if I should broach the subject of₍_____ and the abuse. I chickened out. I couldn't seem to find the courage to raise the topic. It was a perfect opportunity as we were alone between her other clients.

91. I called both‗_____₁and⌐_____₂on₎_____ 2014, straight after court after the OPP dropped all charges and₍_____₎walked free without any consequence. They have not replied to my message. _____₁and₍_____/ ₎can pretend all they like but they are stuck with what he did to us for life. Maybe₍_____₎will feel differently after her first child is born? Time will tell. It will all come out, the truth will keep unravelling the lies whether they like it or not. They are very selfish. They have joined in celebration with the other hypocrites but they can't see they are really celebrating their own self-destruction. Where has the₍_____₎gone who was worried‗_____ had abused her younger sister‗_____₎too and told me she rang⌐_____ to see if he had?

Aunty‗_____

92. My Auntie ₍_____₎was very cross with me for telling the family what‗_____ did to me. When I went to see her about her unexpected response, as we were close, she said to me "You think you're the only one?" She also said "They're not coming forward so you're on your own."

93. My Aunty₍_____ ₎even applied for an intervention order against me in an attempt to silence me. It was withdrawn because it was baseless.

94. On that same day, Tuesday night the‗_____ ~2013 my Melbourne cousins including her daughter‗_____ went out for dinner, I imagine to celebrate Auntie's application, and posted this event on Facebook. This is the bullying that families indulge in when victims dare to speak up! Given the comments of my Aunt and the long term behaviour of‗_____ strongly believe that she, too, is a victim of₍_____

95. I suspect that some of my other cousins may have been victim to₍_____ too. The fact is that intra familial sex abuse is all about opportunity and accessibility. When I think

about it, [   ] had plenty of both. I hate to think who else is silently suffering, relieved that it's me and not them who have come forward.

[   ] disclosure

96. I told her about the abuse in **September 2013** when she visited me at my house with her kids. My parents and husband [   ] were there at the time too. We all had dinner together and shared these experiences after the kids went off and played. She admitted to me that she had a crush on [   ]; that they used to take their clothes off and look at each other's bodies. She also asked me if [   ] had ever used a knitting machine on me, to play with my vagina. I said no, I don't even know what one is. We asked my mum and dad together if she knew what it was and if aunty had one. They confirmed Aunty did have one.

97. Anyway, she said she felt guilty that he abused us girls as she always saw herself as a bit of a mother hen to [   ] and [   ] and said if her parents hadn't broken up forcing her to go to [   ] to live with her mother, then he may not have abused us but played with her instead. My husband and I have talked to her husband [   ] about it and asked him to get her to call me if she's interested in making a statement but I haven't heard from her so I doubt it.

[   ] texts

98. These messages sent to me in **August 2013** are relevant because it shows that [   ] has admitted to what he and [   ] did to us to her, his de facto.

 She says the following to me in text messages:

On 22/8/2013 at 7.59 pm

"....As the wife of one of them I think I deserve an explanation as to why something they did when they were prepubescent is being discussed as if they had an adult concept at the time. From [   ]

On 24/8/2013 at 9.28 am

"....they were children and experimental and curiosity play is not insest.....you have shown us no respect for the adults that are today...."

99. [   ] was in the same year at St [   ], as [   ], a victim of clergy abuse at St [   ] I always wonder whether [   ] himself was abused due to the nature of some of the abuse being so adult, organised with several pieces of equipment and with co-offenders and multiple victims at the one time.

100. I have come to know [___] through being on the Board at [___] and bumping into his wife [___], who volunteers there. I previously knew [___] because her parents are Croatian and friends of the family, including my Aunty [___]. I had a good chat with [___] at [___] funeral and discovered that our children go to [___] College together.

101. She said her husband also lost his family when he disclosed about his abuse. She was disappointed to hear it had happened to me too and could not believe Aunty [___] attitude and bullying behaviour.

DATED ------   2014

Document D — Transcript of the Pre-text Call

PRETEXT TELEPHONE CONVERSATION -

PREAMBLE:

My name is ⎯⎯⎯⎯⎯

I am 39 years old and my date of birth is the ⎯⎯⎯⎯⎯⎯ 1973

Today is Friday the 14th of June, 2013.

I am currently at the ⎯⎯⎯ Police Station and I am the person who has activated this tape recording device.

I activated this device freely and without any inducement or coercion from any other person.

The telephone number that I am about to dial is ⎯⎯⎯⎯⎯

I expect to speak to ⎯⎯⎯⎯⎯

(Dial the telephone number conduct the telephone conversation at conclusion of telephone call)

AFTER PHONE CALL:

The person that I spoke to was ⎯⎯⎯⎯⎯⎯⎯⎯⎯⎯⎯⎯⎯
the time is now.......... am/pm and I will conclude this recording

signed ⎯⎯⎯⎯⎯⎯⎯⎯⎯⎯

VICTORIA POLICE

Transcript of PRE-TEXT
Telephone Conversation conducted on 14/06/2013

_____ My name is _____ I am 39 years old and my date of birth is the _____
_____ 1973. Today is Friday the 14th of June, 2013. I am currently at the ⌐
Police Station and I am the person who has activated this tape recording device. I
activated this device freely and without any inducement or cohesion from any other
person. The telephone number I am about to dial is ⌐   ⌐ I expect to speak to
⌐_____⌐

Dialing....Dialing....

⌐   - Hello. It's ⌐____ ¦speaking.

⌐____¦ Hello ⌐   ¦ this is ⌐   ¦ How are you? Cousin ⌐   ¦ ⁻

⌐⁻⌐

⌐____¦ - Hi.

⌐____¦ - Good thanks.

'   - Yeah, good good. I know this is out of nowhere umm but I just wanted to just
chat with you. Have you got a few minutes?

⌐____¦ - Ahh, yep.

⌐____¦ - Oh great. Thankyou. No it's just I saw at Uncle ⌐____¦ funeral the other day
is saw ⌐____¦ and umm she was telling me that umm that she's been seeing a
counsellor about umm a relationship she's left which was abusive. Do you know
anything about that?

⌐____¦ - Ahh yes. I know a bit of. Yep.

⌐____¦ - Okay, yeah. No, it's just umm it's just got me thinking ⌐   ¦ like just
reflecting on my own life and umm I've just sort of, I was wondering if you could
help me with something that you probably can help me with if you could. Umm I just
been sort of thinking about things that happened in our past. Umm I have a really
memory ⌐   ¦ if you umm you know sexually interfering with me as a kid, and I'm
just wondering if I can get some help from you. Umm, at least..

⌐____¦ Yes, yes. Absolutely.

⌐____¦ Oh, thankyou.

|___| - Yep, alright. I'm not in a position where I can have a chat right now.

|___| - Right.

|___| - But ahh yeah look, I think I think there are certain things that happen when people are young.

|___| - Yes.

|___| - And, you know, and I certainly don't want you to think that that's reflective of who I am or what I am and, umm definantly umm I'm more than happy, for me I look back at those times

|___| - Yes

|___| - And it was silly kids.

|___| - Right

|___| - And umm, and, and if you feel anything then absolutely. More than happy to support you and all that sort of shit. I mean umm umm umm obviously from my perspective I want to make sure you know that you're well and safe and yeah.

|___| - Yeah. Well I've just sort of found the strength to call you I suppose because umm it's really affected me growing up and just me life, particularily having my own children, and umm

|___| - Yep

|___| - I'm really pleased you, that you don't expect me to block it out anymore because it's really difficult. Everytime I've seen you, |___| at for 30 years I've, when I see you I think of it and I always sort of thought to myself, I'm wondering if you're thinking what I'm thinking. Does that make sense to you? Like it's been really difficult to know how to approach you, or like when we just say hello and I think wow we're going through all of these years after year, but I just feel like I've always wanted to talk to you about it but there hasn't been the right time. And umm it's just really painful and just memories flood back I suppose of different things, and even seeing |___| and |___| and |___| umm. When I see them I think how have they processed it what's happened, where do you put all that, and I suppose I'm just looking for answers or a way to survive it. Umm cos I probably thought I was better at keeping it a secret than what I am because it's all come back to haunt me, well it always has been there but umm, I don't know I think you know, I don't know if you're anything like me you sort of look at your life and think ohh but I'm okay, I've had a job or I've had children or I've had happiness but it's still always there. And umm, I don't know. I don't know. But I'm really really glad

|___| I'm really, I'm really happy that you had the courage to call.

|___| - Thankyou.

. , That doesn't make it easy. Don't get me wrong. I'm not saying, and and yeah and there's certain things that I absolutely that's one of the things I've always regretted in my life.

– Yes.

– Always.

– Yes.

– So, and I want you to know that. So it's not something that you can sort of say you can put things behind you. No. It's not.

– No.

And I agree. So. Look I'm not, I can't, I really like to talk to you about it a bit more.

– Yes.

But, I'm not, I'm in a car travelling with people right now so I can't really chat.

– Ahh sure. I understand.

– But I've got your number on my phone here and what I might do is I'll give you a call a little bit later today.

– Okay.

Would that be okay?

– Yeah that would be fine.

I'm not sure what your movements are or

– No No, I'm still just doing the stay at home mum thing. Yeah I'm alright.

Yep.

Yeah. Oh ___ really appreciate it. It will really help me.

Yeah, now look I honestly want you to know that I really really care about you, I really care about your well being.

– Yeah

– And if I can help I will.

– Ah, Thank you. Alright. Thanks so much. Thank you.

▬ And and I'm I'm sorry.

[   ]- Oh thank you. That means a lot to me. I just thought it's 30 years too late. I though wow. That means everything to me that you're sorry. Because

[   ] Absolutely. Absolutely

[   ]- Alright, Alright.

[   ] Alright. I'll talk to you later today okay.

[   ]- Okay. Thanks ▬

[   ] Alright. Speak soon.

[   ]- Okay.

[   ] Take care. Bye.

[   ]- Thank you. Bye. The person I spoke to was ▬▬ The time is now, oh I don't even, 11.14 am and I will conclude this recording now.

Document E — Diagram – Flow Chart of the Criminal IN-Justice System

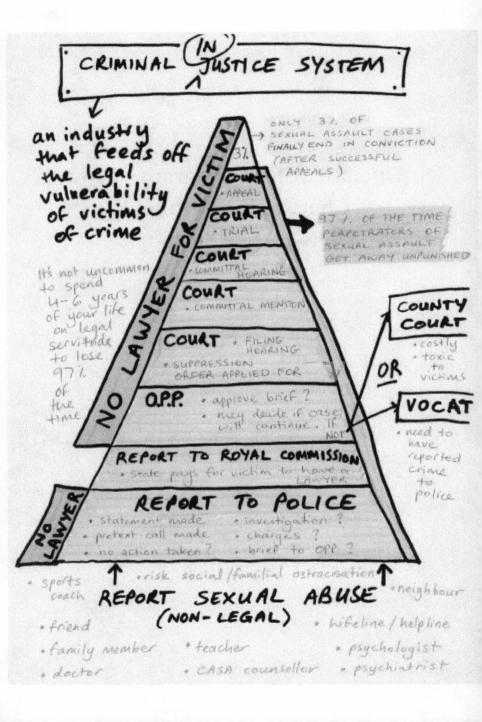

Document F — Email from Cleo to Barnaby Bustard-Braggart at Court Jester Lawyers

From:
Sent: .2018
To:
Subject: FW: Your Incompetent Defamation Claim

Trying to successfully send this to you again – see email below. I am concerned that it will be rejected by you/your computer server once again.

Please confirm once you have received it.

From:
Sent: ,2018
To:
Subject: Your Incompetent Defamation Claim

Dear

Your incompetent Defamation claim

I refer to your letter of   2017 to which I say you have absolutely no cause of action. I have respected your wish for an 'Urgent' response to your correspondence dated   , not taking 28 days as is my entitlement, to not further your distress and to quickly distance myself from your imputation of defamatory e-mail indiscretions.

Before we go any further and lose sight of the simplicity of the matter it is appropriate to remind you of the *Defamation Act 2005* and particularly S 27. Put simply, there is no case to answer. Clearly S 27 provides a 'defense of absolute privilege' for any published material in the course of proceedings in an Australian court or tribunal. Your learned counsel should have made this apparent to you and saved you money and time.

Furthermore, in the event that you persist in making any such application to the Court, I put you on notice that it will be strenuously defended and costs sought against you once again and I will not be letting you off the hook this time.

Your character

Frankly, I consider it surprising that you would seek to engage in a process that would only direct the spotlight on your own character in view of your own distinctly dubious conduct as follows:

1. Your friendship and involvement with   . It is well documented that you   I note with interest that the Court stopped just short of describing you as

2. Your "jail mug shot" posted on the internet, found when I did a simple search of your name on google (clearly you in orange prison uniform)

3. Your totally improper conduct in all aspects where my matters of   are concerned, repeatedly lying to and misleading the court about not receiving correspondence and documents that

were received by every other designated recipient, failing to attend Court and conducting yourself in an embarrassing, petulant and peevish manner to the extent that 3 Judges in the one matter, this matter, made cost orders <u>against you personally</u> because your conduct was so contemptuous. This is most unusual and illustrates how you conduct yourself unethically and in breach of all civil procedure rules and obligations.

4. Your further improper conduct to ride on the coat-tails of the settlement between[   ]. You are not a party to the proceeding, the costs orders against you personally had NOTHING to do with[   ] allegedly (by your own admissions under oath), yet you gutlessly and improperly evaded your responsibility.

5. Your overt sexual harassment of me during mediation in front of 4 witnesses [   ] the mediator, my barrister) sickened me to my stomach and caused my barrister and I to leave the room. Your grandiose gesture to provide us with your ridiculous chart of child sexualised behaviours, followed by your sleazy invitation to "play kiss chasey or spin the bottle" was also highly offensive and inappropriate. You are an embarrassment to yourself and to the profession and caused me to feel intimidated and distressed on an already highly stressful day. What is it about sexual abuse that you and[   ]don't seem to understand?

It is also a fact that your conduct caused[   ][Honour Judge'   ] to threaten to report you to the Legal Services Board and to hold you in contempt, as a result of you, amongst other things, becoming involved in a disgraceful shouting match with [   ]which included you swearing at[   ]shouting "Jesus" in the Court room and being reprimanded for doing so. Under no circumstances can this ever be considered to be conduct becoming of a legal practitioner who should be entitled to hold a practising certificate.

I remind you that[   ][Honour Judge'   ] exclaimed, in an exacerbated tone, the following comments about you and your character:

At transcript p.[   ]line[   ]

,   *HONOUR: I'm far from impressed by the conduct of your instructing solicitor, even the outbursts today, jumping to your side of the Bar table, interfering with the orderly presentation of your submissions. I was trying to ask you questions, he's barking at you. There's an old saying, don't buy a dog and bark yourself. And I thought that it made for a lengthy hearing.*

Didn't need to be such a lengthy hearing. Then there's the affidavit that, some circumstances of which are totally inexplicable. The missing details as to why documents that were apparently served went missing, there's the high-handed manner of dealing with the court by thinking, you just need to make a phone call to somebody called[   ]in registry and then you get your wish as to what happens in court. That is not the way litigation is conducted.

Then there's the most uncivilised manner in which the exchanges between your instructor, speaking over the top of you and then over the top of[   ]. I can understand why things when awry. But in any event it's not the plaintiff's fault that[   ]determined to act on a self-executing order.   [Honour was entitled to take account of the full facts, which [   ]*did as[   ]represented in the order that[   ]made.[   ]was fully aware of the time delay but it was no doubt against a backdrop of non-compliance.*

There is no reason why the plaintiff should be out of pocket in the circumstances. She was entitled to have judgment entered in her favour as the order was a self-executing order. The correspondence was late in the day, no doubt[   ]had already been briefed in any event ready to appear today. So I don't know that such a late service would've altered the obligation to pay counsel's fees.   [only seeking half a day and quite frankly I do not think that it is out of the ballpark.

It's an indulgence that the defendant is seeking from the plaintiff and from the court. And in these circumstances the defendant should pay the actual costs that the plaintiff incurred as a result of the defendant's default. I propose to order that the defendant pay the plaintiffs costs --
MR[   ][   ]Your Honour Mr - - -
,   HONOUR: If you wish to say something,[   ][   ]can call you to give evidence.
MR[   ][   ][ ][   ]is briefed on behalf of the defendant.
[   ][HONOUR: [   ]

2

⌐: He's not briefed on behalf of .

You will certainly be aware that before you can allege that your character has been damaged, it must first be established that you are of a suitably unblemished character and therefore have something to lose. You must establish that the behaviour complained of alone has caused detriment and loss and nothing that you have previously done yourself beforehand has caused people to question your character and to refuse to deal with you. To labour the point, your losses must be attributable to nothing other than the public publication of the criticisms made about you. Defamation laws do not serve to salve hurt feelings or a temporary embarrassment. Clearly if you are in a position to suffer any such embarrassment, loss or hurt it can be clearly established that you brought it upon yourself. Perhaps the most wise of counsel that could be offered to you would be "None is offended but by himself." You have no cause for grievance for your reputation, such as it is, is of your own making.

I point out that once ▮ ▮Judge▮ ▮took over management of the matter, all correspondence was ordered and directed to be sent to ▮associate, the Court and all other parties. It is also well accepted that any correspondence to barristers (and in this case the mediator) involved in matters goes via their clerks who do not involve themselves with the content. To suggest that a letter to the associate of the judge involved in the not-concluded matter, the mediator involved and the clerk of that mediator in a matter where your conduct and attitude was already "legendary" for its deplorable level of contempt could do you damage is laughable. Judge ▮ said in open court, on an occasion you chose not to be there, "*this matter has become legendary dragged kicking and screaming by the defendant's solicitor*", or words to that effect.

One must ask, what has angered you to write such a ridiculous letter of demand now that the matter is over? You're not finished with me yet? I suspect that your male ego has been irreparably wounded to lose the case to me, an unrepresented female at that stage, thanks to you and the money I wasted on legal process and game playing by you. I would not be surprised if your legal bills are unpaid by ▮ and/or that you have boasted to him that you'll get the money back or that you have been reported by numerous members of the judiciary. Judge▮ ▮Judge▮ and Judicial Registrar ▮ made their opinions of you and your conduct well known in open court. Not one of them espoused an opinion of you that was positive! Perhaps you should reflect on why as then you would see the person you can be upset with is yourself. I read with amusement your correspondence to Judge ▮ ▮, complaining about inter-partes correspondence being provided to the court. You caused ▮ Honour to order this through your own outrageous behaviour, lies and subterfuge.

If you have lost any business, it is more than likely due to your own ridiculous conduct. It is fair to say that your reputation precedes you and you have brought any loss of reputation/clients on yourself long before this matter commenced.

Rest assured, I will NEVER apologise to you as there is nothing for me to apologise for. If anyone is to make an apology it is you to me for your utterly deplorable misconduct over the past 4.5 years, however I consider that it would be meaningless like ▮ ▮apology is in any event. His "sorry" in the pretext call is the real apology and the only one worth considering.

I now consider the matters to be over and do not wish to correspond with the likes of you ever again. You are a clearly disgrace to the profession and that you have the misfortune of being ▮ ▮long-time friend is justice in of itself.

Do not waste my time any further or I will produce this letter on the question of costs and seek to have the final Orders set aside and pursue the numerous costs orders made against you personally. The ▮ ▮ ▮are not enforceable where you are concerned as you ▮ ▮you were not a party to the proceeding. The ▮ ▮your attempt at riding in on the coat-tails and continuing litigation now is unconscionable, reprehensible and unlawful. Do you have no bottom line?

Finally, I now warn you to leave me alone. You and ⌐‾‾‾‾‾‾‾‾₁ have surely caused enough damage, and can now be satisfied with the result and have a laugh at the pub together about your success as you grow into older and sadder men. Whether ⌐ instructed you to conduct yourself as you did, or you did it of your own volition, remains a mystery to the court and I. The important point for you to note is that I don't care to know who is responsible anymore, and that's reflected

Furthermore, our office will refuse to act in matters for clients against parties represented by you and your office and I suggest you return the professional courtesy so that we do not cross paths ever again.

Yours faithfully,

⌐ ‾‾‾‾‾‾

Document G — Newspaper article about Cleopatra: 'Lawyer Let Down By Legal System'

Angry ⸋⸋⸋⸋⸋⸋⸋⸋⸋ was left feeling betrayed by the legal system after she came forward against her abuser. PICTURE: KATE HEALY

⸋⸋⸋⸋⸋⸋⸋⸋ was sexually abused over four years as a child. But when she finally came forward and had her assailant charged in 2013, she was left angry and betrayed by a legal system that victimised her all over again.

And the ironic twist is Ms ⸋⸋⸋⸋ is a lawyer.

"As a victim of childhood sexual abuse, I can't get the system to work for me and I'm a lawyer," Ms ⸋⸋⸋⸋ said.

"The (current) system re-victimises people. We shouldn't be asking women and children to have faith in the system and come forward unless we can support them in more meaningful ways.

"The system needs to change to serve the victims' needs. Trying to fit sexual abuse into the legal system is like Cinderella's ugly step sister trying to fit her foot into Cinderella's shoe. It doesn't fit no matter how hard you try."

When Ms ⸋⸋⸋⸋ turned 40, she realised she needed to finally tell the secret she had keept since she was just eight years old.

Over four years, she was repeatedly attacked by a male known to her.

She initially told her family before going to the police, who convinced her to ring her assailant and try to get a taped confession, known as a pretext call.

During the call, he admitted to the abuse, said he was sorry and that he had regretted it all his life. In 2013, he was charged with four counts of rape.

Two days before the committal hearing – and 12 months after she made her initial statement to police – the Office of Public Prosecutions said Ms____ statement needed more detail of the offences and the charges should have been sexual assault of a minor under 10 years, not rape.

The day of the hearing, the OPP informed Ms'___ ney were withdrawing the charges and replacing them with one count of unlawful assault so the matter could be resolved by way of diversion, which is what the OPP agreed to with the defence lawyer.

She was told her assailant had agreed to this as long as no conviction was recorded.

Ms____ refused to have the charges dropped, but was told it was not her choice.

"The problem is it's their case, the police case, you are merely their witness. You have zero control over the case," she said.

However, when the hearing started, Ms____ stood up and asked the magistrate if she could personally address the court, which she did in the witness box.

After hearing her evidence, the magistrate agreed diversion was inappropriate and the matter should be resolved by way of conviction, with the OPP to come back with the correct charges.

The defendant then chose to go to a committal hearing on those charges rather than accept the magistrate's offer of a good behaviour bond with conviction.

Two weeks later at a special hearing, the OPP again asked that the remaining charge of unlawful assault be withdrawn, but did not replace it with new, correct charges, which was the whole reason for that special hearing.

This time, the same magistrate accepted the request.

The remaining charge was then dropped. Despite a taped confession, Ms ____ assailant walked free.

"I said it was an insult to me and to every woman for this matter to be recommended for diversion. "How can four counts of rape be reduced to one count of unlawful assault?" she said.

"It's a magistrate's role to decide if there's enough evidence for it to proceed to trial after the committal has actually run and they've heard the evidence, not for the OPP to cut me off at the courtroom door.

"Four years of offending reduced to one act? This can't be right. What message does this send to the community about men's violence towards women; my right to have my matter heard; the seriousness of the matter; the fact that I have never been told until now about any doubts or weaknesses in my case?"

"Now I have something I will regret for the rest of my life ... but for me, it's coming forward.

"It's impossible to navigate the system, yet I am a practising lawyer. What chance do women, including my clients, have if I can't understand or use it?"

Since her case, Ms ____ has campaigned passionately for changes to the legal system, speaking at White Ribbon Day events and appearing before the Royal Commission into Family Violence.

Among the recommendations she made to the commission were that victims in a criminal matter should be independently legally represented, victims should have a right to private prosecution, and the defendant's right to silence should be repealed if they have admitted the offending.

She also said a defendant's right to make a 'no comment' interview should be repealed if they have confessed; victims should always be a party to the proceedings; and the OPP should not have the power to prevent a committal hearing running when the defendant has made admissions.

She added victims should not be used as "investigators" by the police; that pretext calls where an admission is taped should be enough to proceed with the case; statements to police should be scrutinised by the OPP far earlier to ensure correct charges are laid; and victims should get copies of all court documents, as well as monthly case updates.

Ms'___ also had some advice for sexual assault victims: "Do not go to the police while you are in crisis. Write a chronology and take that instead. Write out dates, times, places, ages, witnesses, evidence and in date order.

"I was overwhelmed by the process. Now, I know my statement suffered for it. I had no time for clear thought, chronology and details of all the offending."

Ms ___ has also recently told her children about what happened to her.

"I'm a confident woman in my 40s – my kids can't believe it had happened to me. But I told them it happened when I was a vulnerable child. No child is immune.

"We can't live in denial. We must accept where sex abuse happens and when it happens and not sweep it under the carpet with all the other inconvenient truths.

"Stranger danger should not be the message. Sexual abuse and other forms of violence are going on everywhere at an alarming rate.

"Good people who know better must do better. Education won't stop abuse, especially when they get away with it so lightly in the court system."

Ms ___ has only now been allowed to speak about her case after having successfully fought to revoke a suppression order that was made "until further order".

It was made on the defendant's application during the criminal proceeding and silenced her, yet she was never served with a copy as she was not a party to the proceeding.

"Victims should not have to fight and pay to get their right to freedom of speech returned to them. We do not need to face another layer of silencing after we fight so hard to break the silence."

___ j@fairfaxmedia.com.au

REFERENCES

GENERAL

- Abbott, T.(1998) Interview by a man named Stavros -a round table discussion including Tony Abbott, and Michael Costa, then a minister from New South Wales, taken from Prime Minister of Australia Julia Gillard's, "Misogyny Speech", delivered in Parliament on 9 October 2012. Canberra.
https://www.youtube.com/watch?v=SOPsxpMzYw4

- Albee, E.(1962) "Who's Afraid of Virginia Woolf?"Play, first staged in 1962, Billy Rose Theatre, NY.

- American Medical Association(1995) Guides to the Evaluation of Permanent Impairment, 4thedition, Chicago: American Medical Association.

- Axiom(1970) "A Little Ray of Sunshine" Album: Axiom Archive 1968-1971, Released 2004.

- Baez J.(1968)"Song In The Blood" A Poem By Jacques Prevert, Translated by Lawrence Ferlinghetti. Baptism. Track 4. Vanguard's 23rdStreet Studio, New York, NY.

- Baez J. (1968) "The Magic Wood" Baptism. (Henry Treece) Track 15. Vanguard's 23rdStreet Studio, New York, NY.

- Beauvoir, S.de(1949). "Le deuxième sexe" [The Second Sex]. NRF essais (in French). 1, Les faits et les mythes [Facts and Myths]. Gallimard. ISBN9782070205134.

- Buddha, G.(c. 563 – c. 483 BC), (quote - unknown date).

- Bugliosi, V.with Gentry, K.(1974) "Helter Skelter The True Story of the Manson Murders" USA, W. W. Norton & Company.
https://www.penguin.co.uk/books/1039062/helter-skelter/

- Busch, W.(1871) "Max und Moritz; A Rascal's History in Seven Tricks." Munchen: Braun und Schneider, 1925

- before Christmas", originally published "The Night Before Christmas", New York Sentinel on December 23. The original publisher hinted at Moore's authorship in 1829. Moore was first credited as author by Charles Fenno Hoffman, ed., The New-York Book of Poetry(New York: George Dearborn, 1837).
https://en.wikipedia.org/wiki/A_Visit_from_St._Nicholas

- Commonwealth, Royal Commission into Institutional Responses to Child Sexual Abuse(2013 – 2017)
https://www.childabuseroyalcommission.gov.au/

- Commonwealth, Royal Commission into Institutional Responses to Child Sexual Abuse(2017) –'Criminal Justice Report'Interim Report – published 14 August 2017. Accessed on 14 August 2017.
https://www.childabuseroyalcommission.gov.au/criminal-justice

- Commonwealth, Royal Commission into Institutional Responses to Child Sexual Abuse(2017) - Final Report Recommendations15 December 2017. Accessed on 18 December 2017.
https://www.childabuseroyalcommission.gov.au/sites/default/files/final_report_-_recommendations.pdf

- Commonwealth, Royal Commission into Institutional Responses to Child Sexual Abuse Terms of Reference (2013)https://www.childabuseroyalcommission.gov.au/search/terms%20of%20reference

- Courtin, J. (2015) "Sexual Assaults and the Catholic Church: Are Victims Finding Justice?", PhD. Monash University, Victoria. Published in Melbourne, p. 20.

- Davies, I. (1987)"Man of Colours"– Icehouse, Man of Colours, Chrysalis Records, Track 4. Accessed July 30, 2017. https://www.azlyrics.com/lyrics/icehouse/manofcolours.html

- Dire Straits(1980) "Romeo and Juliet" Dire Straits; Album Making Movies. Vertigo Records, UK.

- Durrant, J.(2011) 'Public understandings and private metaphor in Ivan Durrant's 'the cow', Art and Australia, Vol. 48/3.

- Elvis Christmas Album(1970) Pickwick Vinyl Record LP 1970 RCA/Camden Records. Australia.

- Epstein, M.W.N., Mendelson G. and Strauss, N.H.M.The Guide to the Evaluation of Psychiatric Impairmnet for Clinicians GEPIC (2006);

- Factor, J.'Unreal Banana Peel' and 'Far Out Brussel Sprout' were common sayings in the 1980s in Conservative Town after the books by the same nameUnreal, Banana Peel]: A Third Collection of Australian Children's Chants and Rhymes Paperback – December 31, 1986. by June Factor (Author, Editor), Peter Viska (Illustrator) ... All Right Vegemite and Far Out Brussel Sprout]: A New Collection of Australian Children's Chants and Rhymes Paperback.

- Forrest Gump(1994), film based on the 1986 novel of the same name by Winston Groom. Directed by Robert Zemeckis. Paramount Pictures, 142 minutes.

- Foster, C. and Kennedy, P.(2010) "Hell on the Way to Heaven",Bantam Books; NY.

- Fox, M., (2002) "The Magic Hat", USA; Harcourt 2002.

- Gillard J.(2012) "Misogyny Speech", Prime Minister of Australia, delivered in Parliament on 9 October 2012. Canberra.
https://www.youtube.com/watch?v=SOPsxpMzYw4

- Gillard J.(2013) "Speech on losing the Prime Ministership of Australia", delivered on 26 June 2013. Canberra.
https://www.youtube.com/watch?v=G0uhHuEw8LY

- Go Betweens(1988) "Streets of your Town." Album 16 Lovers Lane. Studios 301. Sydney

- Hoffmann, H.(1845) Der Struwwelpeter (Slovenly Peter). Rütten & Loening Verlag in Frankfurt am Main, 1871, Germany.

- Jabour, H. (2013) "Julia Gillard's 'small breasts' served up on Liberal party dinner menu", The Guardian, 12 June 2013.
https://www.theguardian.com/world/2013/jun/12/gillard-menu-sexist-liberal-dinner

- Jackson, J.(1982) "Real Men", Album "Night and Day" USA; A & M Records.

- *Jones, Cleopatra(2013) "Eulogy to the Pavlovic Family – on the sad loss of Cleopatra, Julius Caesar and Calpurnia." 27 November 2013 – White Ribbon Day.

- *Jones, Cleopatra(2017) "Flow chart of our Criminal

Injustice System", hand-drawn, 2017. Appended at end of book. (*Pseudonym)

- *Jones, Cleopatra(2017) "Cleopatra's Guide to Pretext Calls", 2017. Appended at end of book. (*Pseudonym)

- Jules. G, and Andrews. M, (2001)"Mad World", Album Trading Snake Oil for Wolftickets. Cover of Tears for Fears Album: The Hurting(1983). Producers Chris Hughes Ross Cullum.

- McClellan, P. (2017). "Seeking Justice for Victims Modern Prosecutors Conference", 13 April 2017. Accessed July 20, 2017 https://www.childabuseroyalcommission.gov.au/media-releases/justice-mcclellan-addresses-modern-prosecutor-conference

- Medical Panel of Psychiatry"**Clinical Guidelines to the Rating of Psychiatric Impairment**", prepared by the Medical Panel of Psychiatry, Melbourne (October 1997)

- Minchin, T. (2016)"Come Home Cardinal Pell" https://www.youtube.com/watch?v=EtHOmforqxk

- Morrison, V. "Brown Eyed Girl" (1967) Album Blowin' Your Mind. Troubadour: Canada.

- Myers, V.(2 August 1930 – 12 February 2003) was an Australian visionary artist, dancer, bohemian and muse whose coverage by the media was mostly in the decades of the 1950s and 1960s in Europe and the United States (Wikipedia).

- Paulina* (2017) "Sinful"*, Rainbow Publishing Co*, Big Smoke. (*Pseudonym)

- Plath, S. (1963)"The Bell Jar" (1stEdition) United States:

Heinemann.

- Prevert J. (1951)"Song In The Blood" (chanson dans le sang) A poem translated by Lawrence Ferlinghetti. https://lyricstranslate.com/en/chanson-dans-le-sang-song-blood.html

- Quadrio, C. (2015) Royal Commission into Institutional Responses to Child Sexual Abuse - Case Study 28 Ballarat, 25 May 2015. Transcript (C81) C8456. https://www.childabuseroyalcommission.gov.au

- Schneider, W.(1974) Frohe Weinachten mit Willy Schneider. Telefunken Records. Germany.

- Scriven, J. M. (1855)Hymn: "What a Friend We Have in Jesus"Accessed June 5, 2017 https://www.hymnal.net/en/hymn/h/789

- Scutt, J. (1991)Women and the Law; Commentary and Materials.Law Book Co of Australasia. 596 pages

- Smith, M* (2004), "Crazy Court Days"*, 2004 Sunset Publishing Company* Big Smoke Victoria. (*Pseudonym and title and details changed)

- Stelarc, (born 1946) is a performance artist who has visually probed and acoustically amplified his body. He has made three films of the inside of his body. Between 1976-1988 he completed 26 body suspension performances with hooks into the skin, and has performed and exhibited in Australia, Japan, Europe and the United States. He has used medical instruments, prosthetics, robotics, Virtual Reality systems, the Internet and biotechnology to engineer intimate and involuntary interfaces with the body. He explores Alternate Anatomical Architectures with augmented and extended body constructs.

- Stevenson, R. (1886) "Strange case of Dr Jekyll and Mr Hyde" UK; Longmans, Green & Co.

- Tchaikovsky (1892) "The Nutcracker Suite, Op. 71a"is a selection of 8 musical numbers Tchaikovsky made from The Nutcracker ballet for a concert performance before the St. Petersburg branch of the Musical Society on March 19, 1892.

- The Warren Cup (5-15 AD) Created Roman 1-15 AD, British Museum http://www.bbc.co.uk/ahistoryoftheworld/objects/D6Xh BBXCTPy-tLxOUvy-FQ

- Transcript of Pretext Telephone Call– between Cleopatra Jones★ and King Claudius★ - made 13 June 2013, made from the Conservative Town★ Police Station. A pretext call is where the receiver of the phone call is unaware that the call is being recorded. (★pseudonyms) A copy of the Transcript is appended at the end of this book.

- Vega, S. (1987)**"Luka"** Solitude Standing, produced by Lenny Kaye and Steve Addabbo (1987), Track 2. https://genius.com/Suzanne-vega-luka-lyrics

- Victoria, Independent Broad-Based Anti-Corruption Commission (IBAC) Inquiry(2016) http://www.ibac.vic.gov.au/

- Wagner, J.(1978) "The Bunyip of Berkley's Creek", Illustrated by Ron Brooks. Picture Puffin: Australia.

- Wikipedia –'pedophilia' definition. Accessed October 2017 https://en.wikipedia.org/wiki/Pedophilia

- Wolf, N. (1990)"The Beauty Myth,"published in 1990 by Chatto & Windus UK.

LEGISLATION

- **County Court Civil Procedure Rules 2008 S.R. No. 148/2008**

- **Crimes Act 1914** (Commonwealth)http://classic.austlii.edu.au/au/legis/cth/consol_act/ca191482/

- **Evidence Act 2008** (Victoria)http://classic.austlii.edu.au/au/legis/vic/consol_act/ea200880/

- **Limitation of Actions Amendment (Child Abuse) Act 2015**(http://www.legislation.vic.gov.au/Domino/Web_Notes/LDMS/PubStatbook.nsf/51dea49770555ea6ca256da4001b90cd/E7B23929426B7541CA257E2E000CC4FE/$FILE/15-009aa%20authorised.pdf

- **Magistrates' Court Act 1989** (Victoria) (http://www7.austlii.edu.au/cgi-bin/viewdb/au/legis/vic/consol_act/mca1989214/

- **Magistrates' Court Act 1989** (Victoria).

- **Open Courts Act2013 (NO. 58 of 2013)**s. 15. http://classic.austlii.edu.au/au/legis/vic/num_act/oca20135802013203/Limitation of Actions Amendment (Child Abuse) Act2015http://www7.austlii.edu.au/cgi-bin/viewdb/au/legis/vic/num_act/loaaaa2015902015426/

- **Service and Execution of Process Act 1992**(Commonwealth). http://www8.austlii.edu.au/cgi-bin/viewdb/au/legis/cth/consol_act/saeopa1992325/

- **The Civil Procedure Act 2010**(Vic)

- **Wrongs Act1958**(Vic)

- http://www7.austlii.edu.au/cgi-bin/viewdb/au/legis/vic/consol_act/wa1958111/

CASE LAW

- **Connellan v Murphy[2017]VSCA 116.**
- *http://www.austlii.edu.au/cgi-bin/viewdoc/au/cases/vic/VSCA/2017/116.html?context=1;query=connellan v murphy;mask_path=*
- **Crown v Pavlovic[2013]**(Criminal matter), Magistrates' Court of Victoria at *Conservative Town, then transferred to *Big Smoke (*names of people and towns have been changed.)
- ***Jones & *Pavlovic & DPP[2015]**(Suppression Order matter), Magistrates' Court of Victoria at *Loganville *names of people and towns have been changed.
- ***Jones– VOCAT Matter 2016/666[2016]**
- ***Jones & *Pavlovic[2016]**(Civil matter), County Court of Victoria at *Big Smoke *names of people and towns have been changed.
- **Lazarus v New South Wales Director of Public Prosecution**[2015] NSWSC 1116 (21August 2015).Accessed 5 June 2018.
- http://www.austlii.edu.au/cgi-bin/viewdoc/au/cases/nsw/NSWSC/2015/1116
- **Re Jamie**(2013)Fam CAFC 110; (31 July 2013) http://www.austlii.edu.au/cgi-bin/sinodisp/au/cases/cth/FamCAFC/2013/110.html?ste

m=0&synonyms=0&query=title(Re%20Jamie%20)

- **Re Willy Panke and Director-General of Social Services**(1981)AATA 65 (23 July 1981). http://www.austlii.edu.au/au/journals/SocSecRpr/1988/17.pdf

- **Trustees of the Roman Catholic Church v Ellis & Anor[2007]**NSWCA 117 (24 May 2007)

- *http://www8.austlii.edu.au/cgi-bin/viewdoc/au/cases/nsw/NSWCA/2007/117.html*

LETTERS/EMAILS

- *Cardinal Carlisle, (2006) untitled letter to his victims, (16 September 2006), sent from Western Paedophile Prison.

- Chief of Staff of the Attorney General(2014) "Regarding the conduct of the DPP in your matter" letter received by Ms

- *Cleopatra Jones (2014) *pseudonym

- DPP *Friarbird, E(2014) "Your request for reasons for my decision" letter received by Ms *Cleopatra Jones (2014) *pseudonym

- *Jones, C., (2018) "Your incompetent defamation claim, email sent to defendant's solicitor *Barnaby Bustard-Braggart at *Court Jester Solicitors, January 2018.(*Pseudonyms)

- VOCAT(Registrar) "Sebastian – VOCAT Award 2016/1234" to Cleopatra Jones* of Jones Lawyers in the matter of Sebastian* (2016)

ART WORKS

- Caravaggio, M.(1593) "Boy with a Basket of Fruit", Biblioteca Ambrosiana (Ambrosian Library), Milan.

- Durrant, I. 'Slaughtered Cow Happening'(1975), National Gallery of Victoria (performance art outside the gallery), Melbourne

- Durrant, I.'Butcher Shop'(1977-1978), National Gallery of Victoria, Melbourne

- *Jones, C.(1991) "What Style of Woman Are You?", Winner of the Year 12 School Art Prize –'Jessie Merrett Award'at Conservative Town Grammar.

NEWSPAPER ARTICLES

- Crabb, A.(2013) "The expectations we have of women who are assaulted" The Age, 23 June 2013. Melbourne. http://www.dailylife.com.au/news-and-views/dl-opinion/the-expectations-we-have-of-women-who-are-assaulted-20130623-2oqey.html

- Hevesi, B.(2017) "They're giving the wrong sentences": Chief Prosecutor slams judges for giving criminals "a slap on the wrist" after rapist who impregnated a 13-year-old was jailed for just five years', 1 July 2017, Daily Mail Australia.

- Gale, L.(2017) "Online sexual predators: How to keep your kids safe"The Courier Mail, 25 August 2017. Queensland.

- *Stevens, F. (2016)"Conservative Town man caught with child porn"*, The Conservative Town* Daily Bugle, 14 June 2016.(*Pseudonyms)

- Taylor, G(2017) "Perth teen who raped neighbour, 9, in 'violent', 'premeditated' attack avoids jail", 12 October 2017, The Western Australian. https://thewest.com.au/news/wa/perth-teen-who-raped-neighbour-9-in-violent-premeditated-attack-avoids-jail-ng-b88625791z

TV/FILM

- **Being Me** (2014) ABC Four Corners, aired 17 November 2014. Melbourne. http://www.abc.net.au/4corners/being-me/5899244

- **Broadchurch** (2013), Television Series, a British fictional crime drama set in a fictional town in Dorset, England. First http://www.abc.net.au/tv/programs/broadchurch/. Created and written by Chris Chibnall and produced by Kudos Film and Television, Shine America, and Imaginary Friends. First aired 4 March 2013.

- **Damien: Omen II**(1978) Directed by Don Taylorand produced by Harvey Bernhard. 20thCentury Fox Films, Released June 9, 1978 US, 107 minutes.

- **Doctor Who** (1963), Television Series,a British science-fiction drama produced by the BBC since 1963.

- **Don't Tell** (2017), film, Directed by Tori Garret and produced by Scott Corfield. Released 18 May 2017, 110 minutes.

- **Forrest Gump**(1994) film based on the 1986 novel of the same name by Winston Groom. The Directed by Robert Zemeckis . Paramount Pictures 142 minutes.

- **Louis Theroux: A place for paedophiles**(2009)written by Louis Theroux, produced byEmma Cooper. Documentary approximately 45 minutes, Released 28 November 2009 https://www.imdb.com/title/tt1433852/

- **Little Children** (2006),Directed by Todd Field, written by Tom Prrotta. New Line Cinema, 137 minutes, Released October 6, 2006.

- **Prisoner** (1979-1986), Television Series, 1978 Reg Grundy Productions, Sydney.

- **Rape on Trial** on SBS program Insight hosted by Jenny Brockie. First aired 27 February 2018 on SBS (https://www.sbs.com.au/ondemand/video/1160813635712/insight-rape-on-trial.

- **Shawshank Redemption** (1994) Castle Rock Entertainment, Columbia Pictures, USA, 142 minutes, released 10 September 1994.

- **Spotlight**, (2015) Boston, USA,Producers:Steve Golin, Michael Sugar, Nicole RocklinBlye, Pagon Faust, 135 minutes. Released 6 Nov 2015 (United States).

- **The Omen**(1976) Director Richard Donner, 20thCentury Fox, Released 23 December 1976 (Australia), 111 minutes.

RADIO PROGRAMS

- Ally Moore, "Under reporting of sexual assault" ABC Radio, Victoria ABC-774 DriveProgram, 1 August 2017. at approximately 5.40 pm talkback radio interview with caller *Cleopatra Jones on the topic of under reporting of sexual assault on university campuses. (*pseudonym).

About the Author

Cleopatra at the grave of her mentor
Simone de Beauvoir, Montparnasse Cemetery,
Paris, France, October 2013

Cleopatra Jones is an experienced lawyer and a proud feminist who can't get the law to work properly for her or her clients when it comes to sexual assault. She was raised in Conservative Town, the Catholic stronghold that was a fertile ground for a paedophile ring that sexually abused children and created inter-generational victims of clergy abuse. A town currently at war; those who support victims against those who pretend to and those who simply don't and who, under the cover of darkness, cut down the loud fence ribbons at St Michael's Cathedral. A town where she still lives with her husband and four children.

She began her education at Conservative Town Grammar School in kindergarten and was a dedicated student through to year 12. She then studied Arts at Traditional University, majoring in Women's Studies and Fine Art History and lived on campus at Crescent College from 1992 to the end of 1993. In 1994 she transferred to Governor University in NSW to study law and returned to Big Smoke to live in 1997, got married and was then admitted to the Supreme Court of Victoria in 1999.

She herself is a victim of childhood sexual abuse but thought that she could vicariously heal, helping other victims of sexual assault and family violence through her legal practice. However, just before her 40th birthday in 2013, she told her secret to the police. Her husband encouraged her, as did her parents. She went to Conservative Town SOCIT, made a statement and made a pretext call where her cousin confessed and apologized, yet one year later the police dropped her case; a case of Doli Incapax and Nolle Prosequi.

She dragged herself and her family though four and a half years of legal fanfaronade in her quest for justice, missing important events of her young children for endless court hearings, psychologist appointments, barrister's conferences and for what? The law utterly betrayed her again and again.

Notwithstanding her absolute frustration with the law, she continues to practice in Conservative Town with her husband in their firm Jones Lawyers, in the hope that she can proudly practice as a victims' lawyer one day. For she believes that just as victims of crime were afforded a lawyer during the Royal Commission into Institutional Responses to Child Sexual Abuse, so too should they have one in criminal matters, where it really counts.

REFERENCES

1. Courtin, J. (2015) "Sexual Assaults and the Catholic Church: Are Victims Finding Justice?", PhD. Monash University, Victoria. Published 2015. p. 20.

2. (Victoria) Independent Broad-based Anti-corruption Commission (IBAC), Victoria, July 2012. http://www.ibac.vic.gov.au/

3. Taylor, G (2017) "Perth teen who raped neighbour, 9, in 'violent', 'premeditated' attack avoids jail". 12 October 2017. The Western Australian, Perth.

4. Axiom, "A Little Ray of Sunshine" (1970) Album: Axiom Archive 1968-1971 Released 2004.

5. Morrison, V. Brown eyed girl (1967) Album Blowin' Your Mind. Troubadour: Canada.

6. Beauvoir, S. de (1949). Le deuxième sexe [The Second Sex]. NRF essais (in French). 1, Les faits et les mythes [Facts and Myths]. Gallimard. ISBN9782070205134.

7. Gary Jules, Michael Andrews (2001) Mad World, Album Trading Snake Oil for Wolftickets. Cover of Tears for Fears Album: The Hurting (1983). Producers Chris Hughes Ross Cullum.

8. Tchaikovsky. The Nutcracker Suite, Op. 71a is a selection of 8 musical numbers Tchaikovsky made from The Nutcracker ballet for a concert performance before the St. Petersburg branch of the Musical Society on March 19,

1892.

9. Dire Straits (1980) Romeo and Juliet" Dire Straits; Album Making Movies. Vertigo Records, UK.

10. **Prisoner -TV Series** (1979-1986) 1978 Reg Grundy Productions, Sydney

11. Durrant, I. 'Slaughtered Cow Happening' (1975), National Gallery of Victoria (performance art outside the gallery), Melbourne

12. **Durrant, J.** *'Public understandings and private metaphor in Ivan Durrant's 'the cow'*, Art and Australia, Vol. 48/3.

13. Vali Myers (2 August 1930 – 12 February 2003) was an Australian visionary artist, dancer, bohemian and muse whose coverage by the media was mostly in the decades of the 1950s and 1960s in Europe and the United States (Wikipedia).

14. 'Unreal banana peel' and 'Far out brussel sprout' were common sayings in the 1980s in Conservative Town after the books by the same name Unreal, Banana Peel]: A Third Collection of Australian Children's Chants and Rhymes Paperback – December 31, 1986. by June Factor (Author, Editor), Peter Viska (Illustrator) ... All Right Vegemite and Far Out Brussel Sprout]: A New Collection of Australian Children's Chants and Rhymes Paperback.

15. Ibid.

16. Scriven, J. M. (1855). Hymn: "What a Friend We Have in Jesus" Accessed June 5, 2017 https://www.hymnal.net/en/hymn/h/789

17. *Jones, C. (1991) "What Style of Woman Are You?", mural - mixed media. Winner of the Year 12 Major School Art Prize

– Jessie Merrett Award at Conservative Town Grammar.

18. Wolf, N. The Beauty Myth, published in 1990 by Chatto & Windus UK.

19. Beauvoir, S. de (1949). Le deuxième sexe [The Second Sex]. NRF essais (in French). 1, Les faits et les mythes [Facts and Myths]. Gallimard. ISBN9782070205134.

20. Plath, S. (1963) The Bell Jar (1st Edition) United States: Heinemann.

21. Albee, E. (1962) Who's Afraid of Virginia Woolf? play first staged in 1962, Billy Rose Theatre, NY.

22. Scutt, J. (1991) Women and the Law; Commentary and Materials. Law Book Co of Australasia. 596 pages

23. Beauvoir, S. de, above n 18.

24. *Jones, C. (2013) 'Eulogy to the Pavlovic Family – on the sad loss of Cleopatra, Julius Caesar and Calpurnia. 27 November 2013 – White Ribbon Day.

25. Busch, W. (1871) Max und Moritz; A Rascal's History in Seven Tricks. Munchen: Braun und Schneider, 1925

26. Hoffmann, H. (1845) Der Struwwelpeter (Slovenly Peter). Rütten & Loening Verlag in Frankfurt am Main, 1871.

27. Wagner, J. (1978) The Bunyip of Berkley's Creek. Illustrated by Ron Brooks. Picture Puffin: Australia.

28. Nutcracker Suite, above n 7

29. **Romeo and Juliet**, above n 8

30. Schneider, W. (1974) Frohe Weinachten mit Willy Schneider. Telefunken Records. Germany.

31. Ibid.

32. Elvis Christmas Album (1970) Pickwick Vinyl Record LP
1970 RCA/Camden Records. Australia.

33. Forrest Gump (1994) film based on the 1986 novel of the
same name by Winston Groom. The Directed by Robert
Zemeckis. Paramount Pictures 142 minutes.

34. Go Betweens (1988) Streets of your Town. Album 16
Lovers Lane. Studios 301. Sydney

35. Commonwealth, Royal Commission into Institutional
Responses to Child Sexual Abuse (2013), Hearings held in
Ballarat, Victoria, May 2014.

36. Quadrio, C. (2015) Royal Commission into Institutional
Responses to Child Sexual Abuse - Case Study 28 Ballarat,
25 May 2015. Transcript (C81) C8456.
https://www.childabuseroyalcommission.gov.au

37. Plath, S. (1963) The Bell Jar (1st Edition) United States:
Heinemann.

38. McClellan, P. (2017). Seeking Justice for Victims Modern
Prosecutors Conference, 13 April 2017. Accessed July 20,
2017
https://www.childabuseroyalcommission.gov.au/media-
releases/justice-mcclellan-addresses-modern-prosecutor-
conference

39. **Lazarus v New South Wales Director of Public
Prosecution[2015] NSWSC 1116 (21 August 2015)** Lazarus
v New South Wales Director of Public Prosecution [2015]
NSWSC 1116 (21 August 2015). Accessed 5 June 2018.
http://www.austlii.edu.au/cgi-
bin/viewdoc/au/cases/nsw/NSWSC/2015/1116

40. Crabb, A. (2013)"The expectations we have of women who

are assaulted" The Age, 23 June 2013. Melbourne.
http://www.dailylife.com.au/news-and-views/dl-
opinion/the-expectations-we-have-of-women-who-are-
assaulted-20130623-2oqey.html

41. Abbott, T. (1998) comments made by then minister Abbott
during a round table discussion, raised by Gillard J. (2012)
Misogyny Speech, Prime Minister of Australia, delivered in
Parliament on 9 October 2012. Canberra.
https://www.youtube.com/watch?v=SOPsxpMzYw4

42. Ibid.

43. Transcript of Pretext Telephone Call – between Cleopatra
Jones* and King Claudius* - 13 June 2013, made from the
Conservative Town* Police Station. A pretext call is where
the receiver of the phone call is unaware that the call is
being recorded. (*pseudonyms) A copy of the Transcript is
appended at the end of this book.

44. Ibid.

45. Jones, C.* "Cleopatra's* Guide to Pretext calls", created
November 2017, a "cheat sheet" for anyone considering
making a pretext call. Appended at the end of this book.
(*Pseudonym)

46. **Open Courts Act 2013** (NO. 58 of 2013) (Victoria)

47. Ibid s. 15

48. **Service and Execution of Process Act 1992**
(Commonwealth).

49. Smith, M* (2004), "Crazy Court Days"*, 2004 Sunset
Publishing Company* Big Smoke Victoria. (*Pseudonym
and title and details changed)

50. Special Issues Committee – a committee set up by the

Catholic Diocese of Conservative Town. It was established by the church to deal with child sexual abuse, as it was being reported to the parish leaders including the bishop. However, it appears that the committee members never reported any of these cases of abuse to the police but kept it "in-house" despite the committee consisting of a serving police officer Luke Fang* and a former priest turned psychologist Dr Butts* among others. (*Pseudonyms)

51. IBAC, n 2.

52. Paulina* (2017) "Sinful"*, Rainbow Publishing Co*, Big Smoke. (*Pseudonym)

53. Open Courts Act 2013, n

54. Magistrates' Court Act 1989 (Victoria)

55. * **Jones & *Pavlovic & DPP(2015)** Magistrates' Court of Victoria at *Loganville *names of people and towns have been changed.

56. *Peterson, Charmion. (2015) "Lawyer says legal system doesn't work" Conservative Town Daily Bugle, April 2015. (*Pseudonyms) See redacted article Appended at the end of this book.

57. Letter from VOCAT to Cleopatra Jones* of Jones Lawyers in the matter of Prospero* (2016)

58. Quadrio, C. n (35)

59. Buddha, G. (c. 563– c. 483 BC), (quote - unknown date).

60. The Civil Procedure Act 2010

61. County Court Civil Procedure Rules 2008 S.R. No. 148/2008

62. Court Connect, County Court online search facility.

https://www.countycourt.vic.gov.au/sites/default/files/f orms/Court%20Connect%20Information%20Sheet.pdf

63. Fox, M (2002) "The Magic Hat", Harcourt 2002.

64. Clarke Moore, C. (1823) "Twas the night before Christmas", originally published "The Night Before Christmas", New York Sentinel on December 23. The original publisher hinted at Moore's authorship in 1829. Moore was first credited as author by Charles Fenno Hoffman, ed., The New-York Book of Poetry (New York: George Dearborn, 1837). https://en.wikipedia.org/wiki/A_Visit_from_St._Nicholas

65. Jones, C (2018) Email to Barnaby Bustard-Braggart at Court Jester Lawyers, January 2018. – see Appendix

66. Clarke Moore, C., above n 63.

67. Jones, Cleopatra (2017) Flow chart of our Criminal Injustice System, hand-drawn, 2017. Appended at end of book.

68. McClellan, P. (2017). Seeking Justice for Victims Modern Prosecutors Conference, 13 April 2017. Accessed July 20, 2017 https://www.childabuseroyalcommission.gov.au/media-releases/justice-mcclellan-addresses-modern-prosecutor-conference

69. Royal Commission into Institutional Responses to Child Sexual Abuse (2017) –'Criminal Justice Report' Interim Report – published 14 August 2017. Accessed on 14 August 2017. https://www.childabuseroyalcommission.gov.au/criminal-justice

70. Ibid.

71. **Shawshank Redemption** (1994) Castle Rock
    Entertainment, Columbia Pictures, USA, 142 minutes,
    released 10 September 1994.

72. Broadchurch, TV Series, a British fictional crime drama set
    in a fictional town in Dorset, England. First
    http://www.abc.net.au/tv/programs/broadchurch/.
    Created and written by Chris Chibnall and produced by
    Kudos Film and Television, Shine America, and Imaginary
    Friends. First aired 4 March 2013.

73. Doctor Who, TV Series, a British science-fiction drama
    produced by the BBC since 1963.

74. Bugliosi, V. with Gentry, K. (1974) Helter Skelter The True
    Story of the Manson Murders. USA, W. W. Norton &
    Company.
    https://www.penguin.co.uk/books/1039062/helter-
    skelter/

75. **Evidence Act 2008** (Victoria)
    http://classic.austlii.edu.au/au/legis/vic/consol_act/ea20
    0880/

76. Chief of Staff of the Attorney General "Regarding the
    conduct of the DPP in your matter" received by Ms
    *Cleopatra Jones (2014) *pseudonym

77. Movies **The Omen** (1976) and **Damien: Omen II** (1978)
    were popular American films of the horror genre that I
    watched as a teenager in Australia in the late 1980s by
    hiring the videos from the local video hire shop.

78. Limitation of Actions Amendment (Child Abuse) Act 2015
    http://www.legislation.vic.gov.au/Domino/Web_Notes/
    LDMS/PubStatbook.nsf/51dea49770555ea6ca256da4001b9
    0cd/E7B23929426B7541CA257E2E000CC4FE/$FILE/15-

009aa%20authorised.pdf

79. **Murphy v Connellan** (2017) VSCA 116

80. **Wrongs Act1958** (Vic) http://www7.austlii.edu.au/cgi-bin/viewdb/au/legis/vic/consol_act/wa1958111/

81. American Medical Association, 1995, Guides to the Evaluation of Permanent Impairment, 4th edition, Chicago: American Medical Association.

82. **Clinical Guidelines to the Rating of Psychiatric Impairment**, prepared by the Medical Panel of Psychiatry, Melbourne (October 1997)

83. Epstein, M.W.N., Mendelson G. and Strauss, N.H.M. The Guide to the Evaluation of Psychiatric Impairment for Clinicians GEPIC (2006);

84. Foster, C. and Kennedy, P. (2010) "Hell on the Way to Heaven" Bantam Books, NY.

85. Gillard J. (2012) Misogyny Speech, Prime Minister of Australia, delivered in Parliament on 9 October 2012. Canberra.
https://www.youtube.com/watch?v=SOPsxpMzYw4

86. Gillard J. (2013) Speech on losing the Prime Ministership of Australia, delivered on 26 June 2013. Canberra.
https://www.youtube.com/watch?v=G0uhHuEw8LY

87. Jabour, H. "Julia Gillard's 'small breasts' served up on Liberal party dinner menu", The Guardian, 12 June 2013.
https://www.theguardian.com/world/2013/jun/12/gillard-menu-sexist-liberal-dinner

88. Gillard, 'Misogyny Speech.'

89. **Re Willy Panke and Director-General of Social Services**

(1981) AATA 65 (23 July 1981).
http://www.austlii.edu.au/au/journals/SocSecRpr/1988/17.pdf

90. A 'Notice of Risk' is a legal document that must be filed
when one makes an application to the court in family law
childrens matters. It raises the risks to a child alleged by a
party so they can be investigated by Department of Health
& Human Services and a report be written for the court to
help the matter be determined.

91. **Little Children** (2006), Directed by Todd Field, written by
Tom Perrotta. New Line Cinema, 137 minutes, Released
October 6, 2006.

92. **Louis Theroux: A place for paedophiles** (2009) written by
Louis Theroux, produced by Emma Cooper. Documentary
approximately 45 minutes, Released 28 November 2009
https://www.imdb.com/title/tt1433852/

93. <u>**Re Jamie**</u> (2013) Fam CAFC 110; (31 July 2013)
http://www.austlii.edu.au/cgi-bin/sinodisp/au/cases/cth/FamCAFC/2013/110.html?stem=0&synonyms=0&query=title(Re%20Jamie%20)

94. **Being Me** (2014) ABC Four Corners, aired 17 November
2014. Melbourne. http://www.abc.net.au/4corners/being-me/5899244

95. <u>**Trustees of the Roman Catholic Church v Ellis &
Anor[2007]**</u> NSWCA 117 (24 May 2007)
http://www8.austlii.edu.au/cgi-bin/viewdoc/au/cases/nsw/NSWCA/2007/117.html

96. Commonwealth, Royal Commission into Institutional
Responses to Child Sexual Abuse - Terms of Reference
(2013)

https://www.childabuseroyalcommission.gov.au/search/t
erms%20of%20reference
https://www.childabuseroyalcommission.gov.au/terms-
reference

97. Ibid.

98. Minchin, T. (2016) "Come Home (Cardinal Pell)"
https://www.youtube.com/watch?v=EtHOmforqxk

99. Wikipedia definition of paedophilia.
https://en.wikipedia.org/wiki/Pedophilia

100 Caravaggio, M. (1593) "Boy with a Basket of Fruit",
Biblioteca Ambrosiana (Ambrosian Library), Milan.

101 The Warren Cup, Created Roman 1-15 AD, British
Museum
http://www.bbc.co.uk/ahistoryoftheworld/objects/D6Xh
BBXCTPy-tLxOUvy-FQ

102 Sunrise is an Australian breakfast television show of news
and current affairs, hosted by David Koch, Natalie Barr and
Samantha Armytage, broadcast by the Seven Network.

103 "Rape on Trial" on SBS program Insight hosted by Jenny
Brockie. First aired 27 February 2018 on SBS
(https://www.sbs.com.au/ondemand/video/11608136357
12/insight-rape-on-trial.

104 Stelarc is a performance artist who has visually probed and
acoustically amplified his body. He has performed and
exhibited in Australia, Japan, Europe and the United States.

105 Travelling Blind, community radio programme in the mid
1980's in Conservative Town, Sounds FM*, Victoria. Guests
include Julius Caesar* and Nym*. Jingle to the show was
Laurie Anderson's song "Language,is a virus." (*

Pseudonyms).

106Livermore, R, (1976) *Betty Blokk-buster Follies*, Album, One-man stage show, Director P. Batey, Bijou Theatre, Sydney Australia.

107Gale, L. (2017) "Online sexual predators: How to keep your kids safe" The Courier Mail, 25 August 2017. Queensland.

108Stevens, F. * "Conservative Town man caught with child porn," The Conservative Town* Daily Bugle, 14 June 2016.(*Pseudonyms)

109Ibid.

110'Loud Fence' is a movement that originated in Conservative Town in 2015 by its creator Maureen Hatcher, whereby colourful ribbons are tied onto the fences of institutions where abuse took place, in a sign of support for survivors and victims of child sexual abuse. Loud Fence has now become a worldwide movement, with supporters tying ribbons on churches and other buildings of significance worldwide, all the way to the Vatican.

111Cade, Jack* is a client of mine and was a victim of multiple incidents of clergy abuse by numerous clergy in Conservative Town.

112Open Courts Act 2013 (NO. 58 of 2013) s. 18.

113Davies, I. (1987) "Man of Colours"– Icehouse, Man of Colours, Chrysalis Records, Track 4. Accessed July 30, 2017. https://www.azlyrics.com/lyrics/icehouse/manofcolours. html

114Hevesi, B. (2017) "They're giving the wrong sentences": Chief Prosecutor slams judges for giving criminals "a slap on the wrist" after rapist who impregnated a 13-year-old was jailed for just five years', 1 July 2017, For Daily Mail Australia.

115Gillard J. (2013) Speech on losing the Prime Ministership of Australia, delivered on 26 June 2013. Canberra. https://www.youtube.com/watch?v=G0uhHuEw8LY

116."Don't Tell" (2017), film, Directed by Tori Garret and produced by Scott Corfield. Released 18 May 2017, 110 minutes.

117Stevenson, R. (1886) "Strange case of Dr Jekyll and Mr Hyde" UK; Longmans, Green & Co.

118Jackson, J. (1982) "Real Men", Album "Night and Day" USA; A & M Records.

119**Spotlight**, (2015) film produced by Boston, USA. Producers: Steve Golin, Michael Sugar, Nicole RocklinBlye, Pagon Faust, 135 minutes. Released 6 Nov 2015 (United States).

120**Ally Moore**, "Under reporting of sexual assault" ABC Radio Victoria ABC 774 Drive 1 August 2017 approximately 5.40 pm talkback radio interview with caller *Cleopatra Jones (on the topic of reporting sexual assault and the underreporting on university campuses.) *pseudonym.

121*Cardinal Carlisle, untitled to his victims, (16 September 2006), sent from Western Paedophile Prison.

122Ophelia Jerkoff, text message sent from Ophelia to Cleopatra Jones in September 2013.

123Beauvoir, S. de (1949). Le deuxième sexe [The Second Sex]. NRF essais (in French). 1, Les faits et les mythes [Facts and Myths]. Gallimard. ISBN9782070205134.

124Prevert J. (1951). "Song In The Blood" (chanson dans le sang) A poem translated by Lawrence Ferlinghetti.

https://lyricstranslate.com/en/chanson-dans-le-sang-song-blood.html

125Baez J.(1968). "Song In The Blood" A Poem By Jacques Prevert
Translated by Lawrence Ferlinghetti. Baptism. Track 4.
Vanguard's 23rd Street Studio, New York, NY.

126Ibid, "The Magic Wood" Baptism. (Henry Treece) Track 15.

CPSIA information can be obtained
at www.ICGtesting.com
Printed in the USA
LVHW051039070623
749110LV00024B/112